Disney
Cruella

BLACK, WHITE, AND RED

BY HACHI ISHIE

VIZ MEDIA

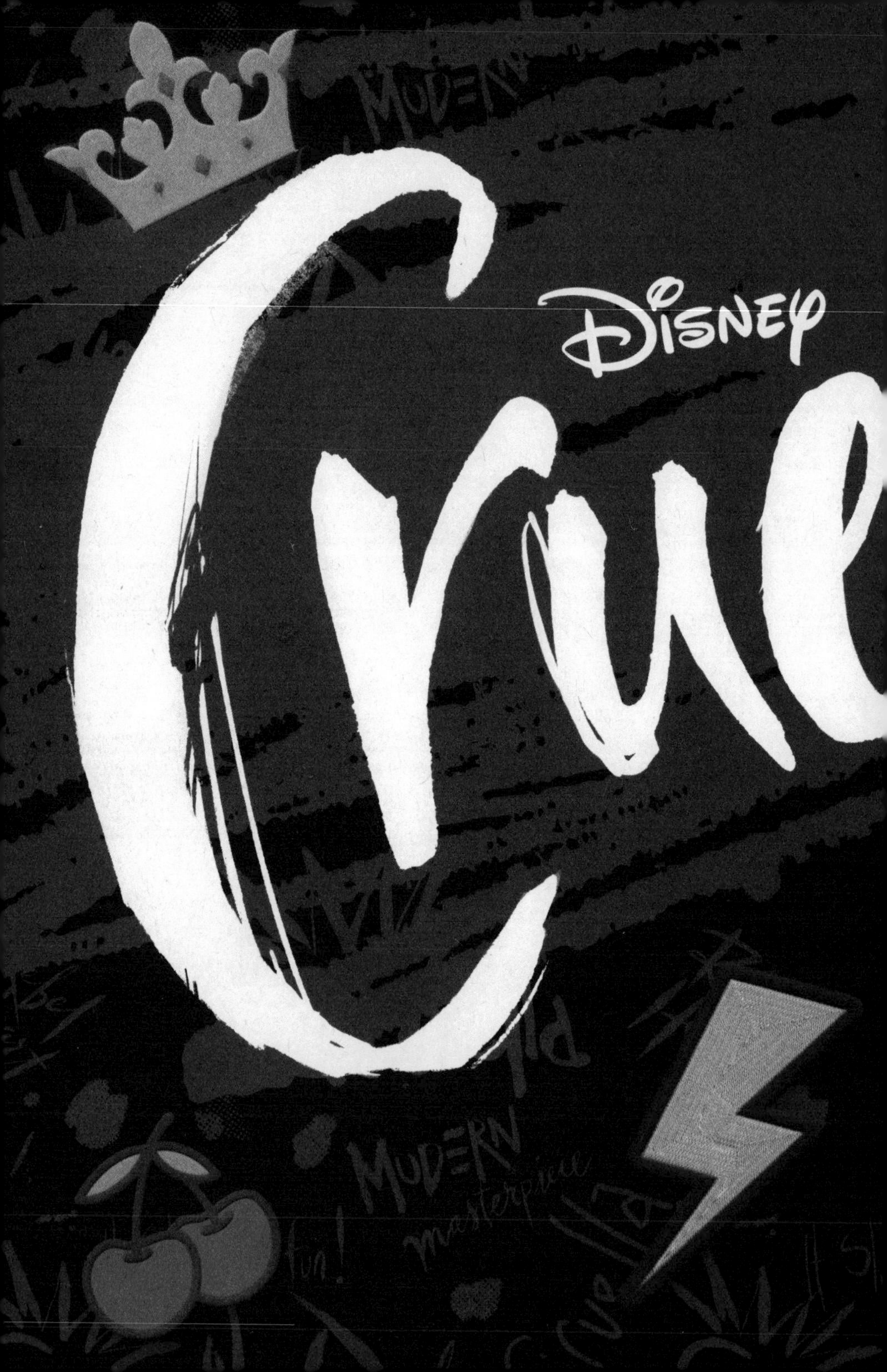
Disney
Crue
MODERN
MODERN
masterpiece
fun!

lla
THE MANGA

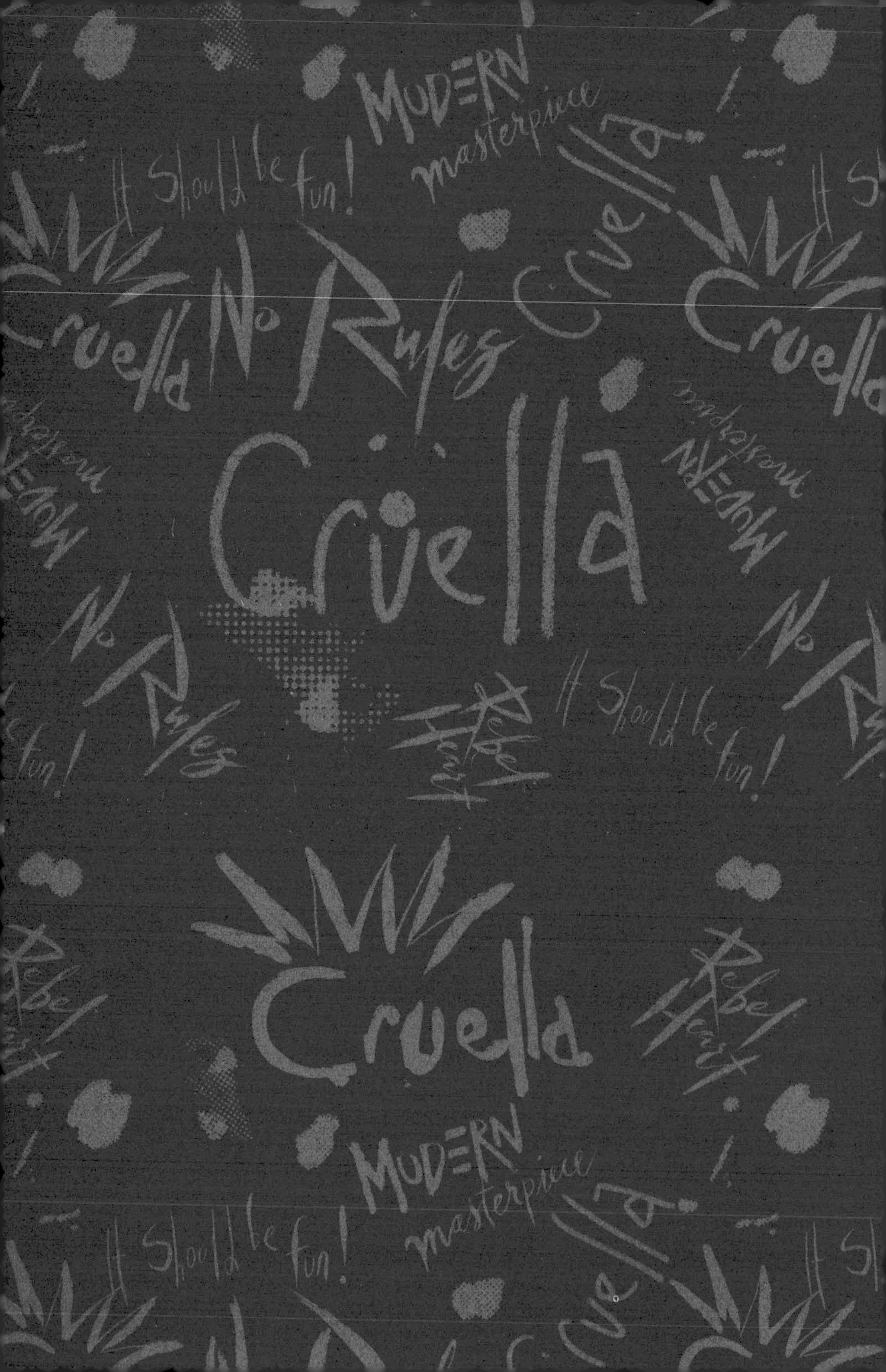
Cruella
No Rules
It Should be fun!
Modern masterpiece
Rebel Heart

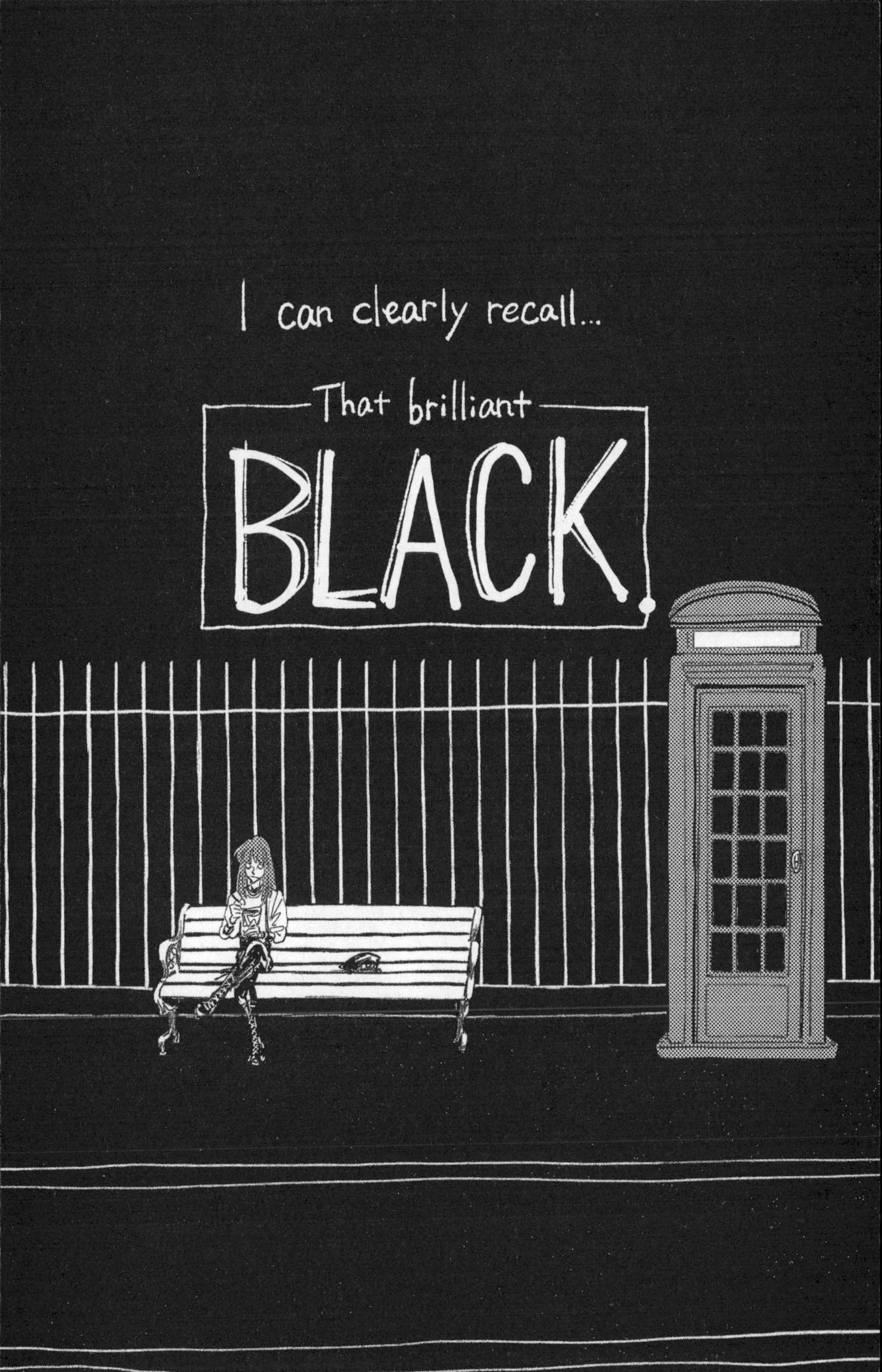
I can clearly recall...
That brilliant
BLACK.

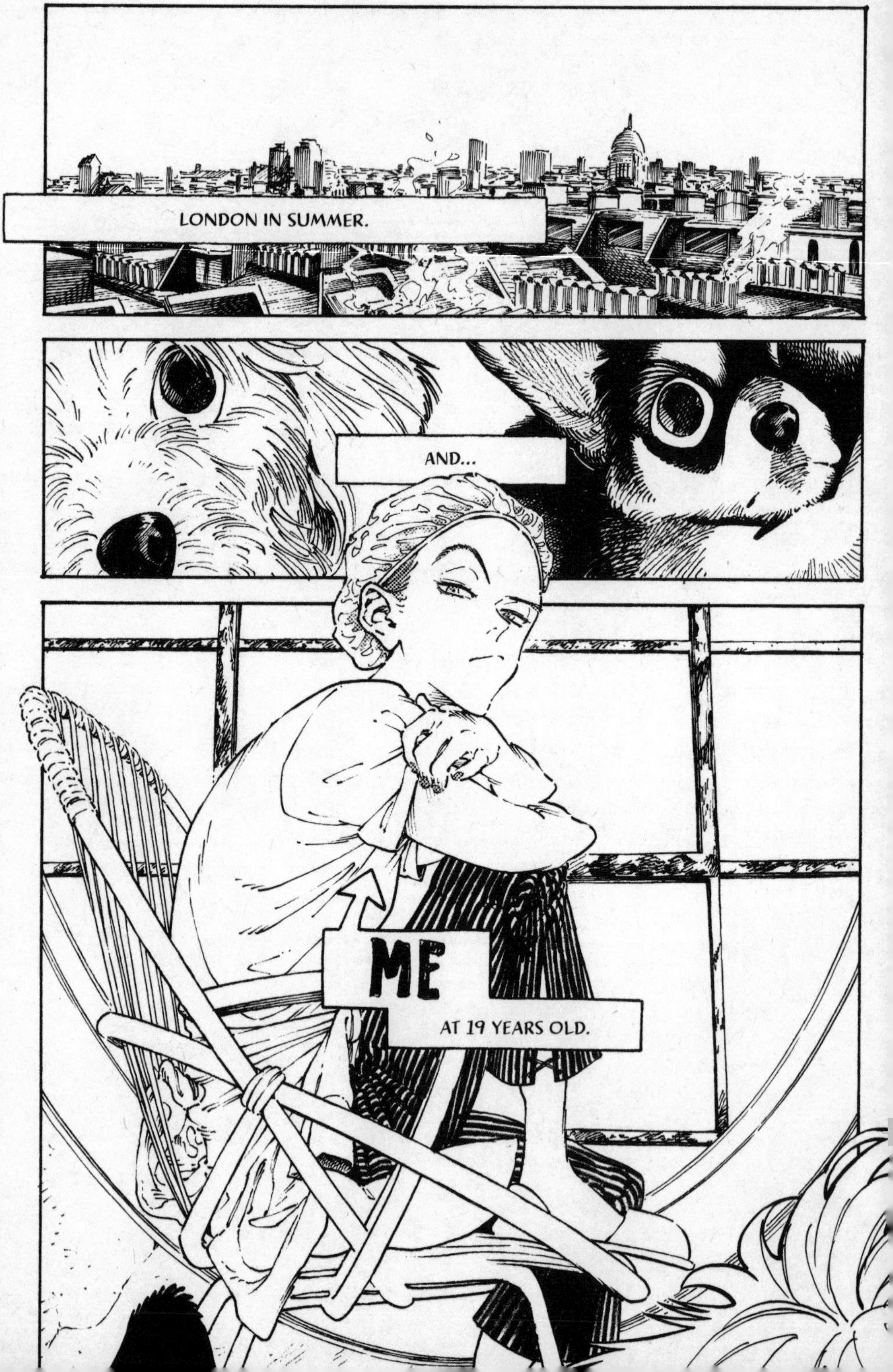
LONDON IN SUMMER.
AND...
ME
AT 19 YEARS OLD.

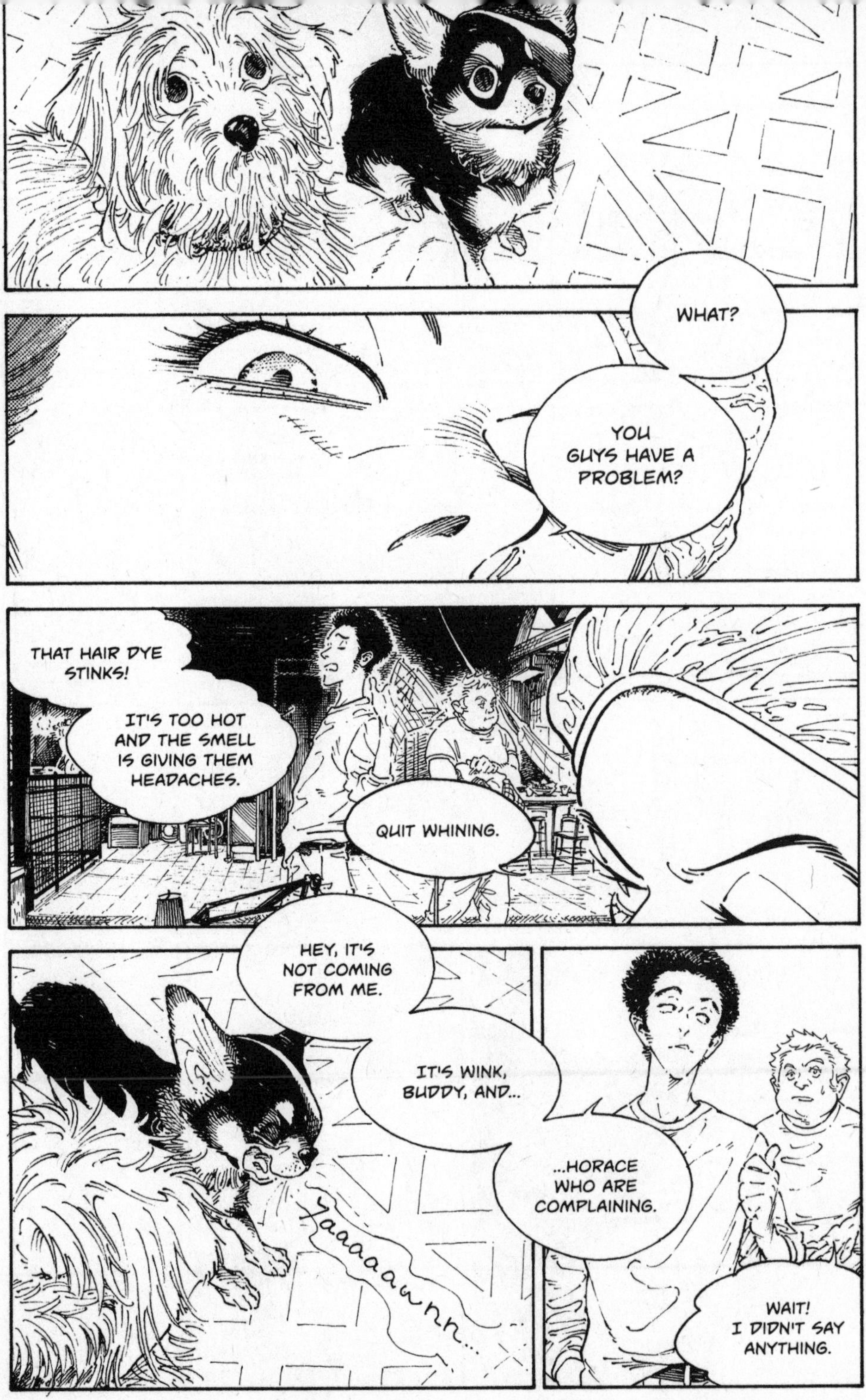
WHAT?
YOU GUYS HAVE A PROBLEM?
THAT HAIR DYE STINKS!
IT'S TOO HOT AND THE SMELL IS GIVING THEM HEADACHES.
QUIT WHINING.
HEY, IT'S NOT COMING FROM ME.
Yaaaaawnn...
IT'S WINK, BUDDY, AND...
...HORACE WHO ARE COMPLAINING.
WAIT! I DIDN'T SAY ANYTHING.

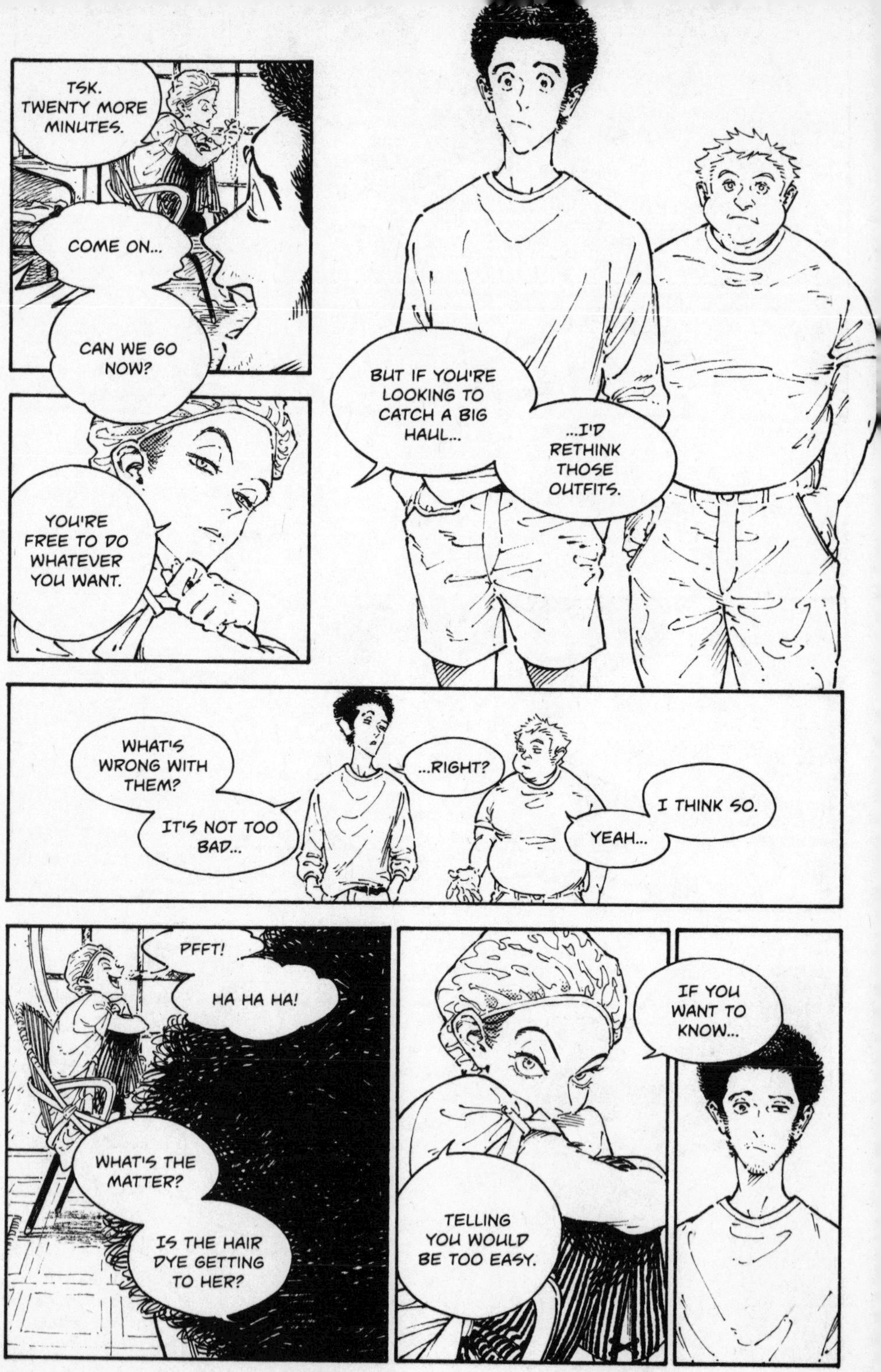
TSK. TWENTY MORE MINUTES.
COME ON...
CAN WE GO NOW?
YOU'RE FREE TO DO WHATEVER YOU WANT.
BUT IF YOU'RE LOOKING TO CATCH A BIG HAUL...
...I'D RETHINK THOSE OUTFITS.
WHAT'S WRONG WITH THEM?
IT'S NOT TOO BAD...
...RIGHT?
I THINK SO.
YEAH...
PFFT!
HA HA HA!
WHAT'S THE MATTER?
IS THE HAIR DYE GETTING TO HER?
IF YOU WANT TO KNOW...
TELLING YOU WOULD BE TOO EASY.

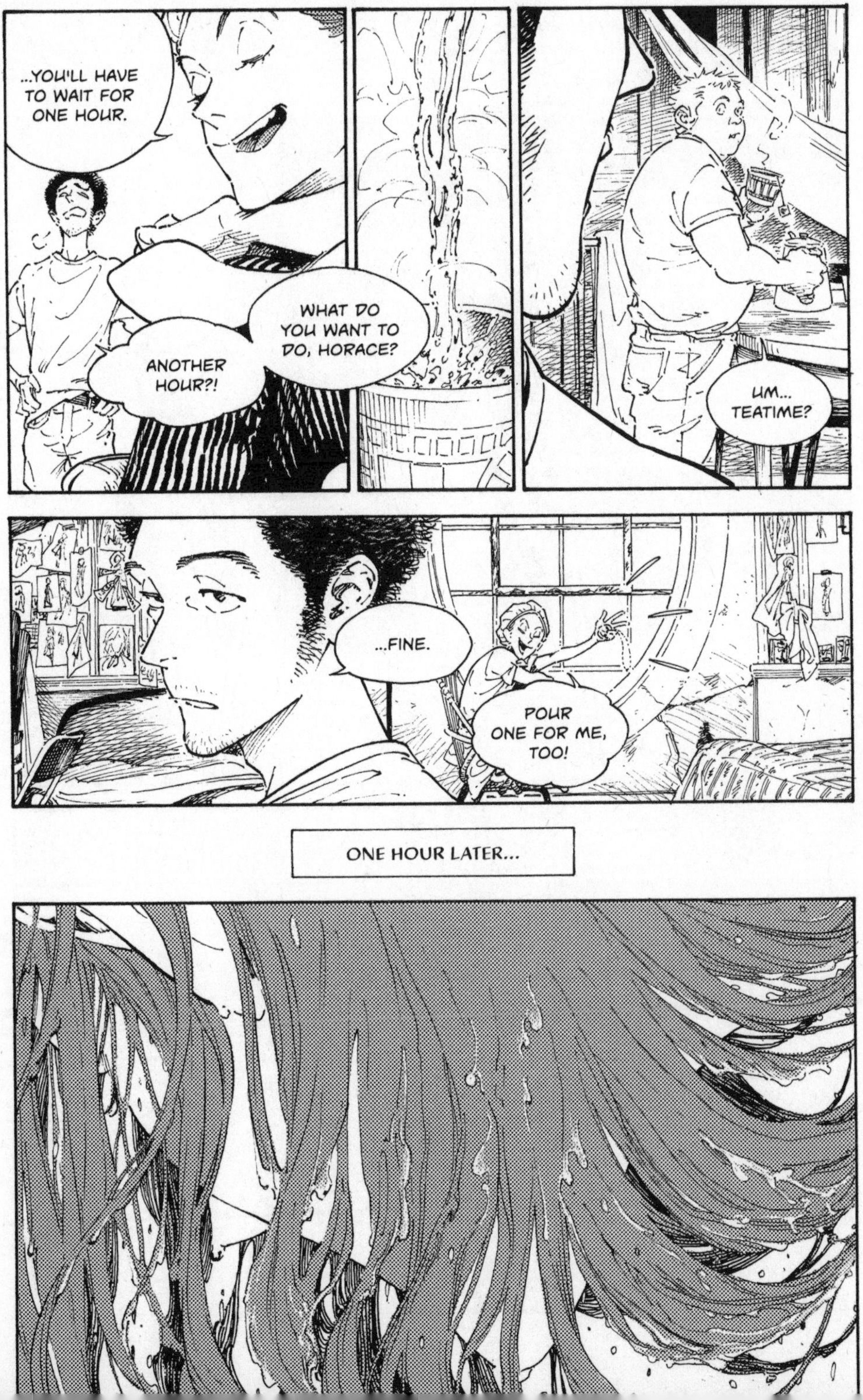
...YOU'LL HAVE TO WAIT FOR ONE HOUR.
ANOTHER HOUR?!
WHAT DO YOU WANT TO DO, HORACE?
UM... TEATIME?
...FINE.
POUR ONE FOR ME, TOO!
ONE HOUR LATER...

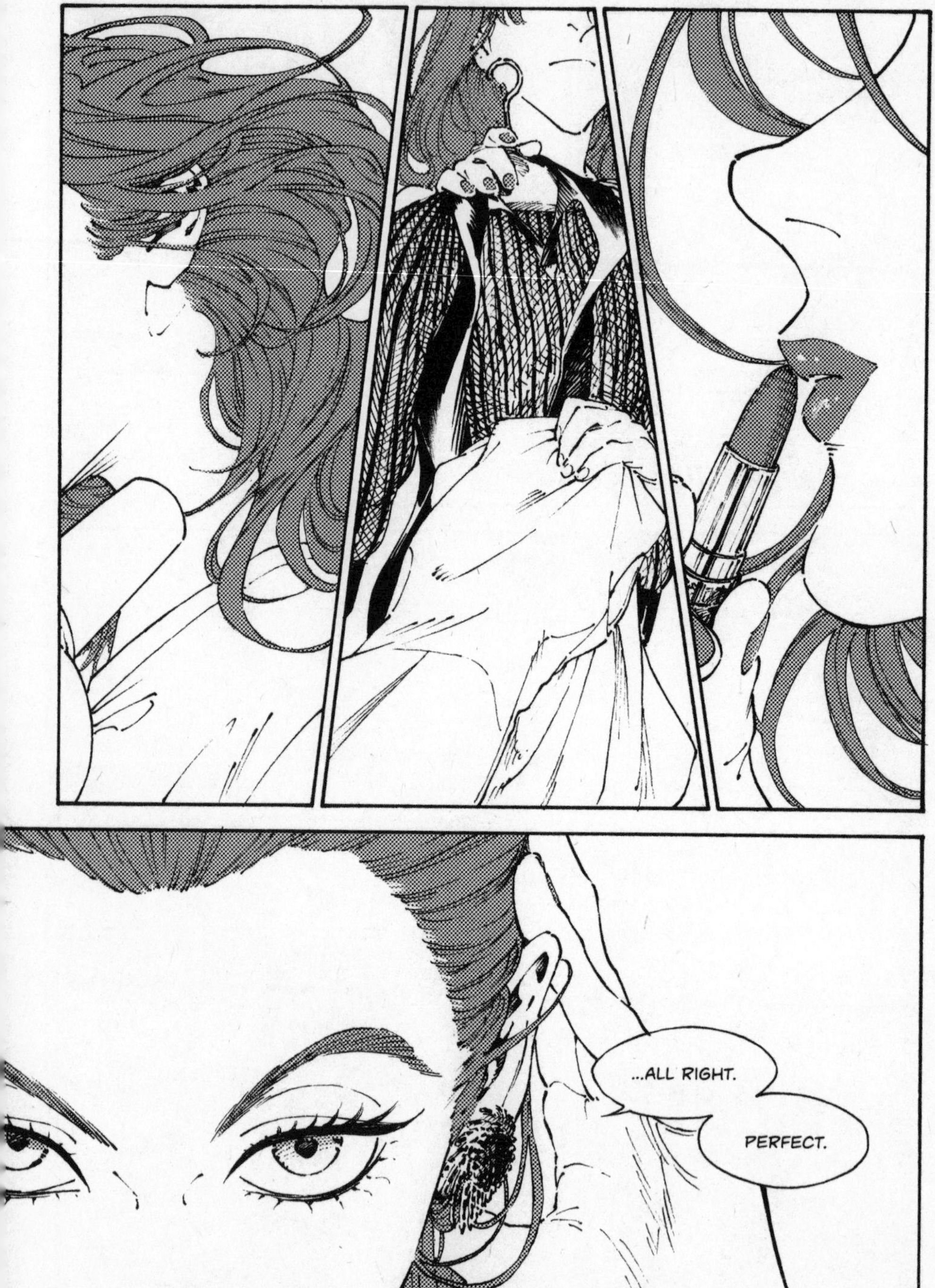
...ALL RIGHT.
PERFECT.

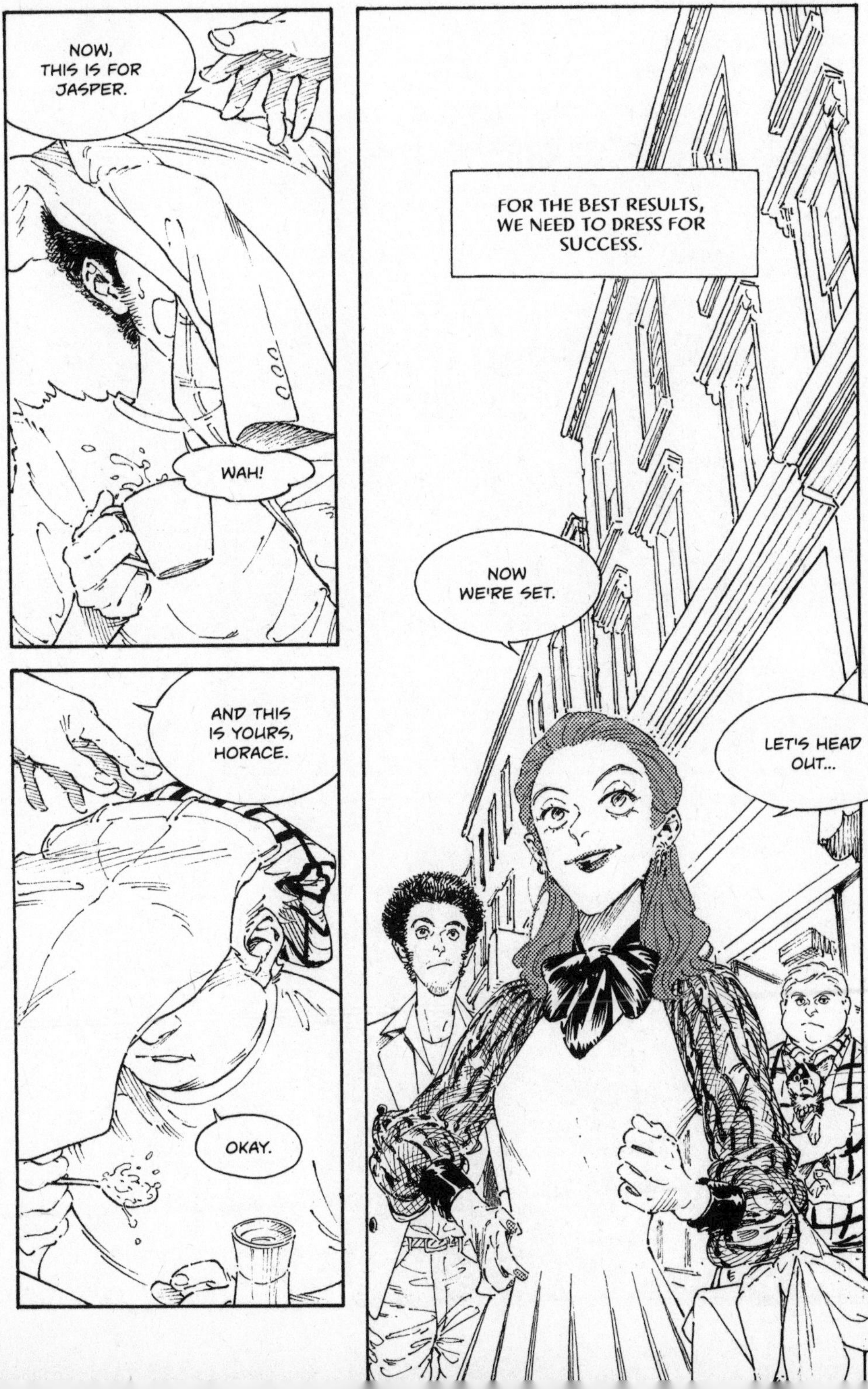
NOW, THIS IS FOR JASPER.
WAH!
AND THIS IS YOURS, HORACE.
OKAY.
FOR THE BEST RESULTS, WE NEED TO DRESS FOR SUCCESS.
NOW WE'RE SET.
LET'S HEAD OUT...

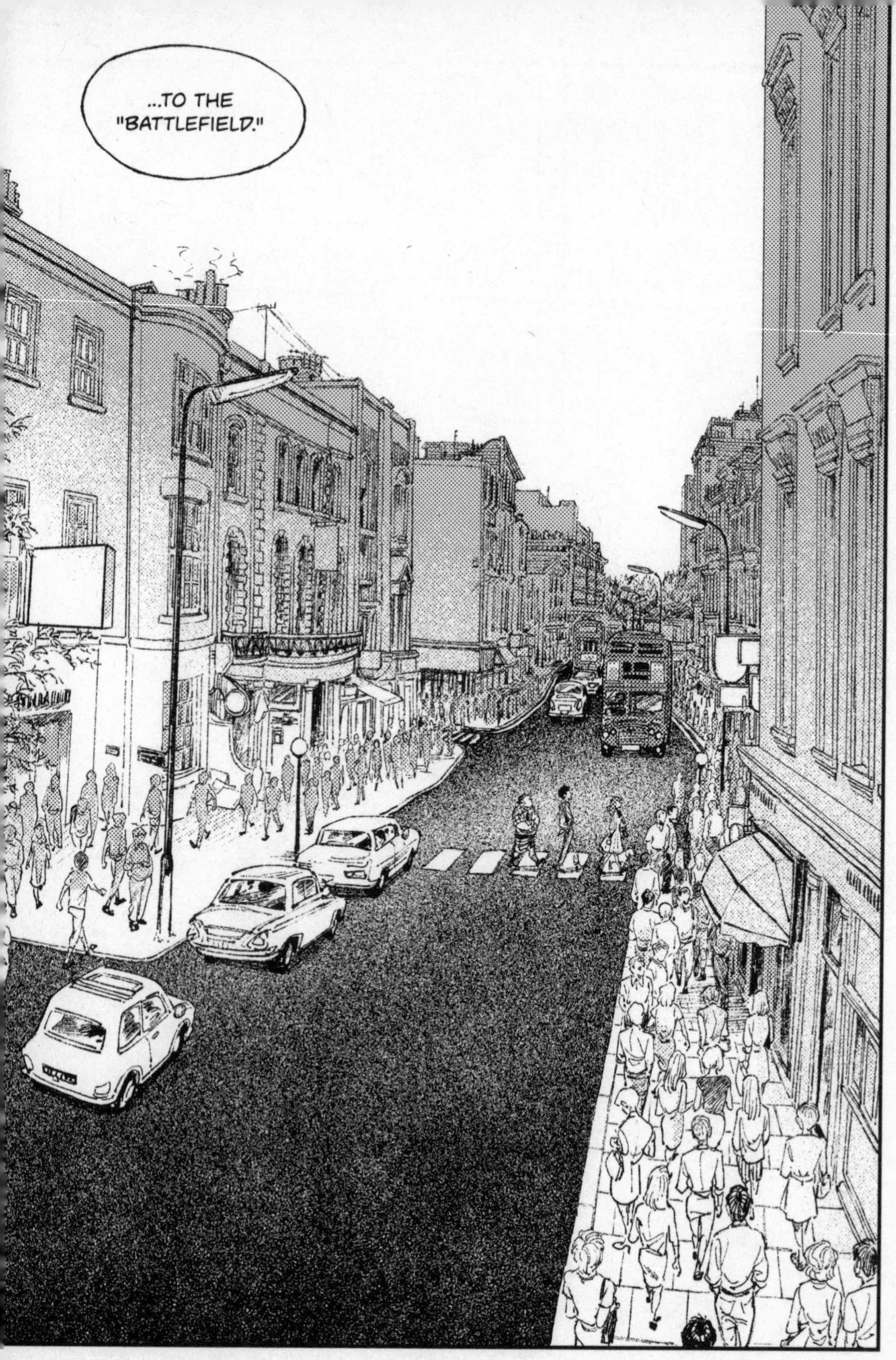
...TO THE "BATTLEFIELD."

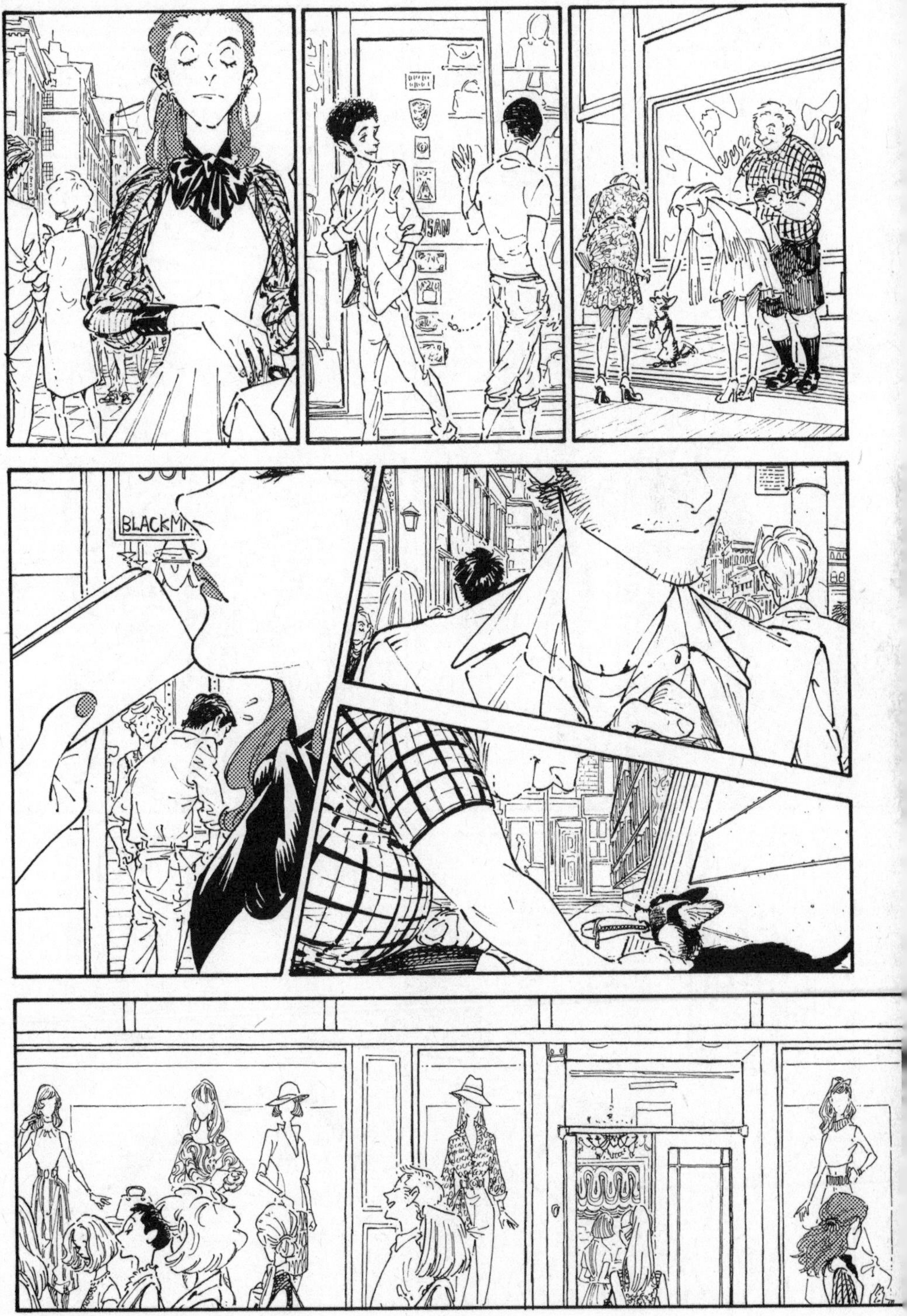
SAN
BLACKM

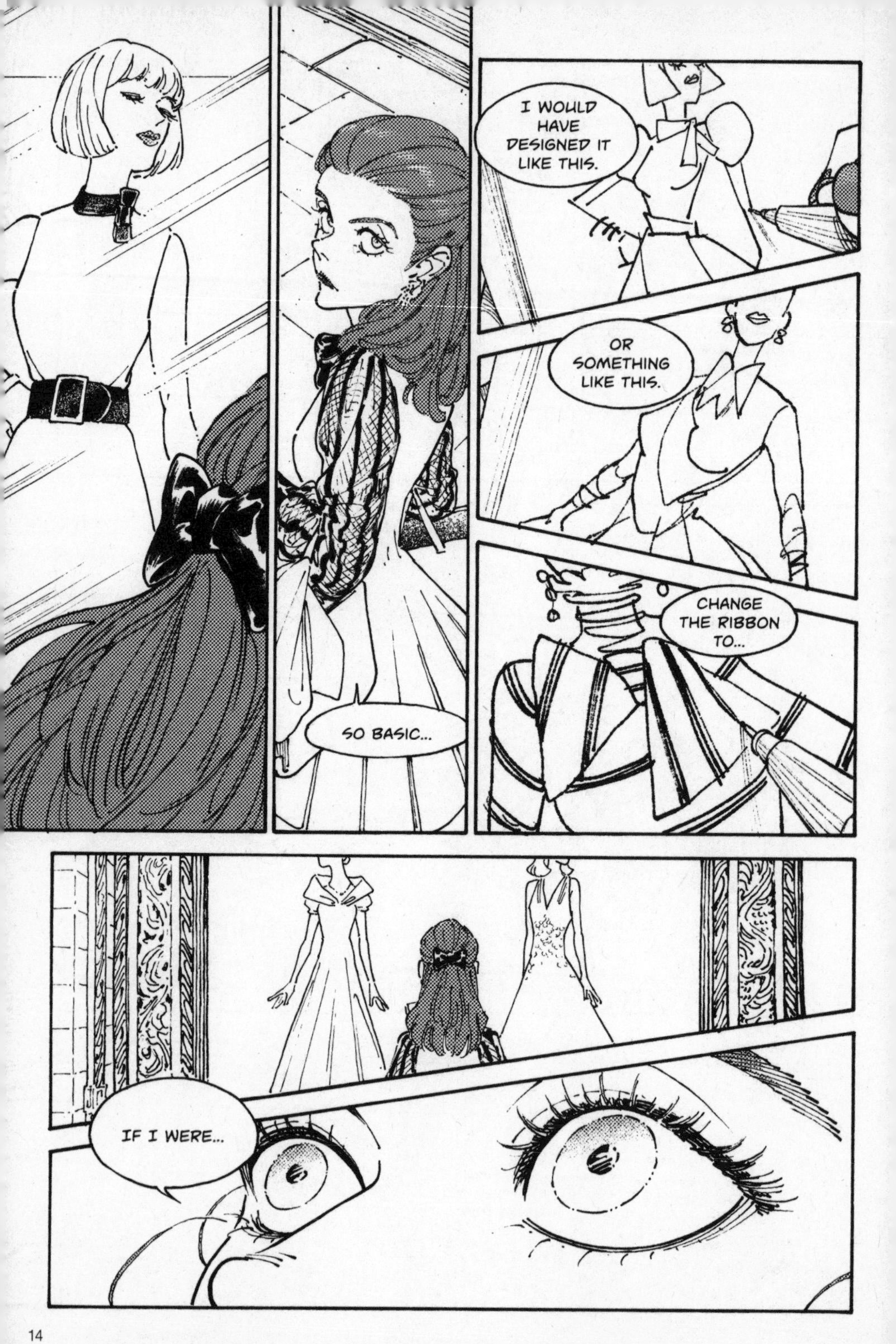
SO BASIC...
I WOULD HAVE DESIGNED IT LIKE THIS.
OR SOMETHING LIKE THIS.
CHANGE THE RIBBON TO...
IF I WERE...

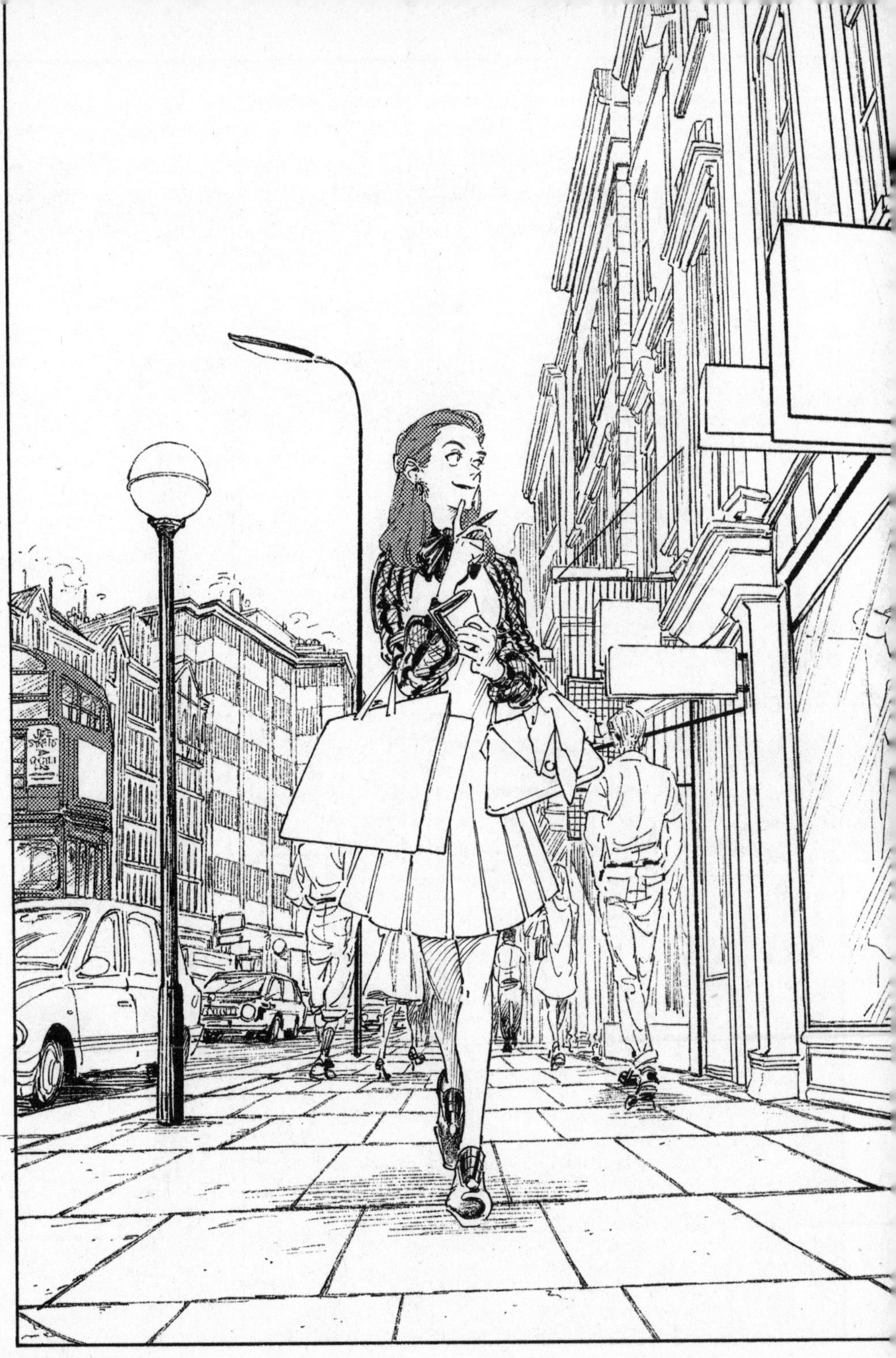

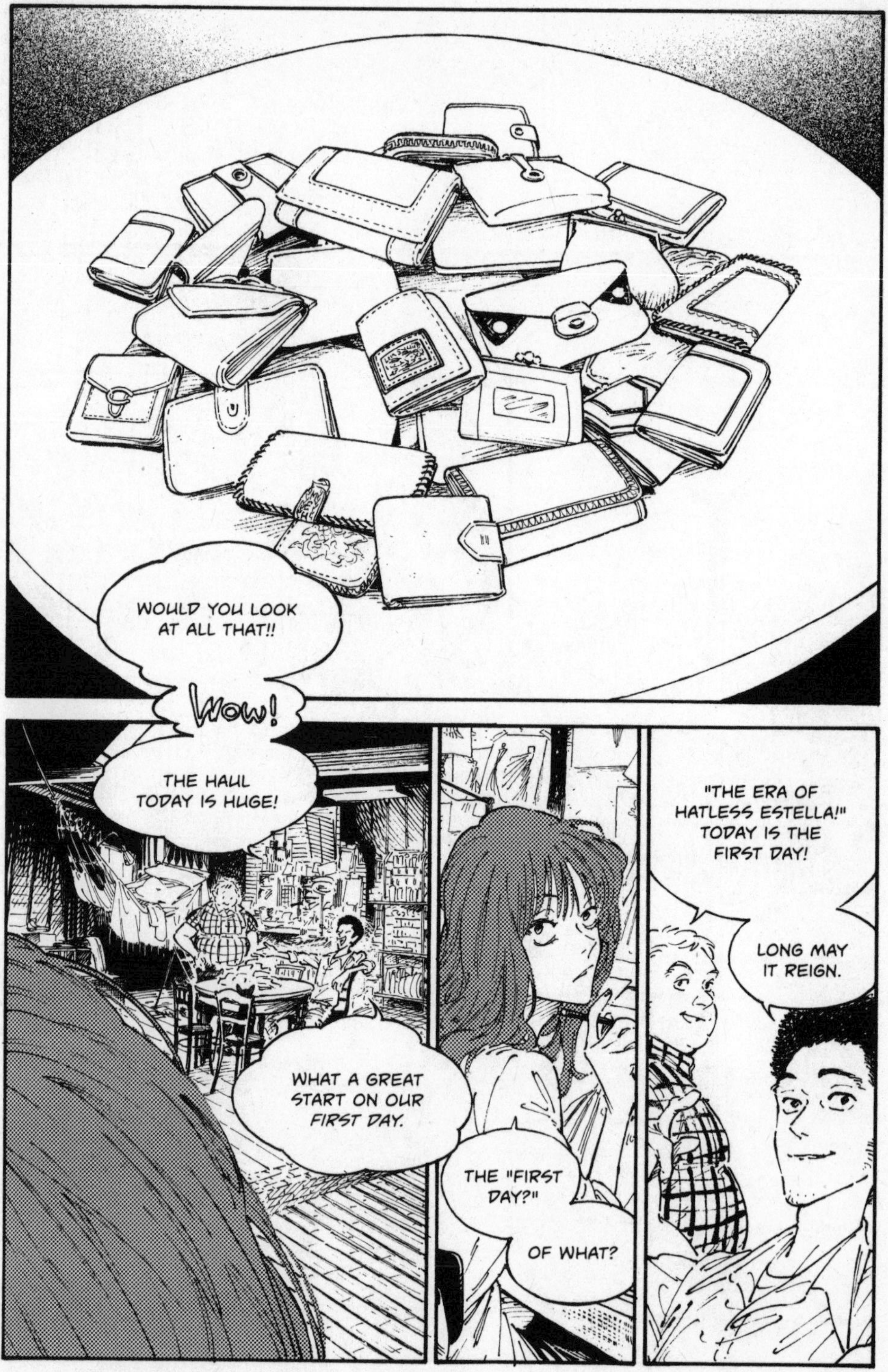
WOULD YOU LOOK AT ALL THAT!!
WOW!
THE HAUL TODAY IS HUGE!
WHAT A GREAT START ON OUR FIRST DAY.
THE "FIRST DAY?"
OF WHAT?
"THE ERA OF HATLESS ESTELLA!" TODAY IS THE FIRST DAY!
LONG MAY IT REIGN.

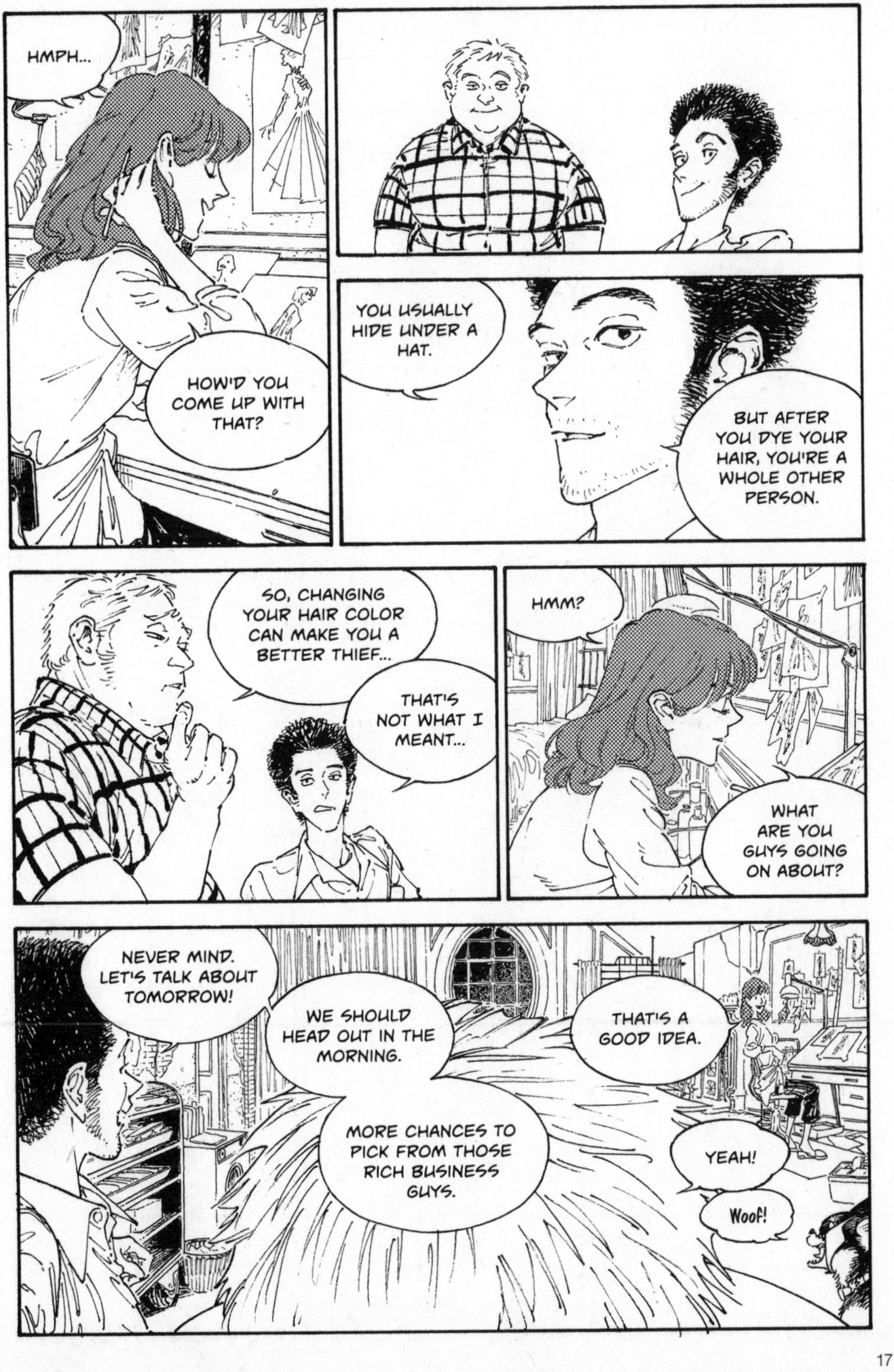
HMPH...
HOW'D YOU COME UP WITH THAT?
YOU USUALLY HIDE UNDER A HAT.
BUT AFTER YOU DYE YOUR HAIR, YOU'RE A WHOLE OTHER PERSON.
SO, CHANGING YOUR HAIR COLOR CAN MAKE YOU A BETTER THIEF...
THAT'S NOT WHAT I MEANT...
HMM?
WHAT ARE YOU GUYS GOING ON ABOUT?
NEVER MIND. LET'S TALK ABOUT TOMORROW!
WE SHOULD HEAD OUT IN THE MORNING.
MORE CHANCES TO PICK FROM THOSE RICH BUSINESS GUYS.
THAT'S A GOOD IDEA.
YEAH!
Woof!

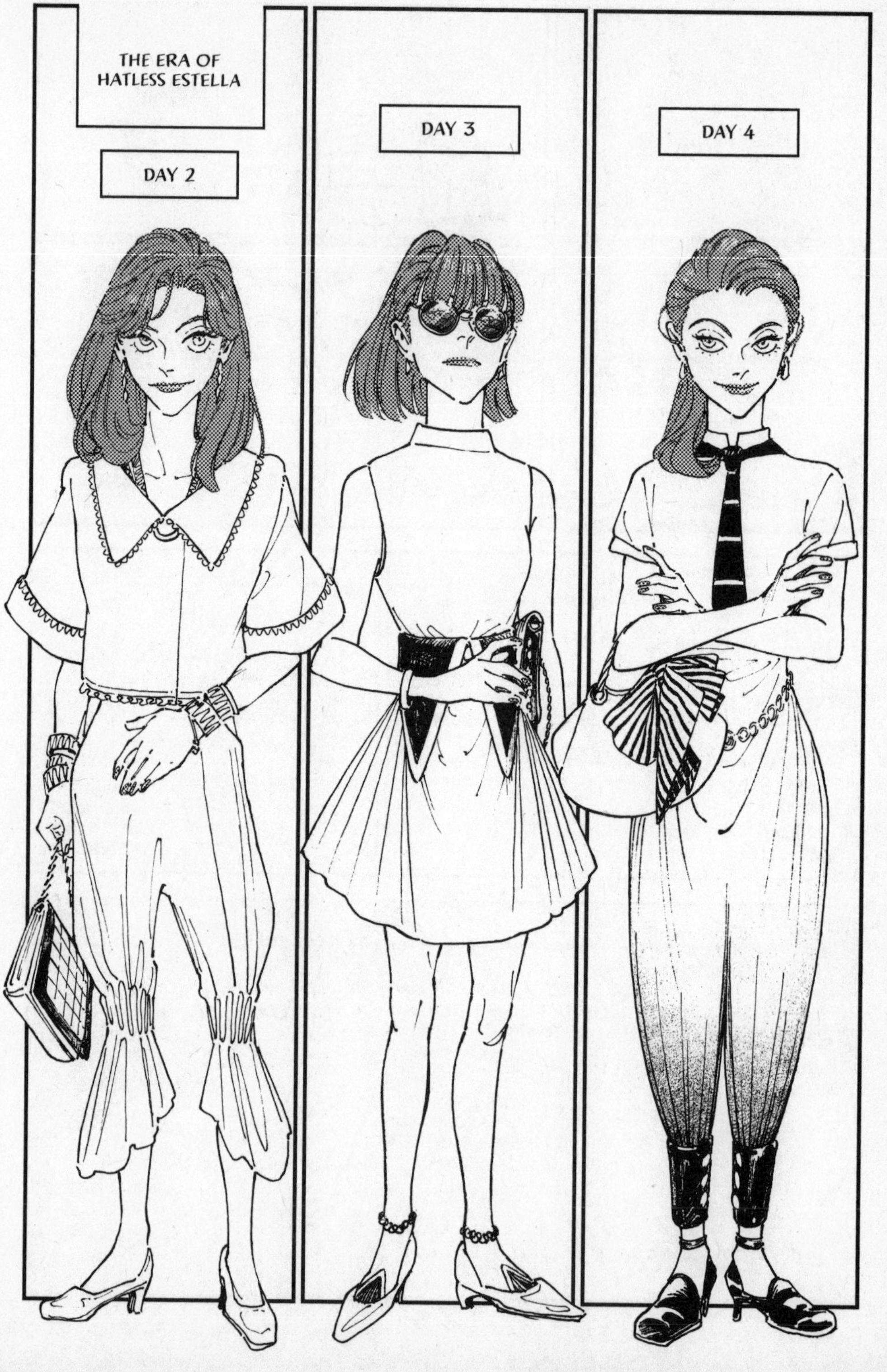
THE ERA OF HATLESS ESTELLA
DAY 2
DAY 3
DAY 4

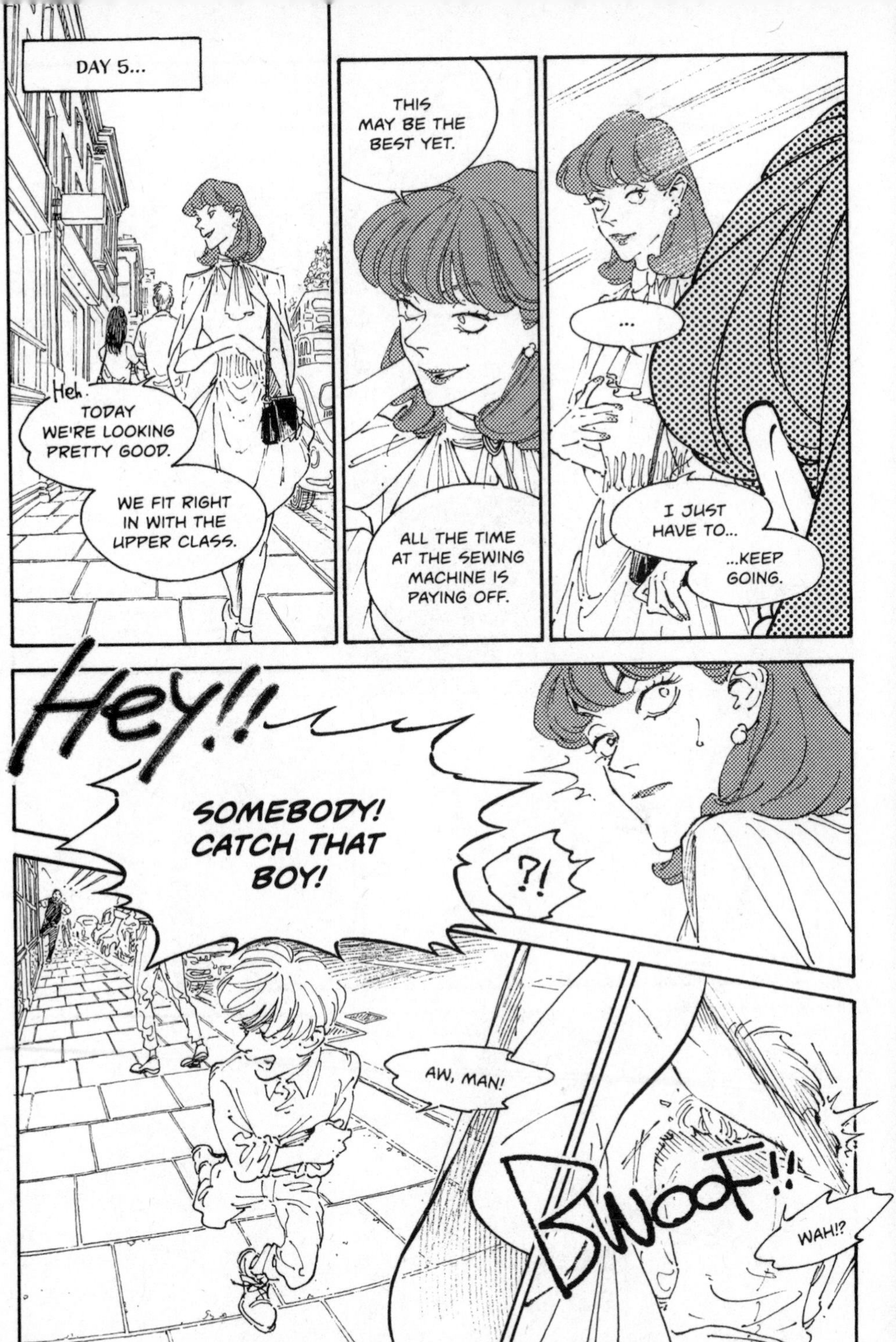
DAY 5...
Heh.
TODAY WE'RE LOOKING PRETTY GOOD.
WE FIT RIGHT IN WITH THE UPPER CLASS.
THIS MAY BE THE BEST YET.
ALL THE TIME AT THE SEWING MACHINE IS PAYING OFF.
...
I JUST HAVE TO...
...KEEP GOING.
Hey!!
SOMEBODY! CATCH THAT BOY!
?!
AW, MAN!
BWOOF!!
WAH!?

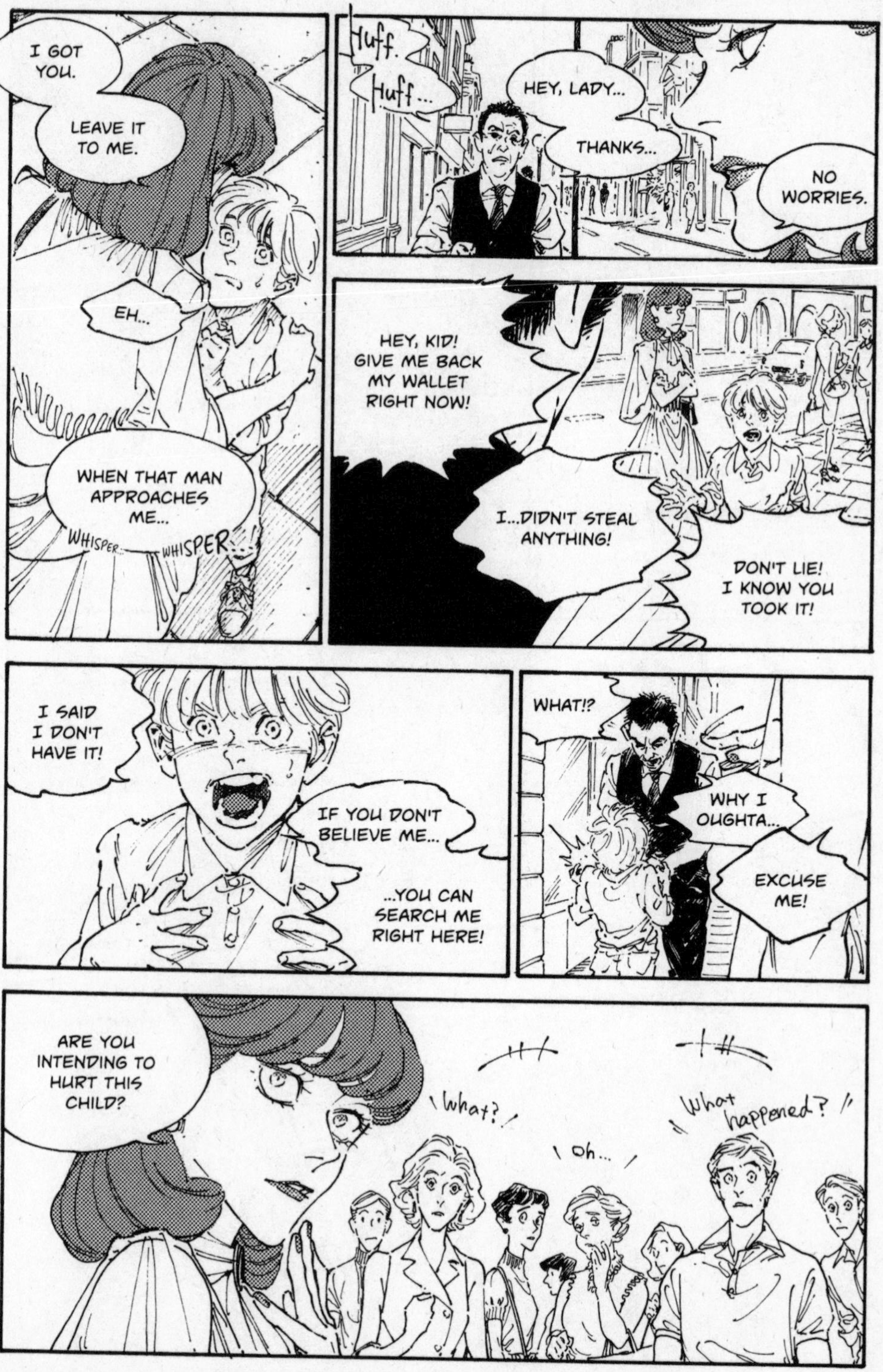
I GOT YOU.
LEAVE IT TO ME.
EH...
WHEN THAT MAN APPROACHES ME...
WHISPER...
WHISPER
Huff.
Huff...
HEY, LADY...
THANKS...
NO WORRIES.
HEY, KID! GIVE ME BACK MY WALLET RIGHT NOW!
I...DIDN'T STEAL ANYTHING!
DON'T LIE! I KNOW YOU TOOK IT!
I SAID I DON'T HAVE IT!
IF YOU DON'T BELIEVE ME...
...YOU CAN SEARCH ME RIGHT HERE!
WHAT!?
WHY I OUGHTA...
EXCUSE ME!
ARE YOU INTENDING TO HURT THIS CHILD?
What?
Oh...
What happened?

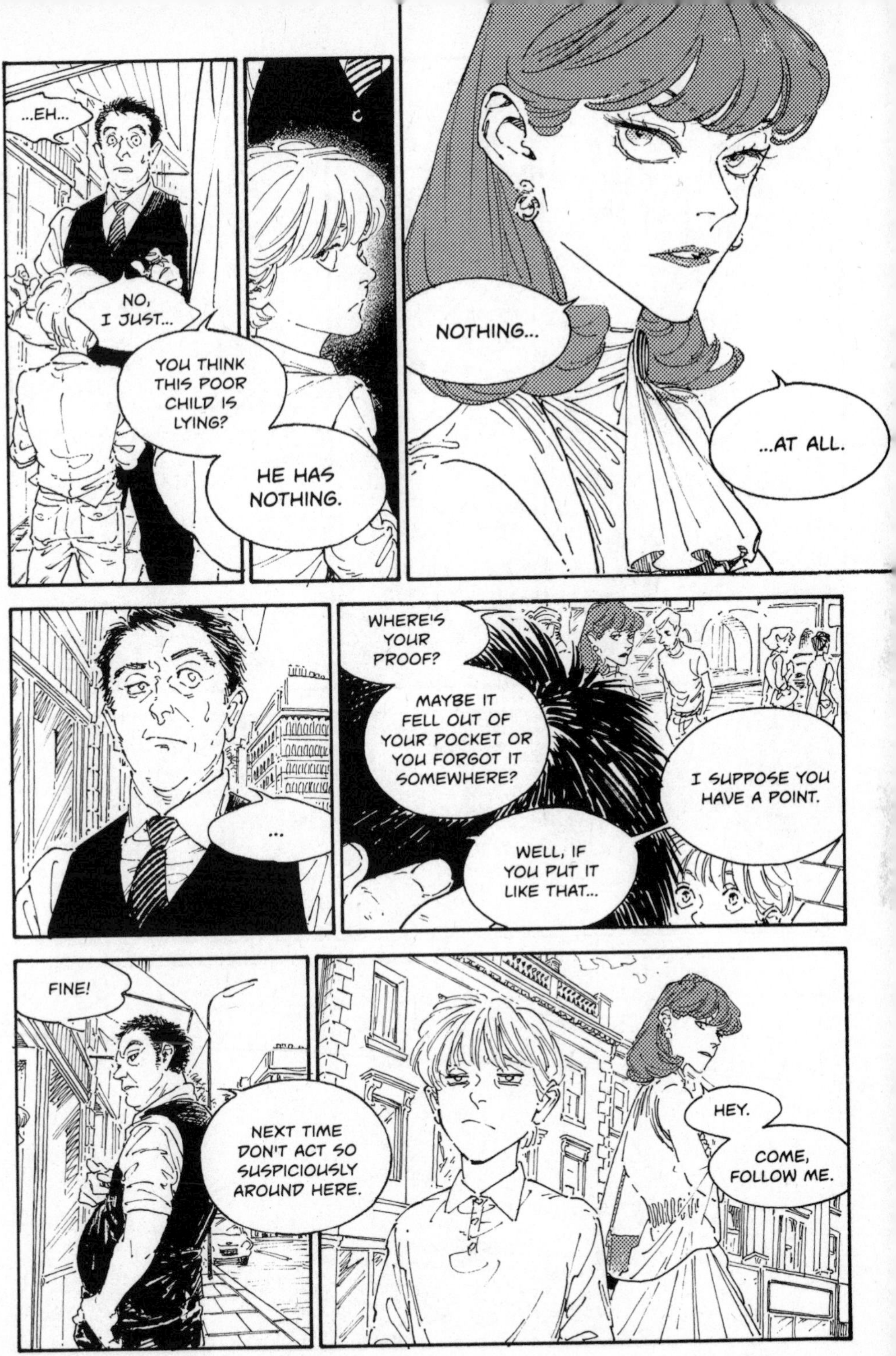
...EH...
NO, I JUST...
YOU THINK THIS POOR CHILD IS LYING?
HE HAS NOTHING.
NOTHING...
...AT ALL.
...
WHERE'S YOUR PROOF?
MAYBE IT FELL OUT OF YOUR POCKET OR YOU FORGOT IT SOMEWHERE?
I SUPPOSE YOU HAVE A POINT.
WELL, IF YOU PUT IT LIKE THAT...
FINE!
NEXT TIME DON'T ACT SO SUSPICIOUSLY AROUND HERE.
HEY.
COME, FOLLOW ME.

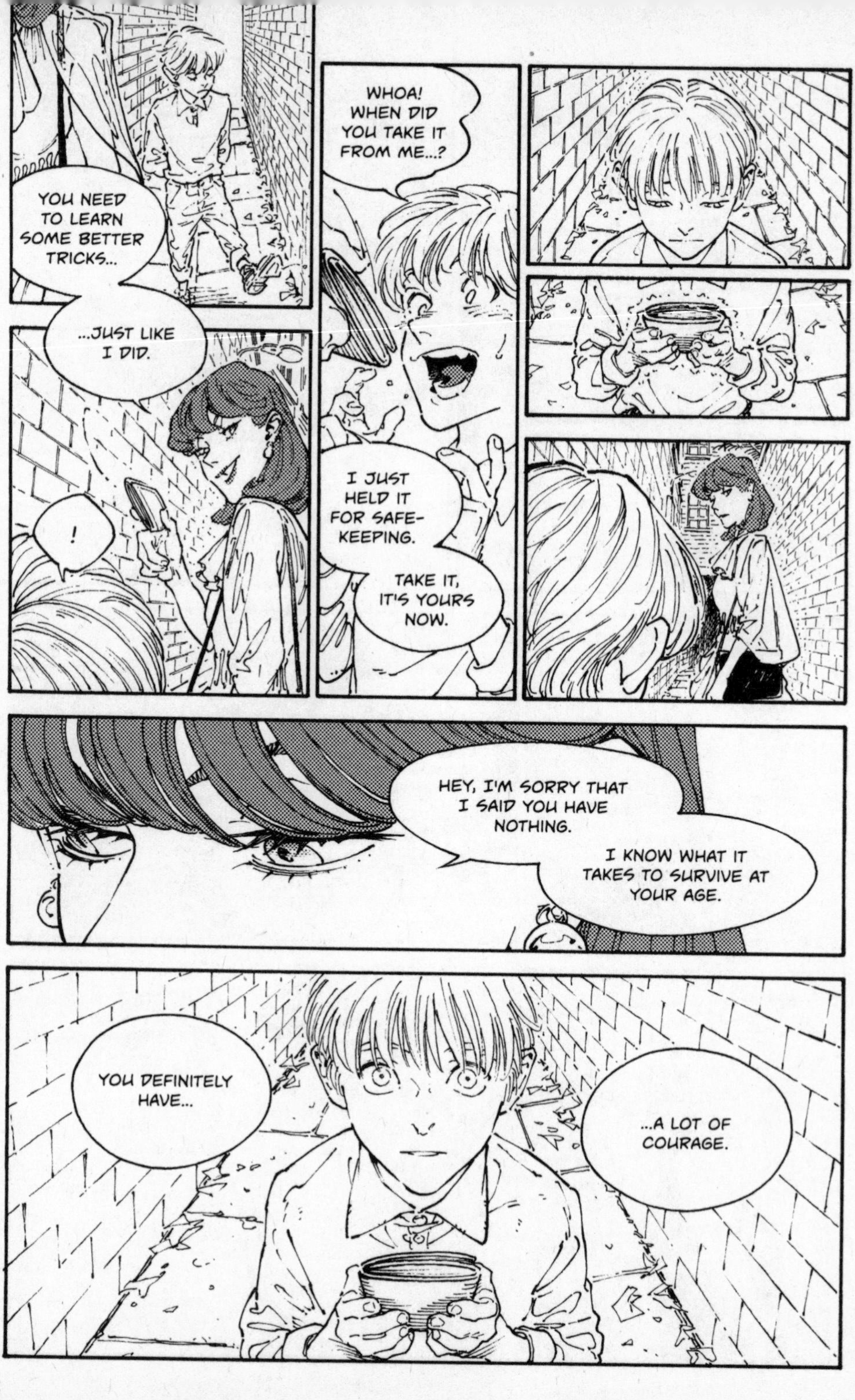
YOU NEED TO LEARN SOME BETTER TRICKS...
...JUST LIKE I DID.
!
WHOA! WHEN DID YOU TAKE IT FROM ME...?
I JUST HELD IT FOR SAFE-KEEPING.
TAKE IT, IT'S YOURS NOW.
HEY, I'M SORRY THAT I SAID YOU HAVE NOTHING.
I KNOW WHAT IT TAKES TO SURVIVE AT YOUR AGE.
YOU DEFINITELY HAVE...
...A LOT OF COURAGE.

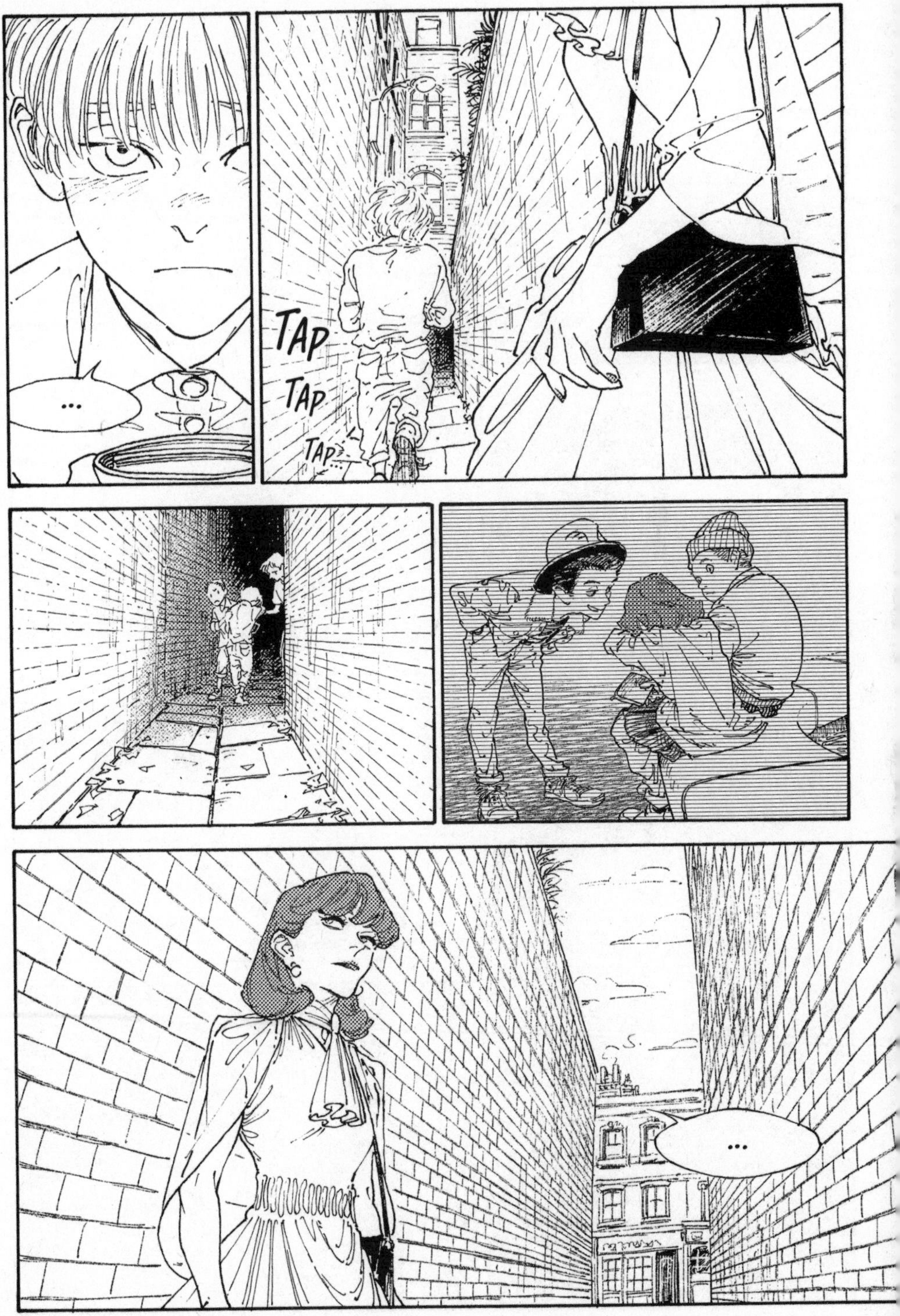
...
TAP
TAP
TAP
...

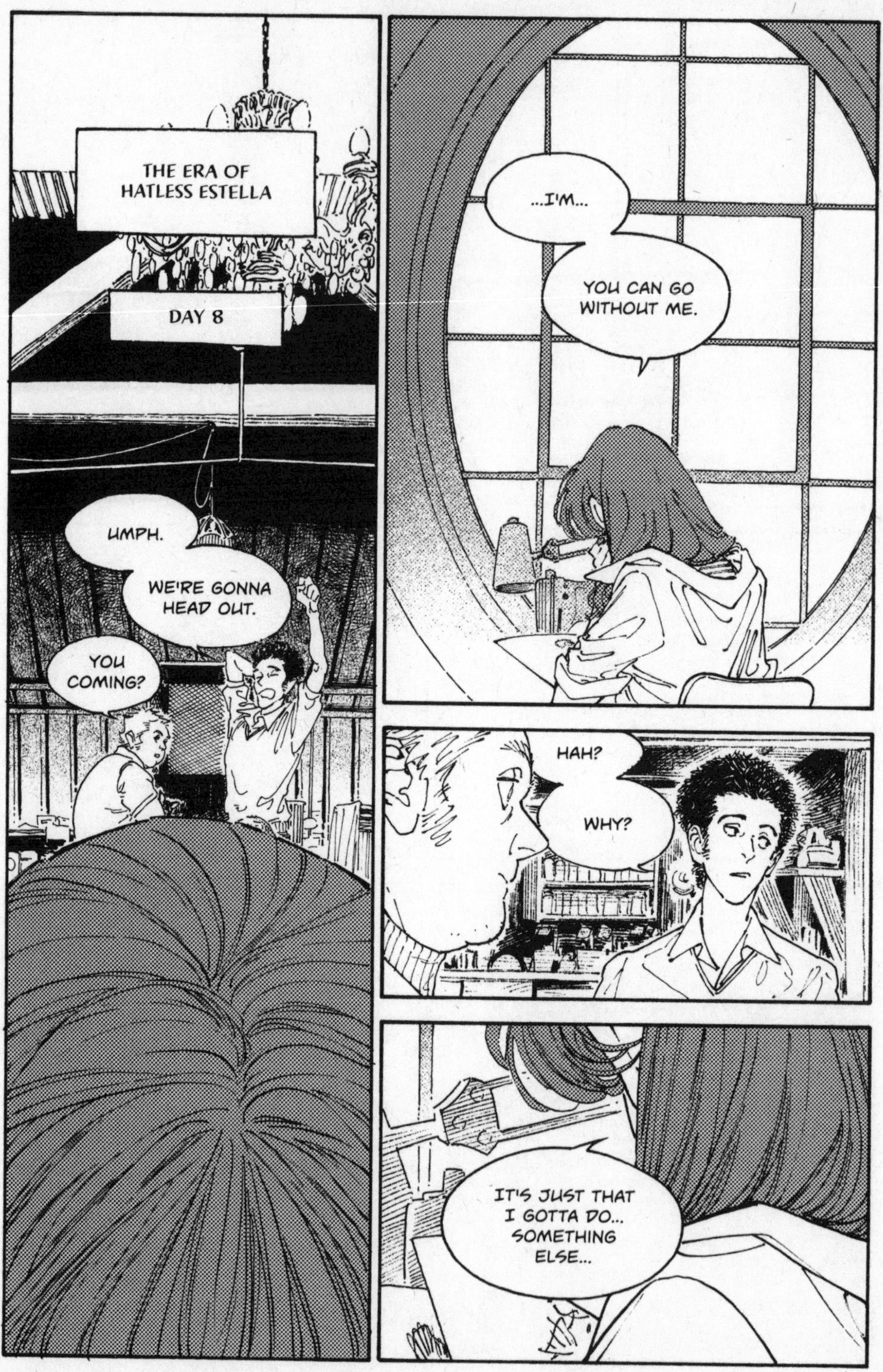
THE ERA OF HATLESS ESTELLA
DAY 8
UMPH.
WE'RE GONNA HEAD OUT.
YOU COMING?
...I'M...
YOU CAN GO WITHOUT ME.
HAH?
WHY?
IT'S JUST THAT I GOTTA DO... SOMETHING ELSE...

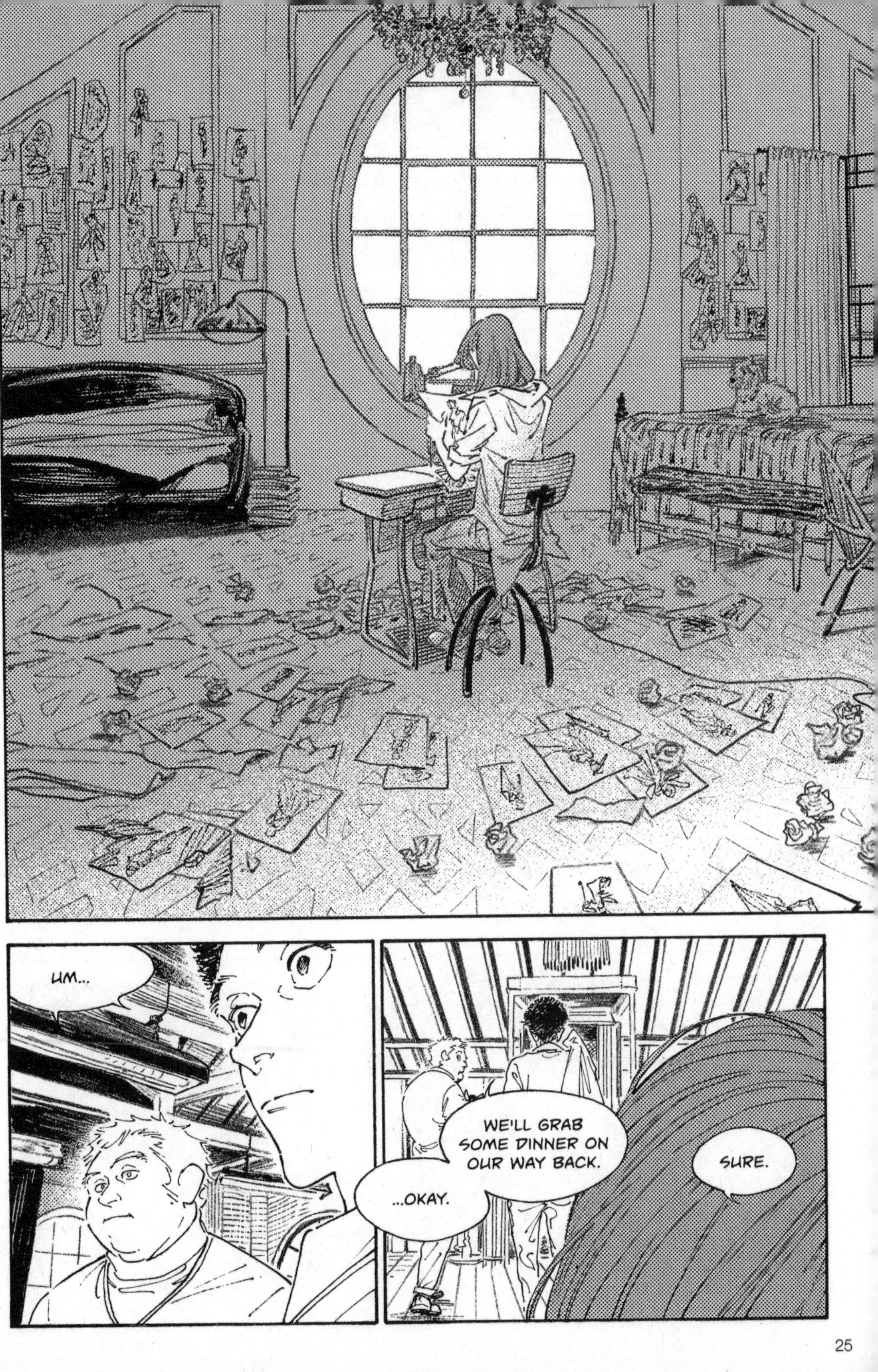
UM...
WE'LL GRAB SOME DINNER ON OUR WAY BACK.
...OKAY.
SURE.

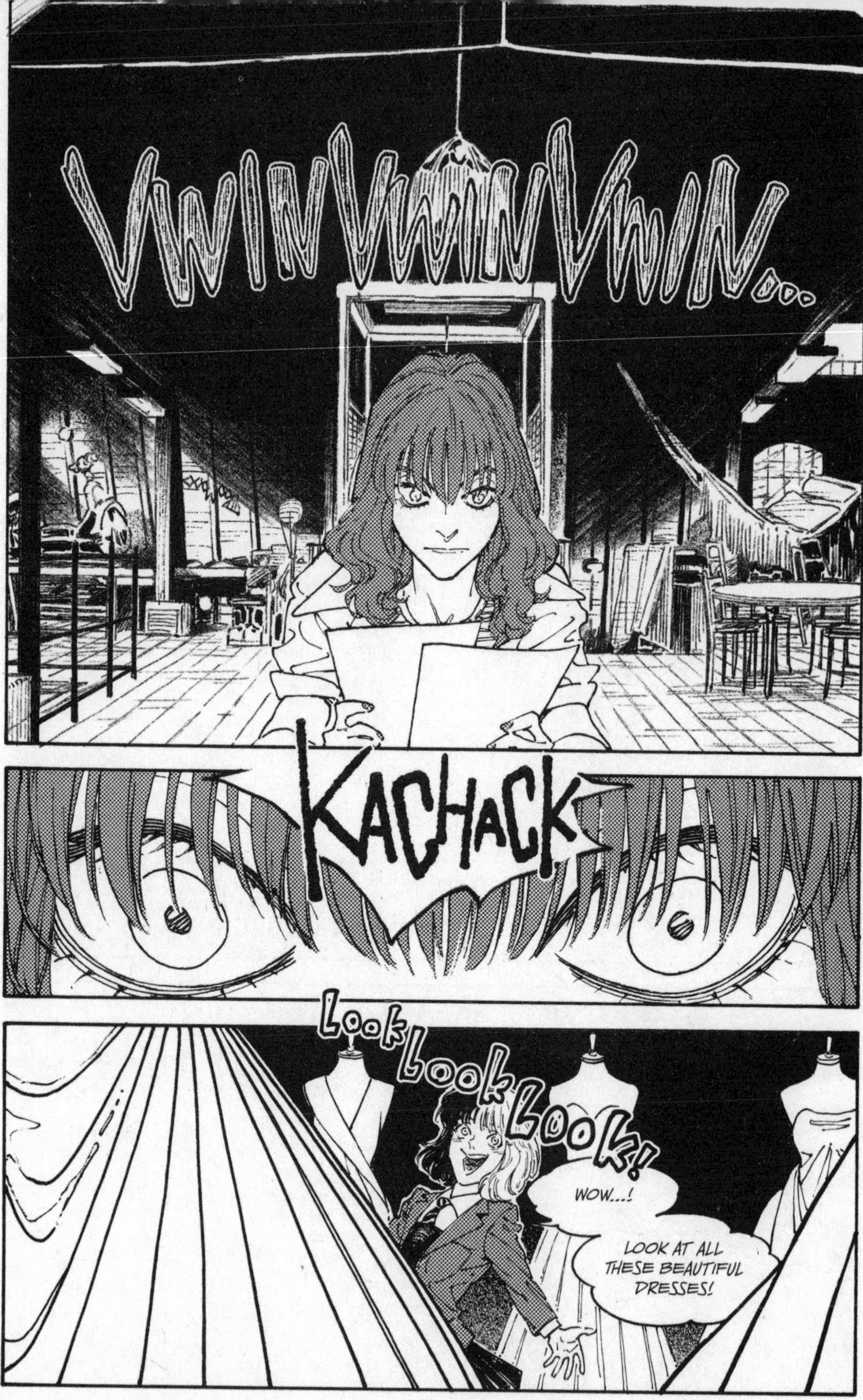
VWIN VWIN VWIN...
KACHACK
LOOK LOOK LOOK!
WOW...!
LOOK AT ALL THESE BEAUTIFUL DRESSES!

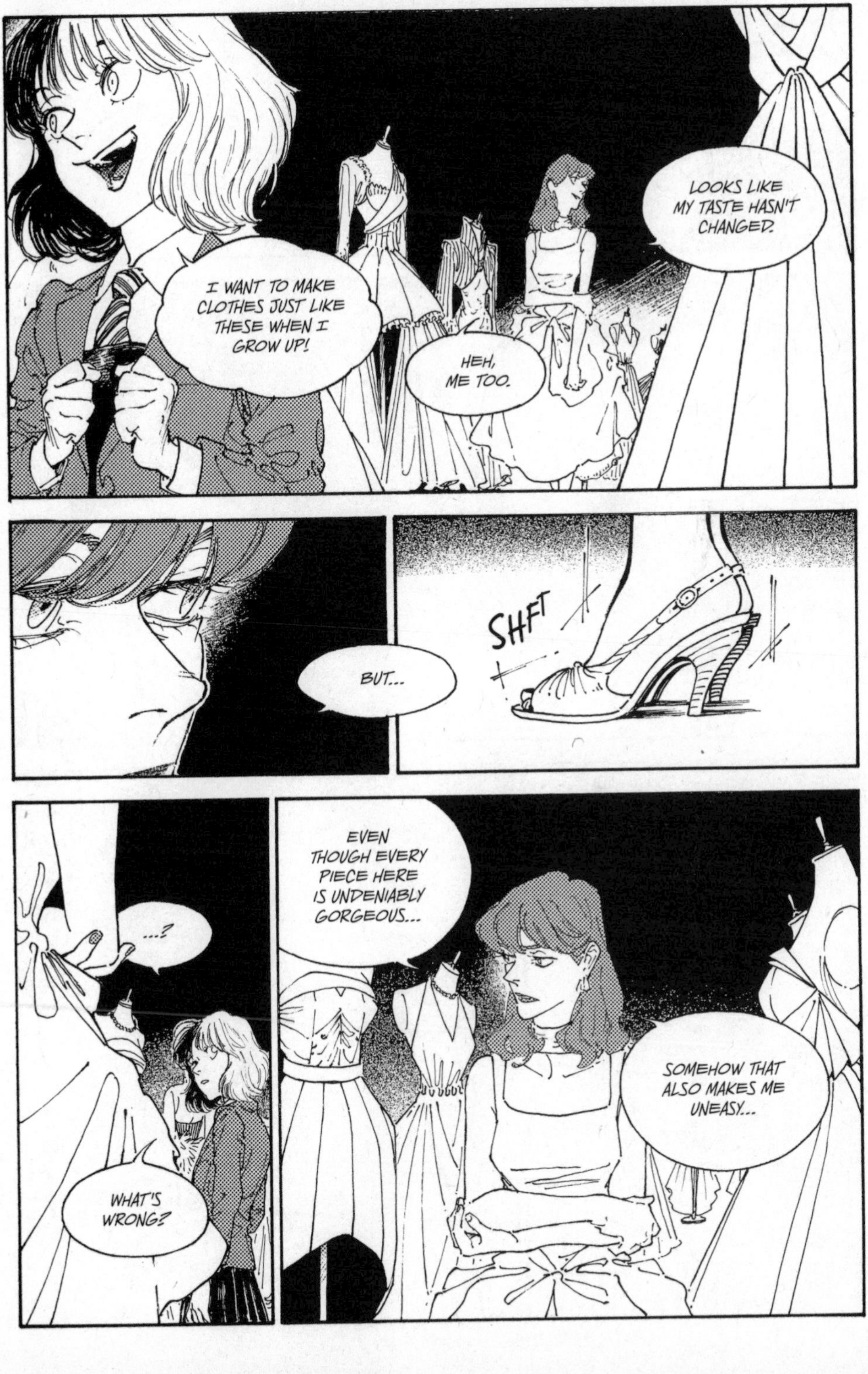
I WANT TO MAKE CLOTHES JUST LIKE THESE WHEN I GROW UP!
HEH, ME TOO.
LOOKS LIKE MY TASTE HASN'T CHANGED.
BUT...
SHFT
...?
WHAT'S WRONG?
EVEN THOUGH EVERY PIECE HERE IS UNDENIABLY GORGEOUS...
SOMEHOW THAT ALSO MAKES ME UNEASY...

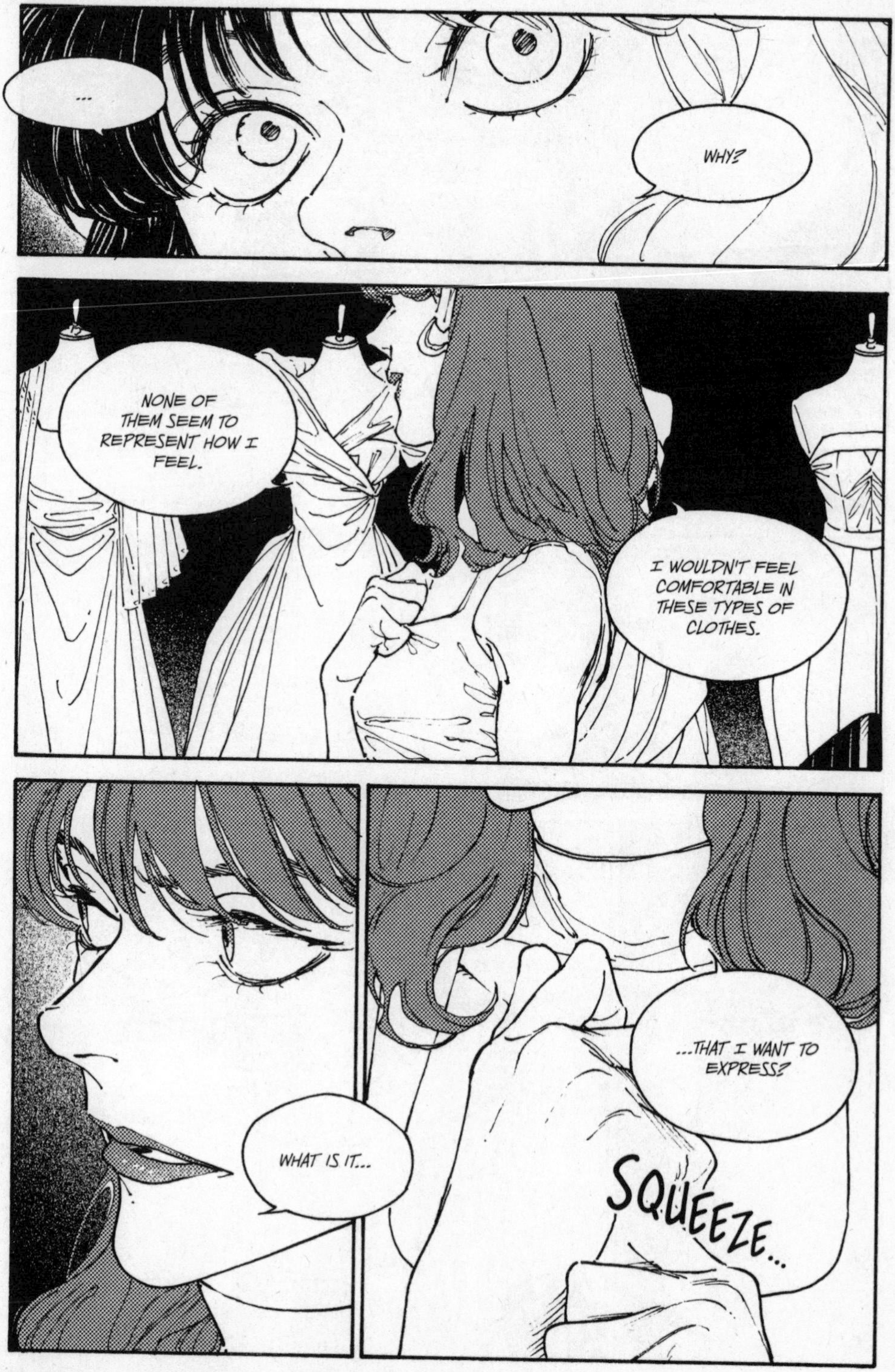
...
WHY?
NONE OF THEM SEEM TO REPRESENT HOW I FEEL.
I WOULDN'T FEEL COMFORTABLE IN THESE TYPES OF CLOTHES.
WHAT IS IT...
...THAT I WANT TO EXPRESS?
SQUEEZE...

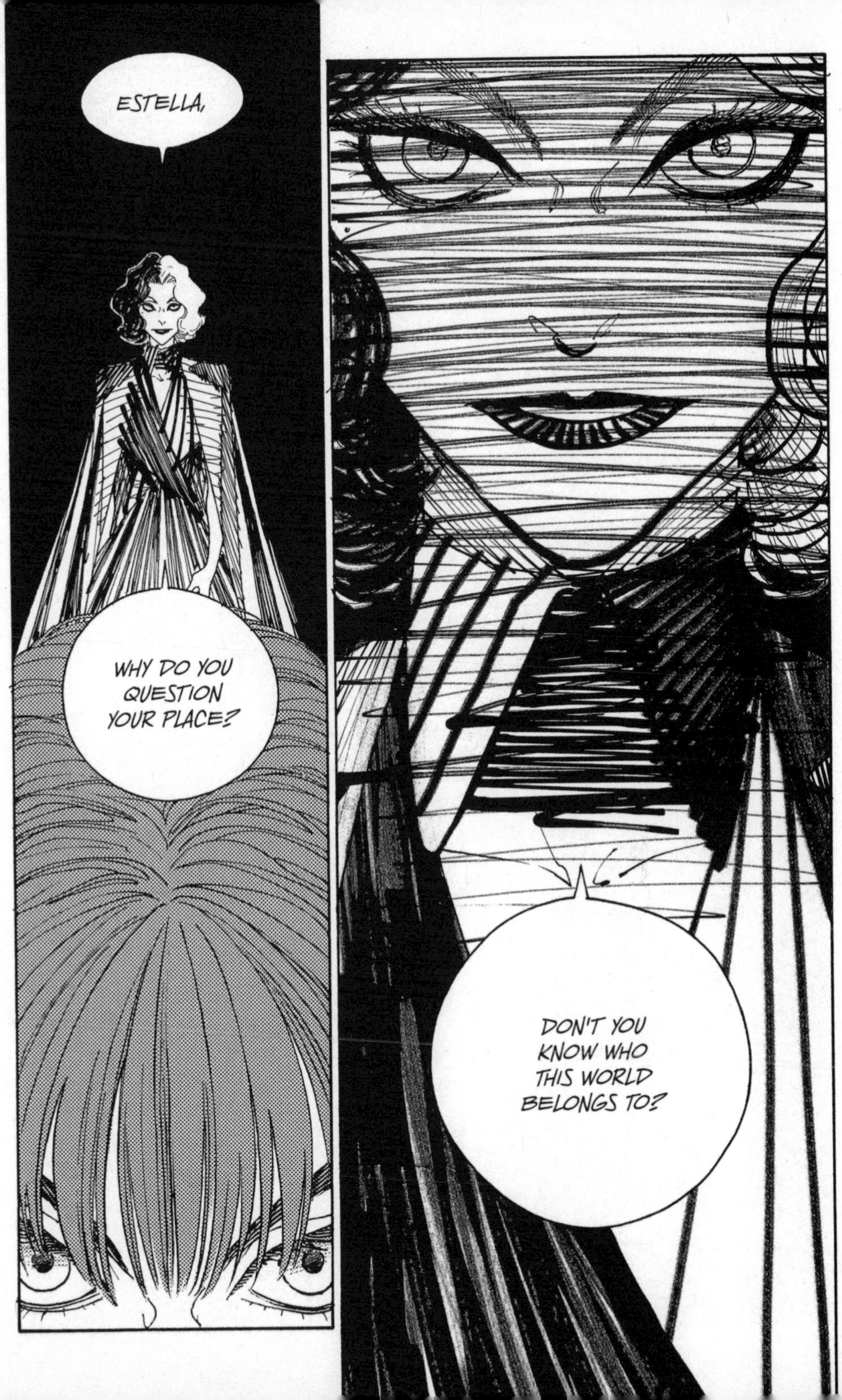
ESTELLA,
WHY DO YOU QUESTION YOUR PLACE?
DON'T YOU KNOW WHO THIS WORLD BELONGS TO?

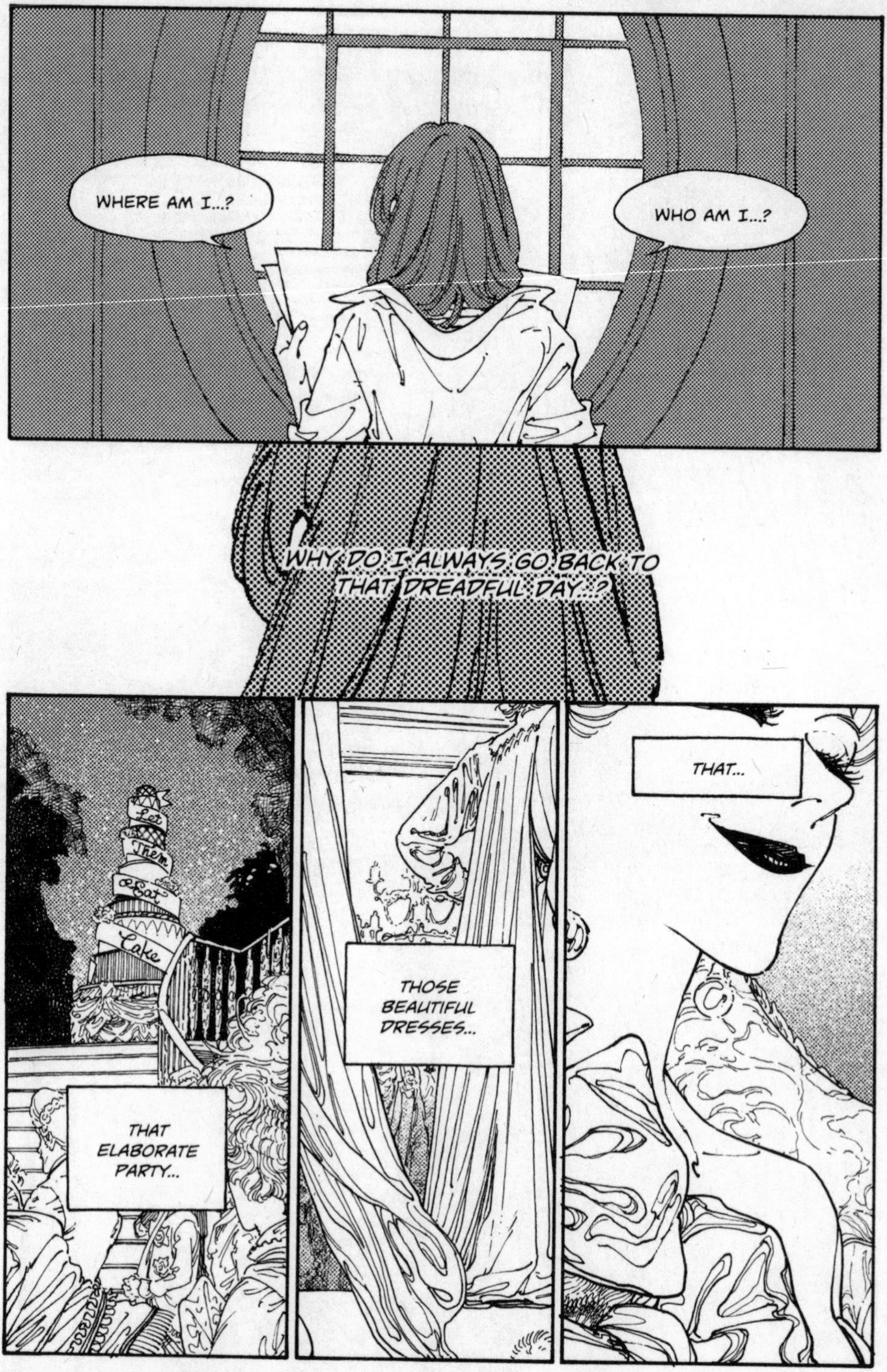
WHERE AM I...?
WHO AM I...?
WHY DO I ALWAYS GO BACK TO THAT DREADFUL DAY...?
Let Them Eat Cake
THAT ELABORATE PARTY...
THOSE BEAUTIFUL DRESSES...
THAT...

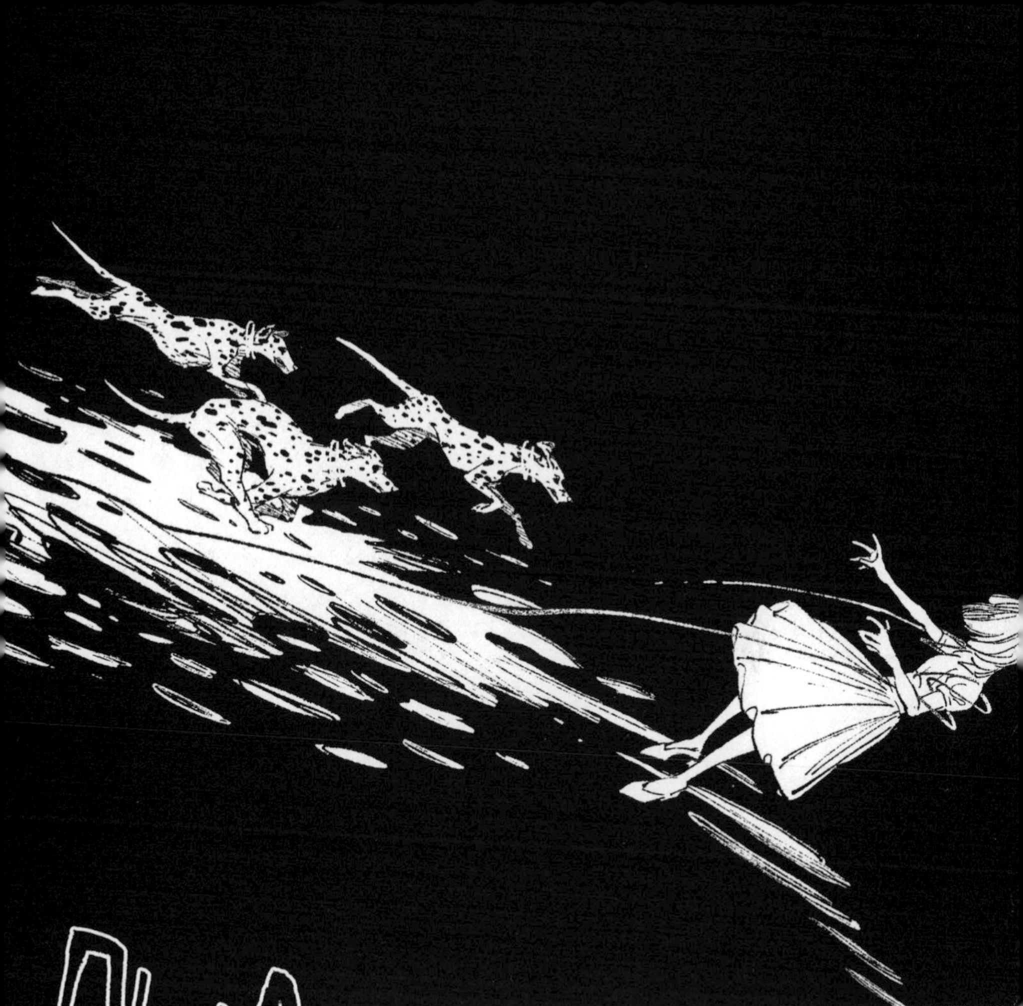

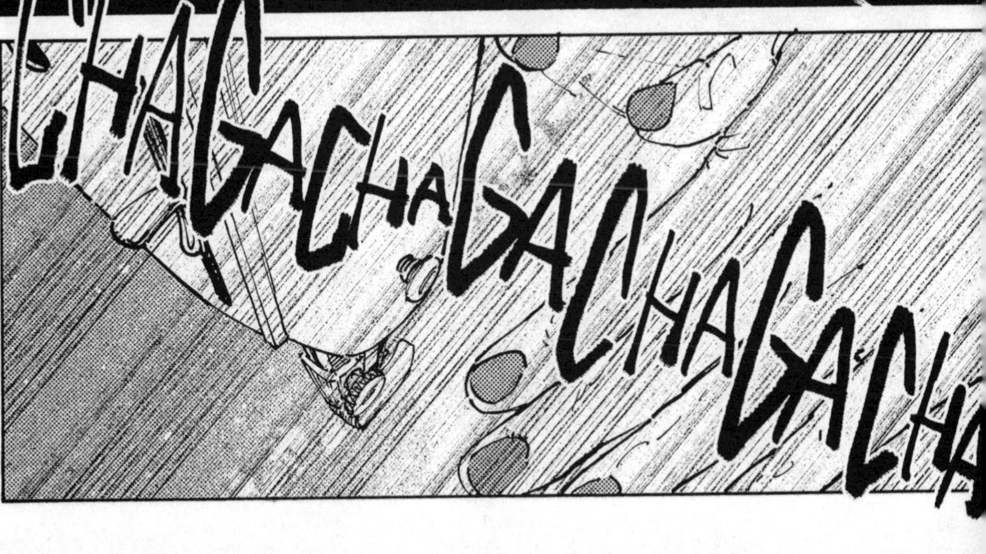
CHAGACHAGACHAGACHA

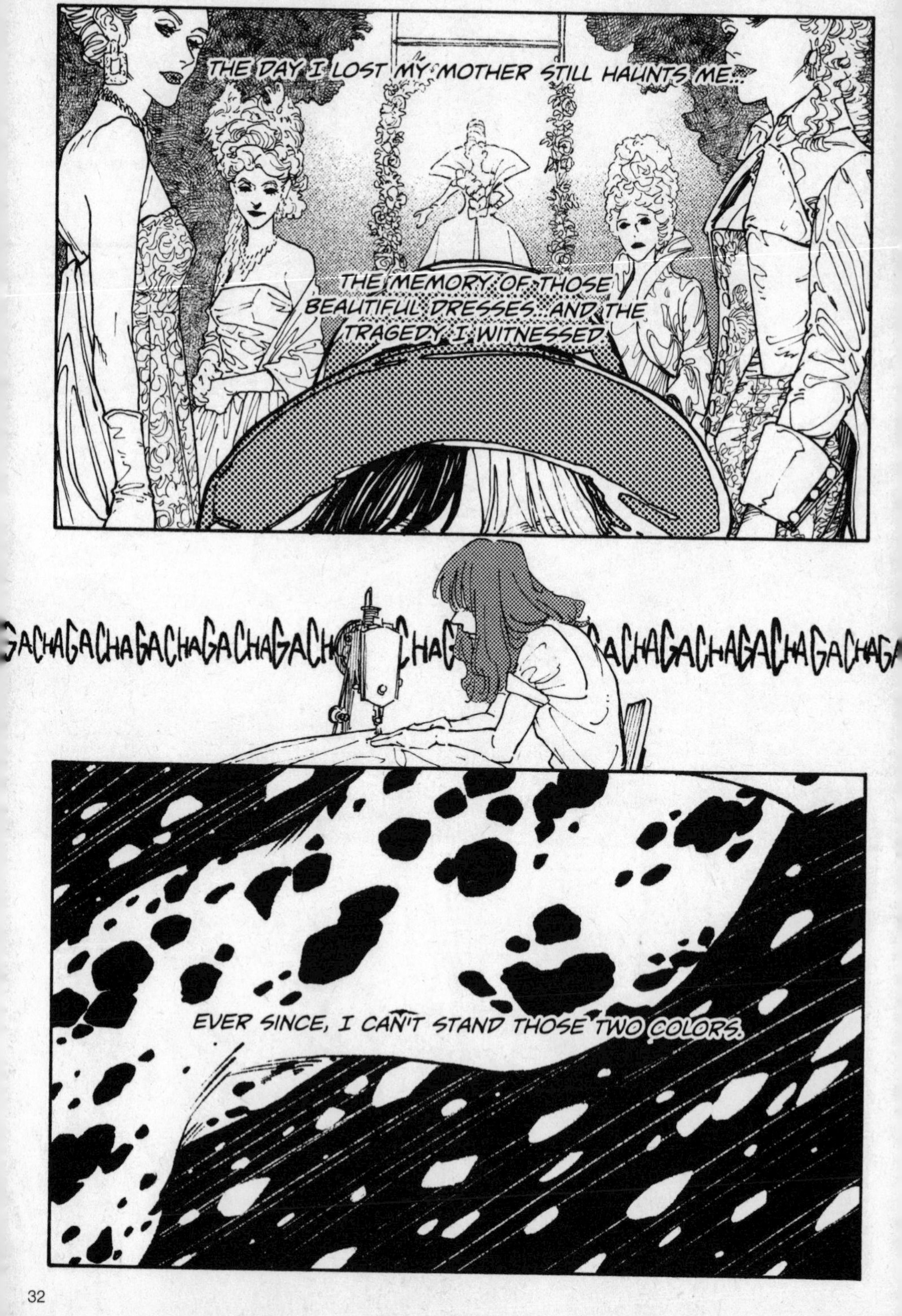
THE DAY I LOST MY MOTHER STILL HAUNTS ME...
THE MEMORY OF THOSE BEAUTIFUL DRESSES...AND THE TRAGEDY I WITNESSED.
GACHAGACHAGACHAGACHAGACH CHAG GACHAGACHAGACHAGACHAGA
EVER SINCE, I CAN'T STAND THOSE TWO COLORS.

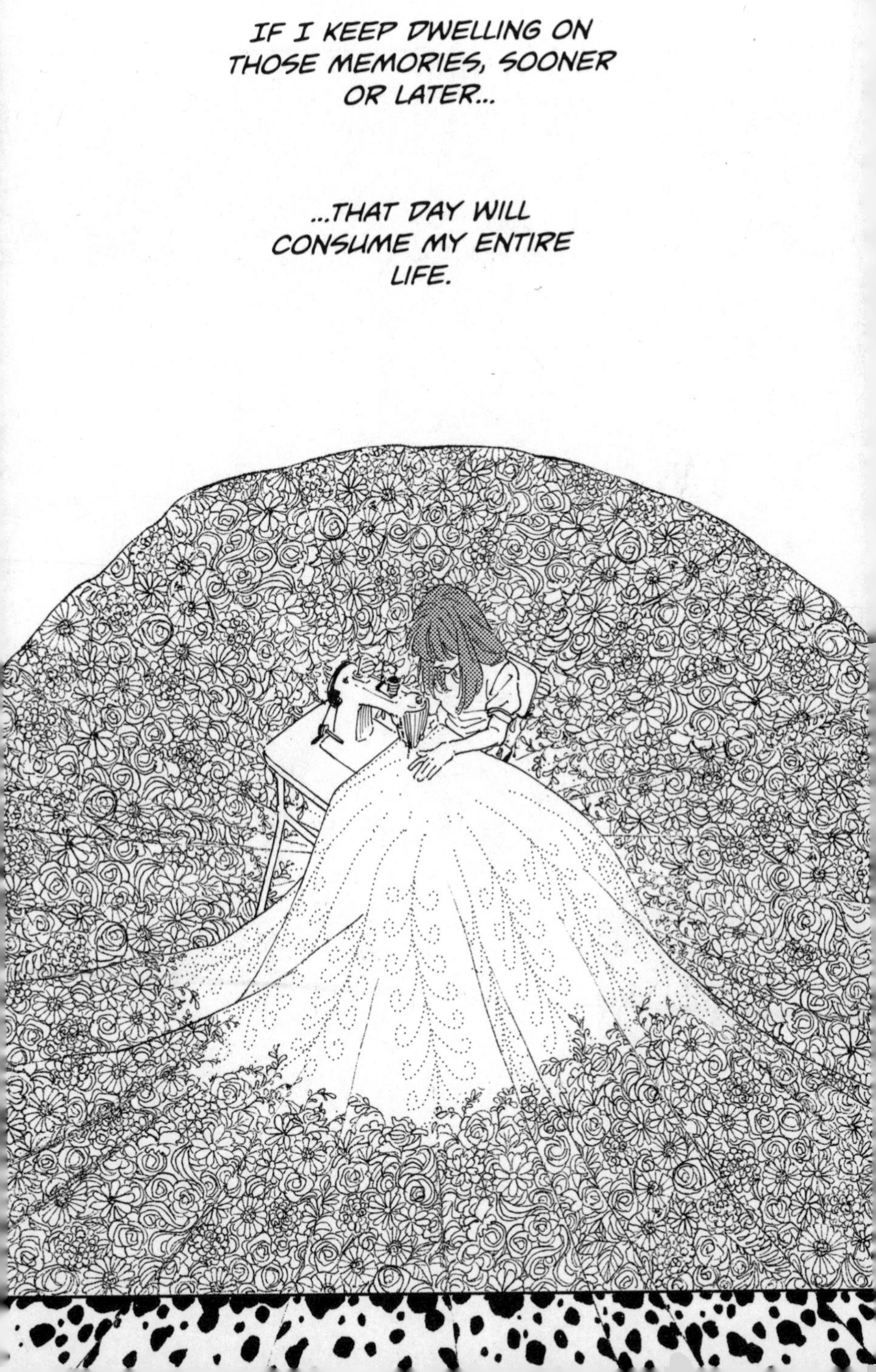
IF I KEEP DWELLING ON THOSE MEMORIES, SOONER OR LATER...
...THAT DAY WILL CONSUME MY ENTIRE LIFE.

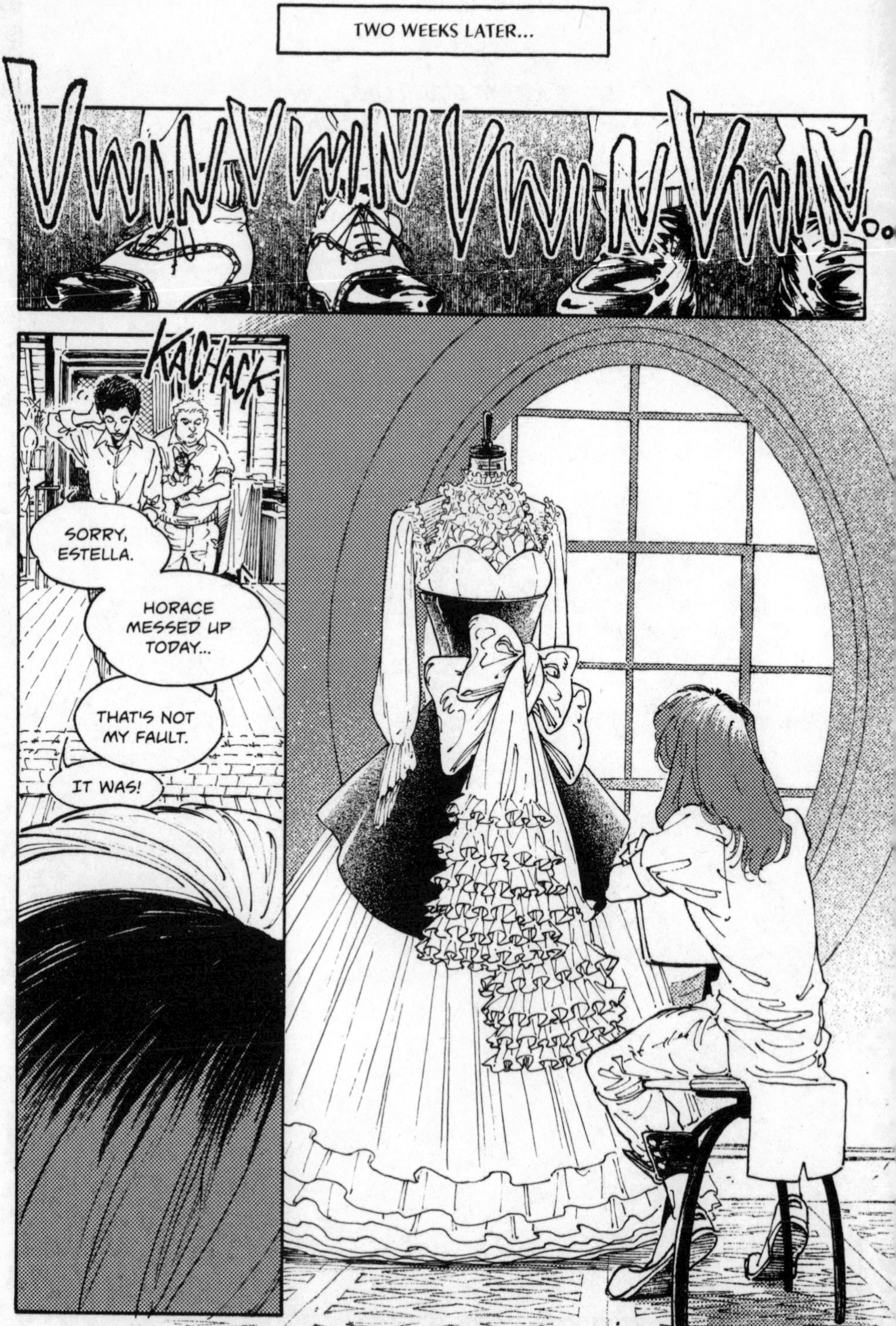

TWO WEEKS LATER...
VWIN VWIN VWIN VWIN...
KACHACK
SORRY, ESTELLA.
HORACE MESSED UP TODAY...
THAT'S NOT MY FAULT.
IT WAS!

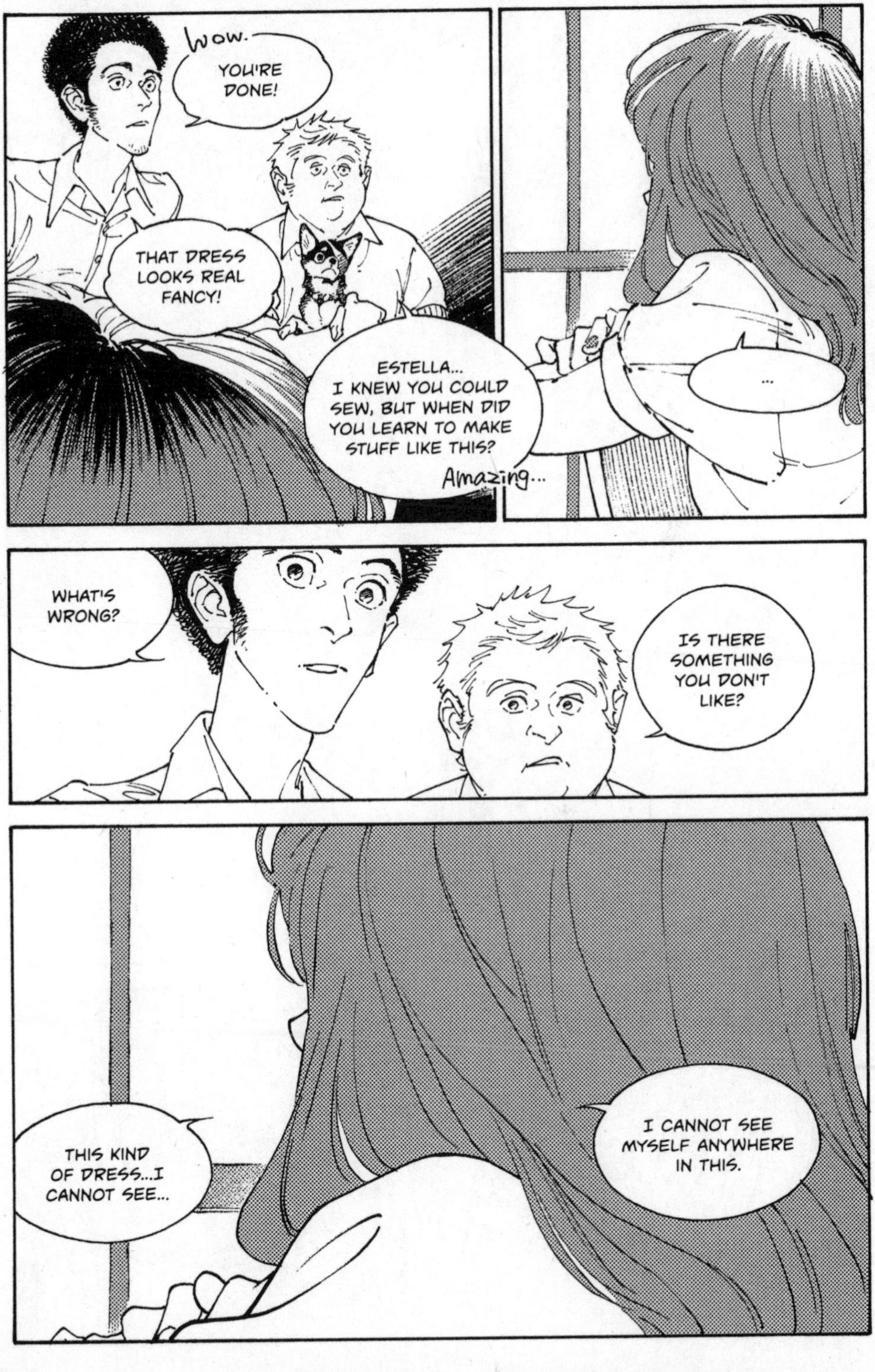
Wow.
YOU'RE DONE!
THAT DRESS LOOKS REAL FANCY!
ESTELLA... I KNEW YOU COULD SEW, BUT WHEN DID YOU LEARN TO MAKE STUFF LIKE THIS?
Amazing...
...
WHAT'S WRONG?
IS THERE SOMETHING YOU DON'T LIKE?
THIS KIND OF DRESS...I CANNOT SEE...
I CANNOT SEE MYSELF ANYWHERE IN THIS.

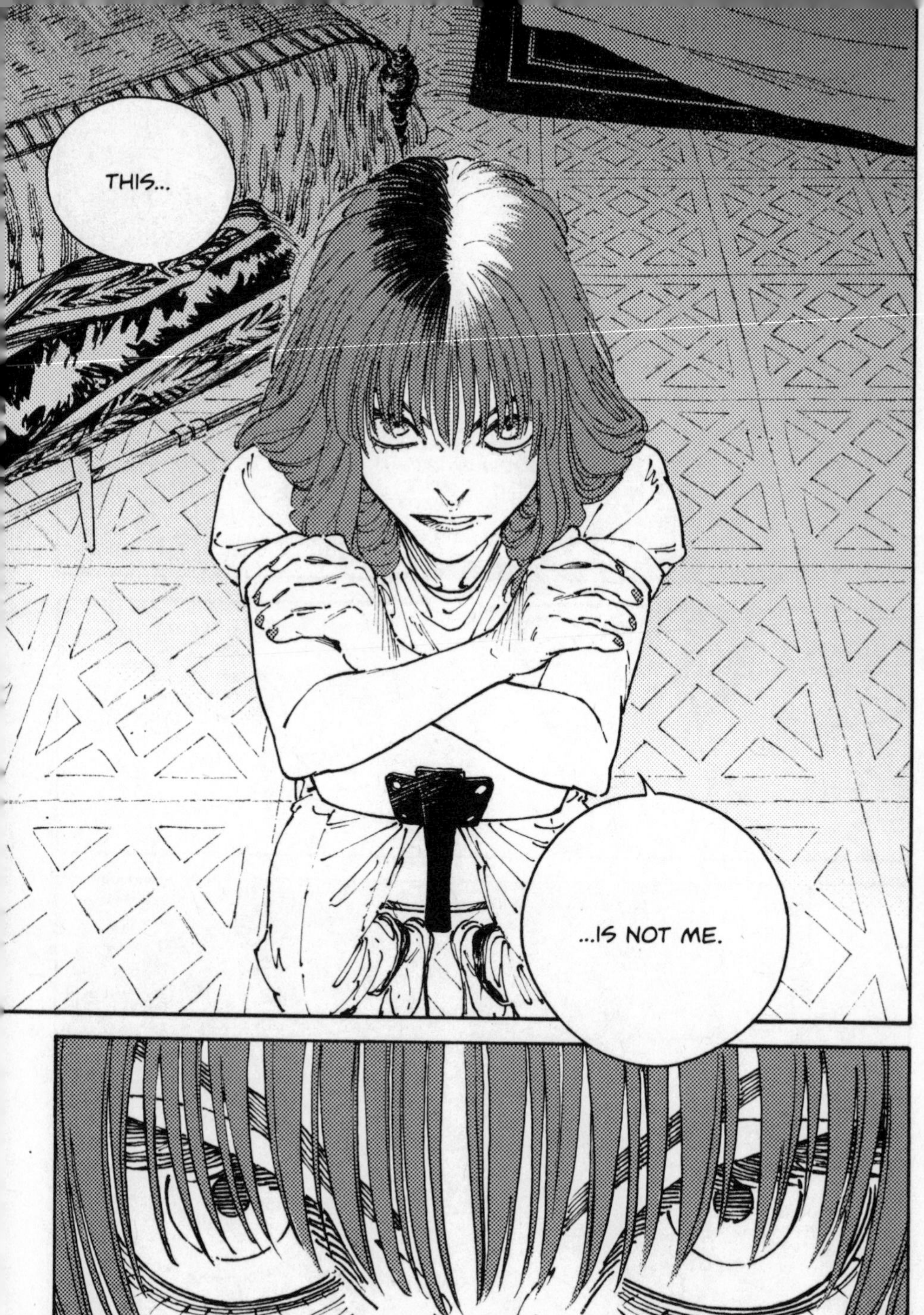
THIS...
...IS NOT ME.

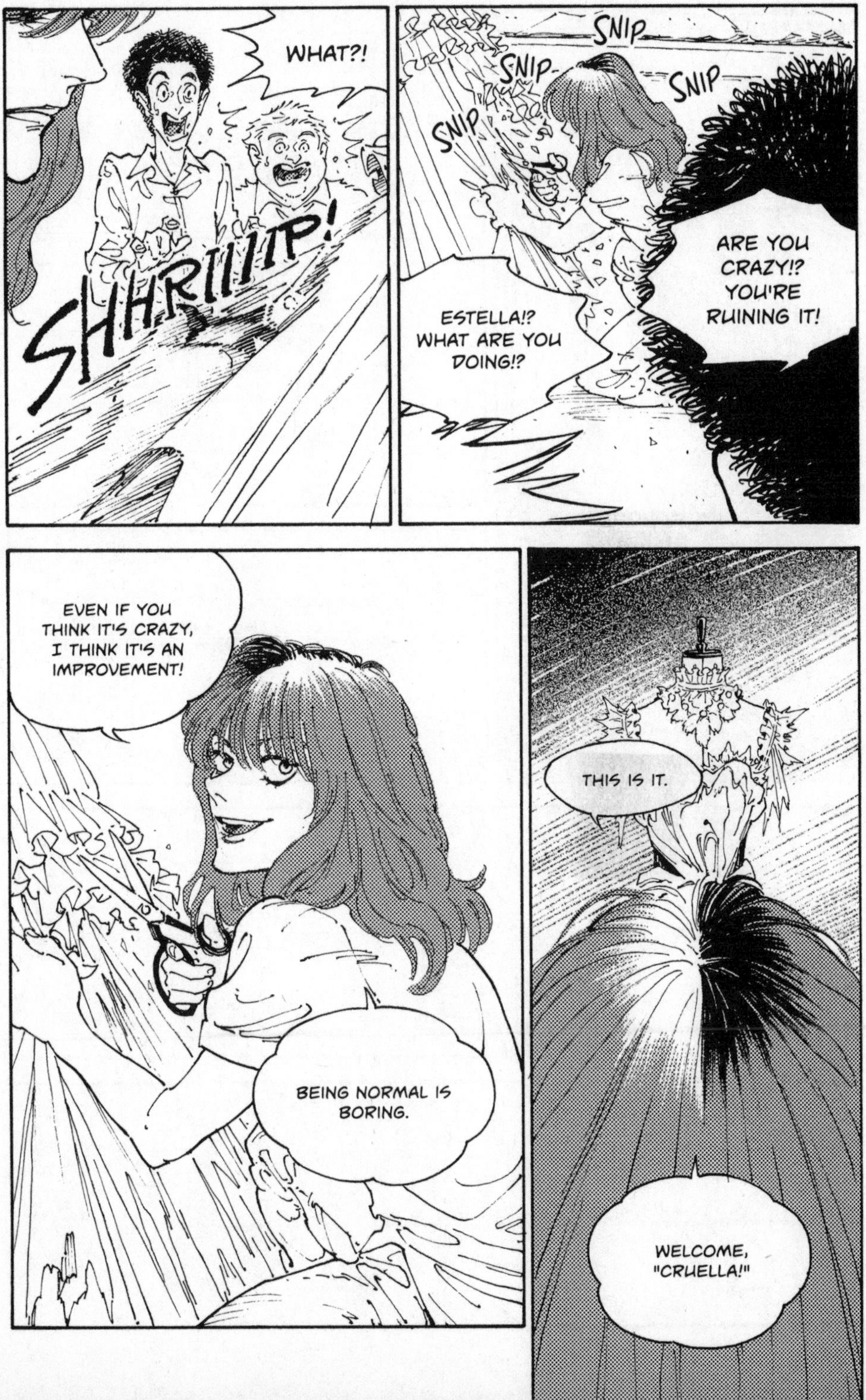

WHAT?!
SHHRIIIIP!
SNIP
SNIP
SNIP
SNIP
ESTELLA!? WHAT ARE YOU DOING!?
ARE YOU CRAZY!? YOU'RE RUINING IT!
EVEN IF YOU THINK IT'S CRAZY, I THINK IT'S AN IMPROVEMENT!
BEING NORMAL IS BORING.
THIS IS IT.
WELCOME, "CRUELLA!"

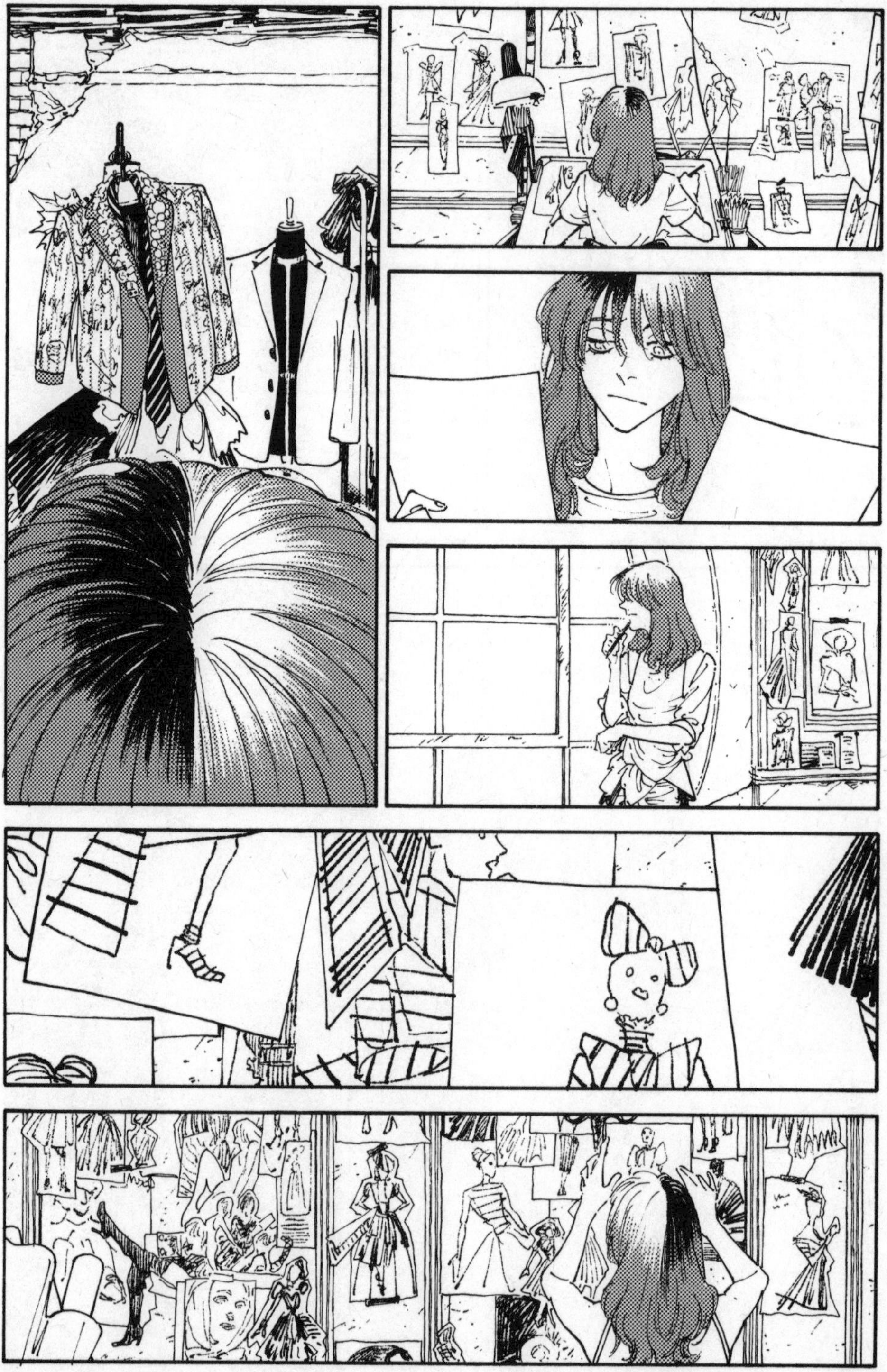

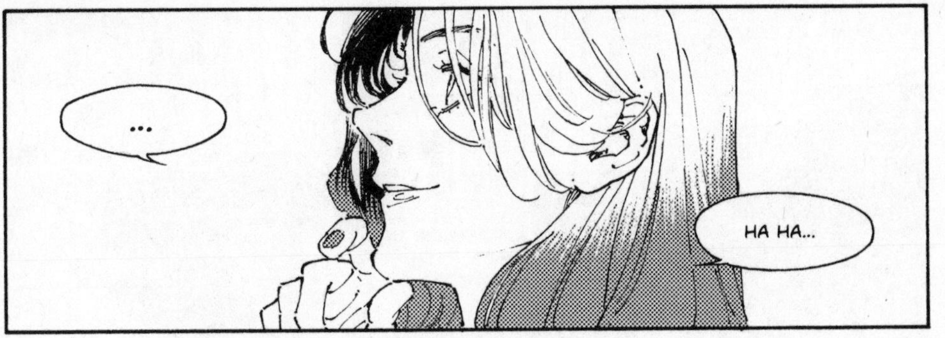
...
HA HA...

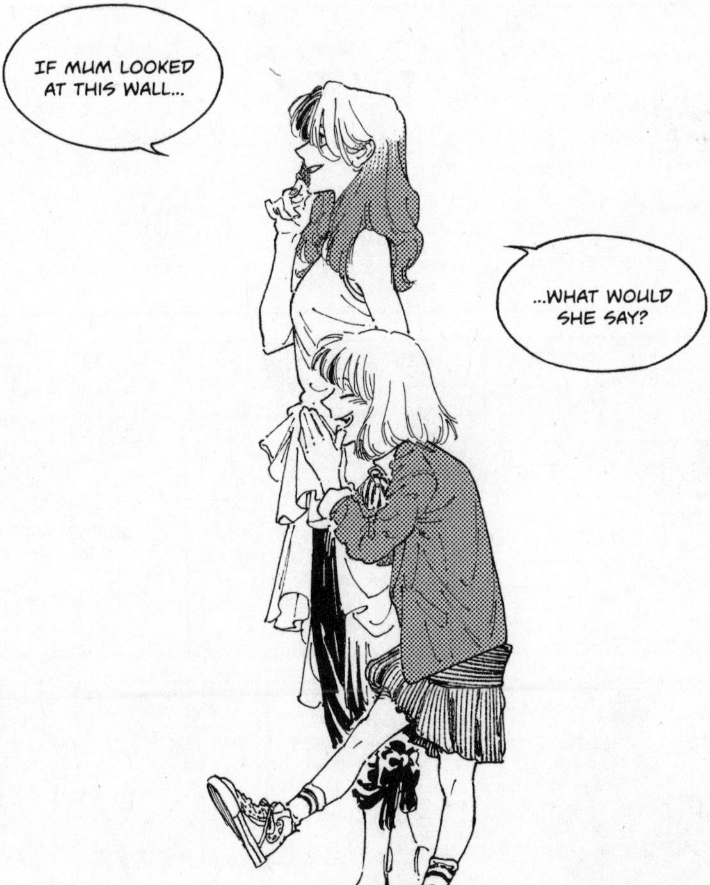
IF MUM LOOKED AT THIS WALL...
...WHAT WOULD SHE SAY?

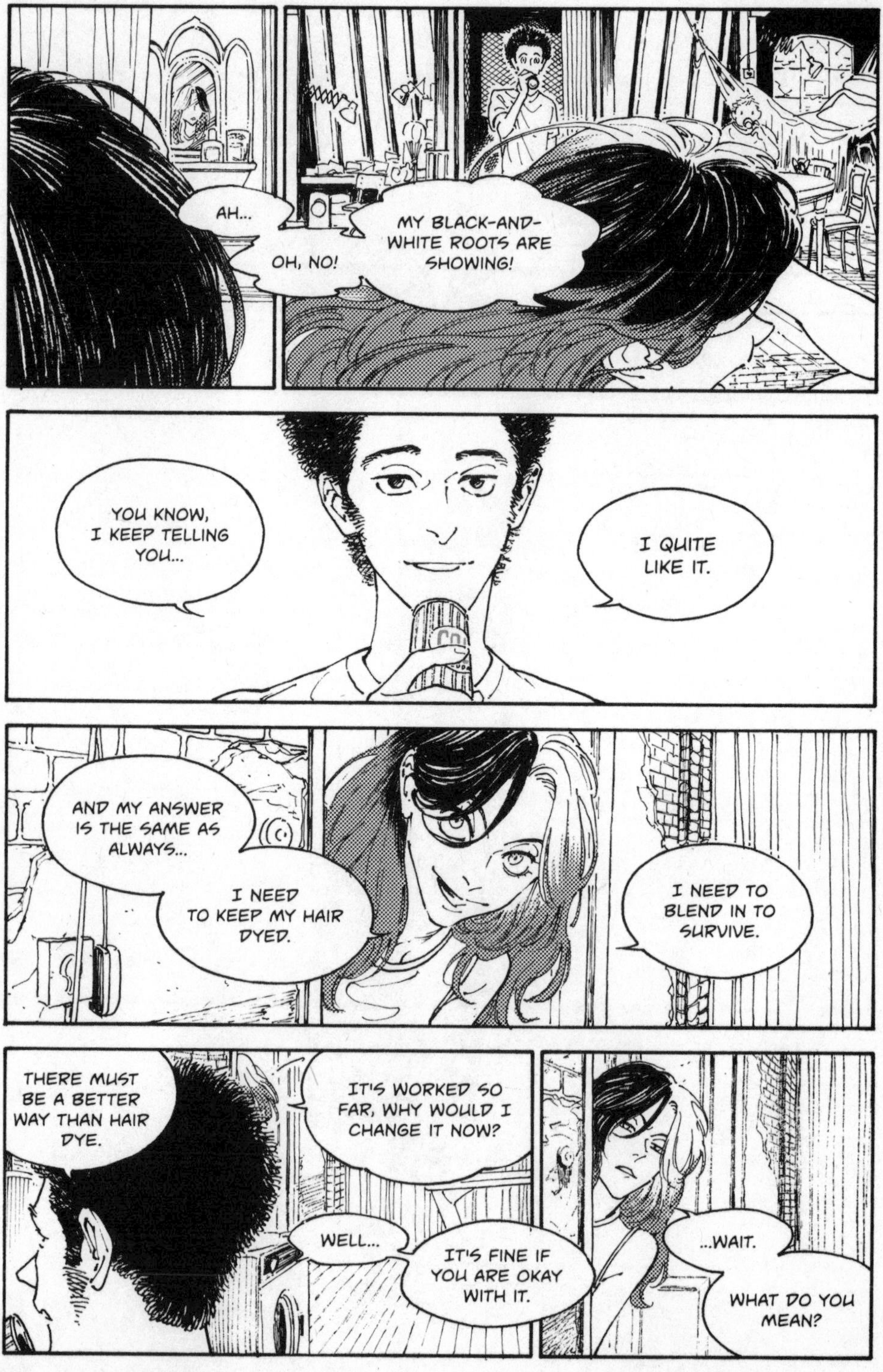
AH...
OH, NO!
MY BLACK-AND-WHITE ROOTS ARE SHOWING!
YOU KNOW, I KEEP TELLING YOU...
I QUITE LIKE IT.
AND MY ANSWER IS THE SAME AS ALWAYS...
I NEED TO KEEP MY HAIR DYED.
I NEED TO BLEND IN TO SURVIVE.
THERE MUST BE A BETTER WAY THAN HAIR DYE.
IT'S WORKED SO FAR, WHY WOULD I CHANGE IT NOW?
WELL...
IT'S FINE IF YOU ARE OKAY WITH IT.
...WAIT.
WHAT DO YOU MEAN?

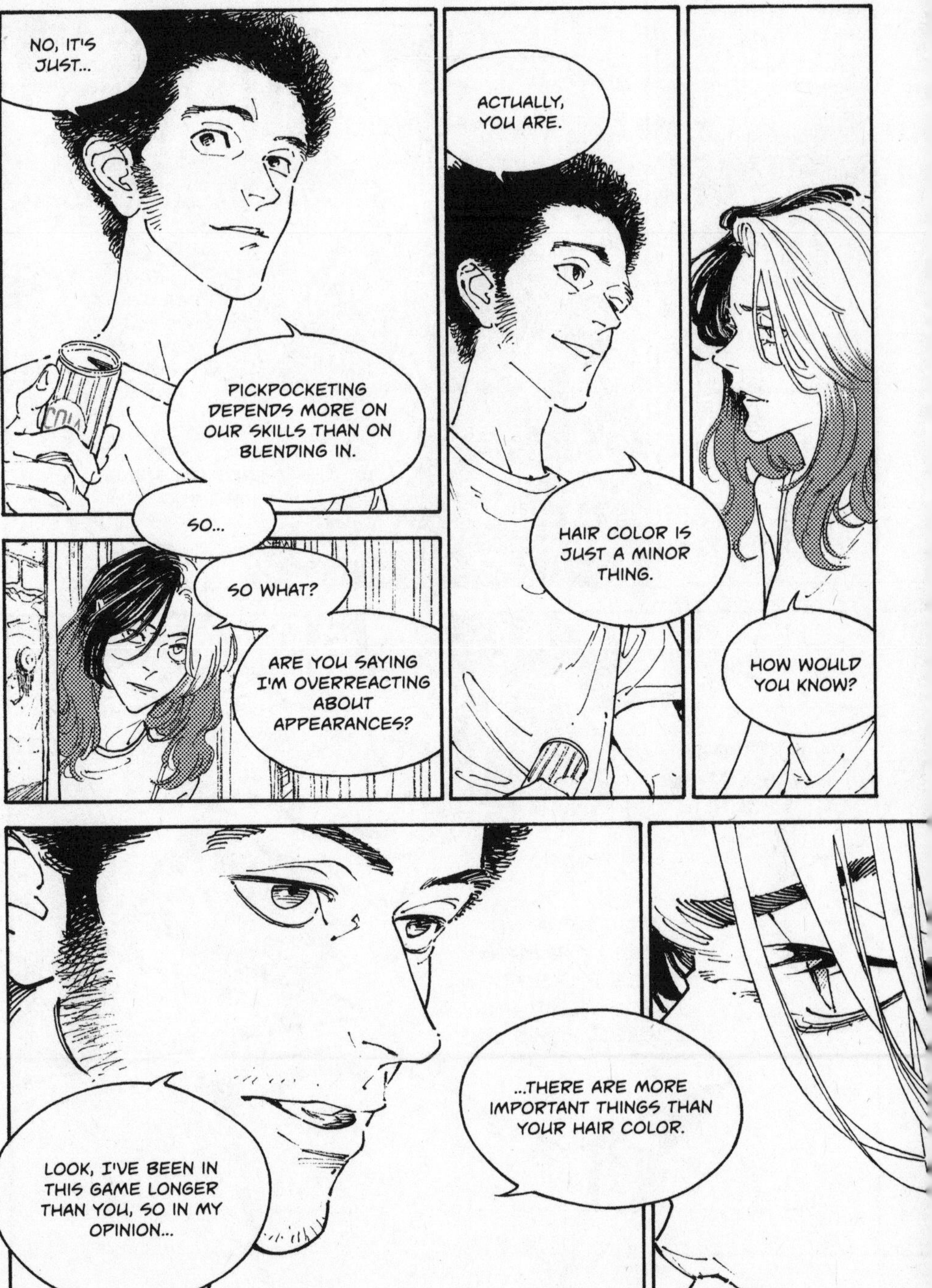
NO, IT'S JUST...
PICKPOCKETING DEPENDS MORE ON OUR SKILLS THAN ON BLENDING IN.
SO...
SO WHAT?
ARE YOU SAYING I'M OVERREACTING ABOUT APPEARANCES?
ACTUALLY, YOU ARE.
HAIR COLOR IS JUST A MINOR THING.
HOW WOULD YOU KNOW?
LOOK, I'VE BEEN IN THIS GAME LONGER THAN YOU, SO IN MY OPINION...
...THERE ARE MORE IMPORTANT THINGS THAN YOUR HAIR COLOR.

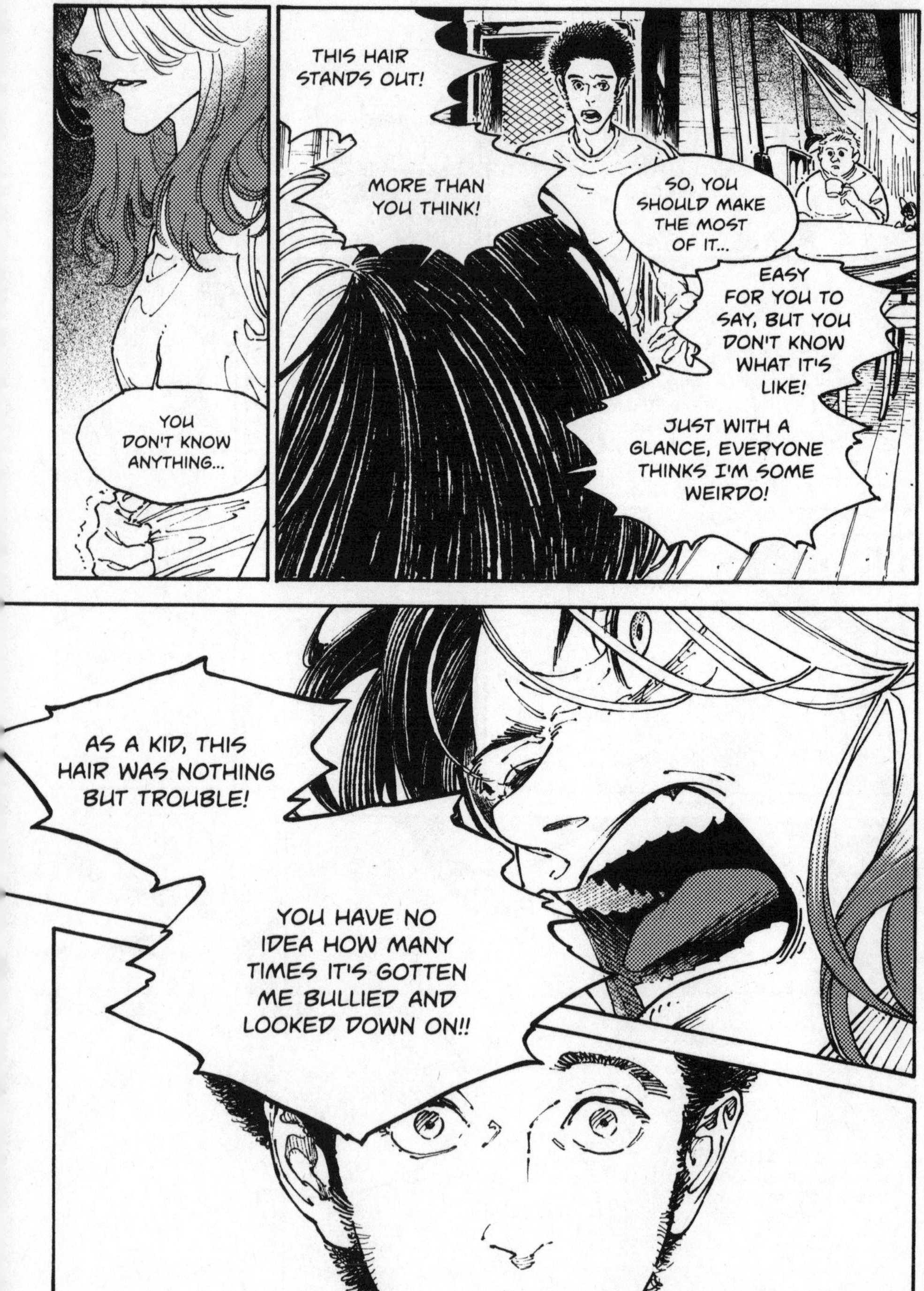
YOU DON'T KNOW ANYTHING...
THIS HAIR STANDS OUT!
MORE THAN YOU THINK!
SO, YOU SHOULD MAKE THE MOST OF IT...
EASY FOR YOU TO SAY, BUT YOU DON'T KNOW WHAT IT'S LIKE!
JUST WITH A GLANCE, EVERYONE THINKS I'M SOME WEIRDO!
AS A KID, THIS HAIR WAS NOTHING BUT TROUBLE!
YOU HAVE NO IDEA HOW MANY TIMES IT'S GOTTEN ME BULLIED AND LOOKED DOWN ON!!

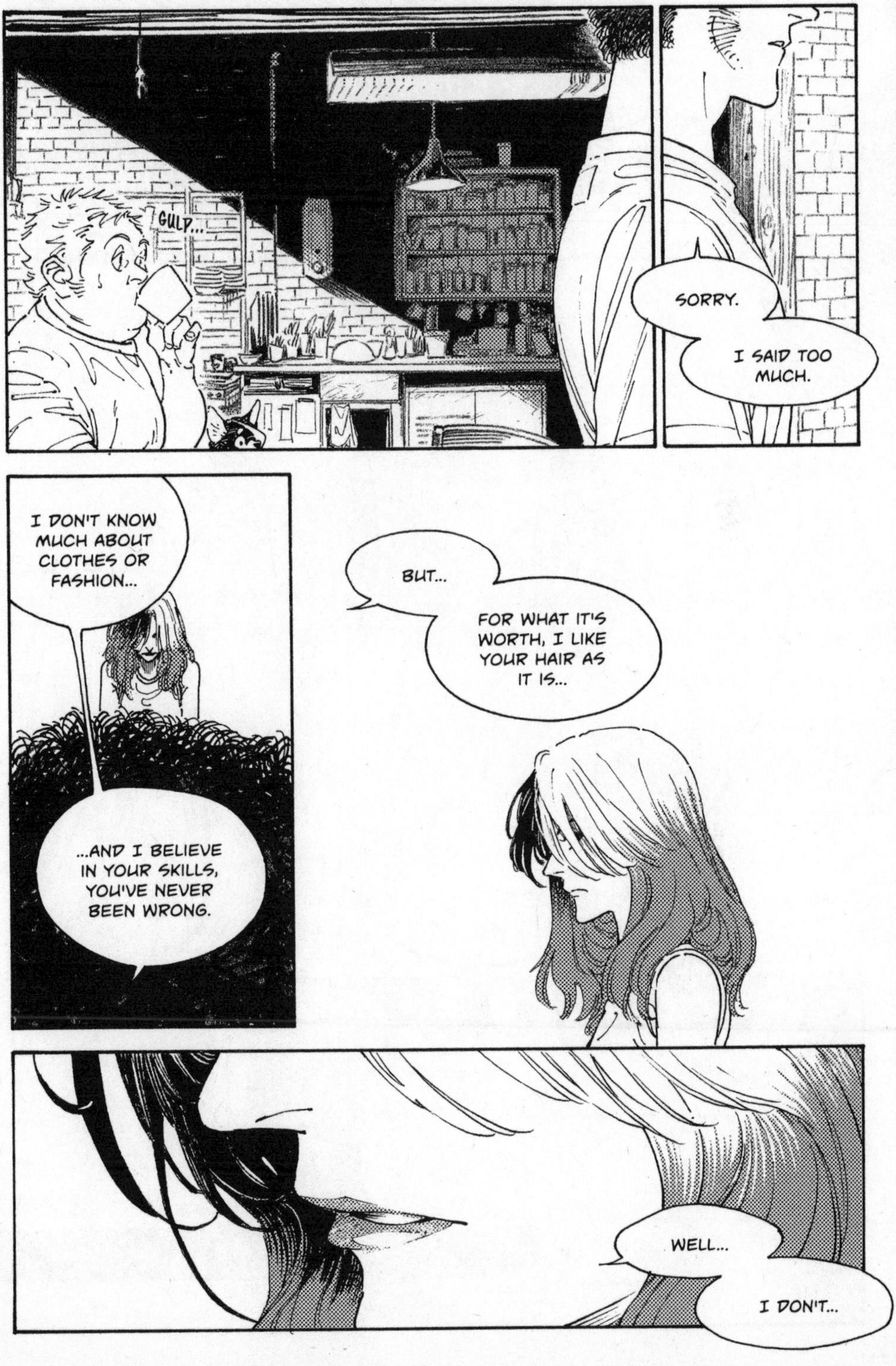
GULP...
SORRY.
I SAID TOO MUCH.
I DON'T KNOW MUCH ABOUT CLOTHES OR FASHION...
...AND I BELIEVE IN YOUR SKILLS, YOU'VE NEVER BEEN WRONG.
BUT...
FOR WHAT IT'S WORTH, I LIKE YOUR HAIR AS IT IS...
WELL...
I DON'T...

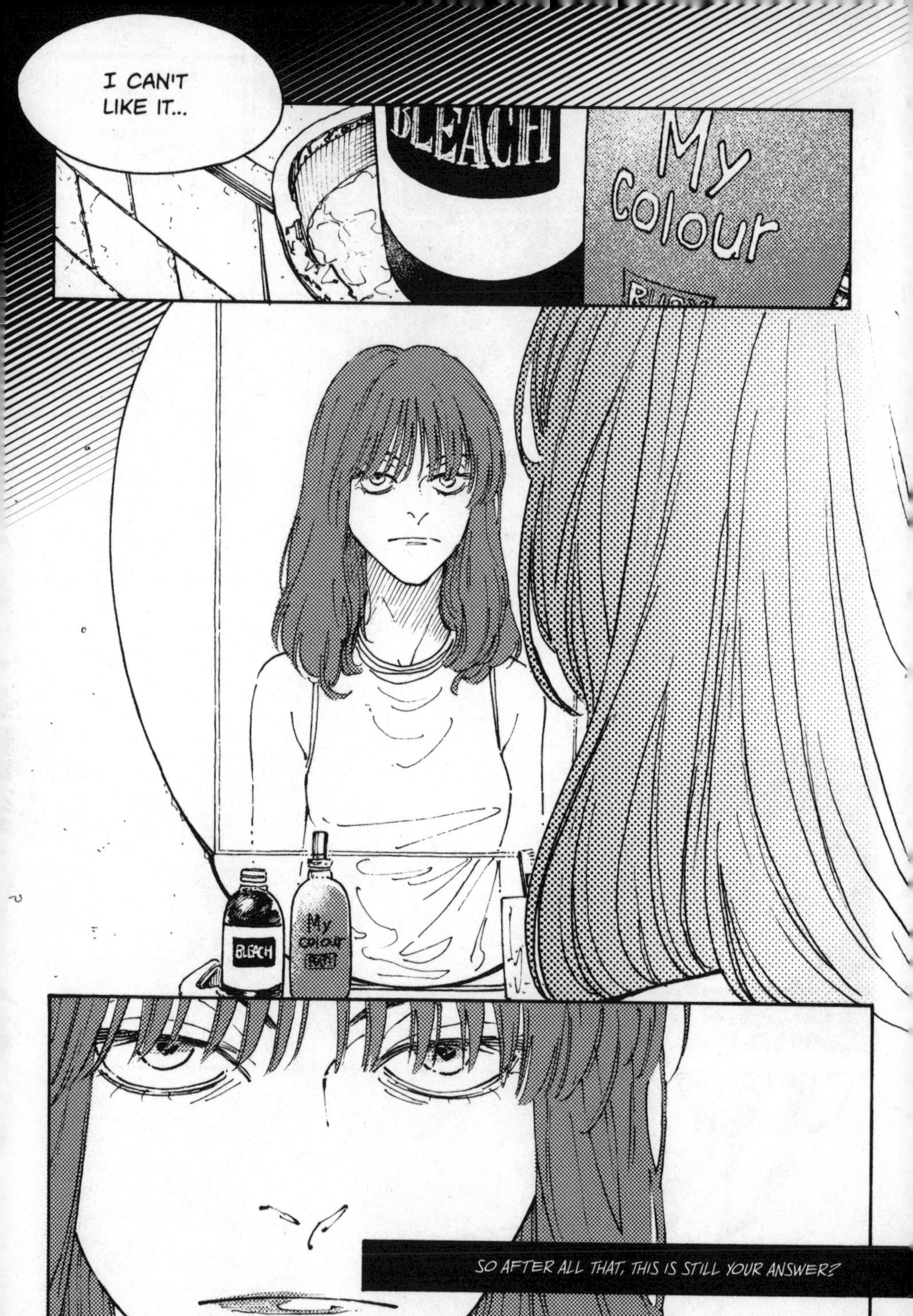
I CAN'T LIKE IT...
BLEACH
My Colour
BLEACH
My colour
SO AFTER ALL THAT, THIS IS STILL YOUR ANSWER?

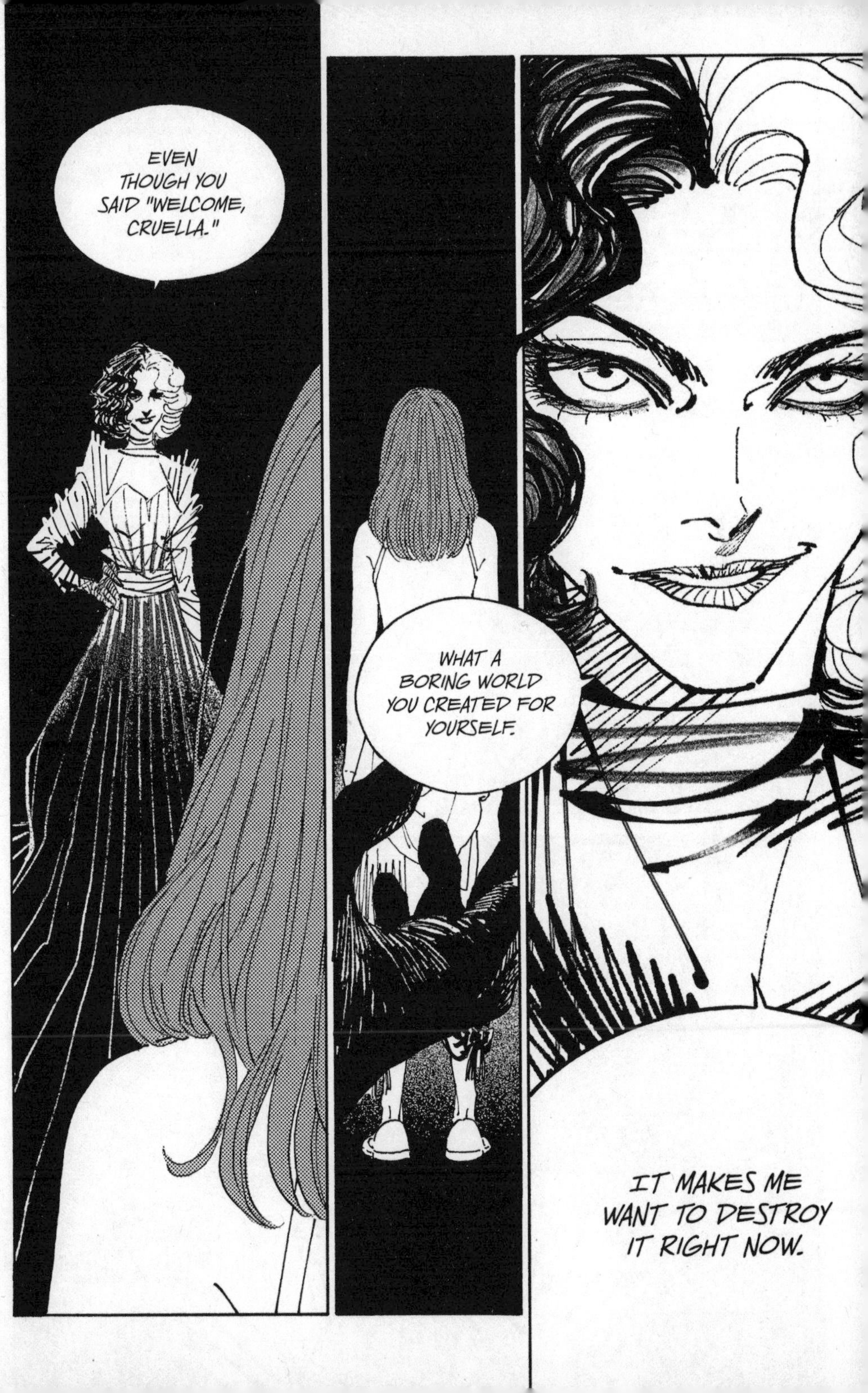
EVEN THOUGH YOU SAID "WELCOME, CRUELLA."
WHAT A BORING WORLD YOU CREATED FOR YOURSELF.
IT MAKES ME WANT TO DESTROY IT RIGHT NOW.

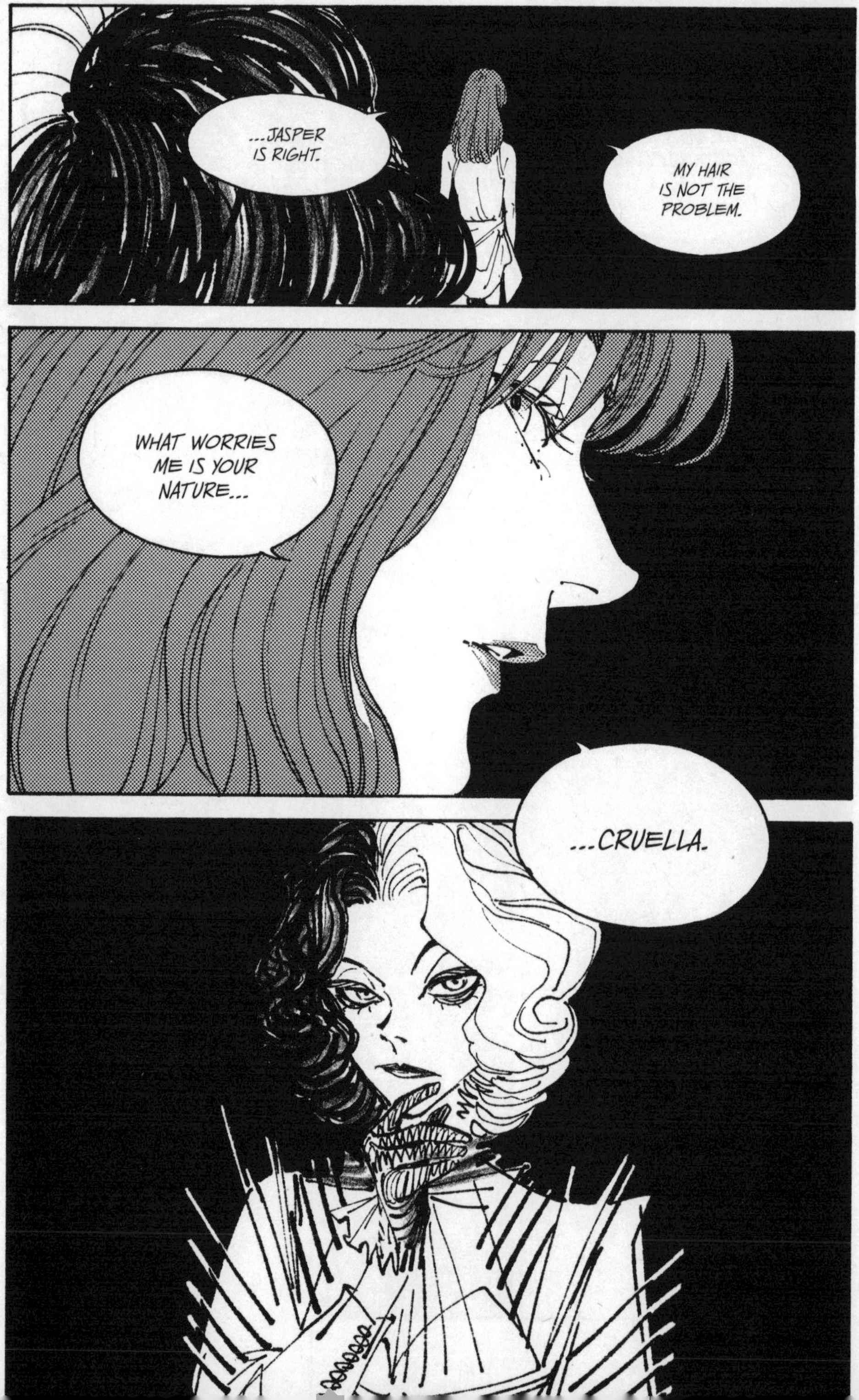
...JASPER IS RIGHT.
MY HAIR IS NOT THE PROBLEM.
WHAT WORRIES ME IS YOUR NATURE...
...CRUELLA.

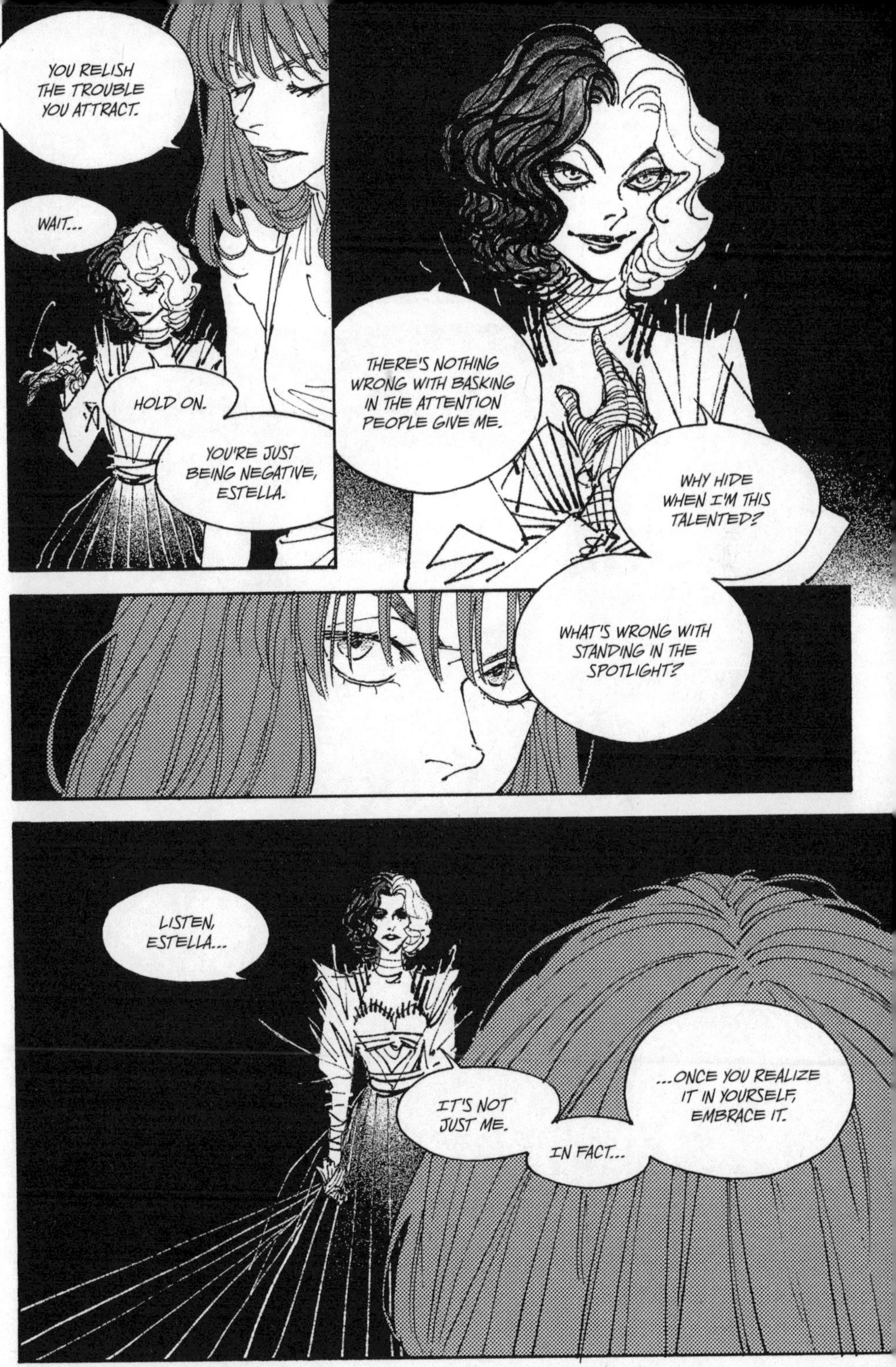
YOU RELISH THE TROUBLE YOU ATTRACT.
WAIT...
HOLD ON.
YOU'RE JUST BEING NEGATIVE, ESTELLA.
THERE'S NOTHING WRONG WITH BASKING IN THE ATTENTION PEOPLE GIVE ME.
WHY HIDE WHEN I'M THIS TALENTED?
WHAT'S WRONG WITH STANDING IN THE SPOTLIGHT?
LISTEN, ESTELLA...
IT'S NOT JUST ME.
IN FACT...
...ONCE YOU REALIZE IT IN YOURSELF, EMBRACE IT.

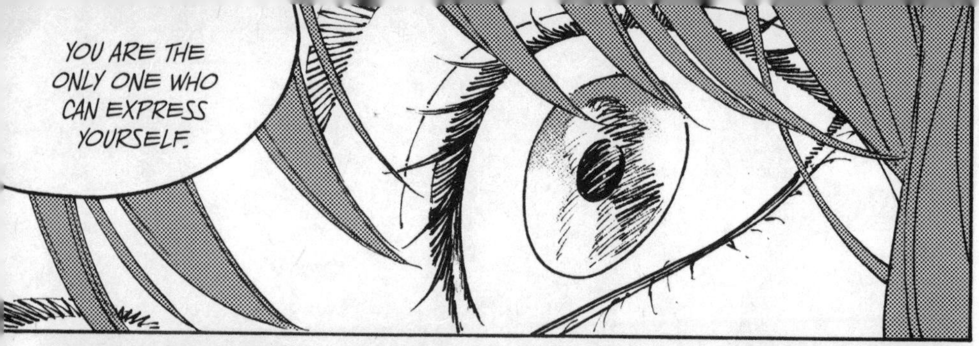
YOU ARE THE ONLY ONE WHO CAN EXPRESS YOURSELF.

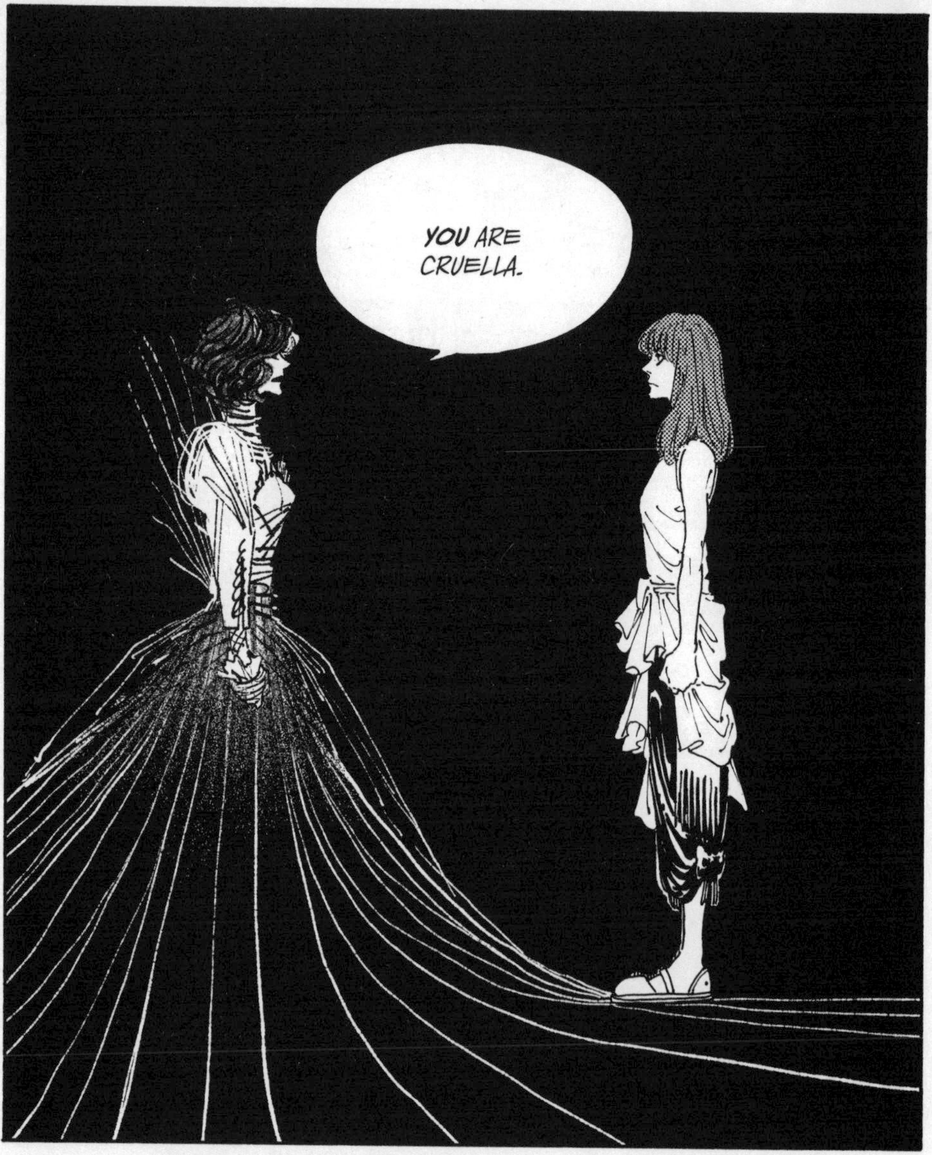
YOU ARE CRUELLA.

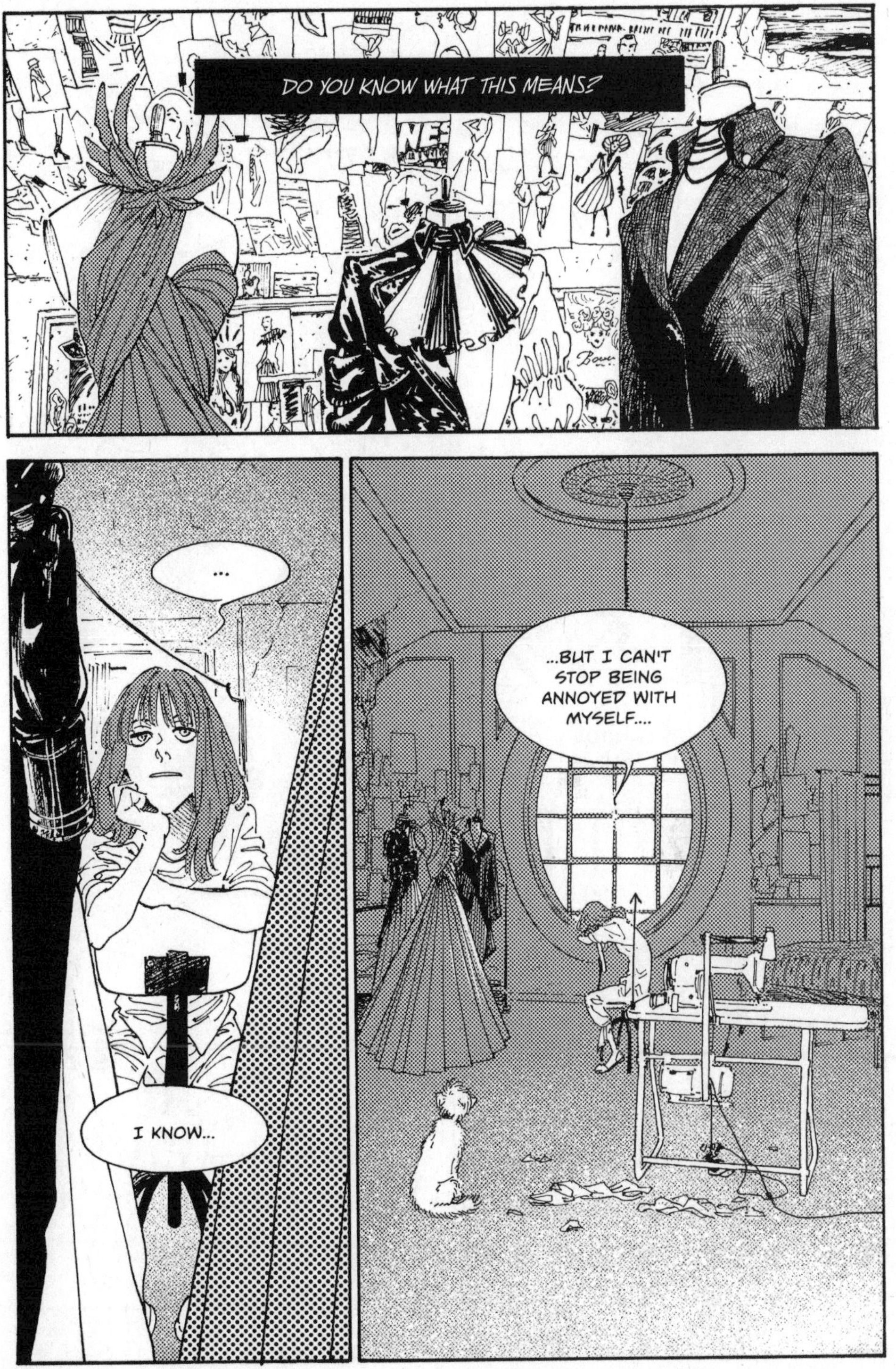
DO YOU KNOW WHAT THIS MEANS?
...
I KNOW...
...BUT I CAN'T STOP BEING ANNOYED WITH MYSELF....

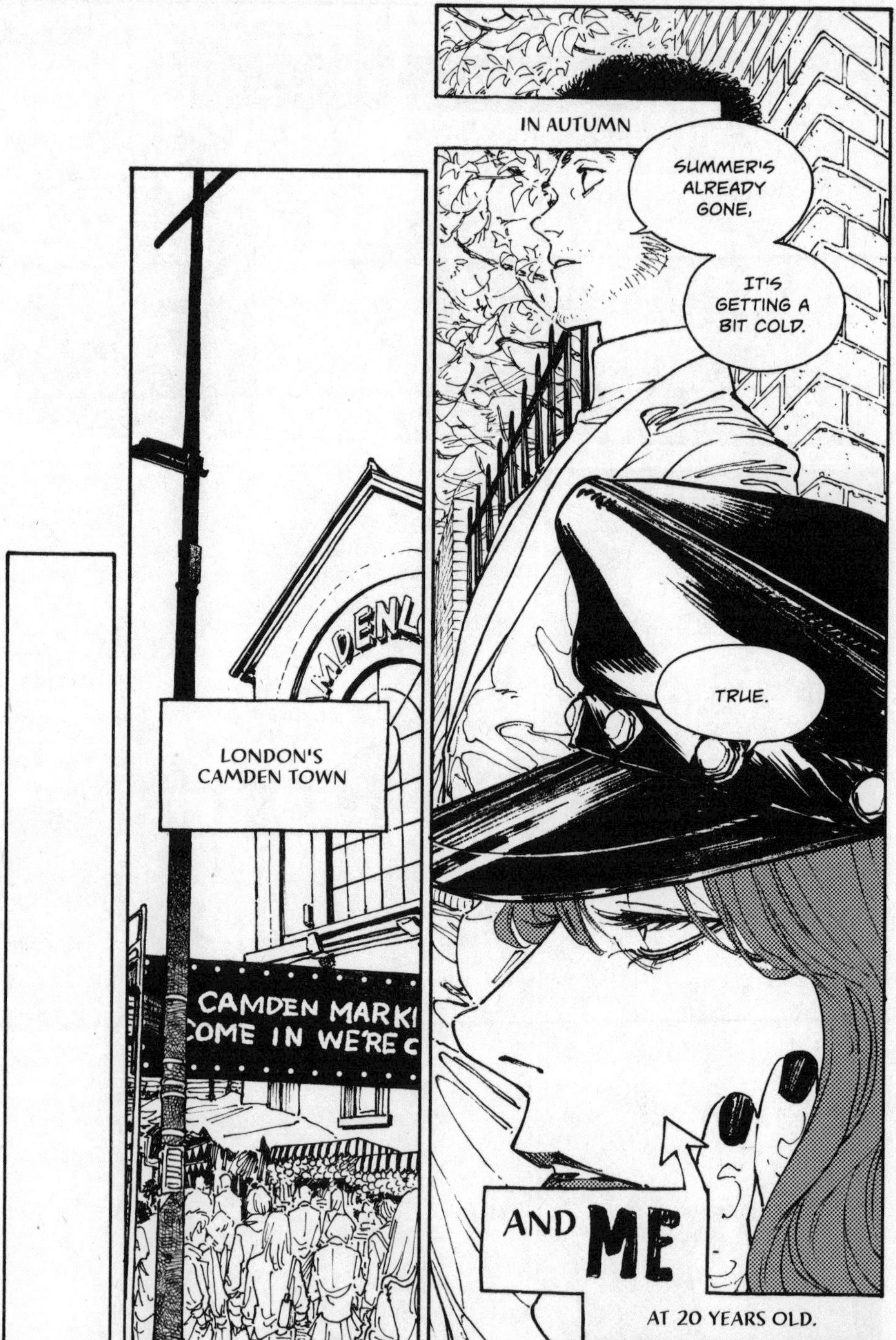
LONDON'S CAMDEN TOWN
CAMDEN
COME IN
IN AUTUMN
SUMMER'S ALREADY GONE,
IT'S GETTING A BIT COLD.
TRUE.
AND ME
AT 20 YEARS OLD.

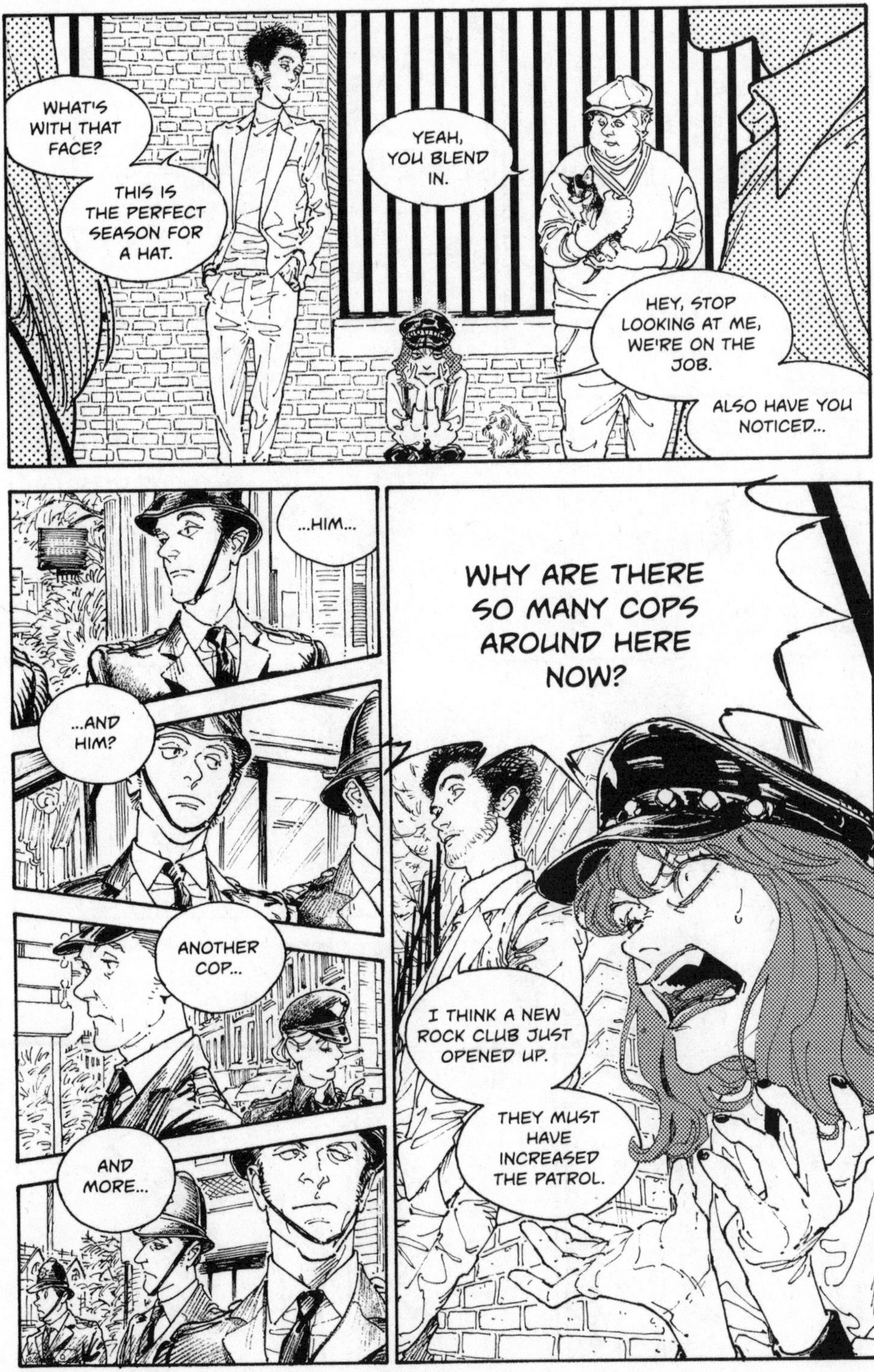
WHAT'S WITH THAT FACE?
THIS IS THE PERFECT SEASON FOR A HAT.
YEAH, YOU BLEND IN.
HEY, STOP LOOKING AT ME, WE'RE ON THE JOB.
ALSO HAVE YOU NOTICED...
...HIM...
...AND HIM?
ANOTHER COP...
AND MORE...
WHY ARE THERE SO MANY COPS AROUND HERE NOW?
I THINK A NEW ROCK CLUB JUST OPENED UP.
THEY MUST HAVE INCREASED THE PATROL.

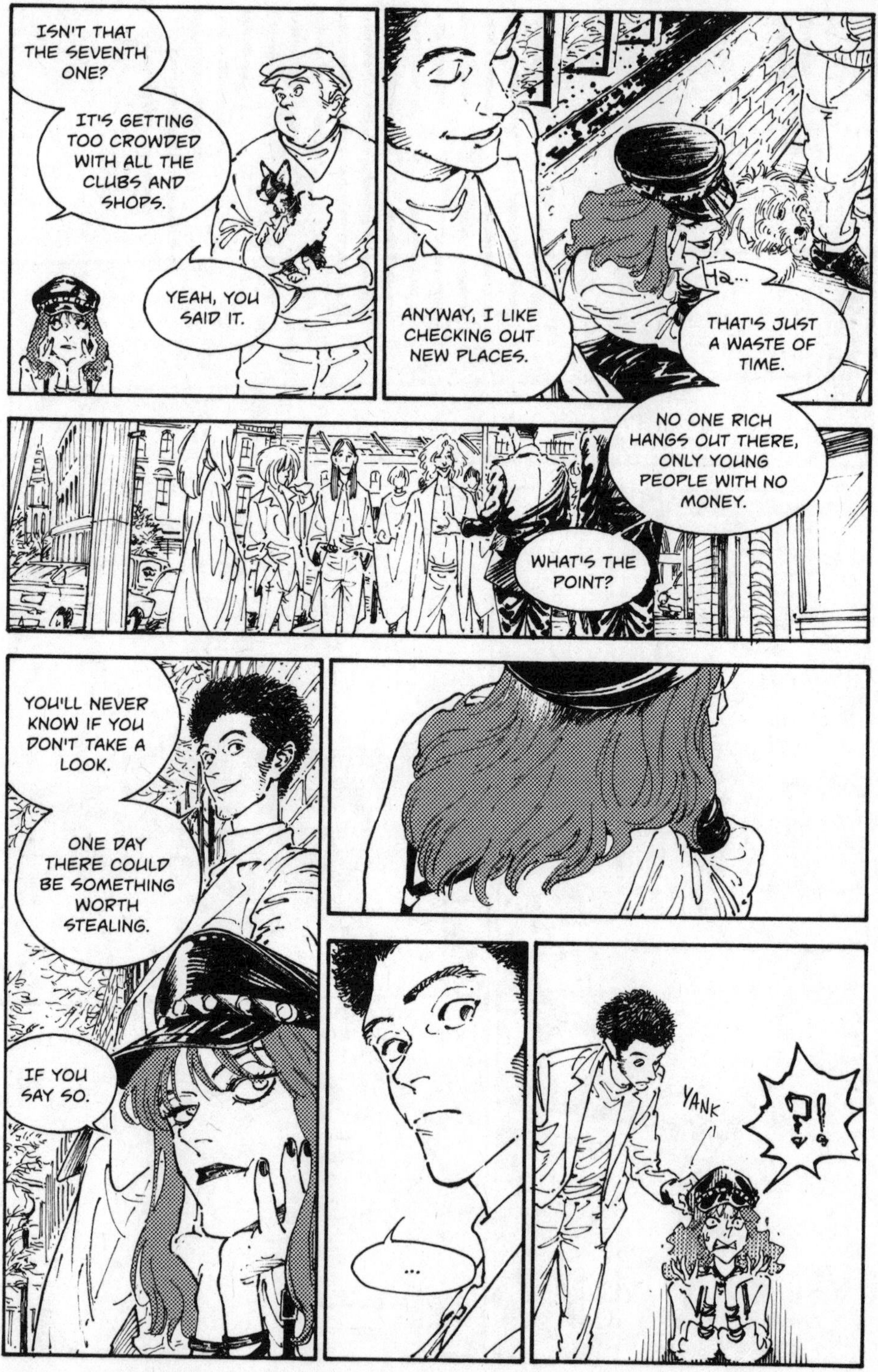

ISN'T THAT THE SEVENTH ONE?
IT'S GETTING TOO CROWDED WITH ALL THE CLUBS AND SHOPS.
YEAH, YOU SAID IT.
ANYWAY, I LIKE CHECKING OUT NEW PLACES.
HA...
THAT'S JUST A WASTE OF TIME.
NO ONE RICH HANGS OUT THERE, ONLY YOUNG PEOPLE WITH NO MONEY.
WHAT'S THE POINT?
YOU'LL NEVER KNOW IF YOU DON'T TAKE A LOOK.
ONE DAY THERE COULD BE SOMETHING WORTH STEALING.
IF YOU SAY SO.
...
YANK
?!

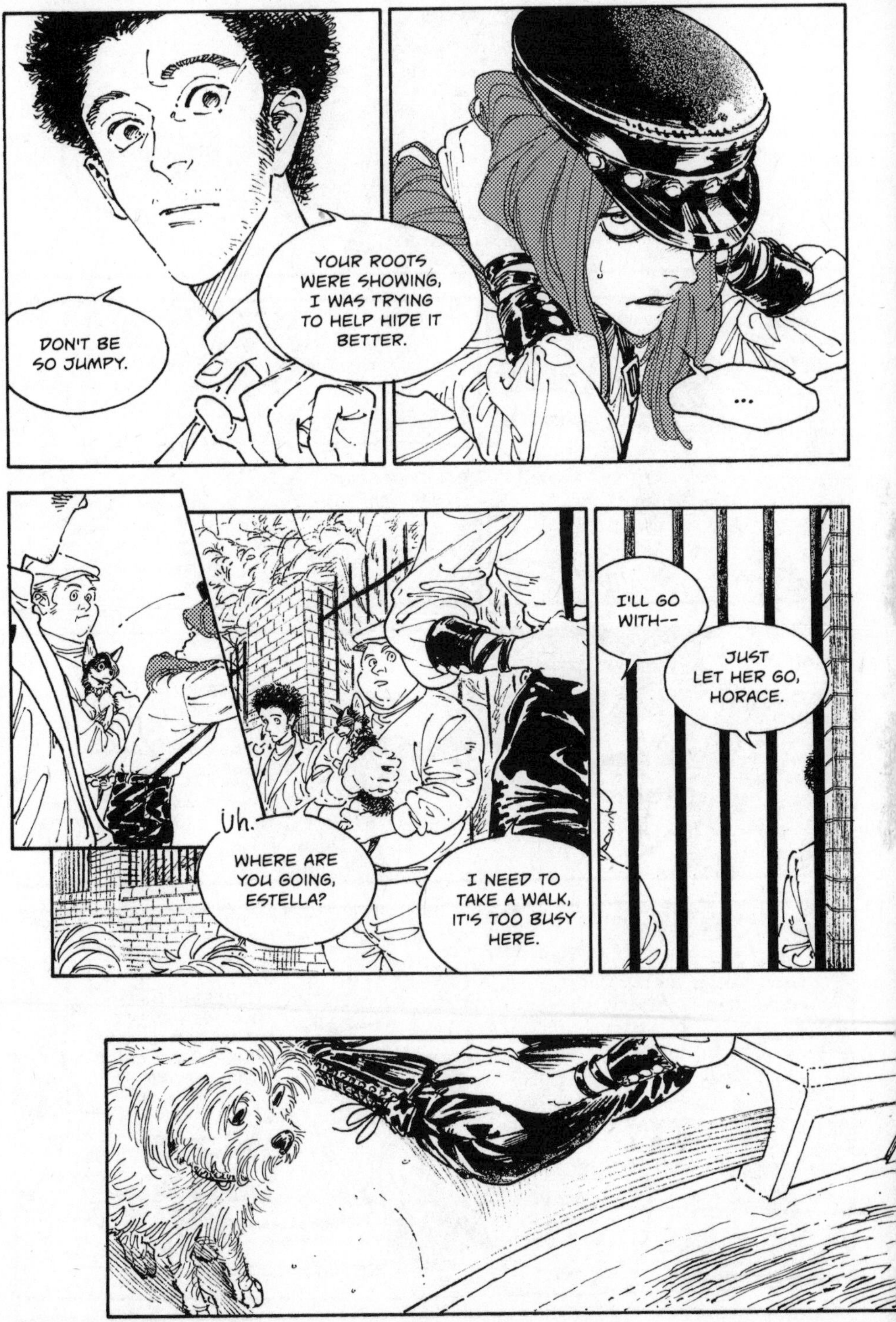
DON'T BE SO JUMPY.
YOUR ROOTS WERE SHOWING, I WAS TRYING TO HELP HIDE IT BETTER.
...
Uh.
WHERE ARE YOU GOING, ESTELLA?
I NEED TO TAKE A WALK, IT'S TOO BUSY HERE.
I'LL GO WITH--
JUST LET HER GO, HORACE.

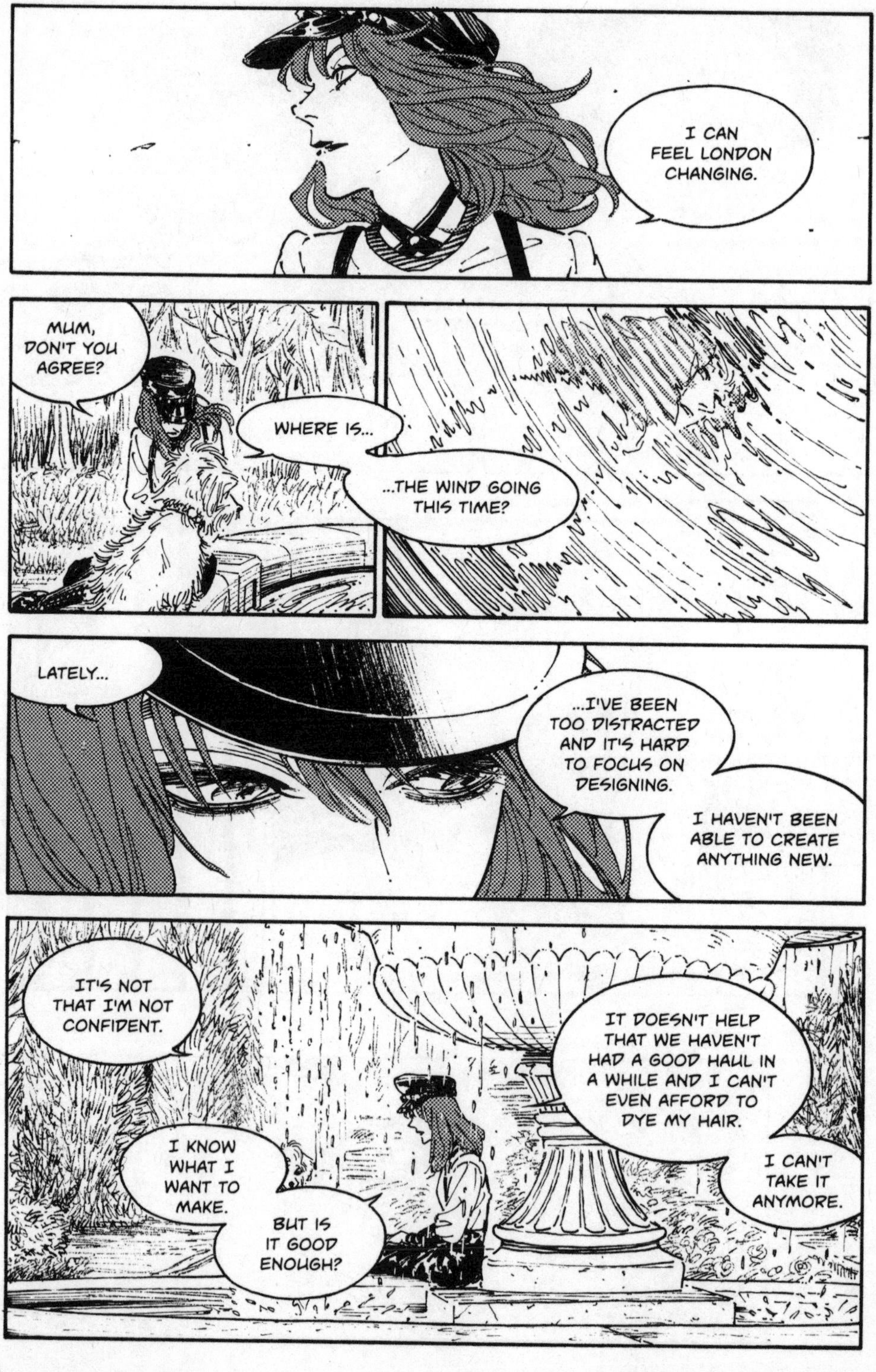
I CAN FEEL LONDON CHANGING.
MUM, DON'T YOU AGREE?
WHERE IS...
...THE WIND GOING THIS TIME?
LATELY...
...I'VE BEEN TOO DISTRACTED AND IT'S HARD TO FOCUS ON DESIGNING.
I HAVEN'T BEEN ABLE TO CREATE ANYTHING NEW.
IT'S NOT THAT I'M NOT CONFIDENT.
I KNOW WHAT I WANT TO MAKE.
BUT IS IT GOOD ENOUGH?
IT DOESN'T HELP THAT WE HAVEN'T HAD A GOOD HAUL IN A WHILE AND I CAN'T EVEN AFFORD TO DYE MY HAIR.
I CAN'T TAKE IT ANYMORE.

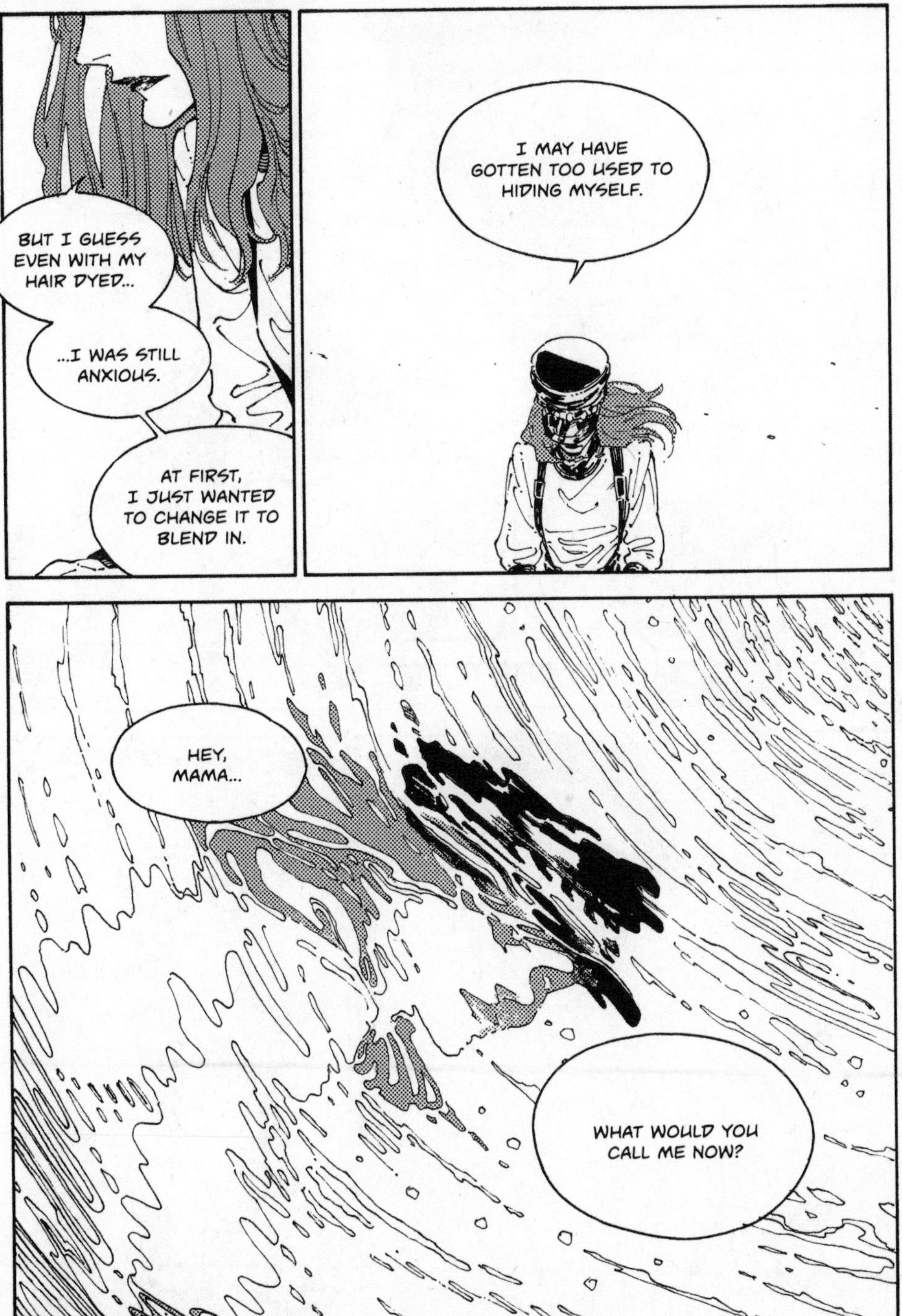
BUT I GUESS EVEN WITH MY HAIR DYED...
...I WAS STILL ANXIOUS.
AT FIRST, I JUST WANTED TO CHANGE IT TO BLEND IN.
I MAY HAVE GOTTEN TOO USED TO HIDING MYSELF.
HEY, MAMA...
WHAT WOULD YOU CALL ME NOW?

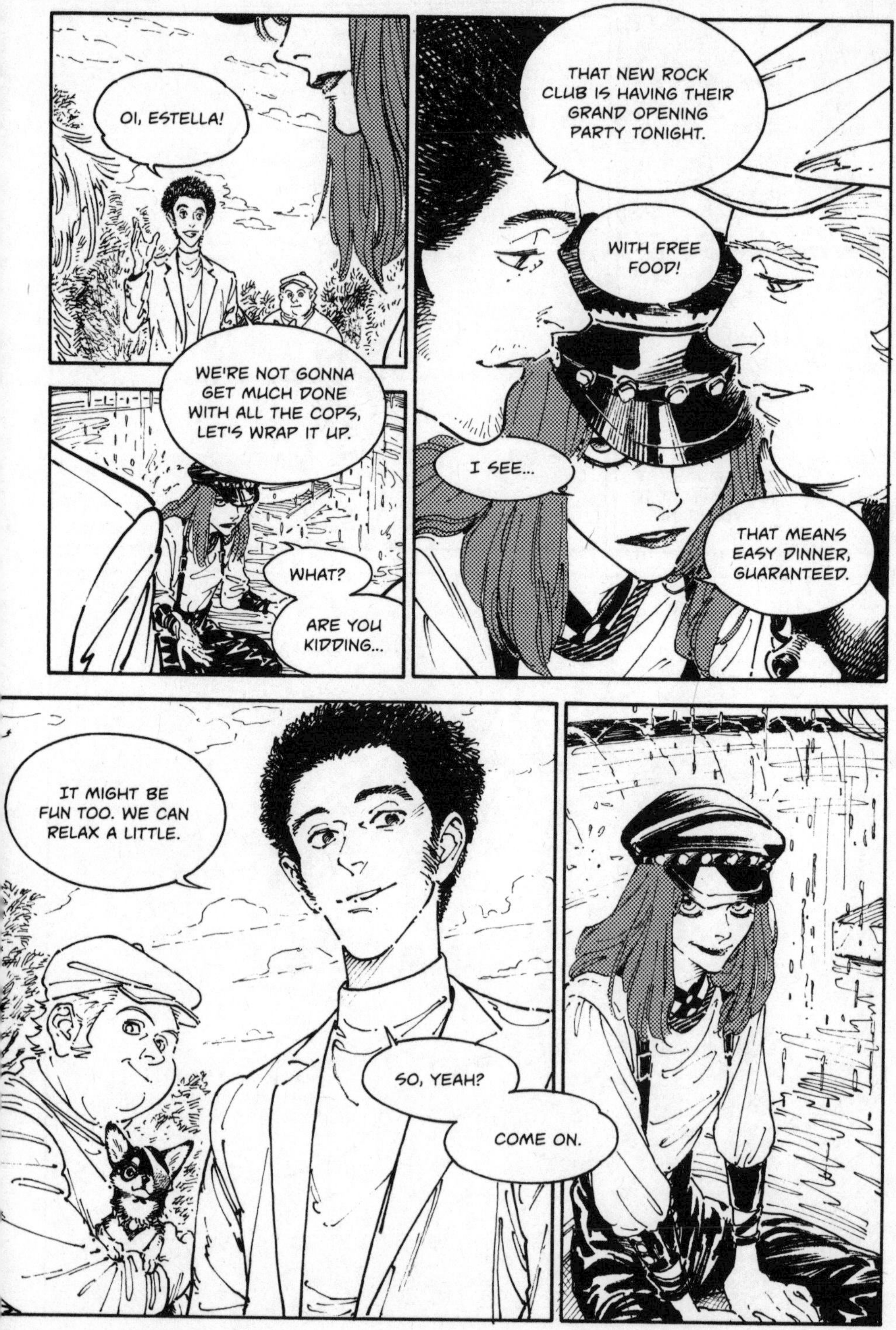
OI, ESTELLA!
WE'RE NOT GONNA GET MUCH DONE WITH ALL THE COPS, LET'S WRAP IT UP.
WHAT?
ARE YOU KIDDING...
THAT NEW ROCK CLUB IS HAVING THEIR GRAND OPENING PARTY TONIGHT.
WITH FREE FOOD!
I SEE...
THAT MEANS EASY DINNER, GUARANTEED.
IT MIGHT BE FUN TOO. WE CAN RELAX A LITTLE.
SO, YEAH?
COME ON.

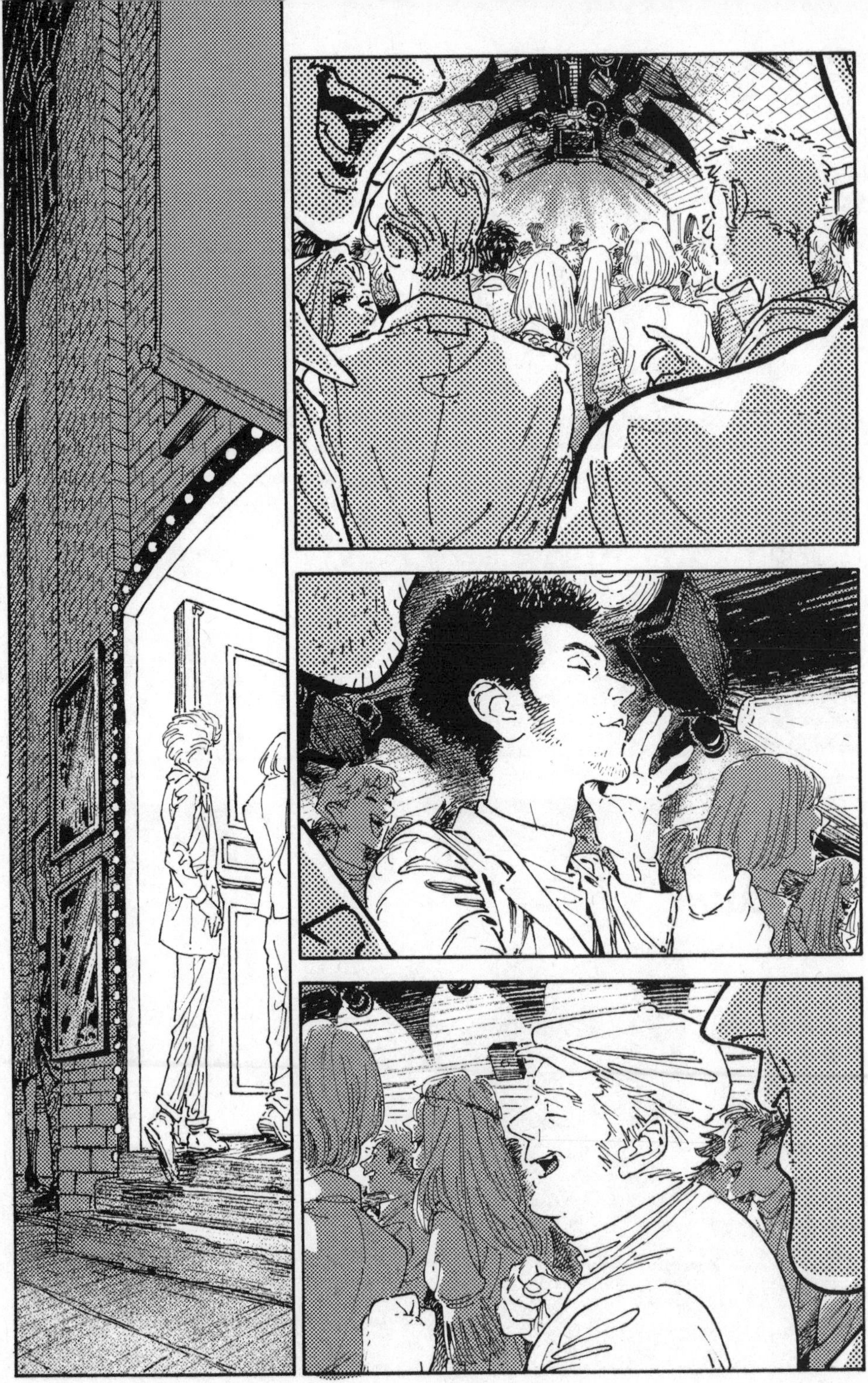

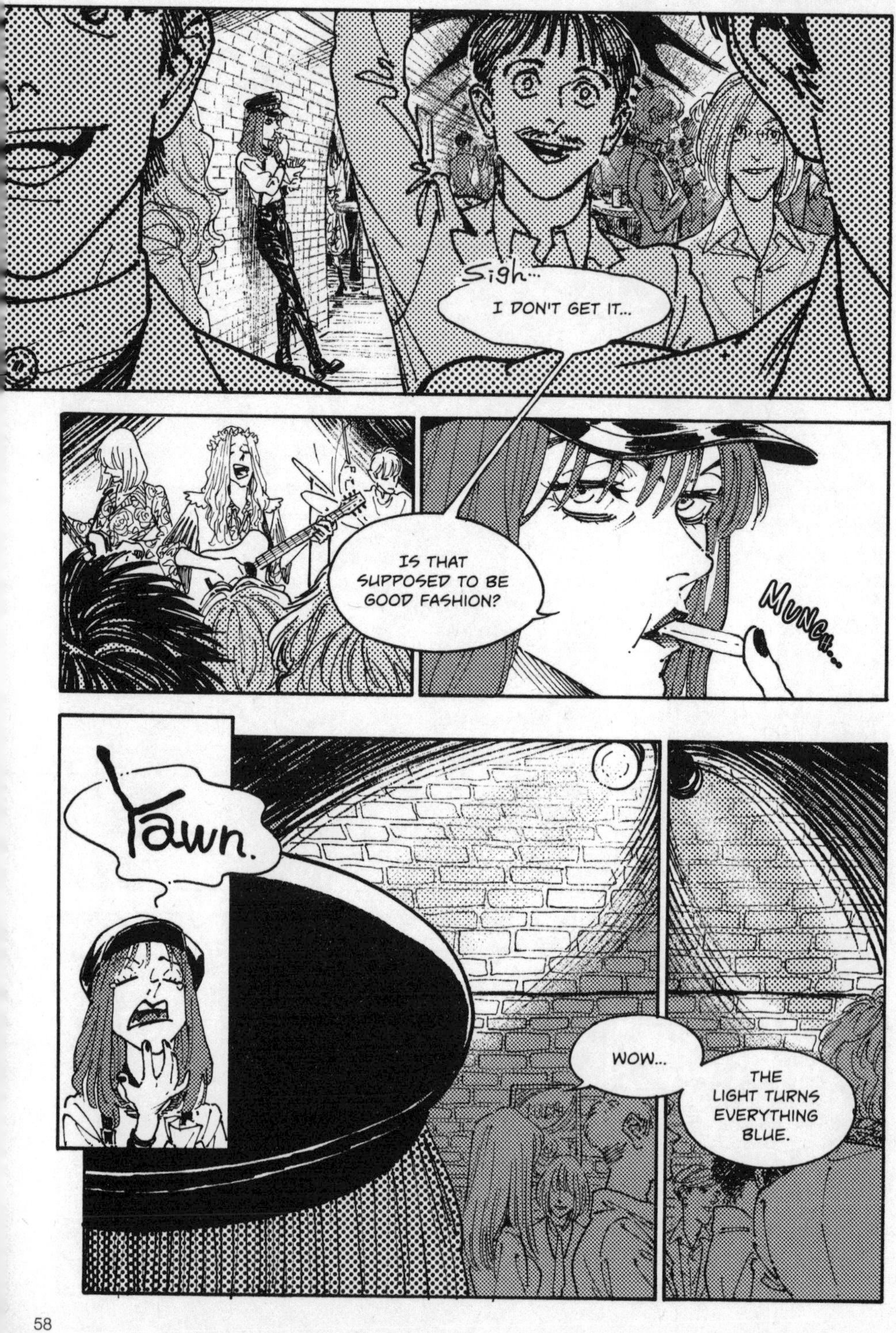
Sigh...
I DON'T GET IT...
IS THAT SUPPOSED TO BE GOOD FASHION?
MUNCH...
Yawn.
WOW...
THE LIGHT TURNS EVERYTHING BLUE.

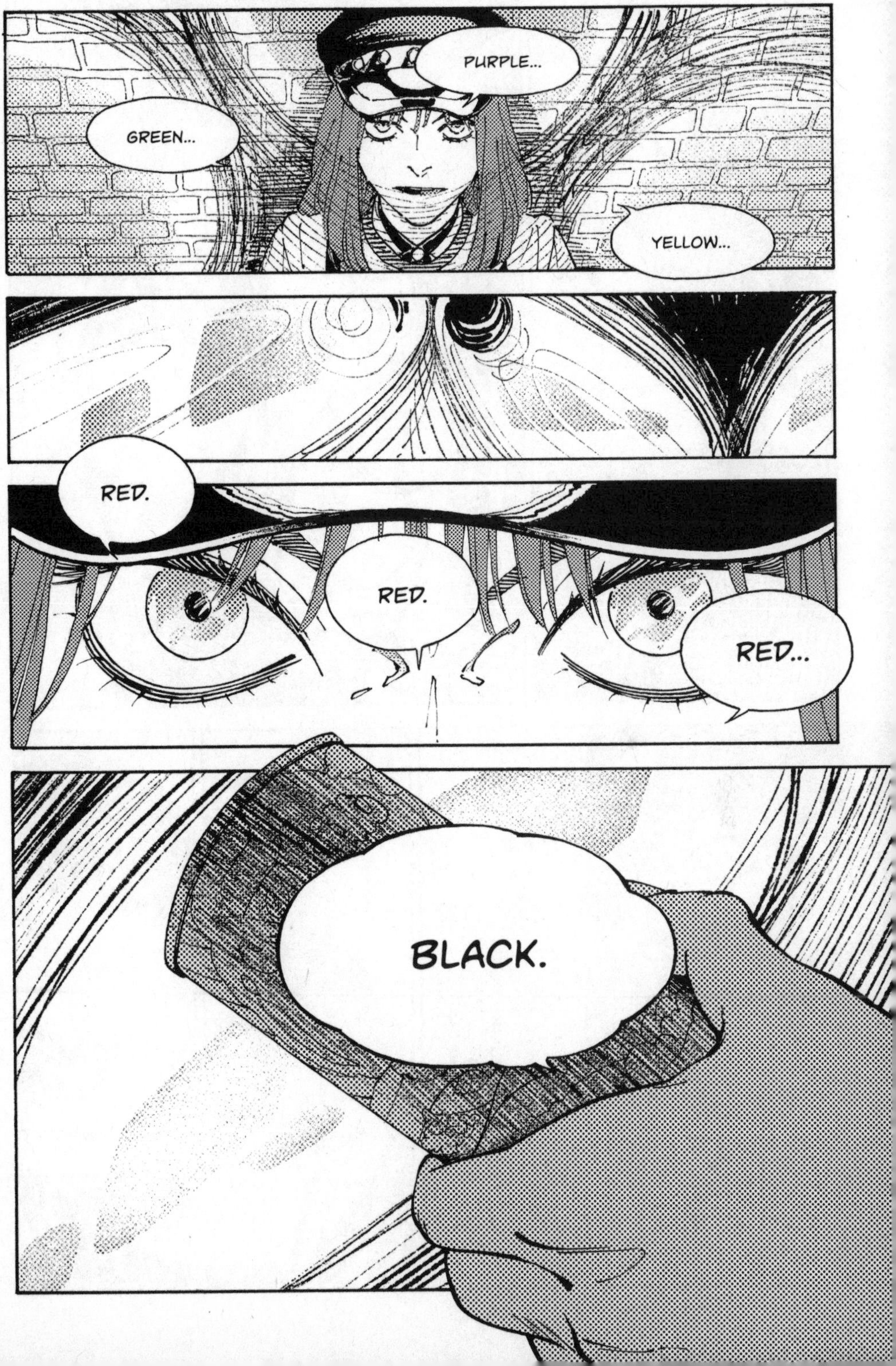
GREEN...
PURPLE...
YELLOW...
RED.
RED.
RED...
BLACK.

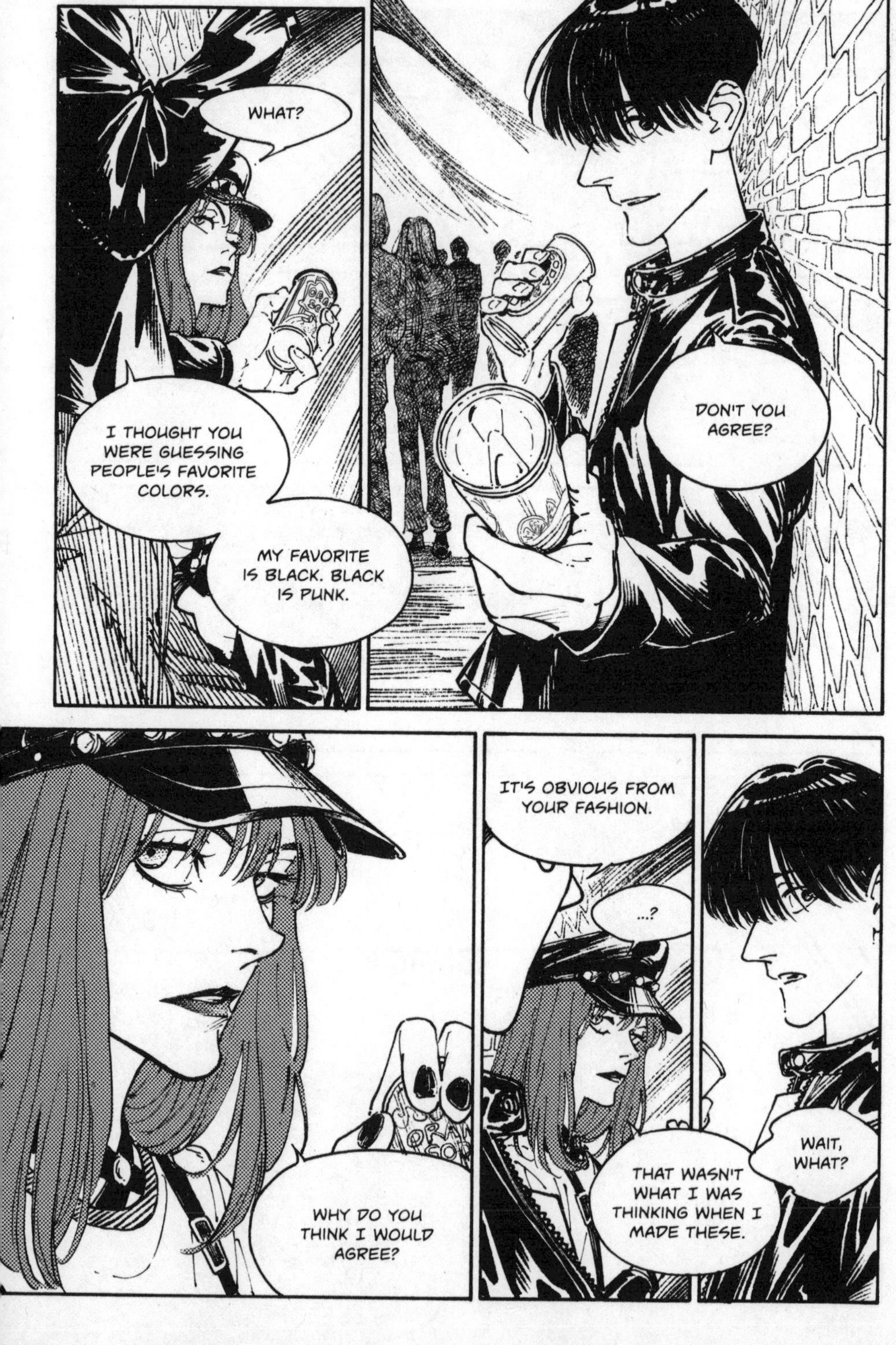
WHAT?
I THOUGHT YOU WERE GUESSING PEOPLE'S FAVORITE COLORS.
MY FAVORITE IS BLACK. BLACK IS PUNK.
DON'T YOU AGREE?
WHY DO YOU THINK I WOULD AGREE?
IT'S OBVIOUS FROM YOUR FASHION.
...?
THAT WASN'T WHAT I WAS THINKING WHEN I MADE THESE.
WAIT, WHAT?

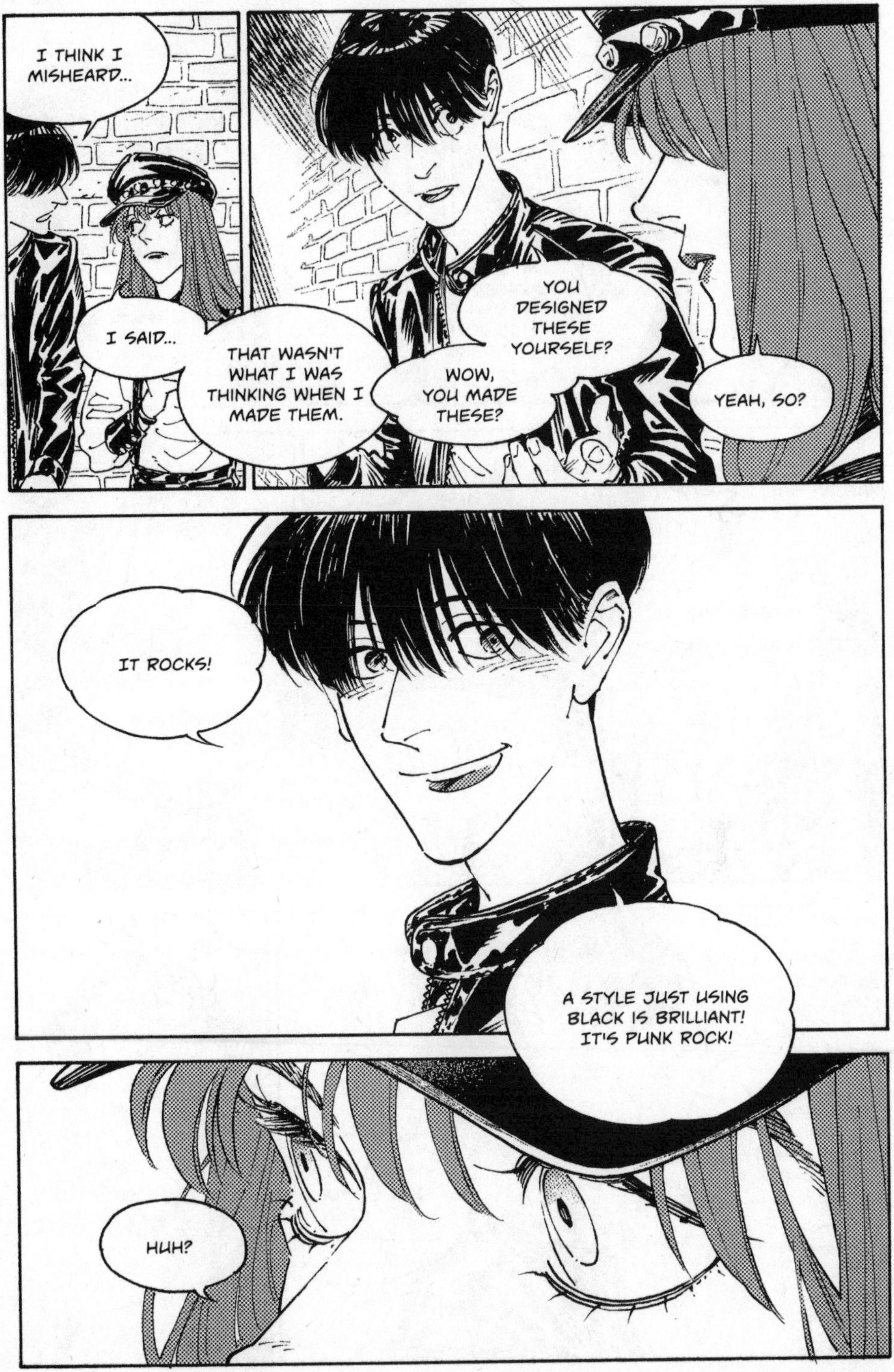
YOU DESIGNED THESE YOURSELF?
YEAH, SO?
WOW, YOU MADE THESE?
I THINK I MISHEARD...
I SAID...
THAT WASN'T WHAT I WAS THINKING WHEN I MADE THEM.
IT ROCKS!
A STYLE JUST USING BLACK IS BRILLIANT! IT'S PUNK ROCK!
HUH?

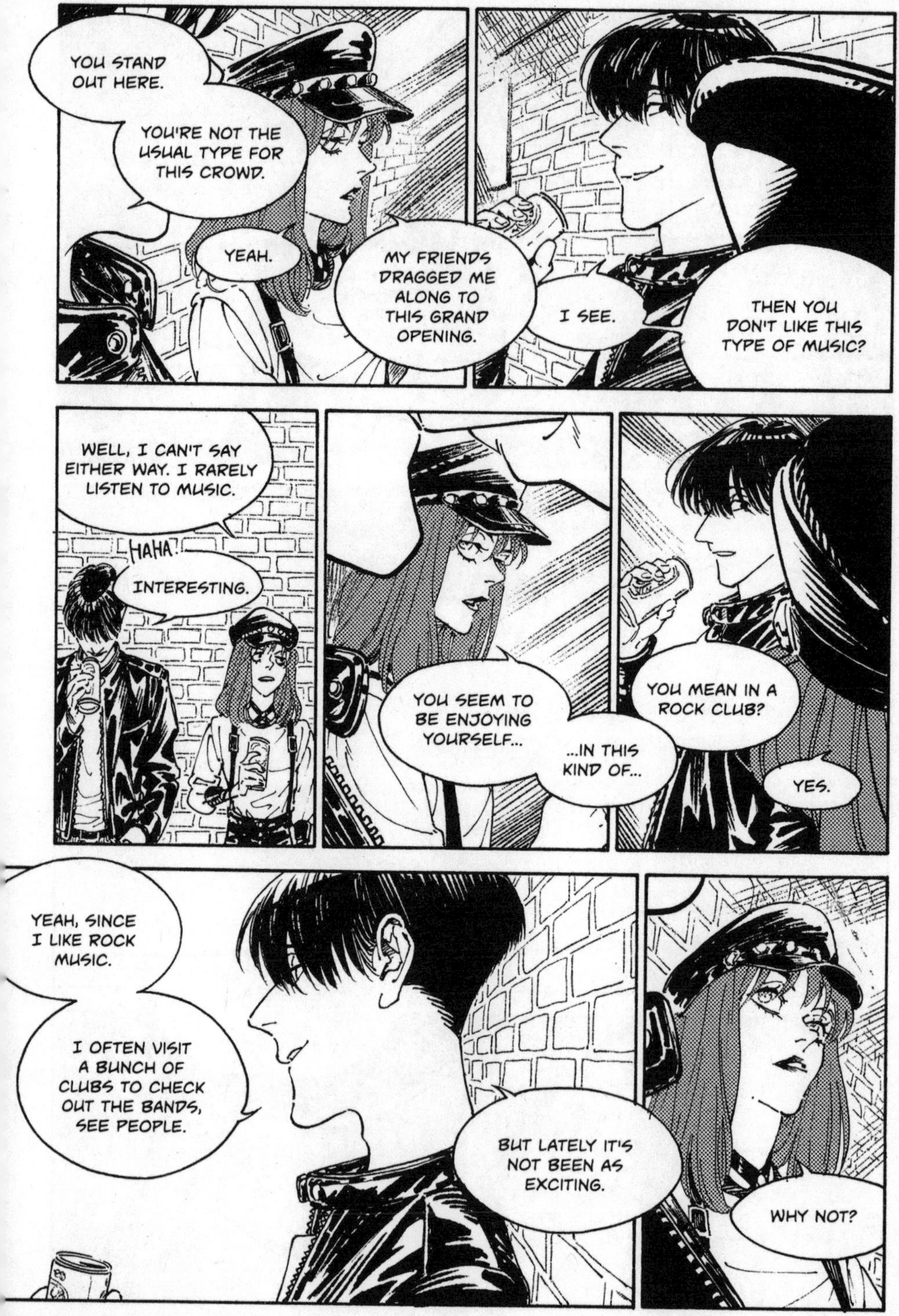
YOU STAND OUT HERE.
YOU'RE NOT THE USUAL TYPE FOR THIS CROWD.
YEAH.
MY FRIENDS DRAGGED ME ALONG TO THIS GRAND OPENING.
I SEE.
THEN YOU DON'T LIKE THIS TYPE OF MUSIC?
WELL, I CAN'T SAY EITHER WAY. I RARELY LISTEN TO MUSIC.
HAHA!
INTERESTING.
YOU SEEM TO BE ENJOYING YOURSELF...
...IN THIS KIND OF...
YOU MEAN IN A ROCK CLUB?
YES.
YEAH, SINCE I LIKE ROCK MUSIC.
I OFTEN VISIT A BUNCH OF CLUBS TO CHECK OUT THE BANDS, SEE PEOPLE.
BUT LATELY IT'S NOT BEEN AS EXCITING.
WHY NOT?

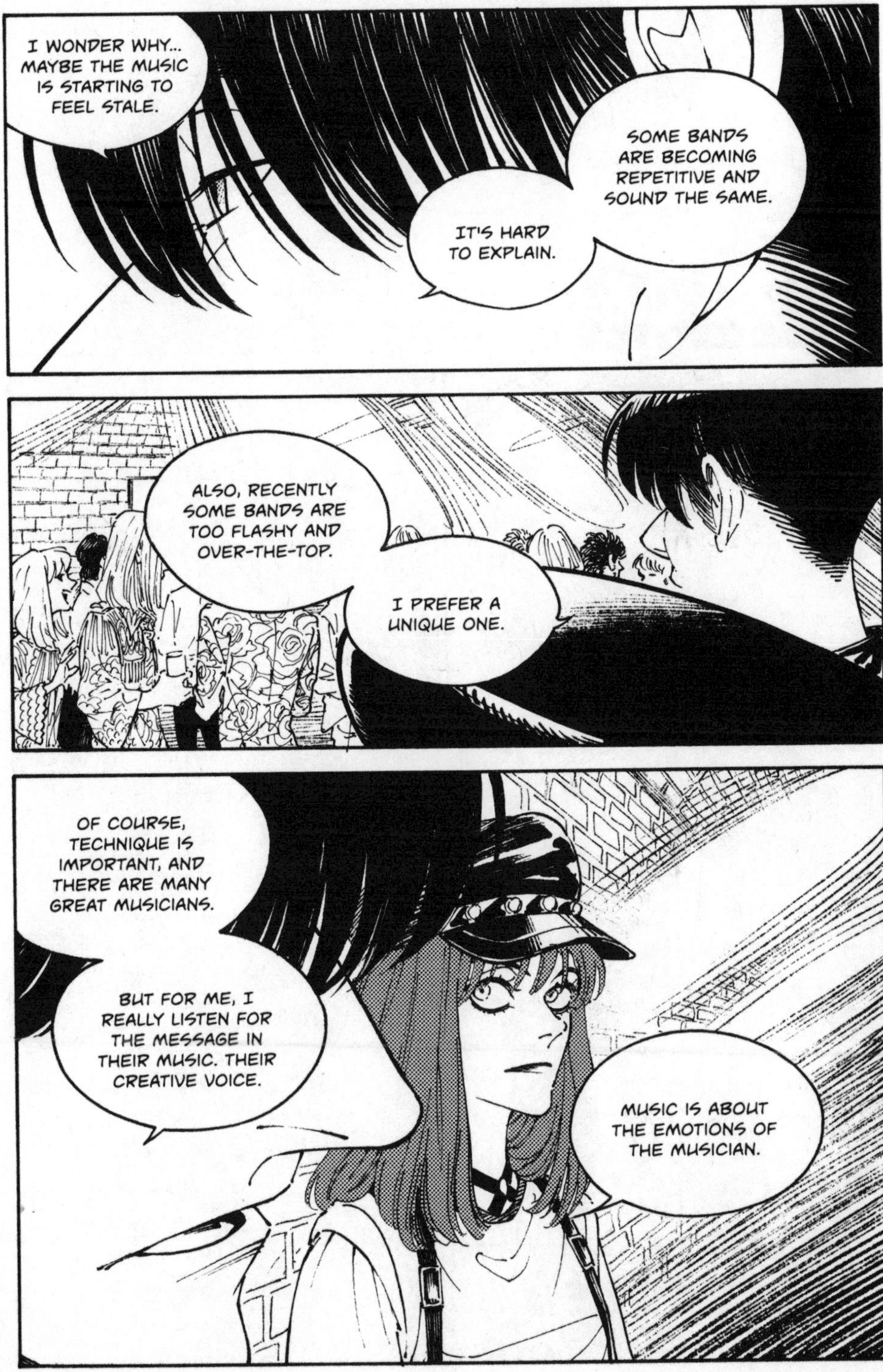

I WONDER WHY... MAYBE THE MUSIC IS STARTING TO FEEL STALE.
IT'S HARD TO EXPLAIN.
SOME BANDS ARE BECOMING REPETITIVE AND SOUND THE SAME.
ALSO, RECENTLY SOME BANDS ARE TOO FLASHY AND OVER-THE-TOP.
I PREFER A UNIQUE ONE.
OF COURSE, TECHNIQUE IS IMPORTANT, AND THERE ARE MANY GREAT MUSICIANS.
BUT FOR ME, I REALLY LISTEN FOR THE MESSAGE IN THEIR MUSIC. THEIR CREATIVE VOICE.
MUSIC IS ABOUT THE EMOTIONS OF THE MUSICIAN.

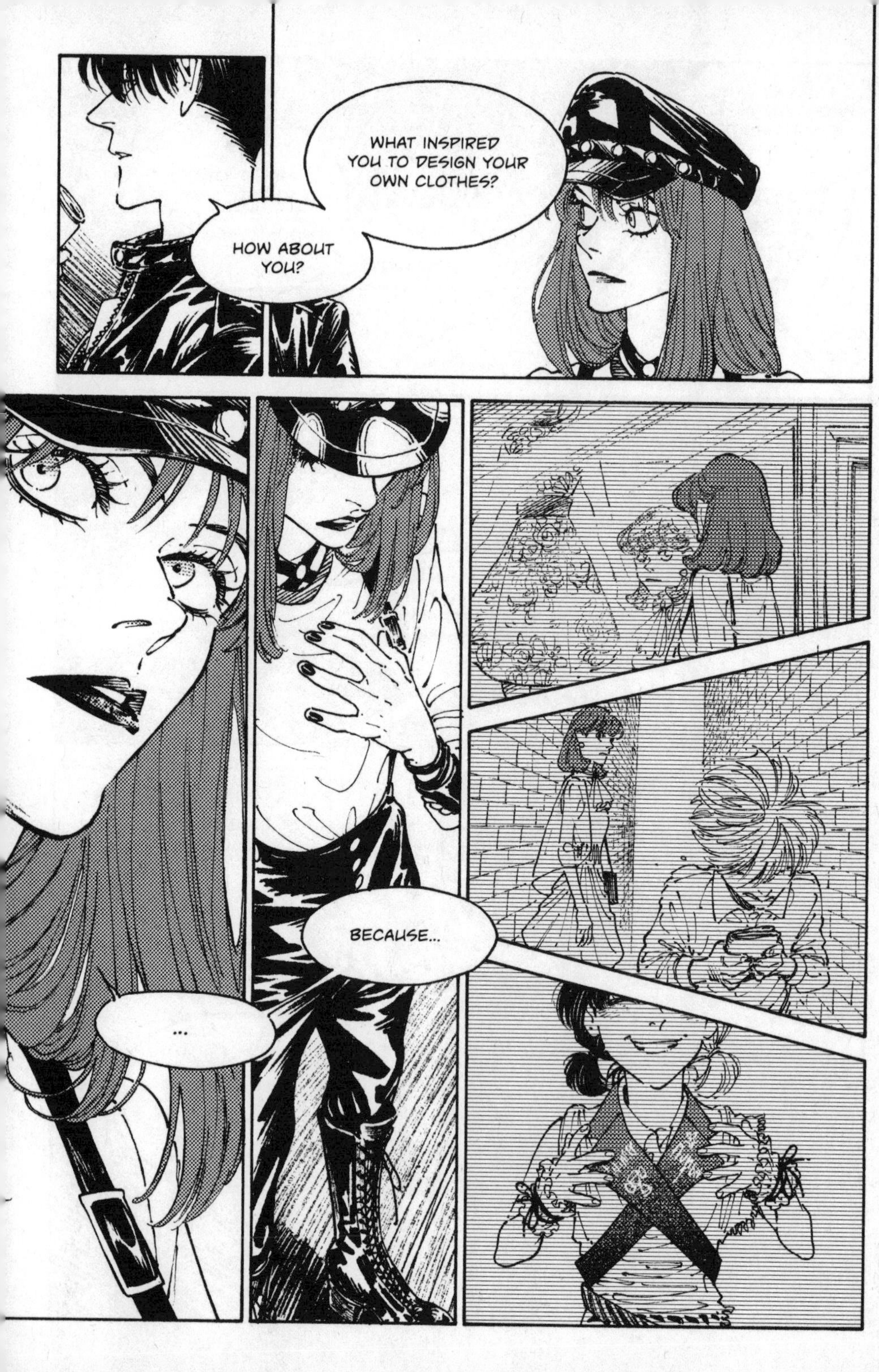
WHAT INSPIRED YOU TO DESIGN YOUR OWN CLOTHES?
HOW ABOUT YOU?
...
BECAUSE...

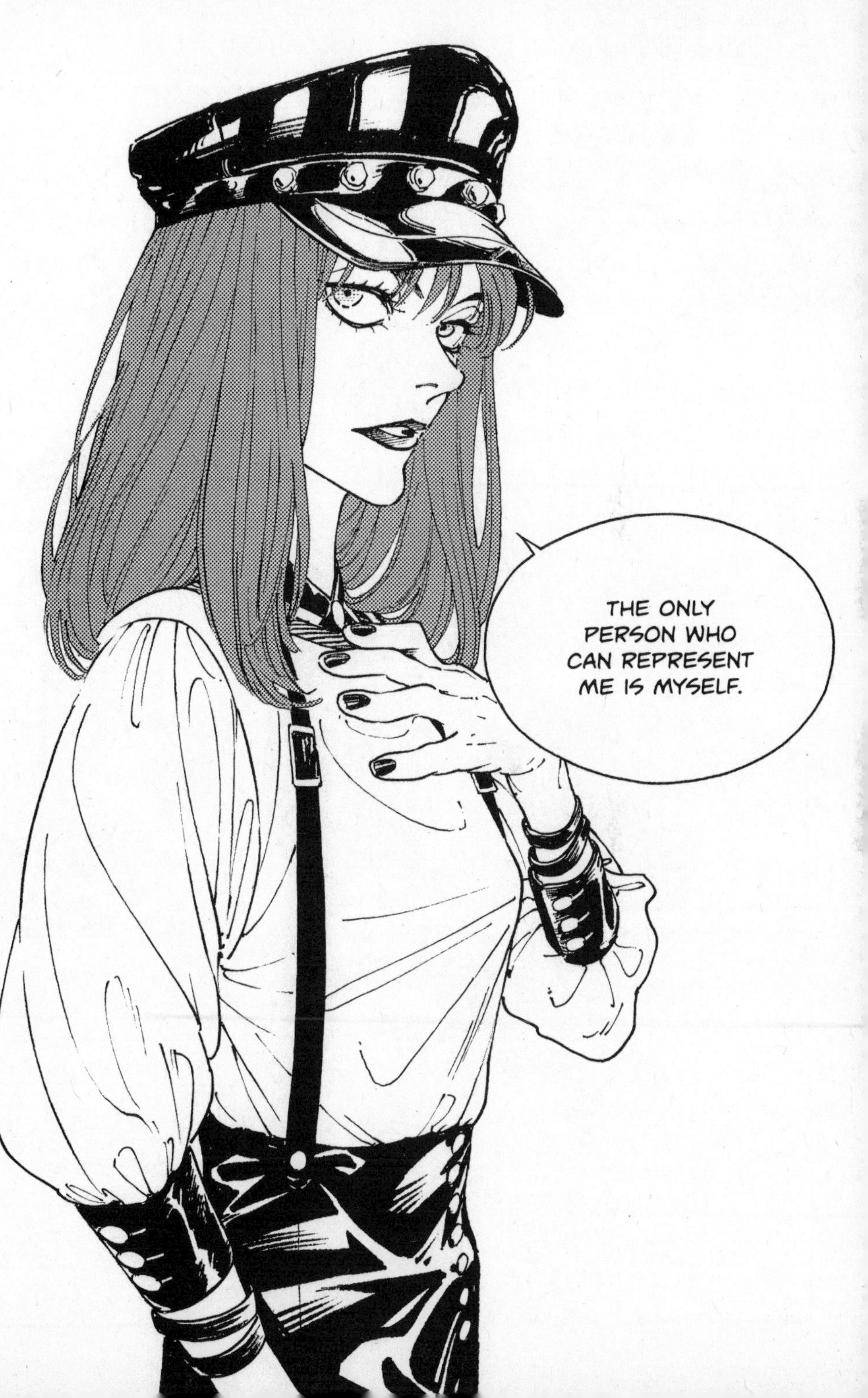
THE ONLY PERSON WHO CAN REPRESENT ME IS MYSELF.

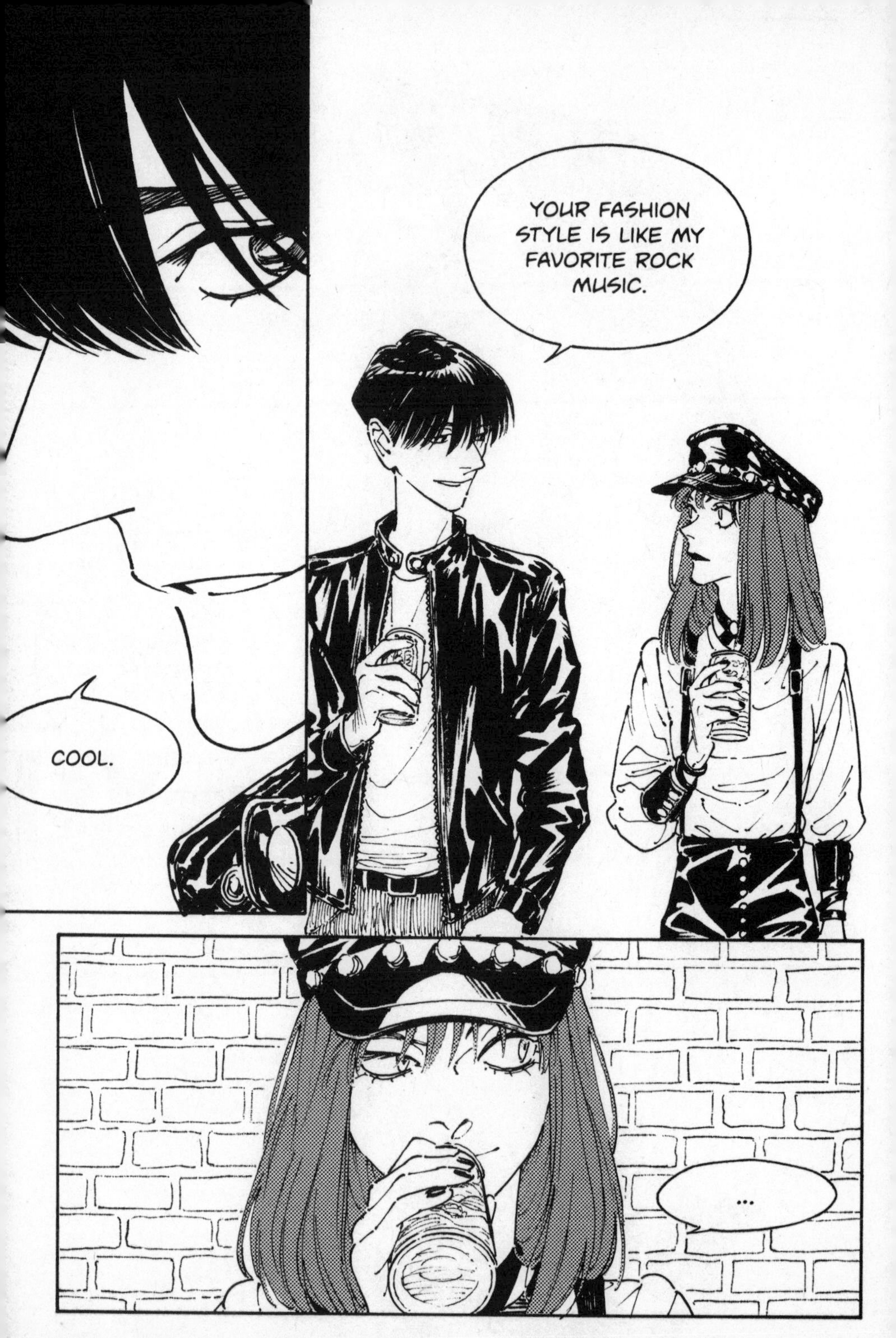
COOL.
YOUR FASHION STYLE IS LIKE MY FAVORITE ROCK MUSIC.
...

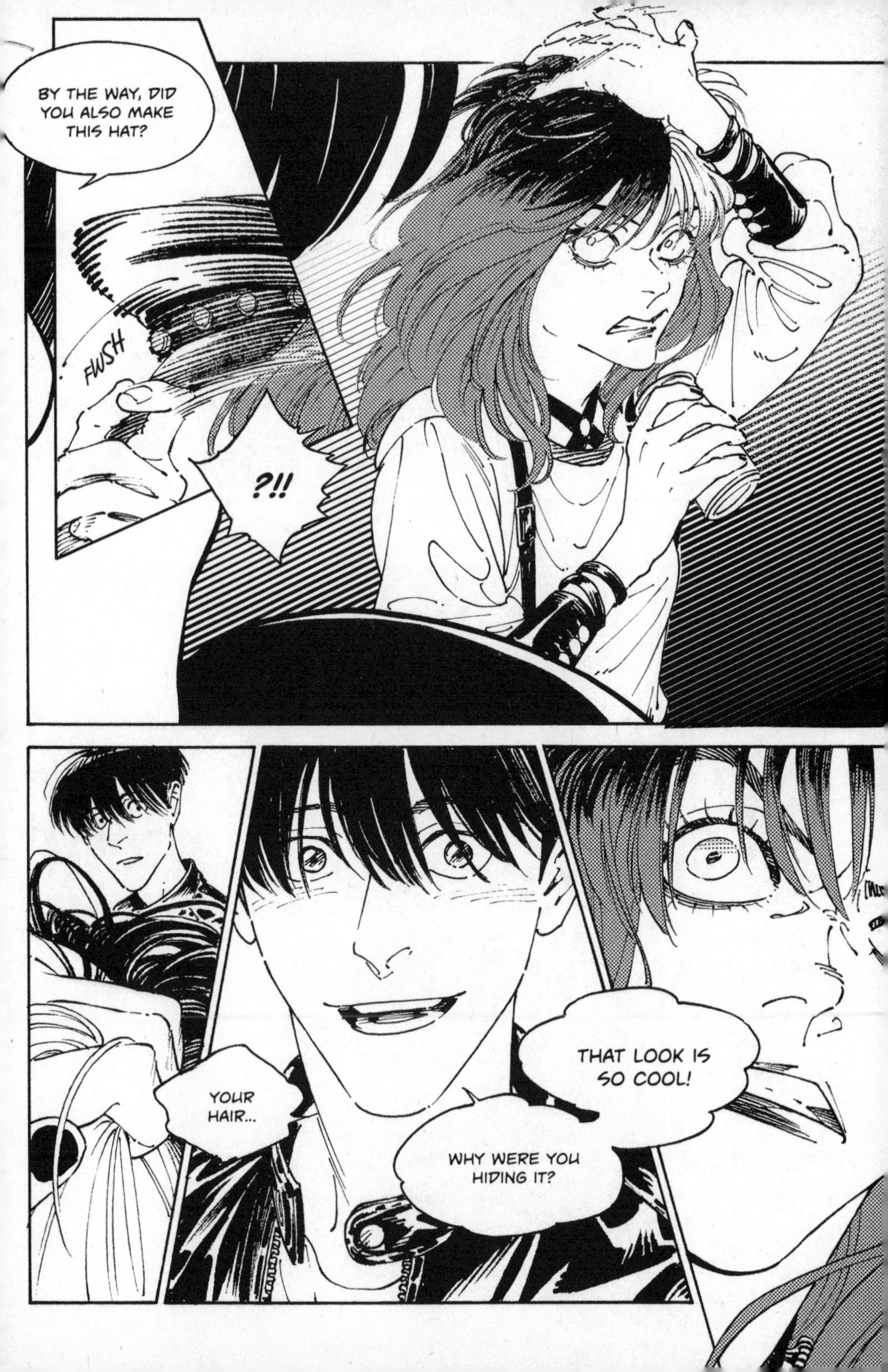

BY THE WAY, DID YOU ALSO MAKE THIS HAT?
FWSH
?!!
YOUR HAIR...
THAT LOOK IS SO COOL!
WHY WERE YOU HIDING IT?

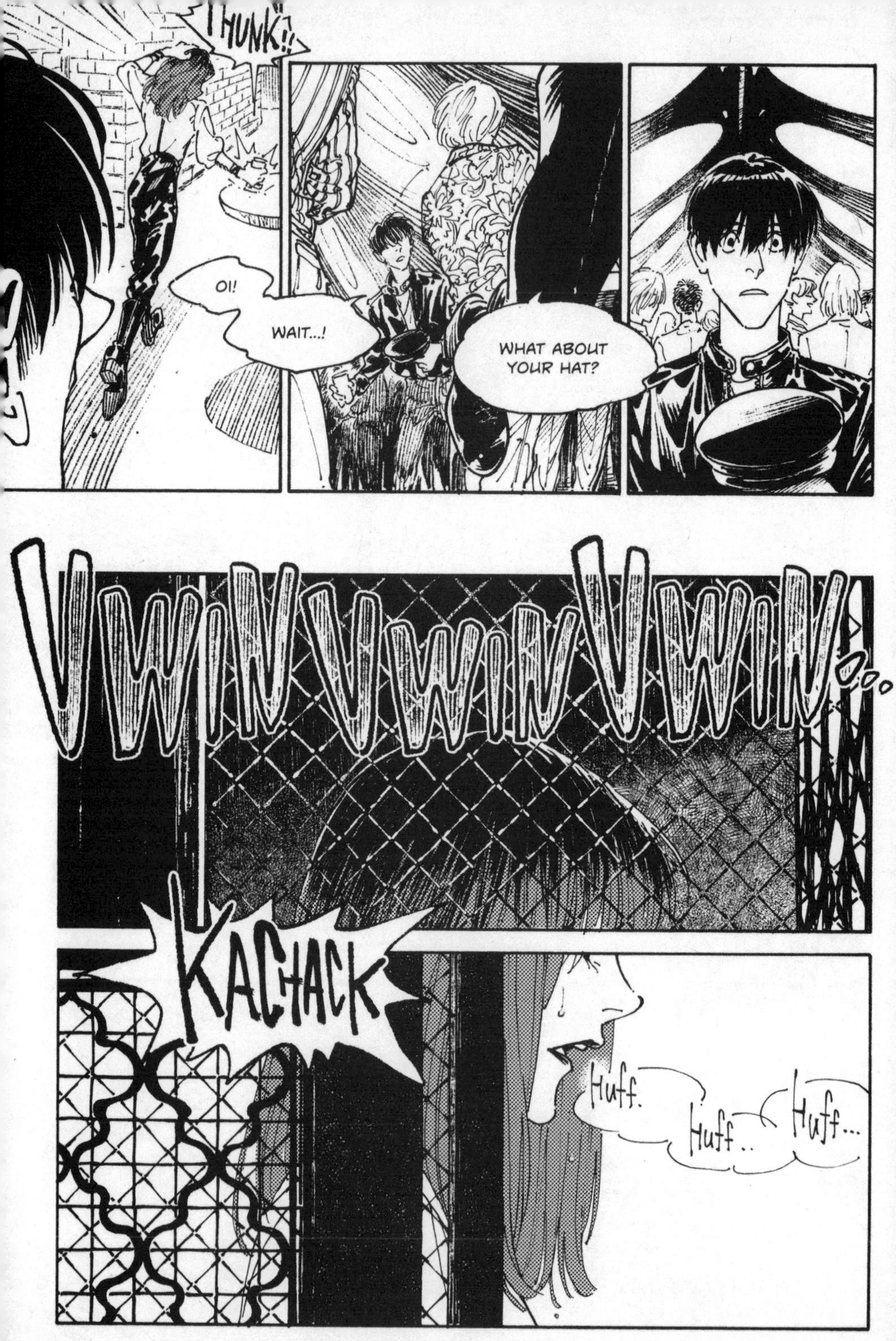
THUNK!!
OI!
WAIT...!
WHAT ABOUT YOUR HAT?
VWIN VWIN VWIN...
KACHACK
Huff.
Huff..
Huff...

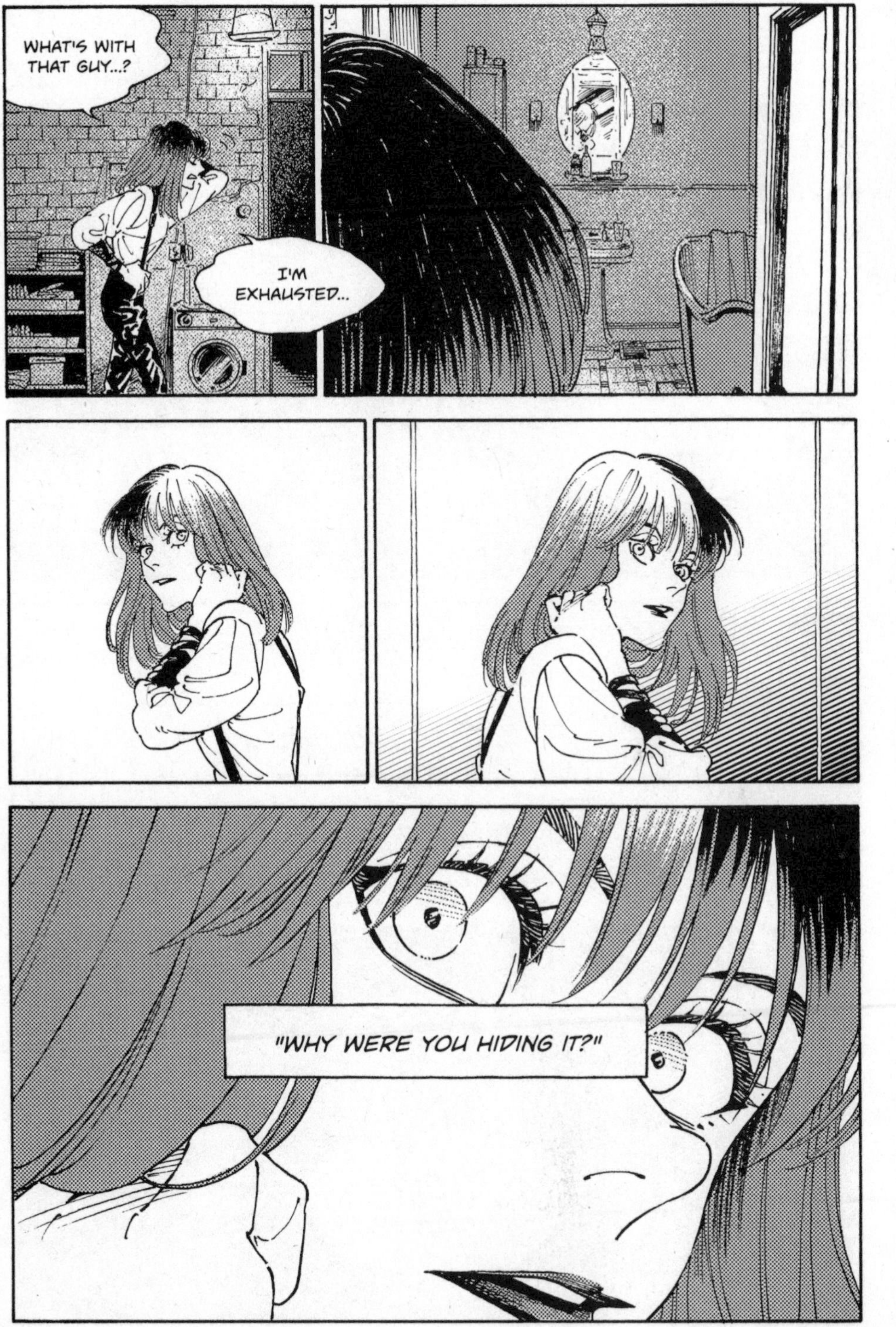
WHAT'S WITH THAT GUY...?
I'M EXHAUSTED...
"WHY WERE YOU HIDING IT?"

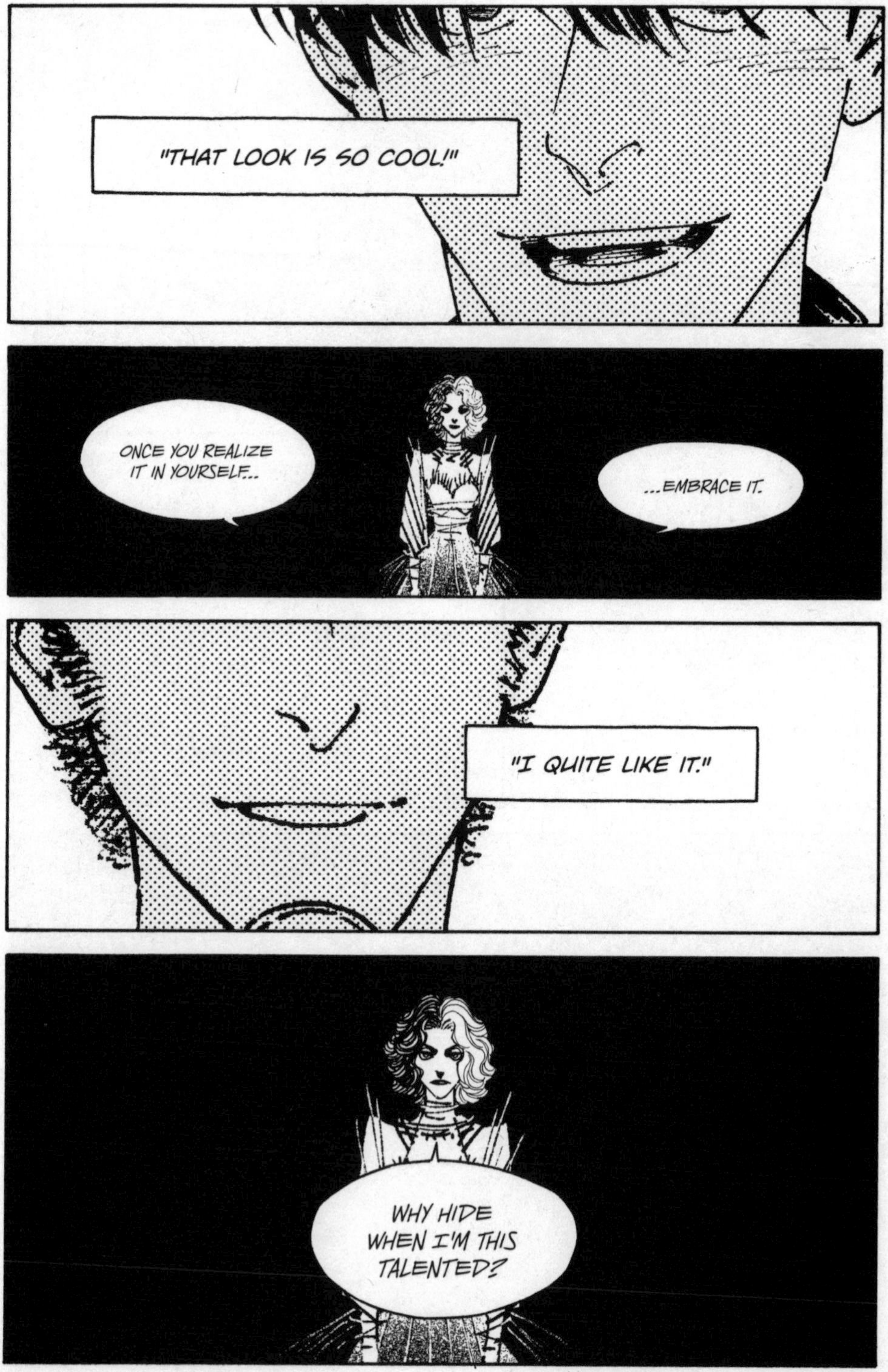
"THAT LOOK IS SO COOL!"
ONCE YOU REALIZE IT IN YOURSELF...
...EMBRACE IT.
"I QUITE LIKE IT."
WHY HIDE WHEN I'M THIS TALENTED?

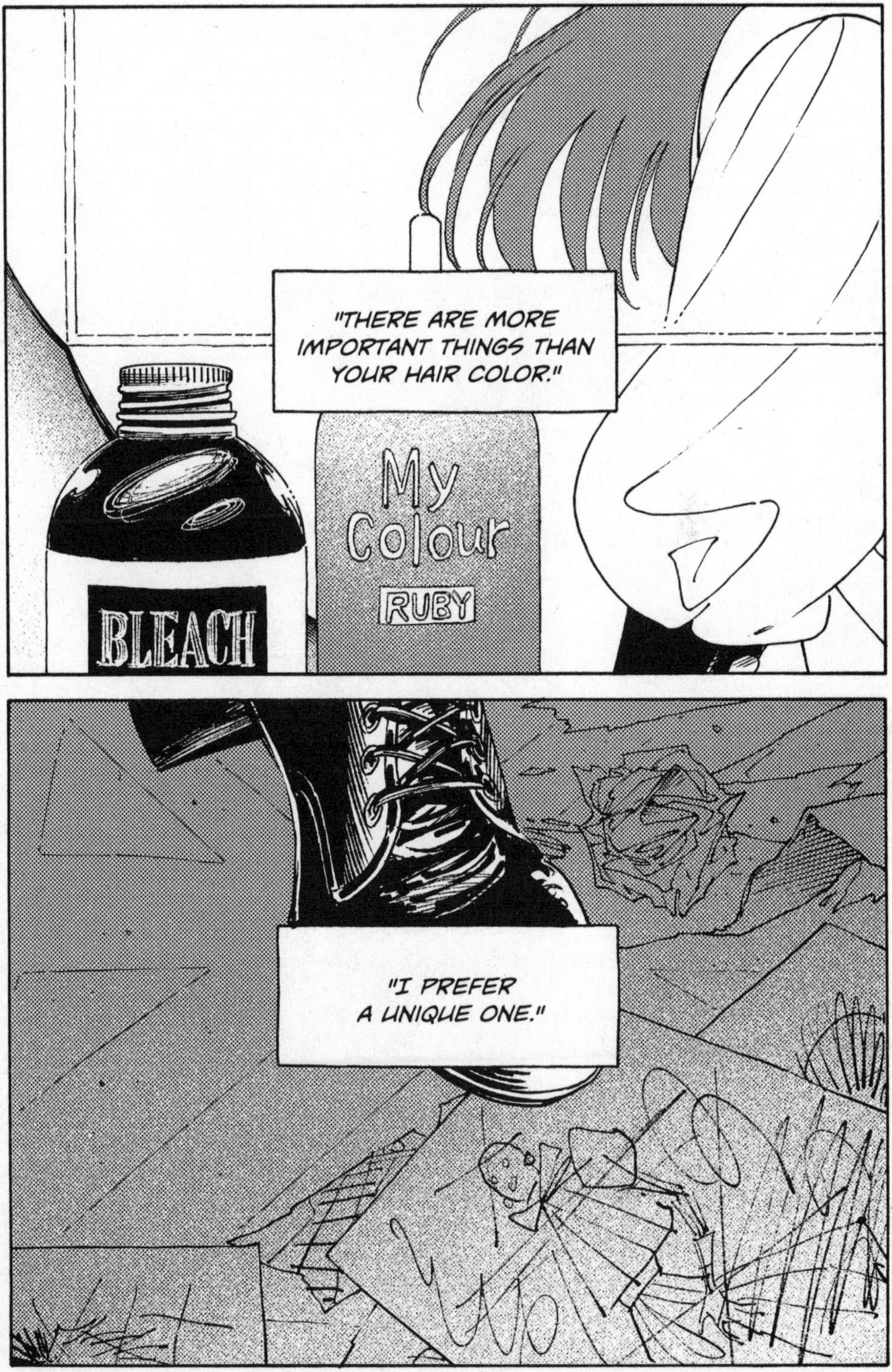
"THERE ARE MORE IMPORTANT THINGS THAN YOUR HAIR COLOR."
BLEACH
My Colour
RUBY
"I PREFER A UNIQUE ONE."

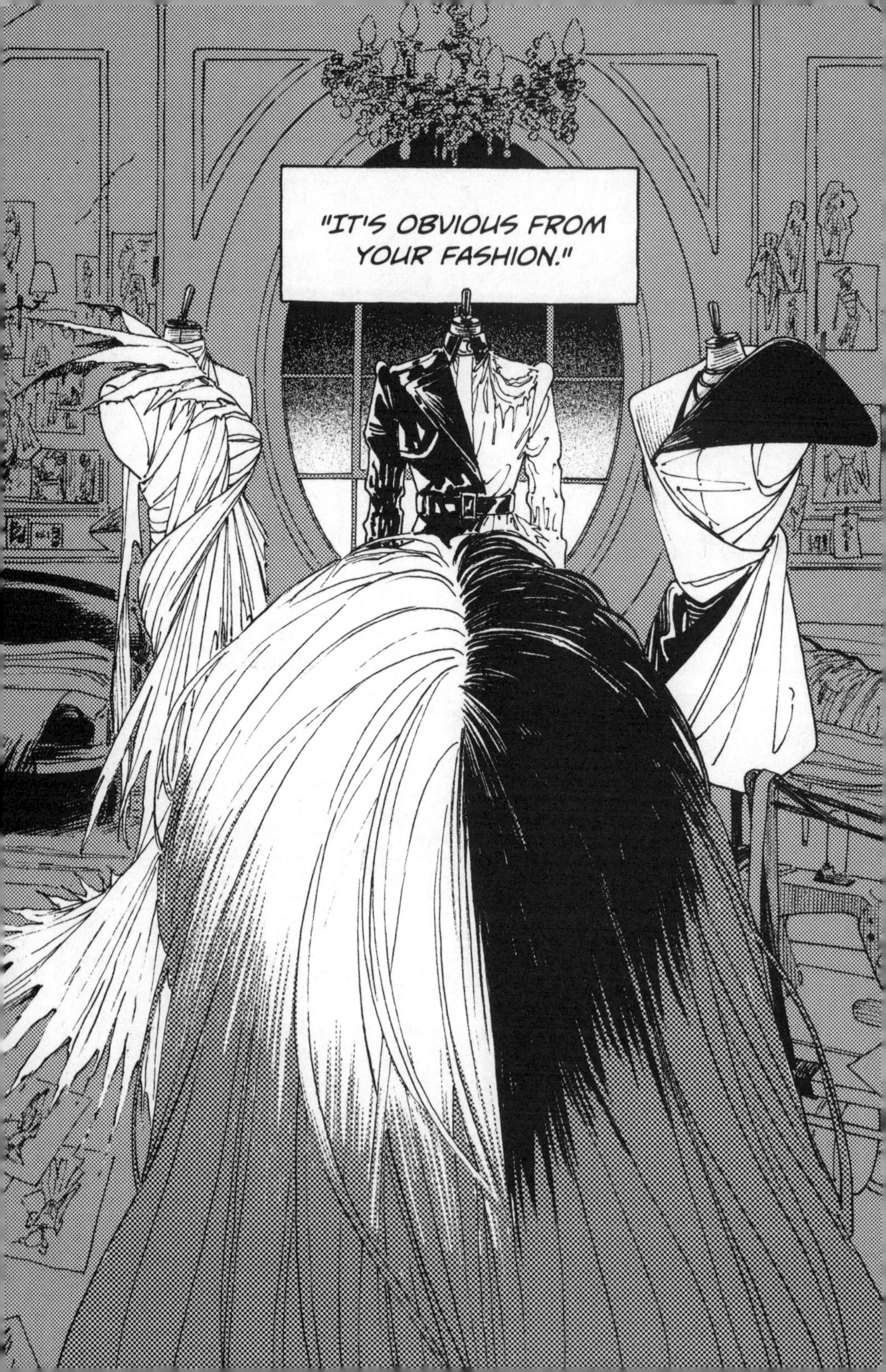
"IT'S OBVIOUS FROM YOUR FASHION."

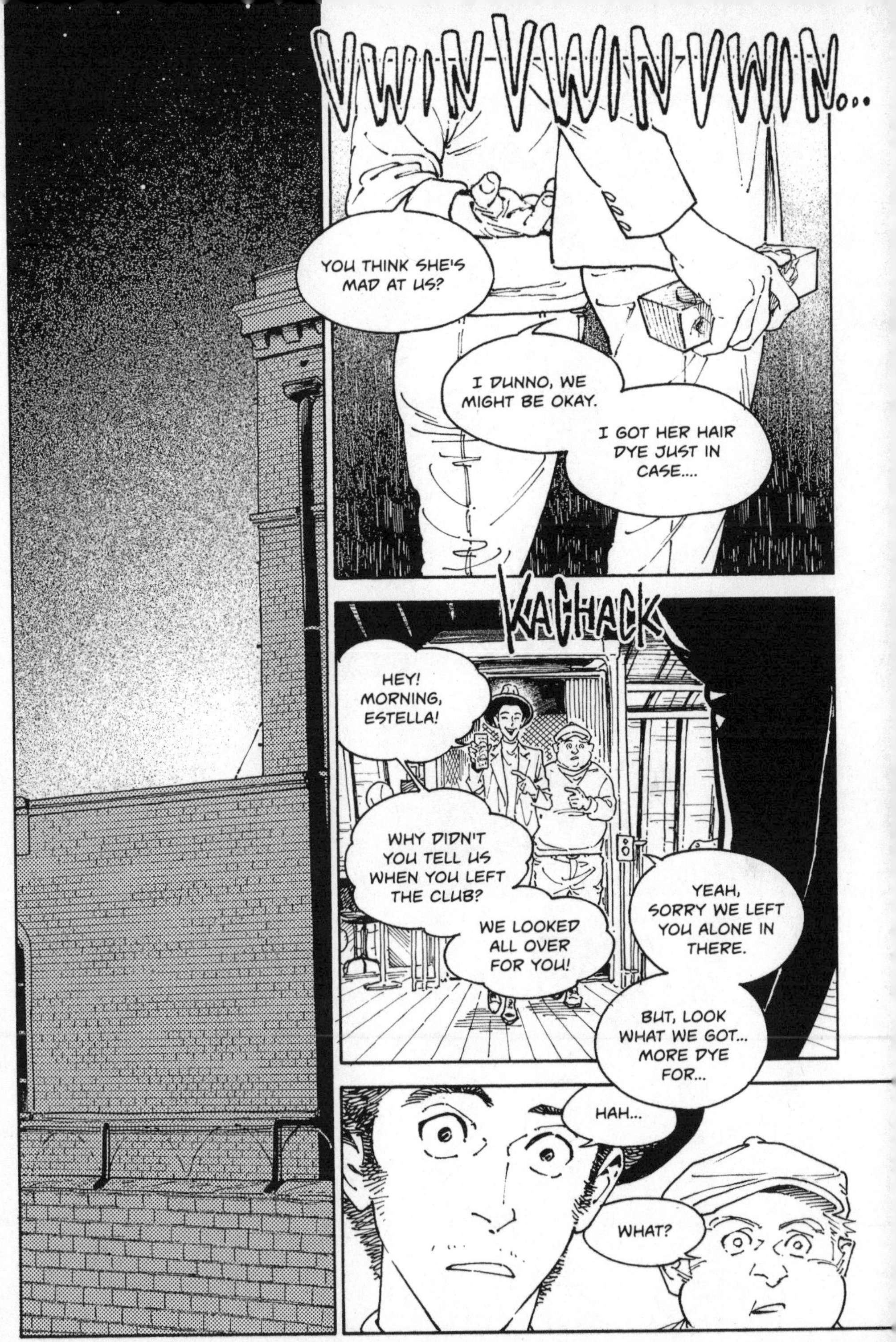
VWIN VWIN VWIN...
YOU THINK SHE'S MAD AT US?
I DUNNO, WE MIGHT BE OKAY.
I GOT HER HAIR DYE JUST IN CASE....
KACHACK
HEY! MORNING, ESTELLA!
WHY DIDN'T YOU TELL US WHEN YOU LEFT THE CLUB?
WE LOOKED ALL OVER FOR YOU!
YEAH, SORRY WE LEFT YOU ALONE IN THERE.
BUT, LOOK WHAT WE GOT... MORE DYE FOR...
HAH...
WHAT?

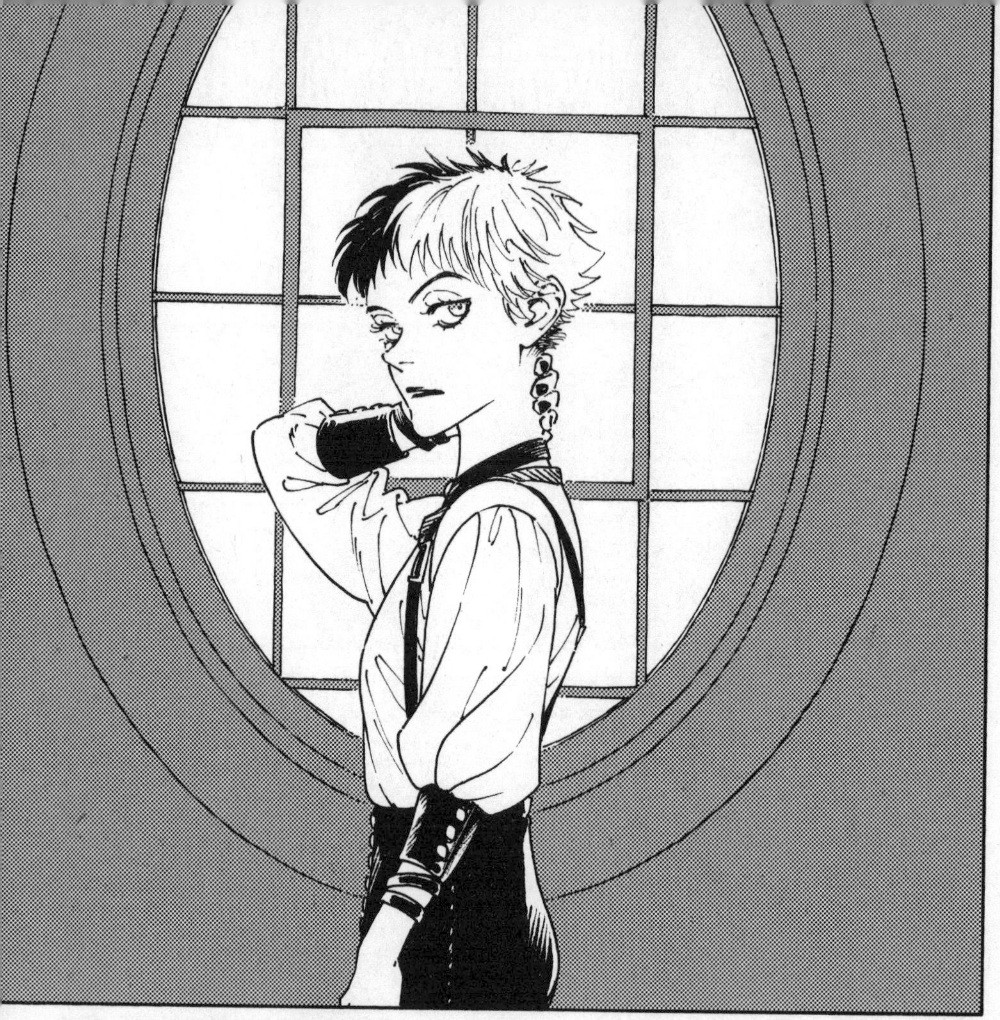

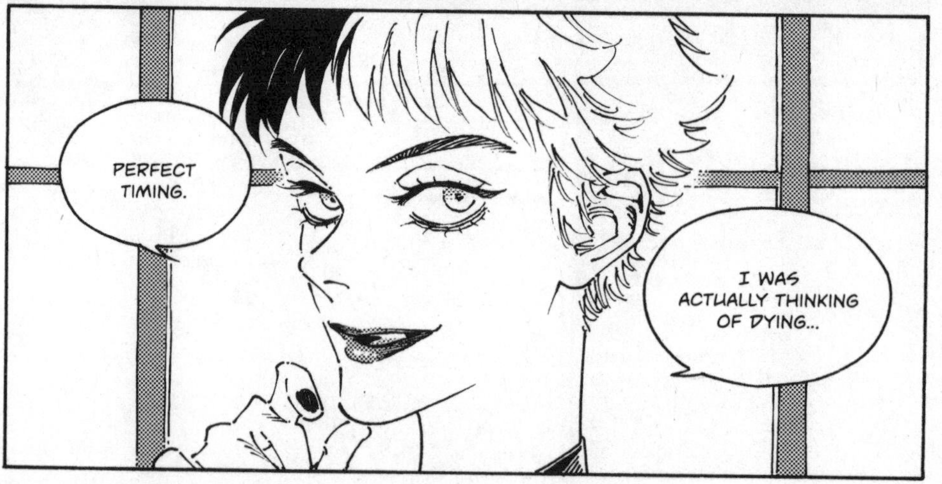
PERFECT TIMING.
I WAS ACTUALLY THINKING OF DYING...

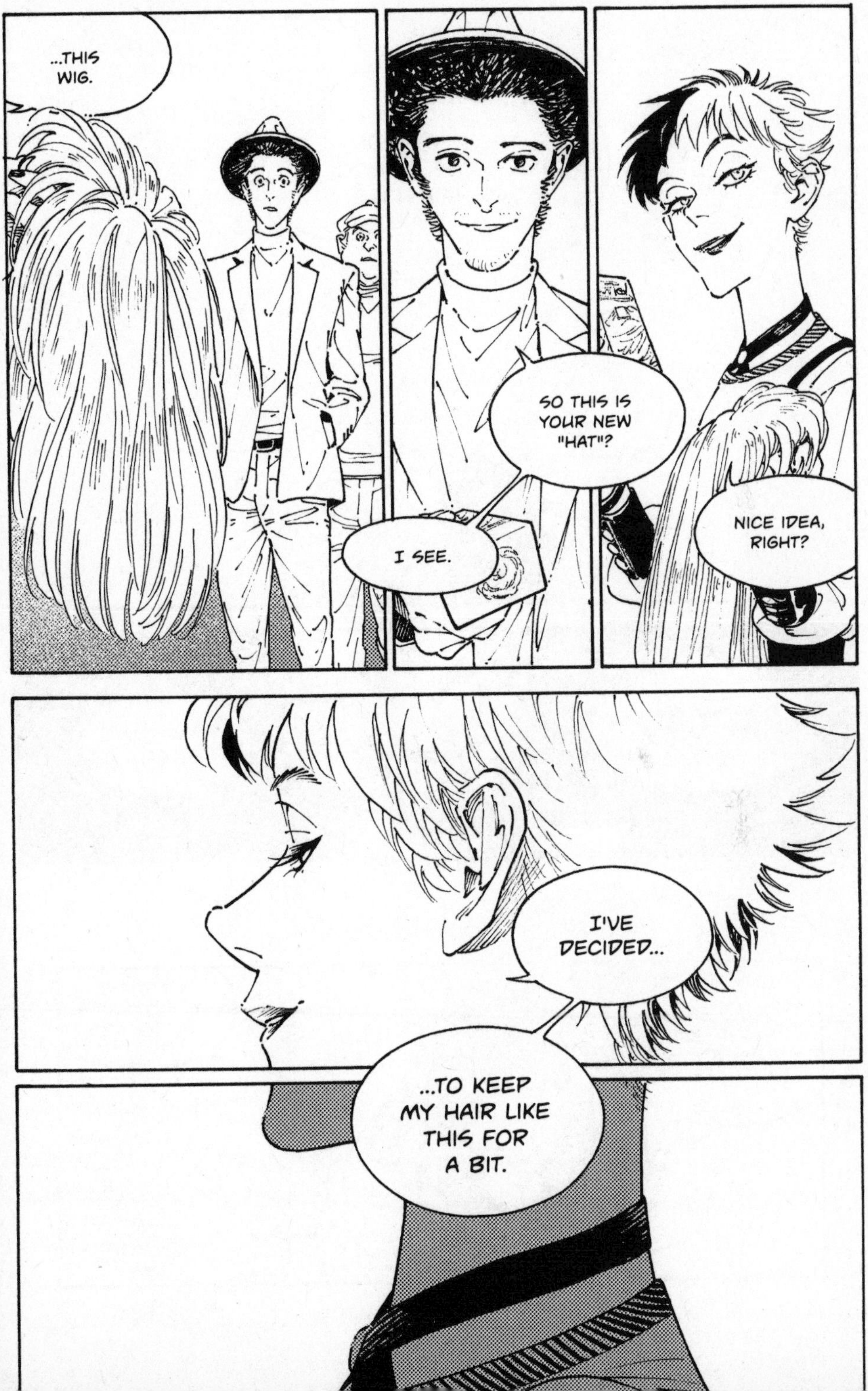
...THIS WIG.
SO THIS IS YOUR NEW "HAT"?
I SEE.
NICE IDEA, RIGHT?
I'VE DECIDED...
...TO KEEP MY HAIR LIKE THIS FOR A BIT.

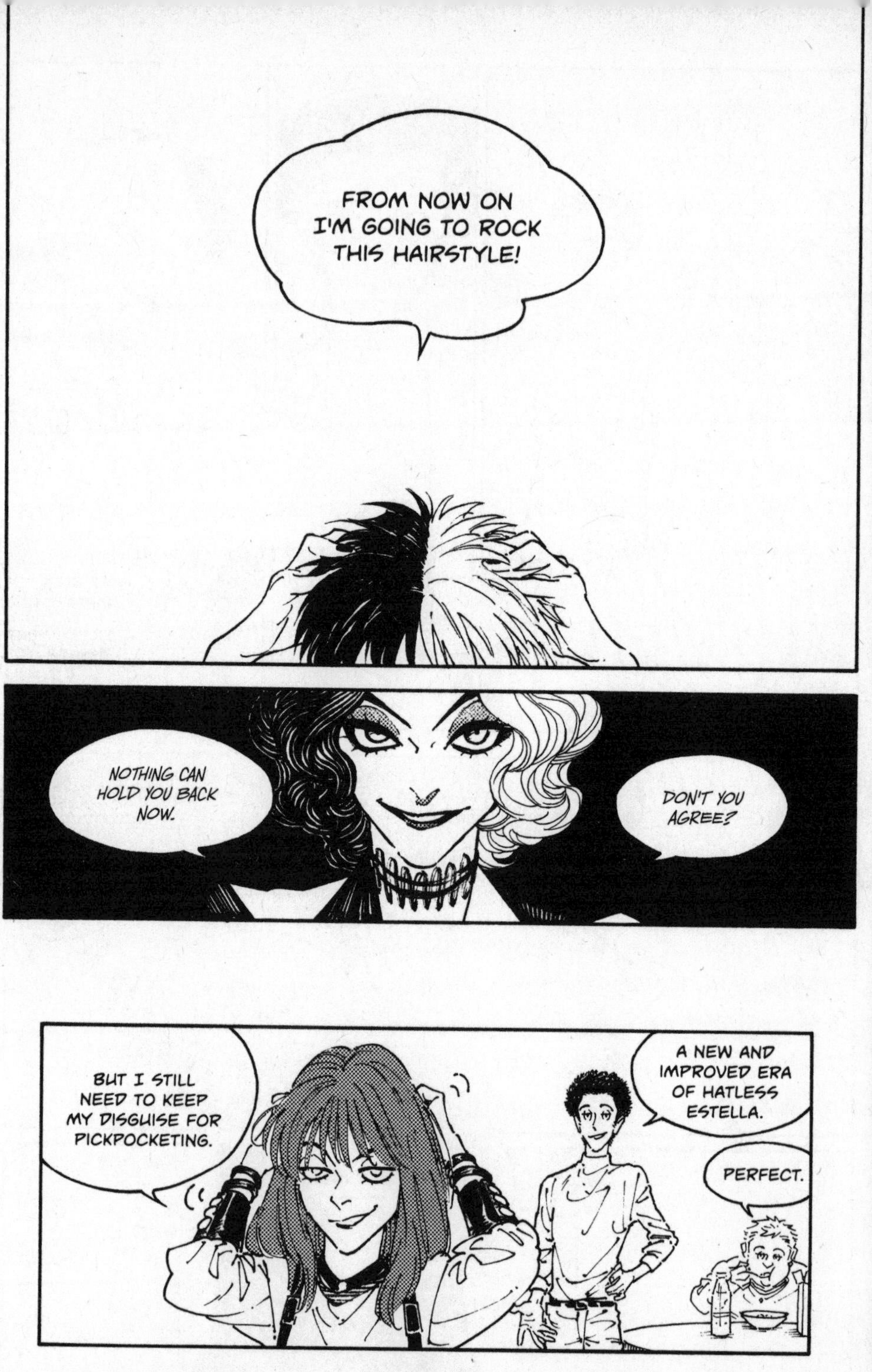
FROM NOW ON I'M GOING TO ROCK THIS HAIRSTYLE!
NOTHING CAN HOLD YOU BACK NOW.
DON'T YOU AGREE?
BUT I STILL NEED TO KEEP MY DISGUISE FOR PICKPOCKETING.
A NEW AND IMPROVED ERA OF HATLESS ESTELLA.
PERFECT.

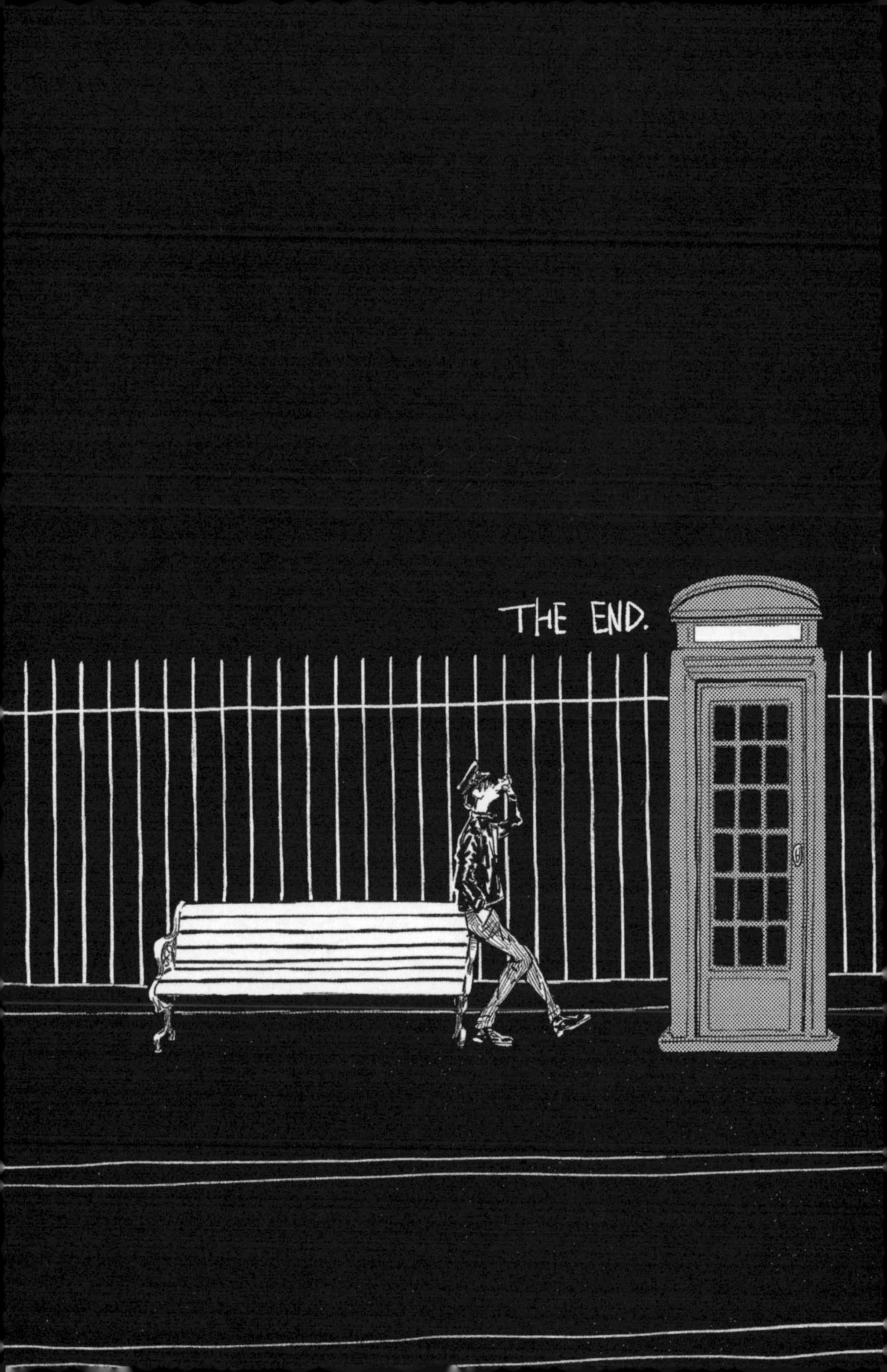
THE END.

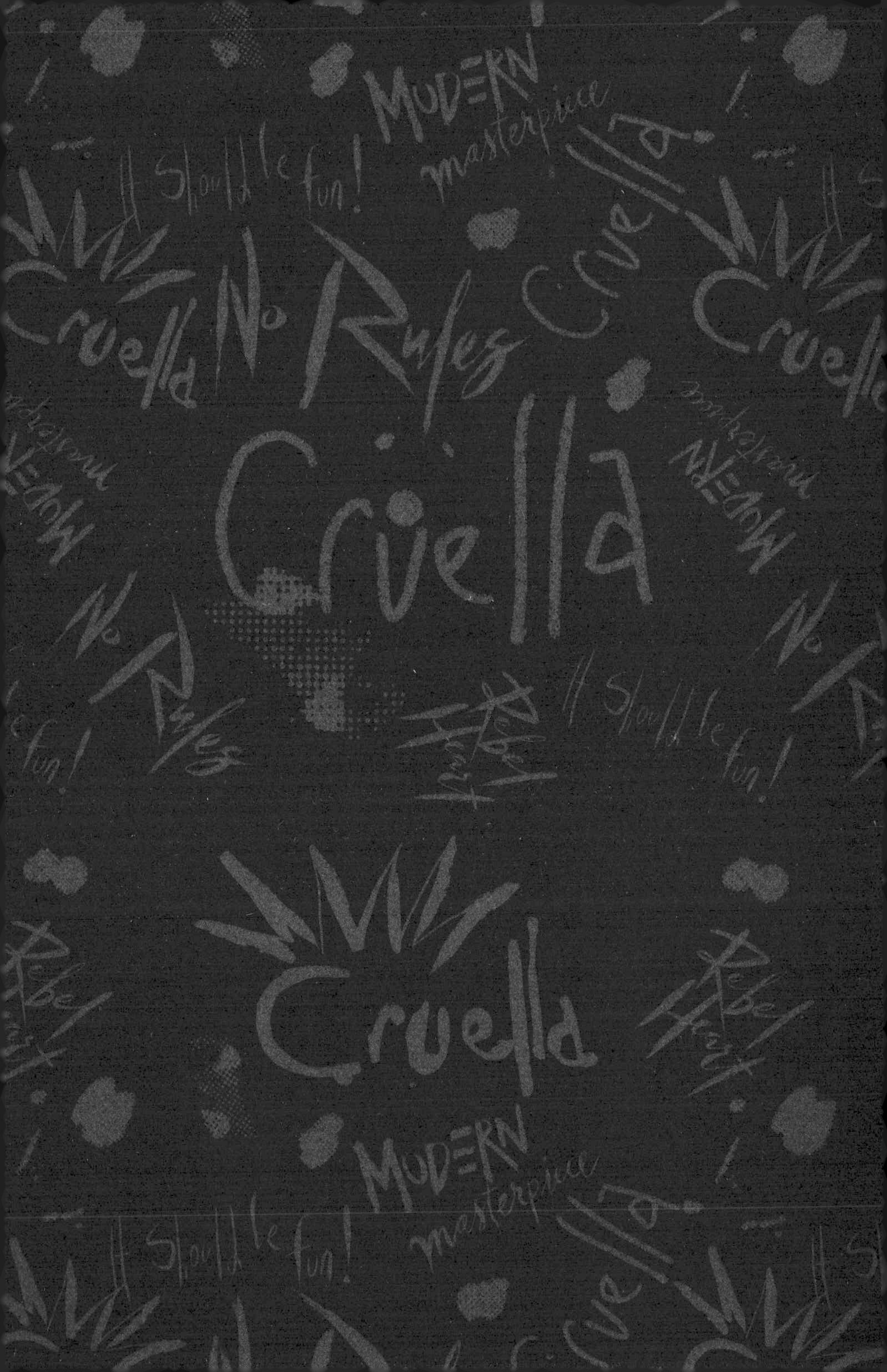
Cruella
No Rules
It should be fun!
MODERN masterpiece
Rebel Heart

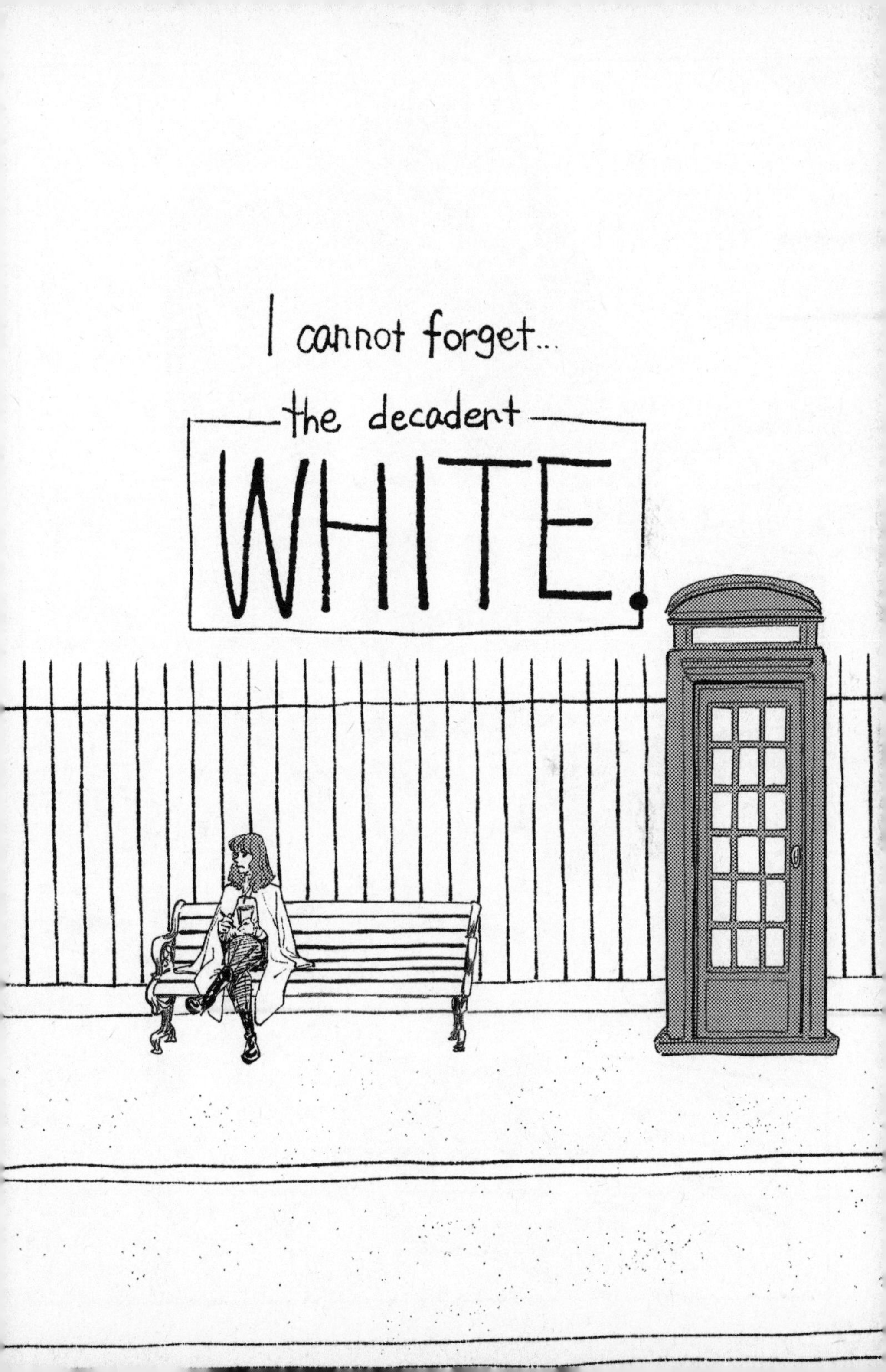
I cannot forget...
the decadent
WHITE.

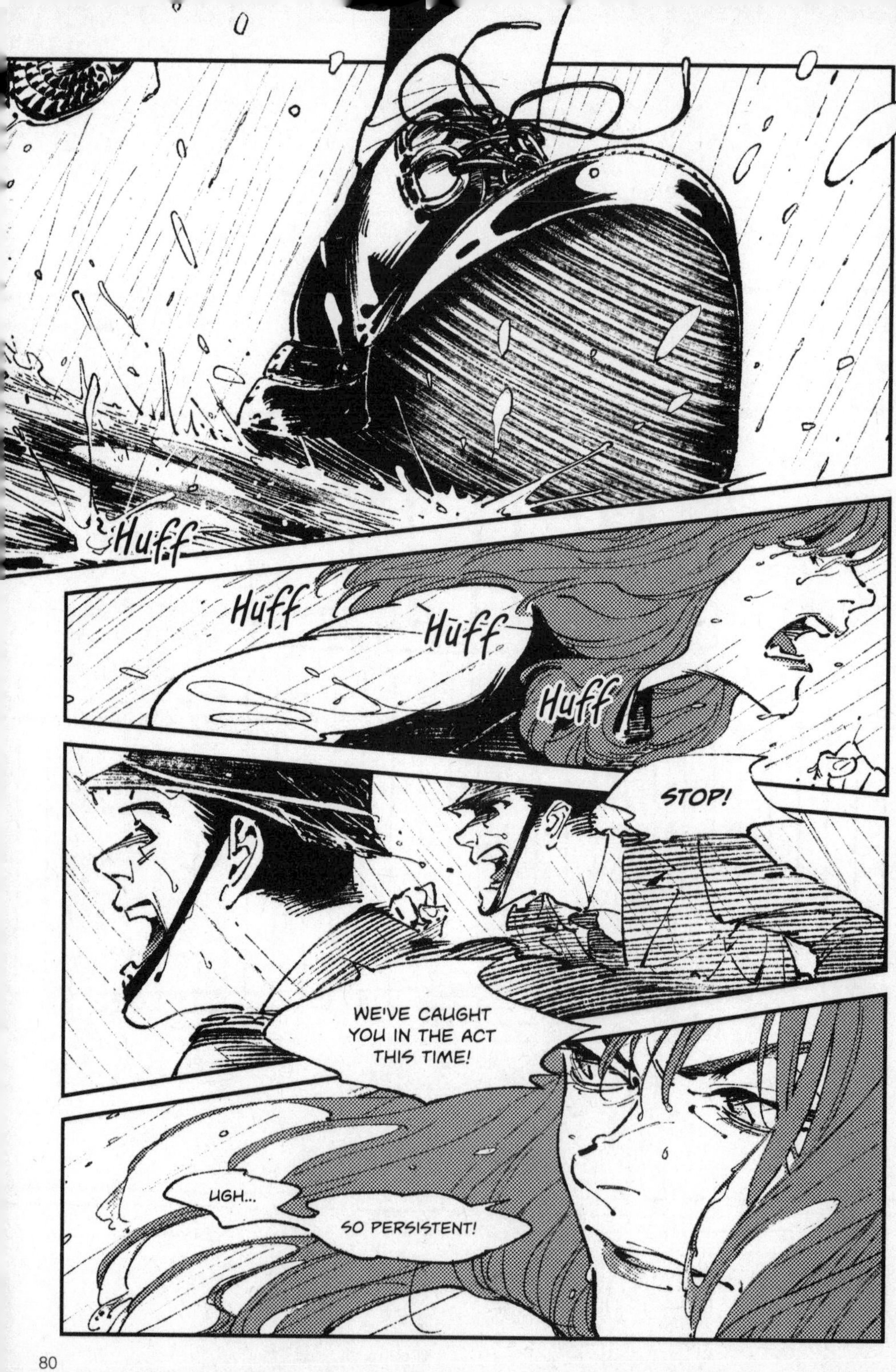
Huff
Huff
Huff
Huff
STOP!
WE'VE CAUGHT YOU IN THE ACT THIS TIME!
UGH...
SO PERSISTENT!

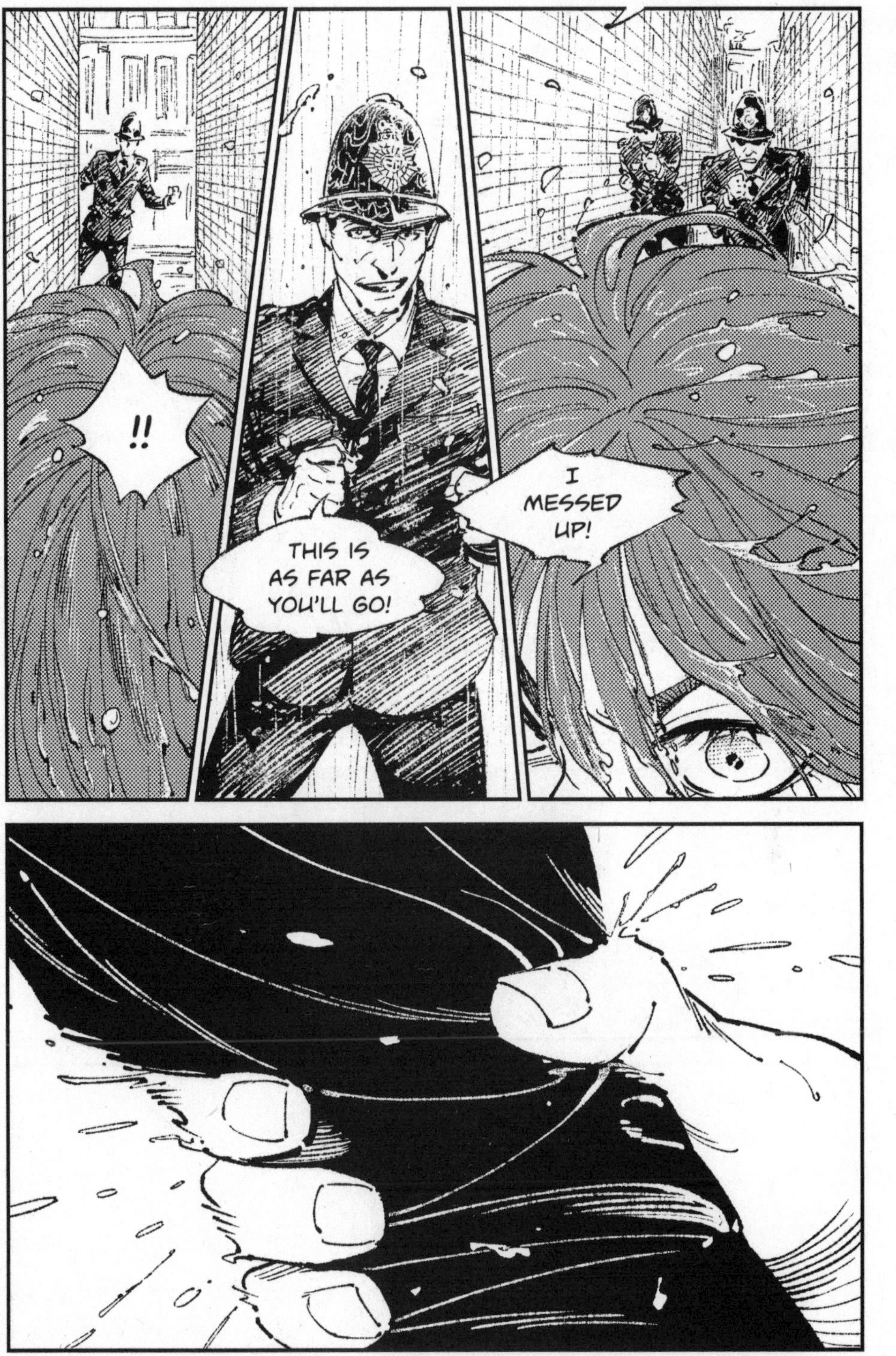
!!
THIS IS AS FAR AS YOU'LL GO!
I MESSED UP!

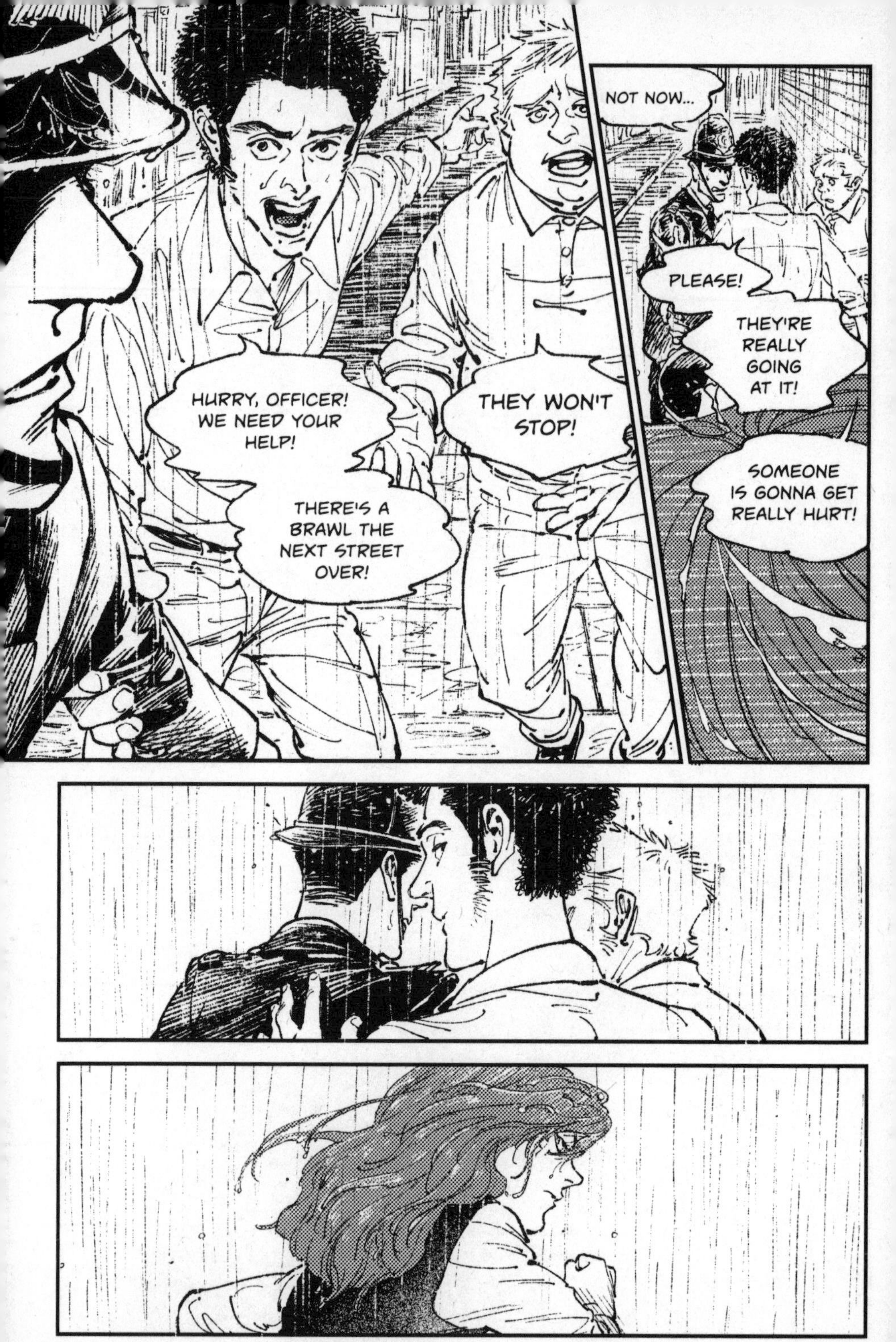
HURRY, OFFICER! WE NEED YOUR HELP!
THERE'S A BRAWL THE NEXT STREET OVER!
THEY WON'T STOP!
NOT NOW...
PLEASE!
THEY'RE REALLY GOING AT IT!
SOMEONE IS GONNA GET REALLY HURT!

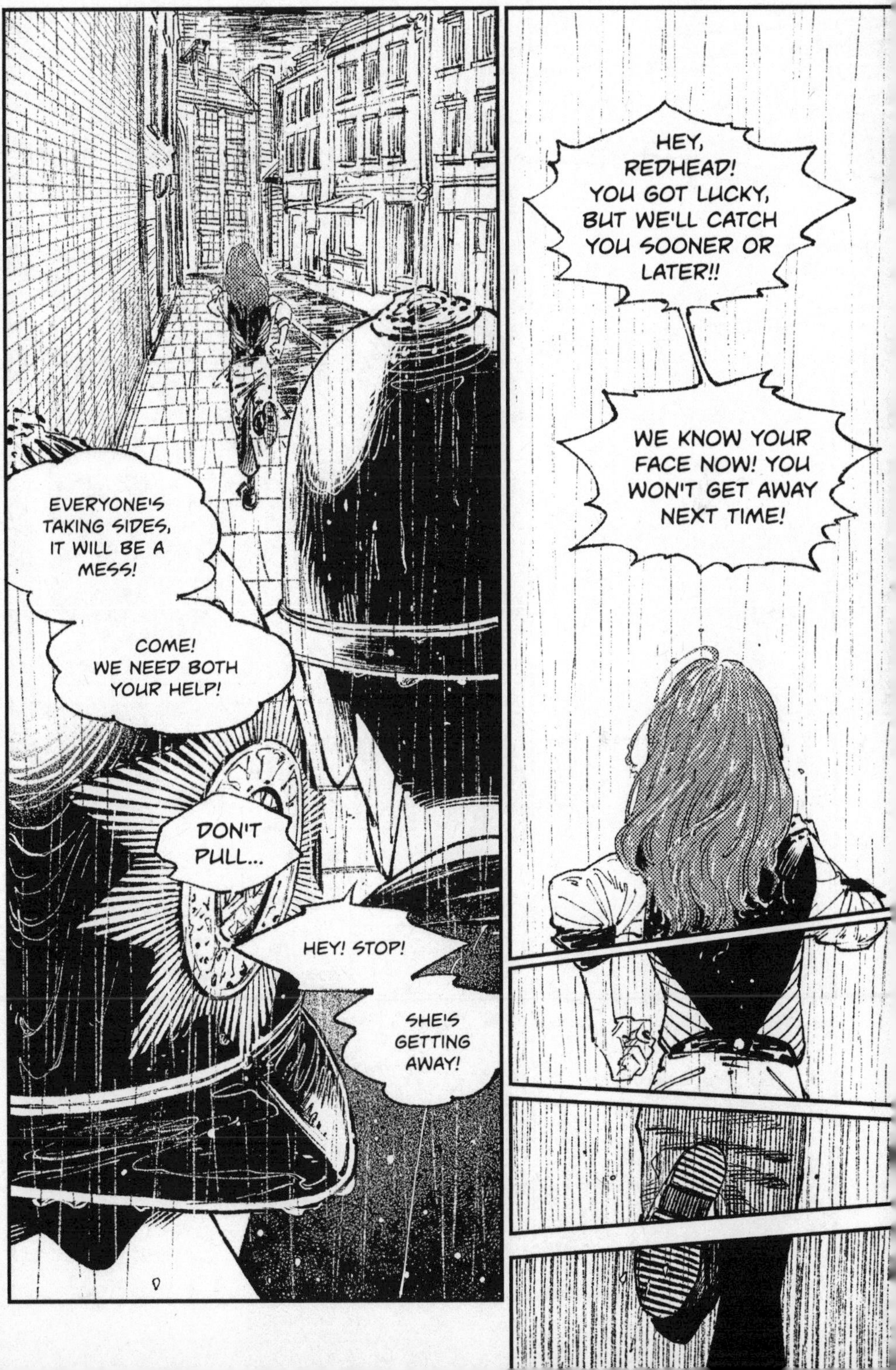
EVERYONE'S TAKING SIDES, IT WILL BE A MESS!
COME! WE NEED BOTH YOUR HELP!
DON'T PULL...
HEY! STOP!
SHE'S GETTING AWAY!
HEY, REDHEAD! YOU GOT LUCKY, BUT WE'LL CATCH YOU SOONER OR LATER!!
WE KNOW YOUR FACE NOW! YOU WON'T GET AWAY NEXT TIME!

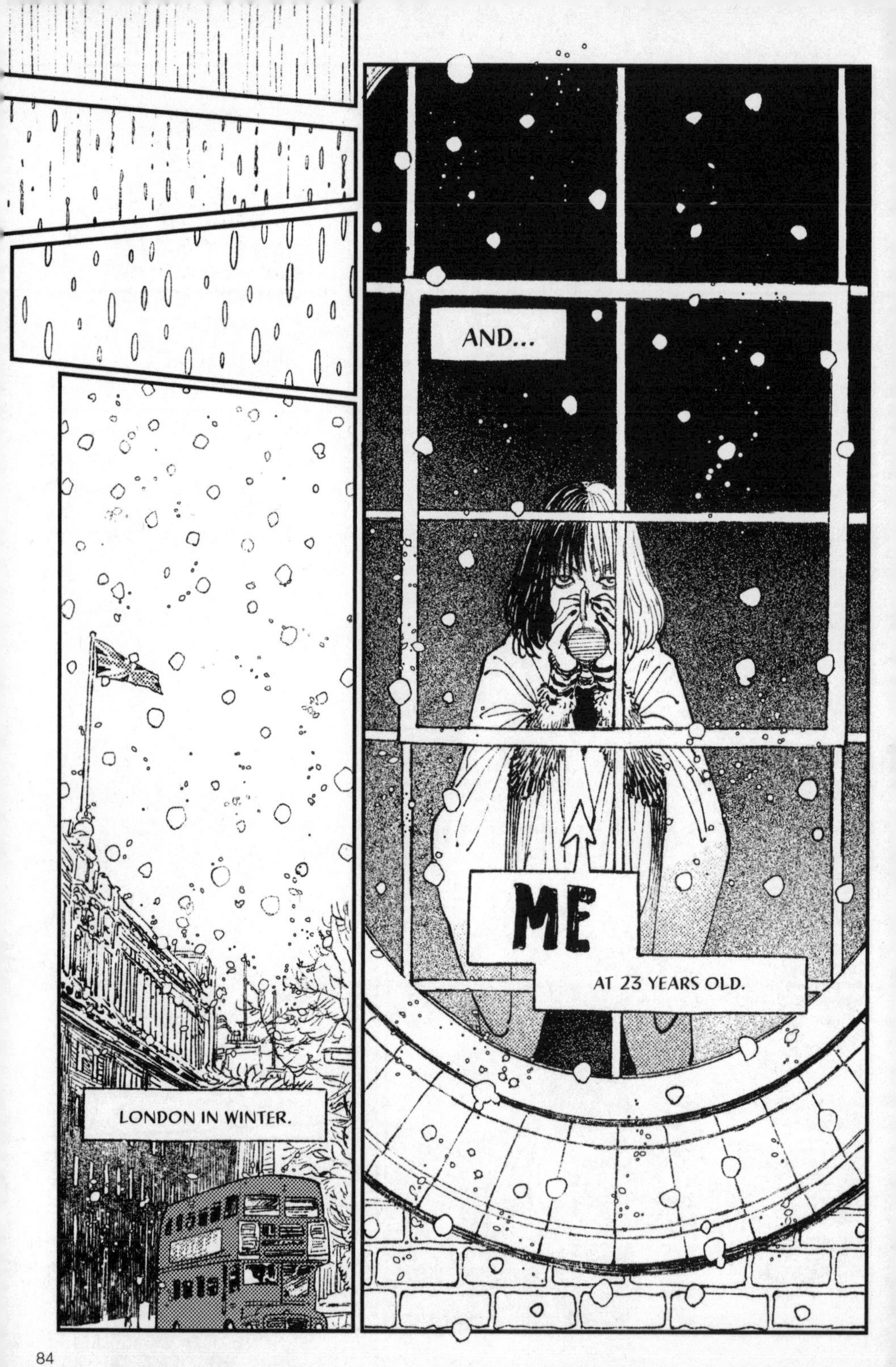
LONDON IN WINTER.
AND...
ME
AT 23 YEARS OLD.

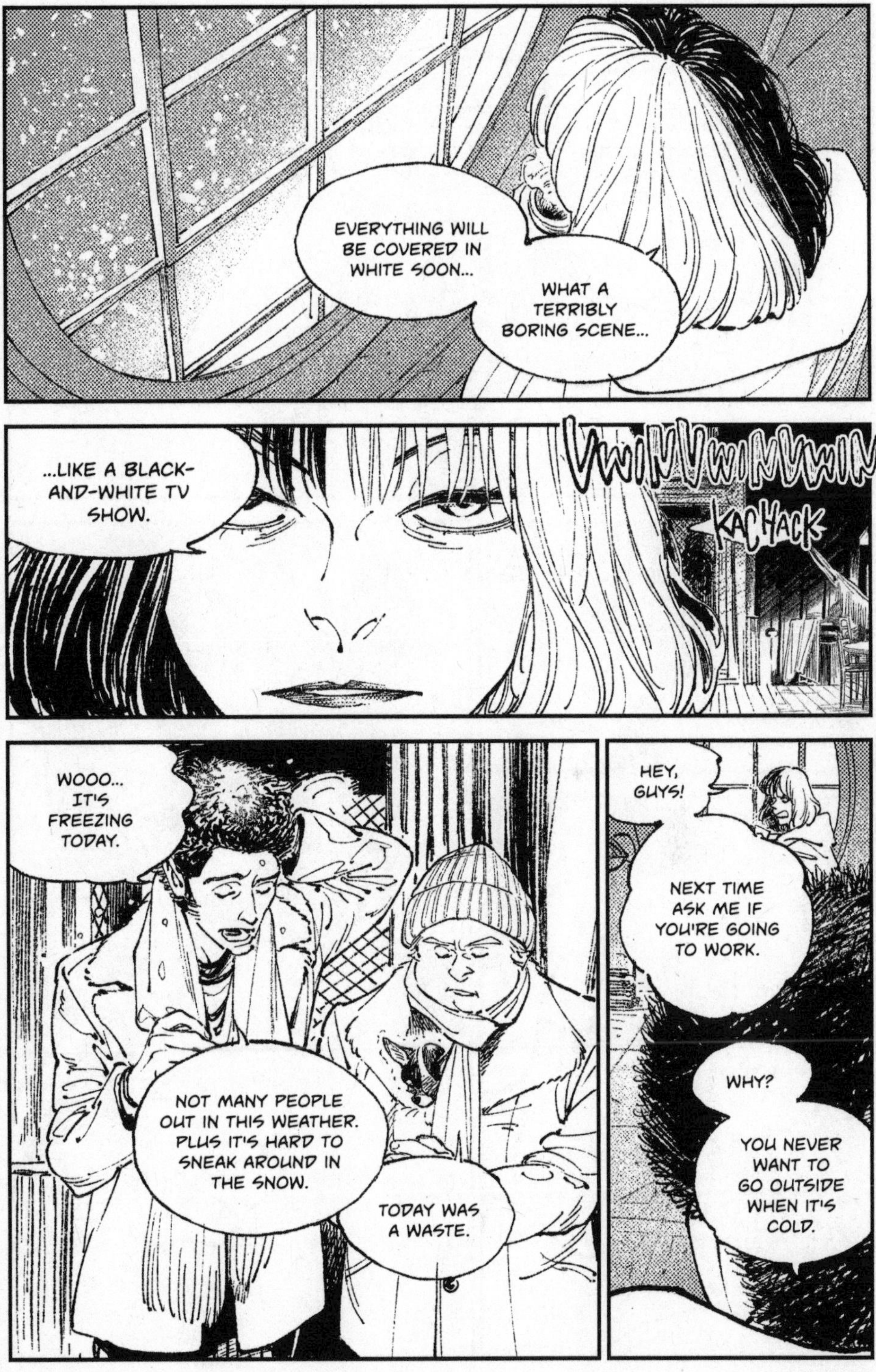
EVERYTHING WILL BE COVERED IN WHITE SOON...
WHAT A TERRIBLY BORING SCENE...
...LIKE A BLACK-AND-WHITE TV SHOW.
VWINVWINVWIN...
KACHACK
WOOO... IT'S FREEZING TODAY.
NOT MANY PEOPLE OUT IN THIS WEATHER. PLUS IT'S HARD TO SNEAK AROUND IN THE SNOW.
TODAY WAS A WASTE.
HEY, GUYS!
NEXT TIME ASK ME IF YOU'RE GOING TO WORK.
WHY?
YOU NEVER WANT TO GO OUTSIDE WHEN IT'S COLD.

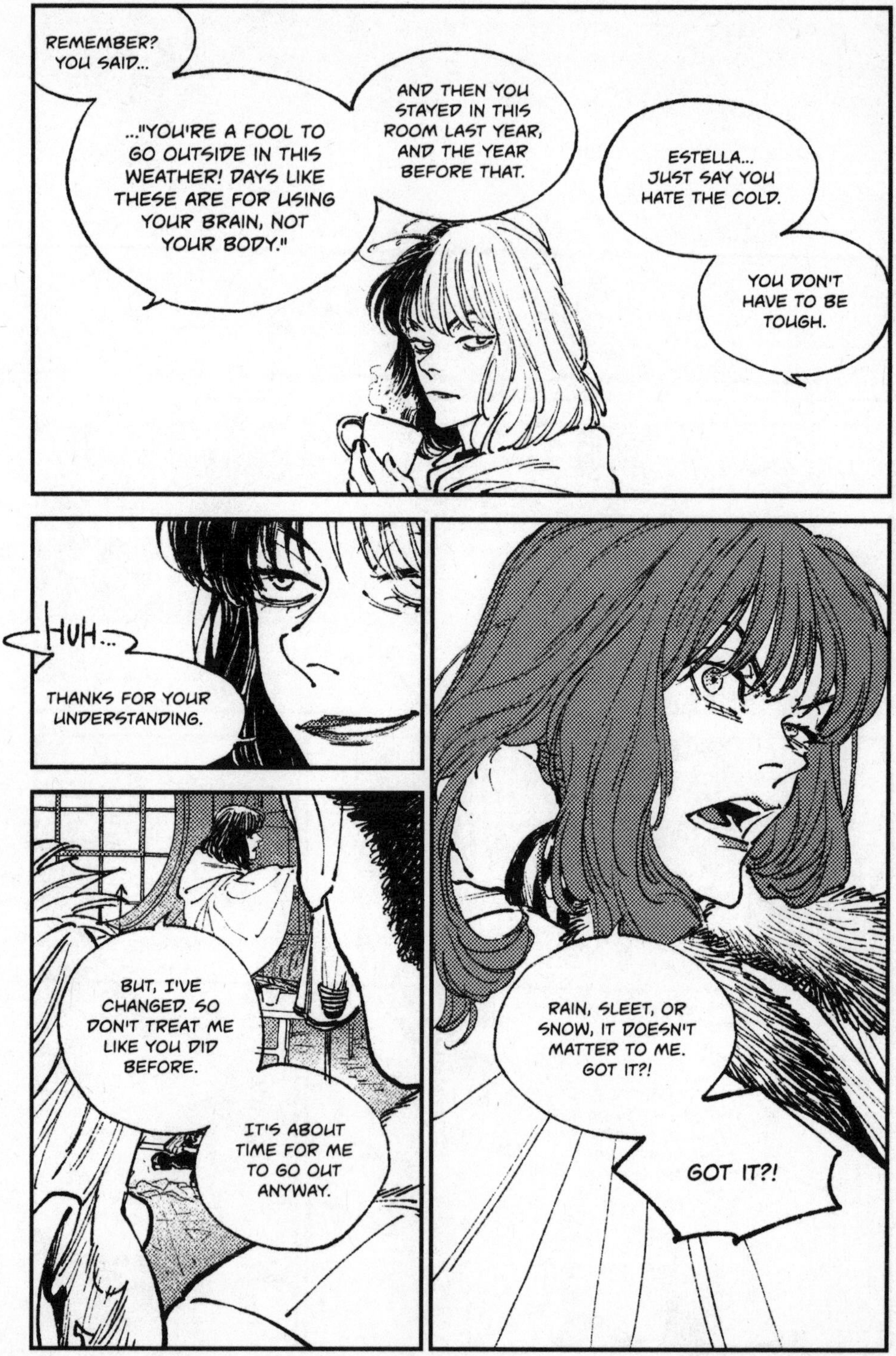
REMEMBER? YOU SAID...
..."YOU'RE A FOOL TO GO OUTSIDE IN THIS WEATHER! DAYS LIKE THESE ARE FOR USING YOUR BRAIN, NOT YOUR BODY."
AND THEN YOU STAYED IN THIS ROOM LAST YEAR, AND THE YEAR BEFORE THAT.
ESTELLA... JUST SAY YOU HATE THE COLD.
YOU DON'T HAVE TO BE TOUGH.
HUH...
THANKS FOR YOUR UNDERSTANDING.
BUT, I'VE CHANGED. SO DON'T TREAT ME LIKE YOU DID BEFORE.
IT'S ABOUT TIME FOR ME TO GO OUT ANYWAY.
RAIN, SLEET, OR SNOW, IT DOESN'T MATTER TO ME. GOT IT?!
GOT IT?!

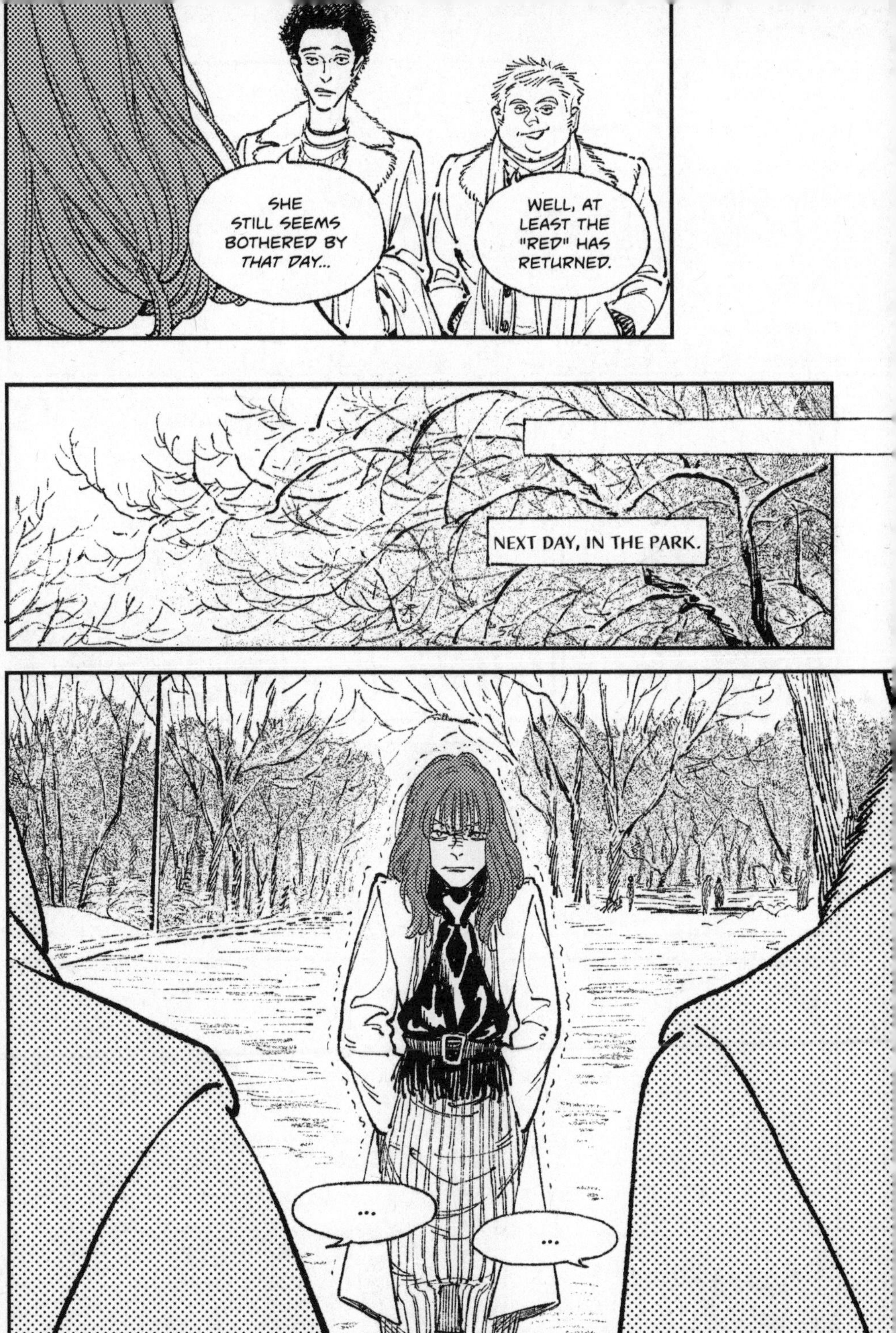
SHE STILL SEEMS BOTHERED BY *THAT DAY*...
WELL, AT LEAST THE "RED" HAS RETURNED.
NEXT DAY, IN THE PARK.
...
...

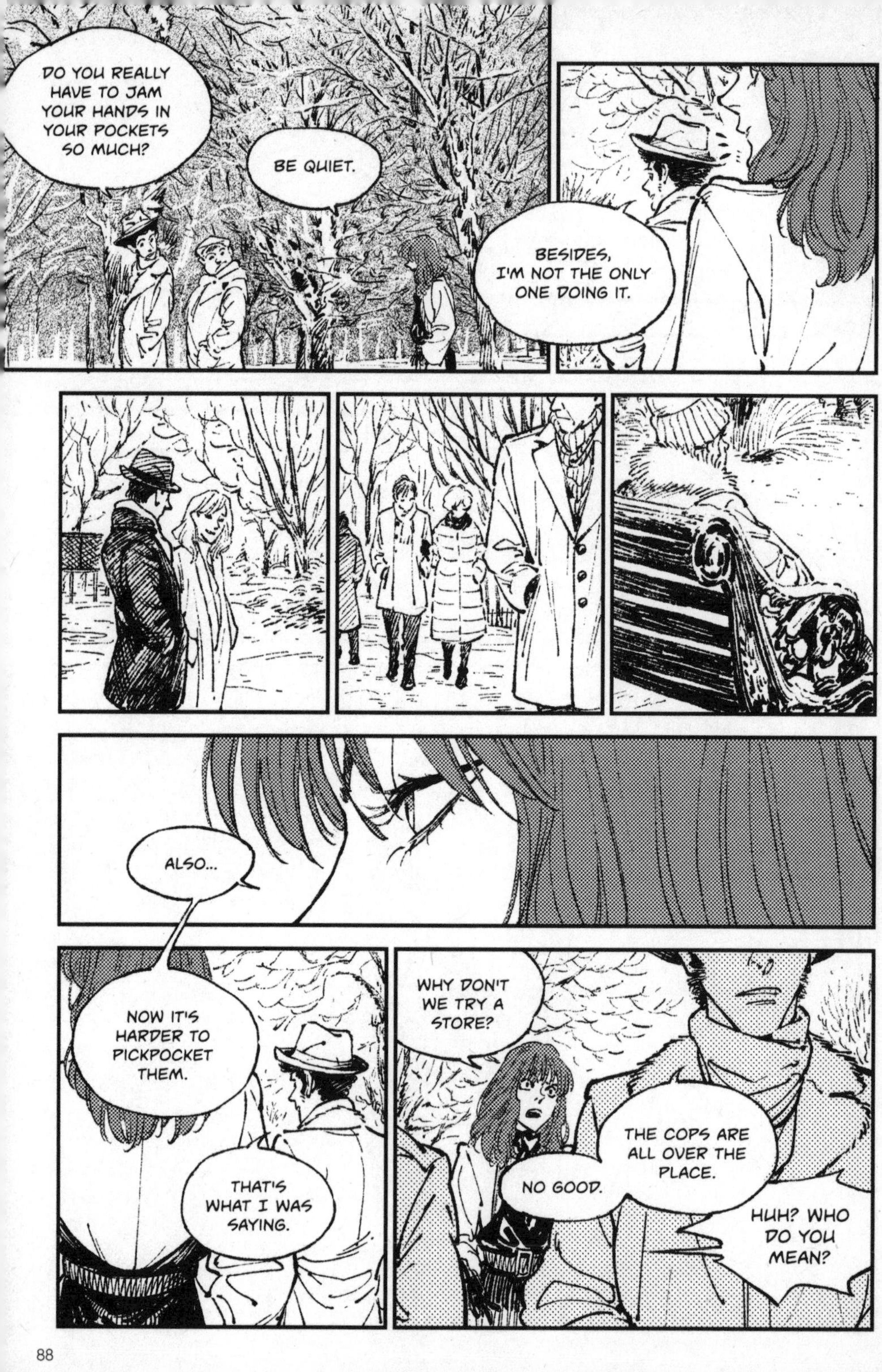
DO YOU REALLY HAVE TO JAM YOUR HANDS IN YOUR POCKETS SO MUCH?
BE QUIET.
BESIDES, I'M NOT THE ONLY ONE DOING IT.
ALSO...
NOW IT'S HARDER TO PICKPOCKET THEM.
THAT'S WHAT I WAS SAYING.
WHY DON'T WE TRY A STORE?
NO GOOD.
THE COPS ARE ALL OVER THE PLACE.
HUH? WHO DO YOU MEAN?

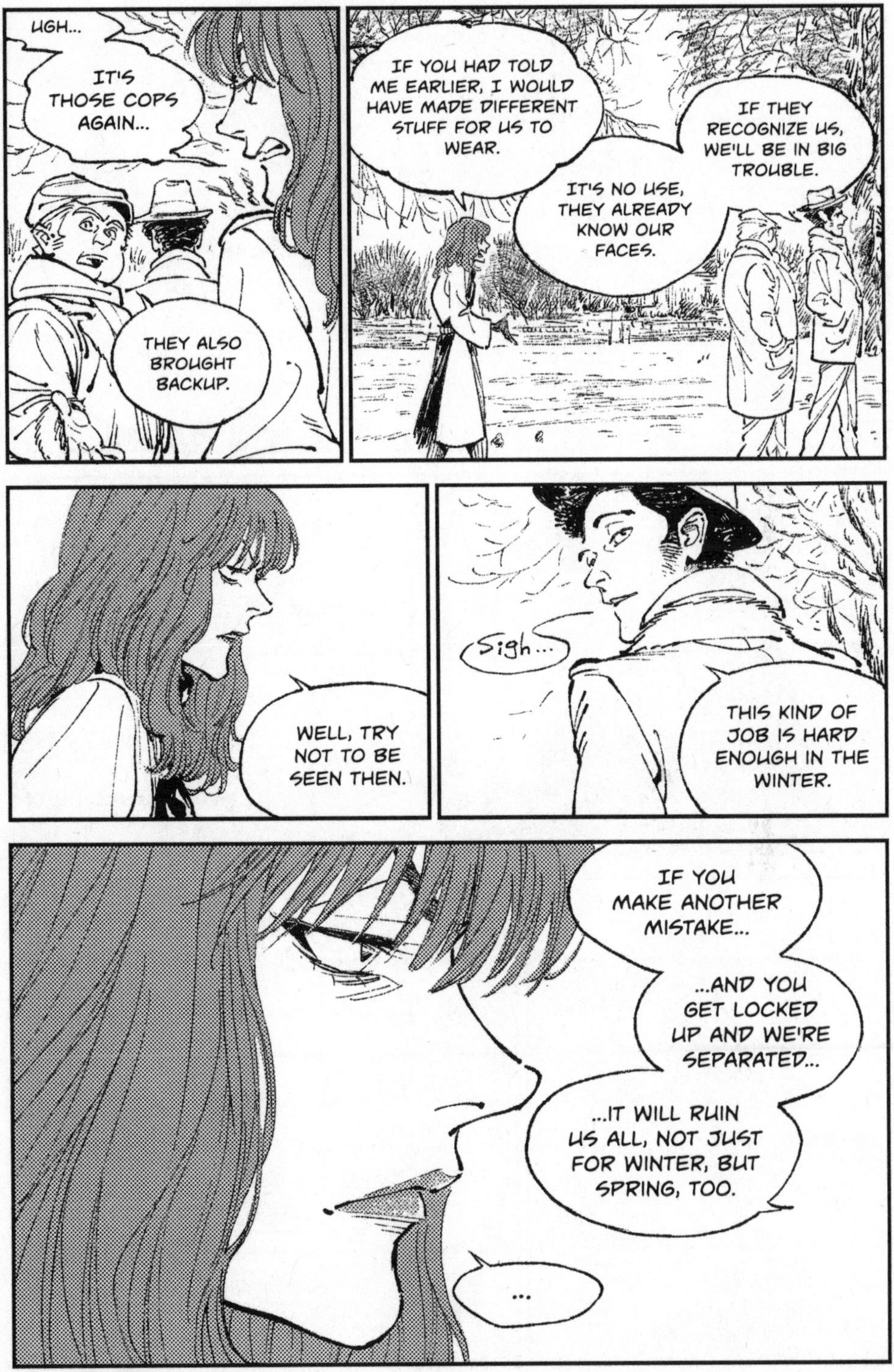
UGH...
IT'S THOSE COPS AGAIN...
THEY ALSO BROUGHT BACKUP.
IF YOU HAD TOLD ME EARLIER, I WOULD HAVE MADE DIFFERENT STUFF FOR US TO WEAR.
IF THEY RECOGNIZE US, WE'LL BE IN BIG TROUBLE.
IT'S NO USE, THEY ALREADY KNOW OUR FACES.
WELL, TRY NOT TO BE SEEN THEN.
Sigh...
THIS KIND OF JOB IS HARD ENOUGH IN THE WINTER.
IF YOU MAKE ANOTHER MISTAKE...
...AND YOU GET LOCKED UP AND WE'RE SEPARATED...
...IT WILL RUIN US ALL, NOT JUST FOR WINTER, BUT SPRING, TOO.
...

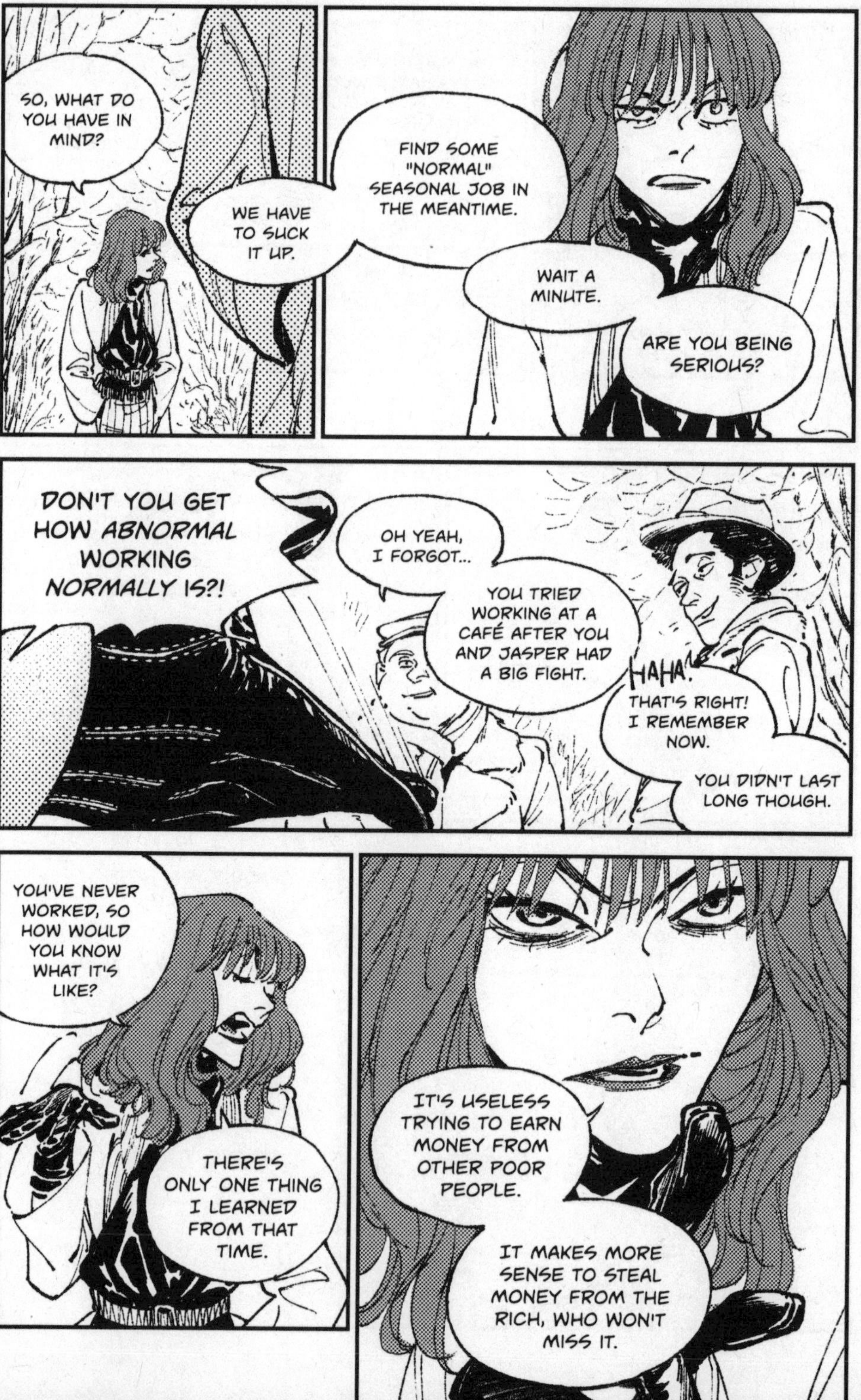
SO, WHAT DO YOU HAVE IN MIND?
WE HAVE TO SUCK IT UP.
FIND SOME "NORMAL" SEASONAL JOB IN THE MEANTIME.
WAIT A MINUTE.
ARE YOU BEING SERIOUS?
DON'T YOU GET HOW *ABNORMAL* WORKING *NORMALLY* IS?!
OH YEAH, I FORGOT...
YOU TRIED WORKING AT A CAFÉ AFTER YOU AND JASPER HAD A BIG FIGHT.
HAHA!
THAT'S RIGHT! I REMEMBER NOW.
YOU DIDN'T LAST LONG THOUGH.
YOU'VE NEVER WORKED, SO HOW WOULD YOU KNOW WHAT IT'S LIKE?
THERE'S ONLY ONE THING I LEARNED FROM THAT TIME.
IT'S USELESS TRYING TO EARN MONEY FROM OTHER POOR PEOPLE.
IT MAKES MORE SENSE TO STEAL MONEY FROM THE RICH, WHO WON'T MISS IT.

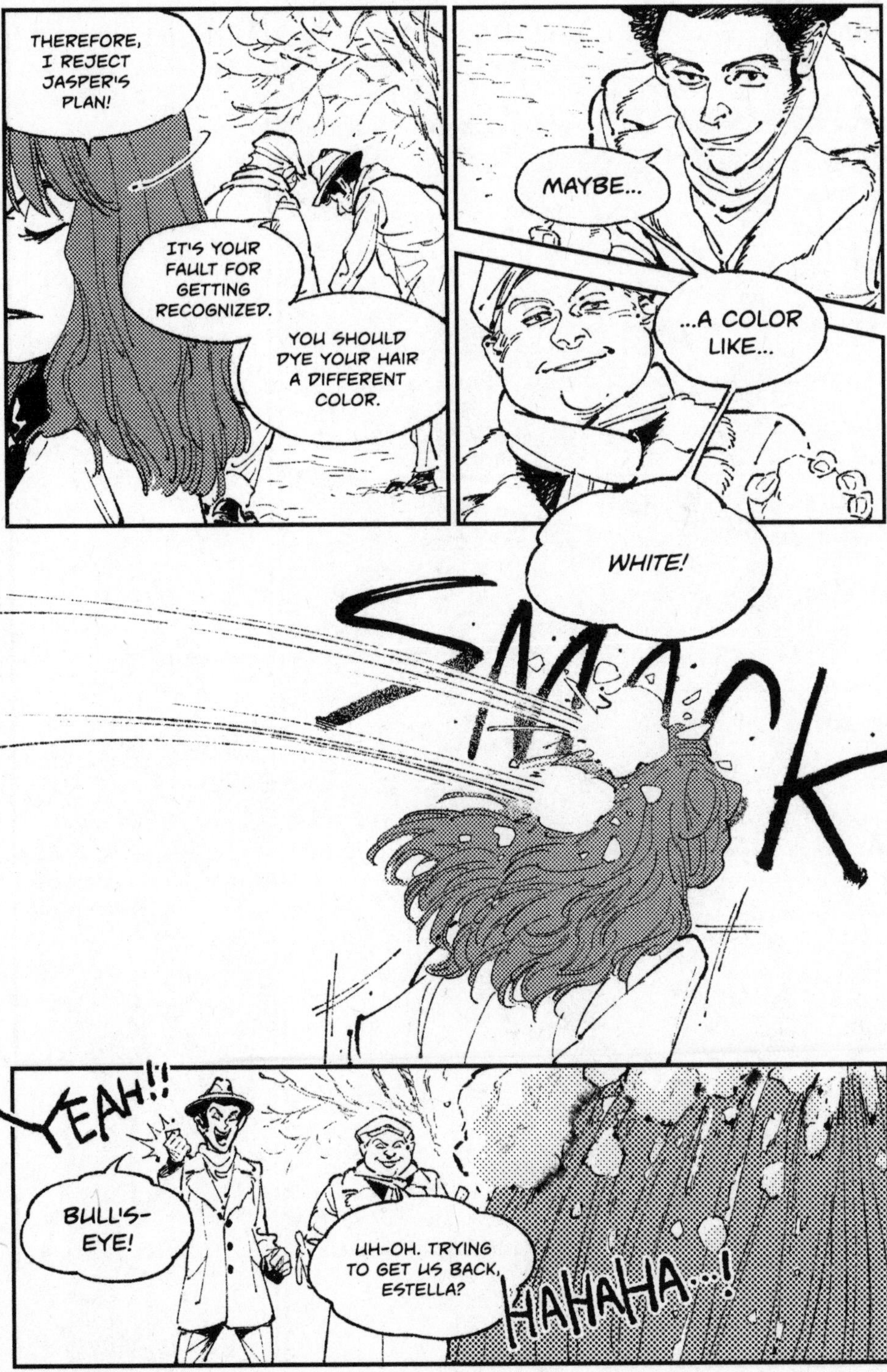
THEREFORE, I REJECT JASPER'S PLAN!
IT'S YOUR FAULT FOR GETTING RECOGNIZED.
YOU SHOULD DYE YOUR HAIR A DIFFERENT COLOR.
MAYBE...
...A COLOR LIKE...
WHITE!
SMACK
YEAH!!
BULL'S-EYE!
UH-OH. TRYING TO GET US BACK, ESTELLA?
HAHAHA...!

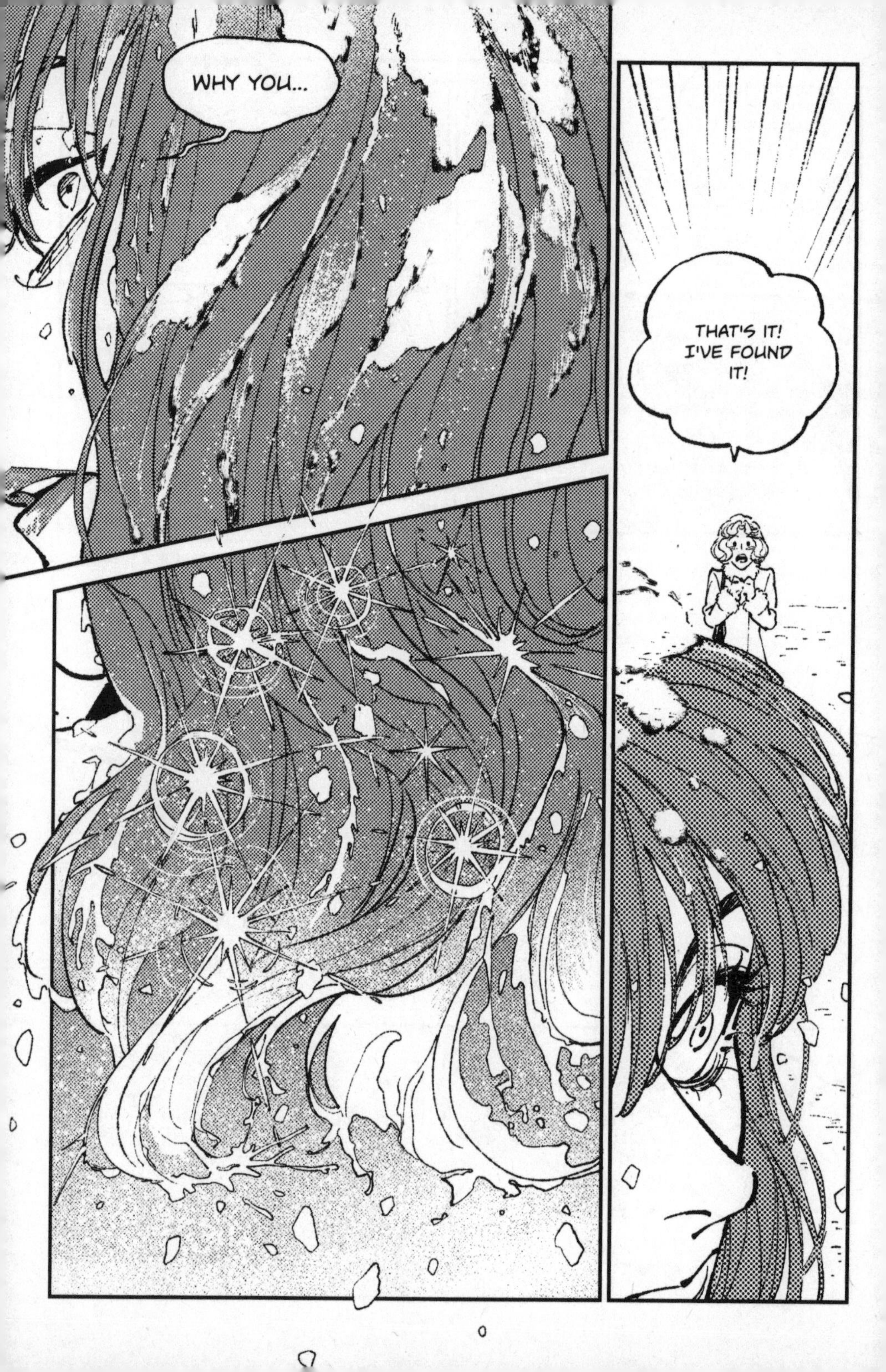
WHY YOU...
THAT'S IT! I'VE FOUND IT!

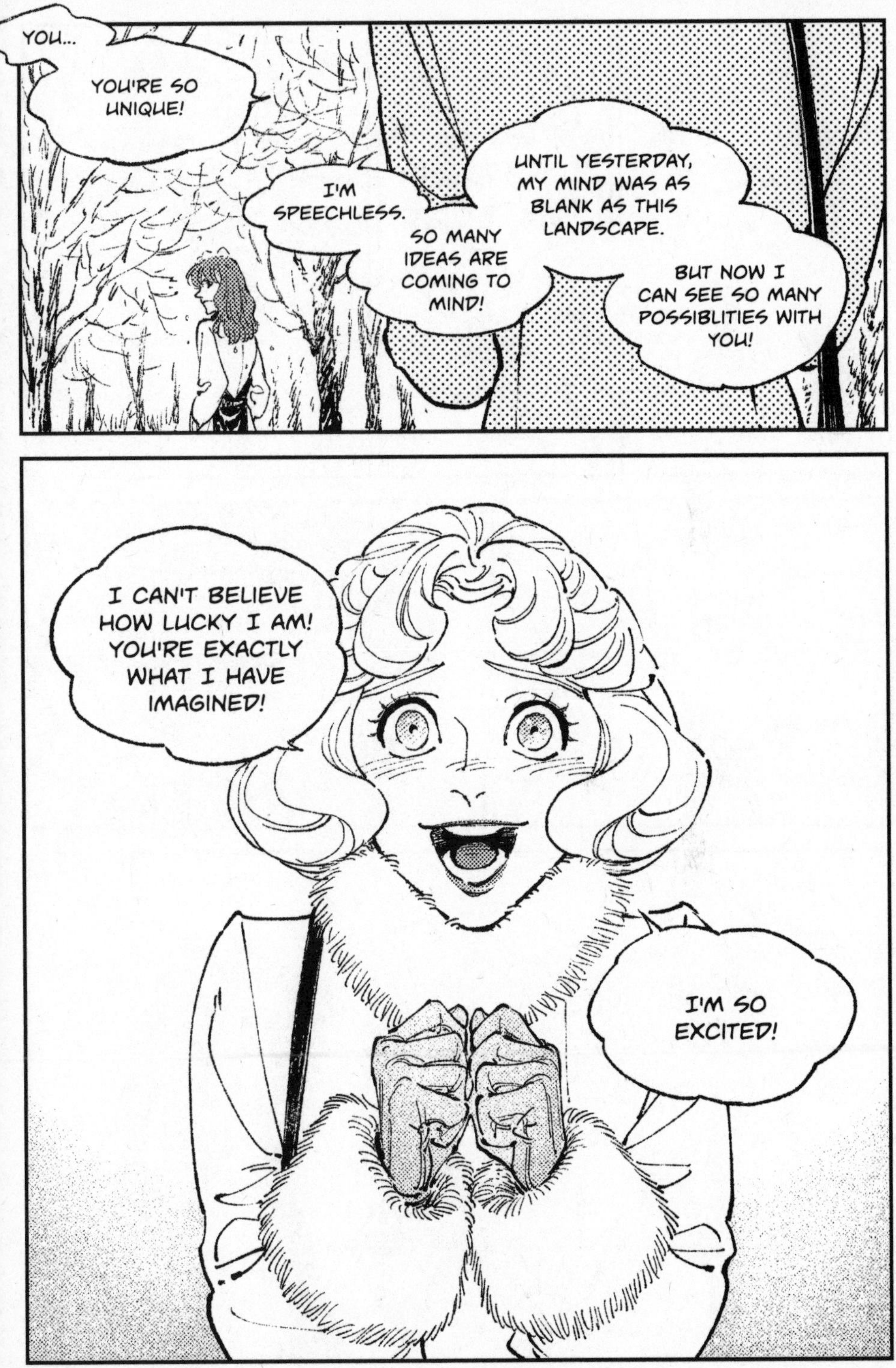
YOU...
YOU'RE SO UNIQUE!
I'M SPEECHLESS.
SO MANY IDEAS ARE COMING TO MIND!
UNTIL YESTERDAY, MY MIND WAS AS BLANK AS THIS LANDSCAPE.
BUT NOW I CAN SEE SO MANY POSSIBLITIES WITH YOU!
I CAN'T BELIEVE HOW LUCKY I AM! YOU'RE EXACTLY WHAT I HAVE IMAGINED!
I'M SO EXCITED!

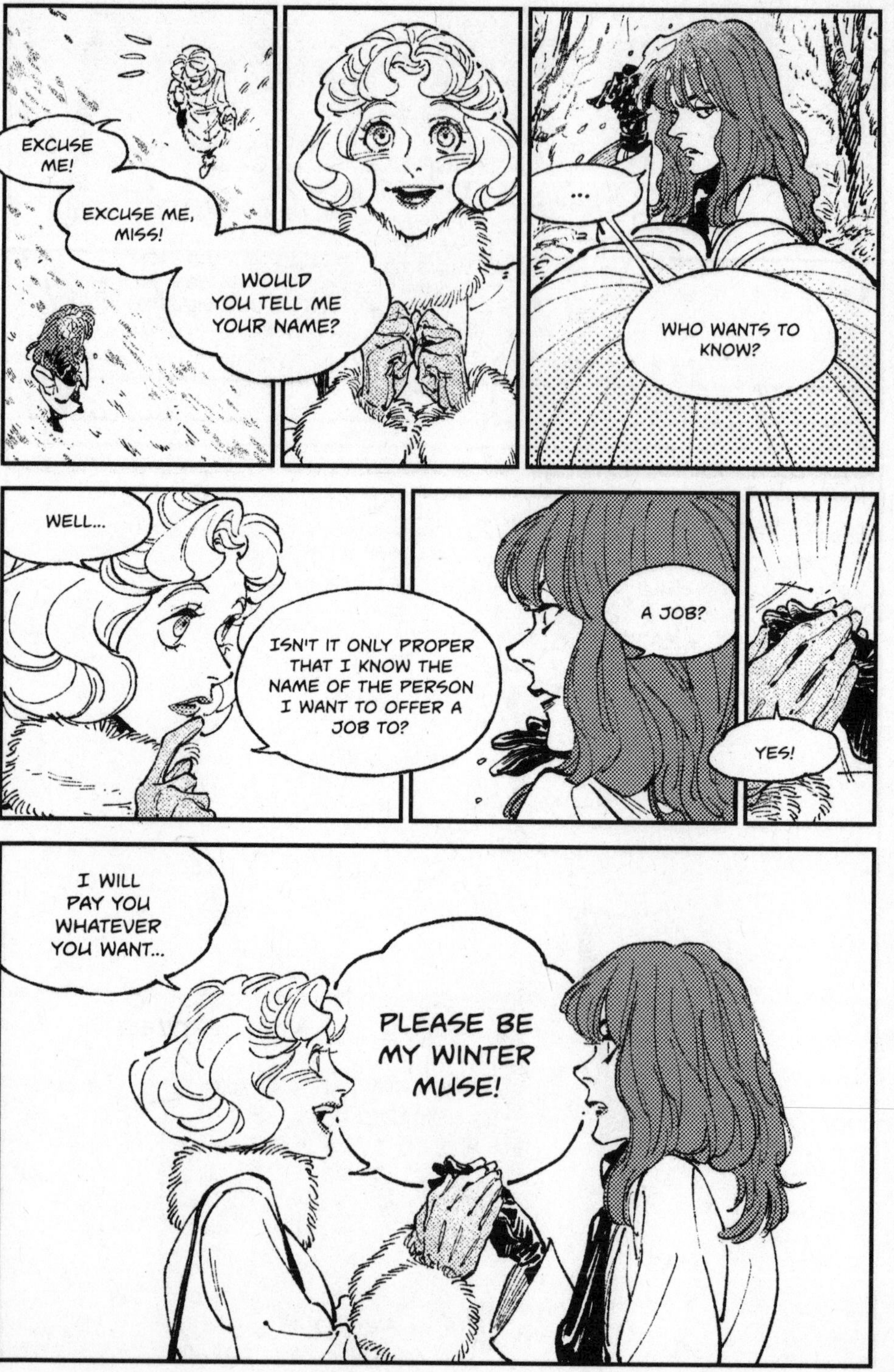
EXCUSE ME!
EXCUSE ME, MISS!
WOULD YOU TELL ME YOUR NAME?
...
WHO WANTS TO KNOW?
WELL...
ISN'T IT ONLY PROPER THAT I KNOW THE NAME OF THE PERSON I WANT TO OFFER A JOB TO?
A JOB?
YES!
I WILL PAY YOU WHATEVER YOU WANT...
PLEASE BE MY WINTER MUSE!

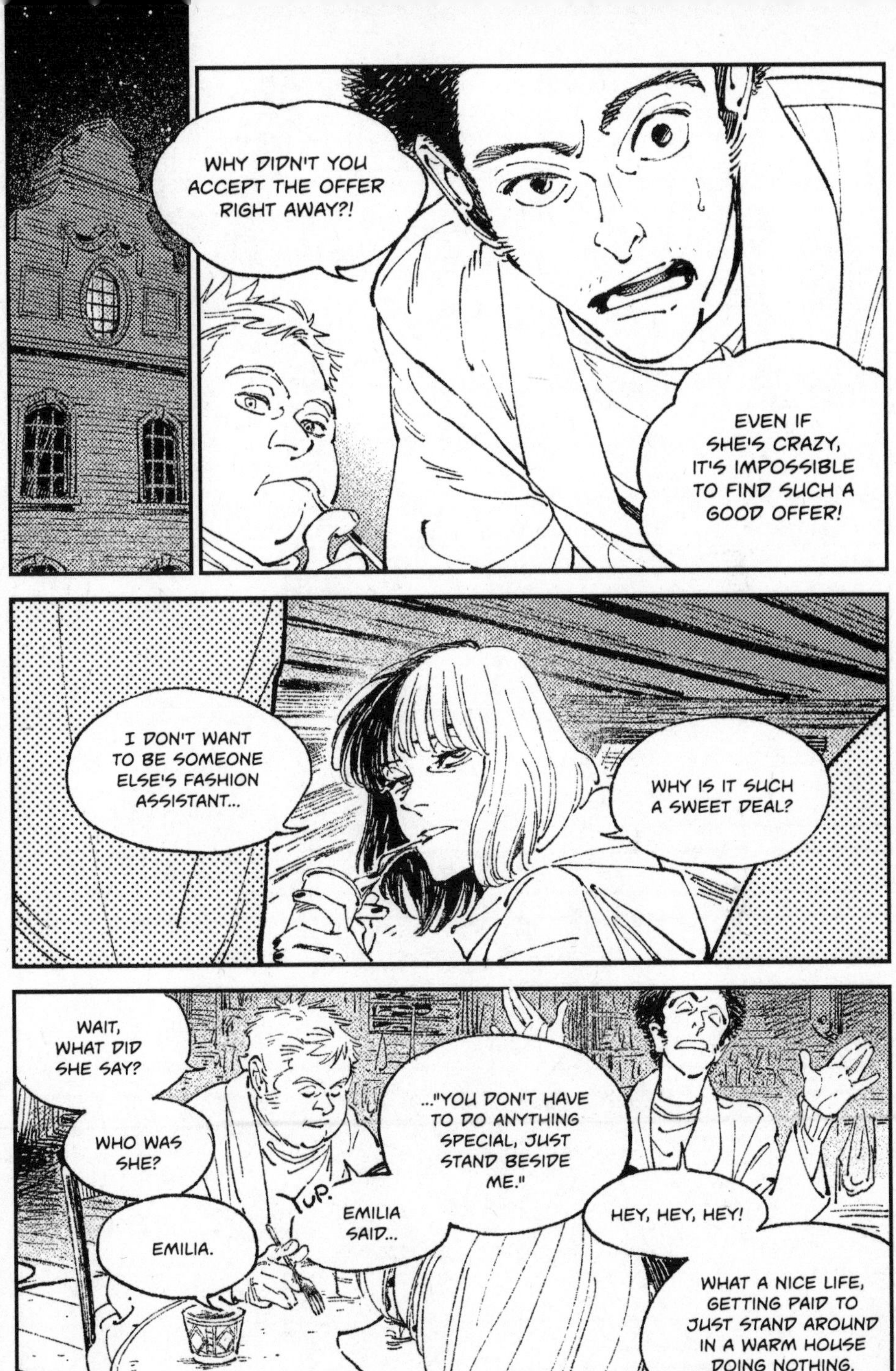
WHY DIDN'T YOU ACCEPT THE OFFER RIGHT AWAY?!
EVEN IF SHE'S CRAZY, IT'S IMPOSSIBLE TO FIND SUCH A GOOD OFFER!
I DON'T WANT TO BE SOMEONE ELSE'S FASHION ASSISTANT...
WHY IS IT SUCH A SWEET DEAL?
WAIT, WHAT DID SHE SAY?
WHO WAS SHE?
EMILIA.
YUP.
EMILIA SAID...
..."YOU DON'T HAVE TO DO ANYTHING SPECIAL, JUST STAND BESIDE ME."
HEY, HEY, HEY!
WHAT A NICE LIFE, GETTING PAID TO JUST STAND AROUND IN A WARM HOUSE DOING NOTHING.

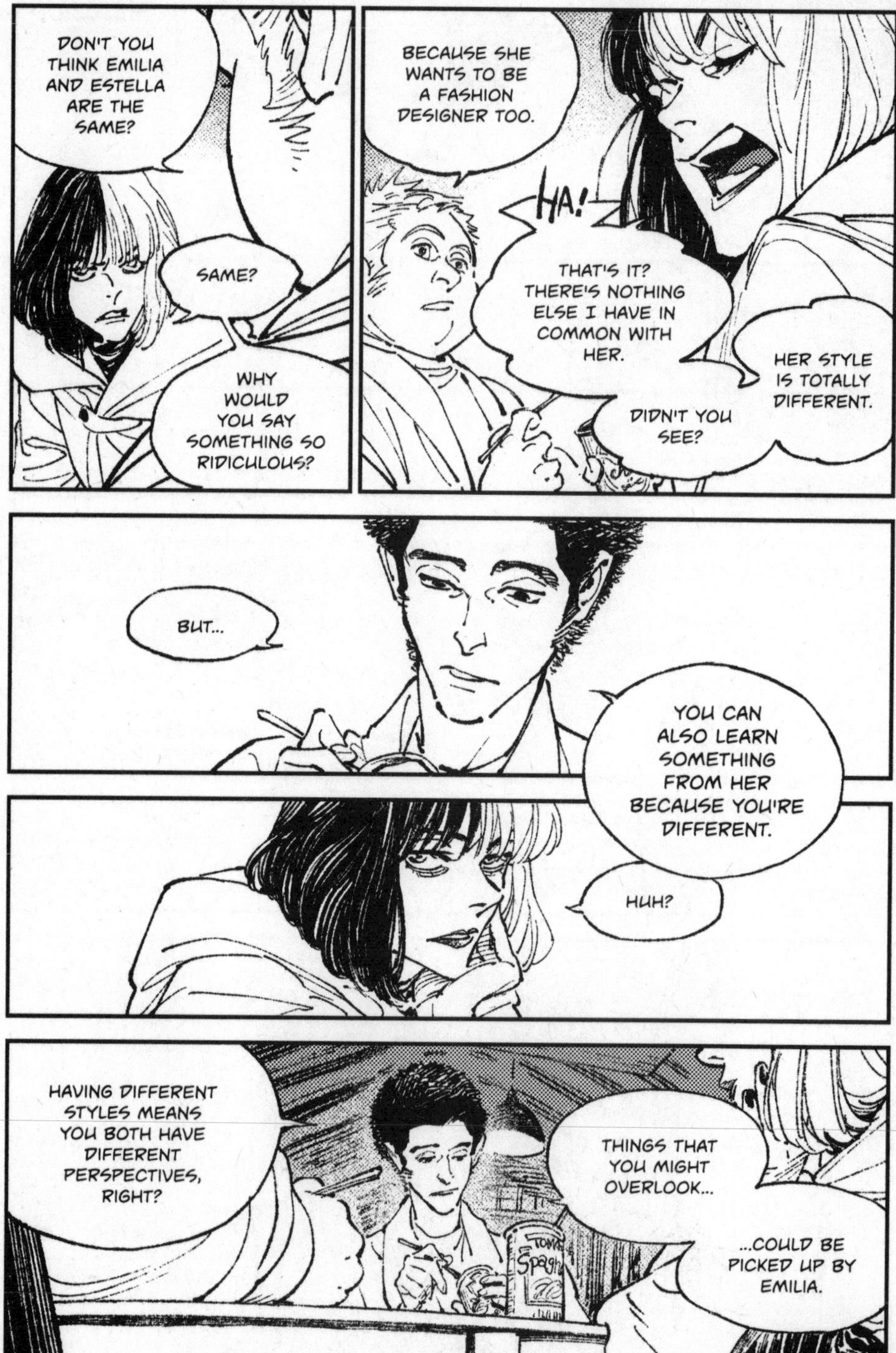
DON'T YOU THINK EMILIA AND ESTELLA ARE THE SAME?
SAME?
WHY WOULD YOU SAY SOMETHING SO RIDICULOUS?
BECAUSE SHE WANTS TO BE A FASHION DESIGNER TOO.
HA!
THAT'S IT? THERE'S NOTHING ELSE I HAVE IN COMMON WITH HER.
HER STYLE IS TOTALLY DIFFERENT.
DIDN'T YOU SEE?
BUT...
YOU CAN ALSO LEARN SOMETHING FROM HER BECAUSE YOU'RE DIFFERENT.
HUH?
HAVING DIFFERENT STYLES MEANS YOU BOTH HAVE DIFFERENT PERSPECTIVES, RIGHT?
THINGS THAT YOU MIGHT OVERLOOK...
...COULD BE PICKED UP BY EMILIA.

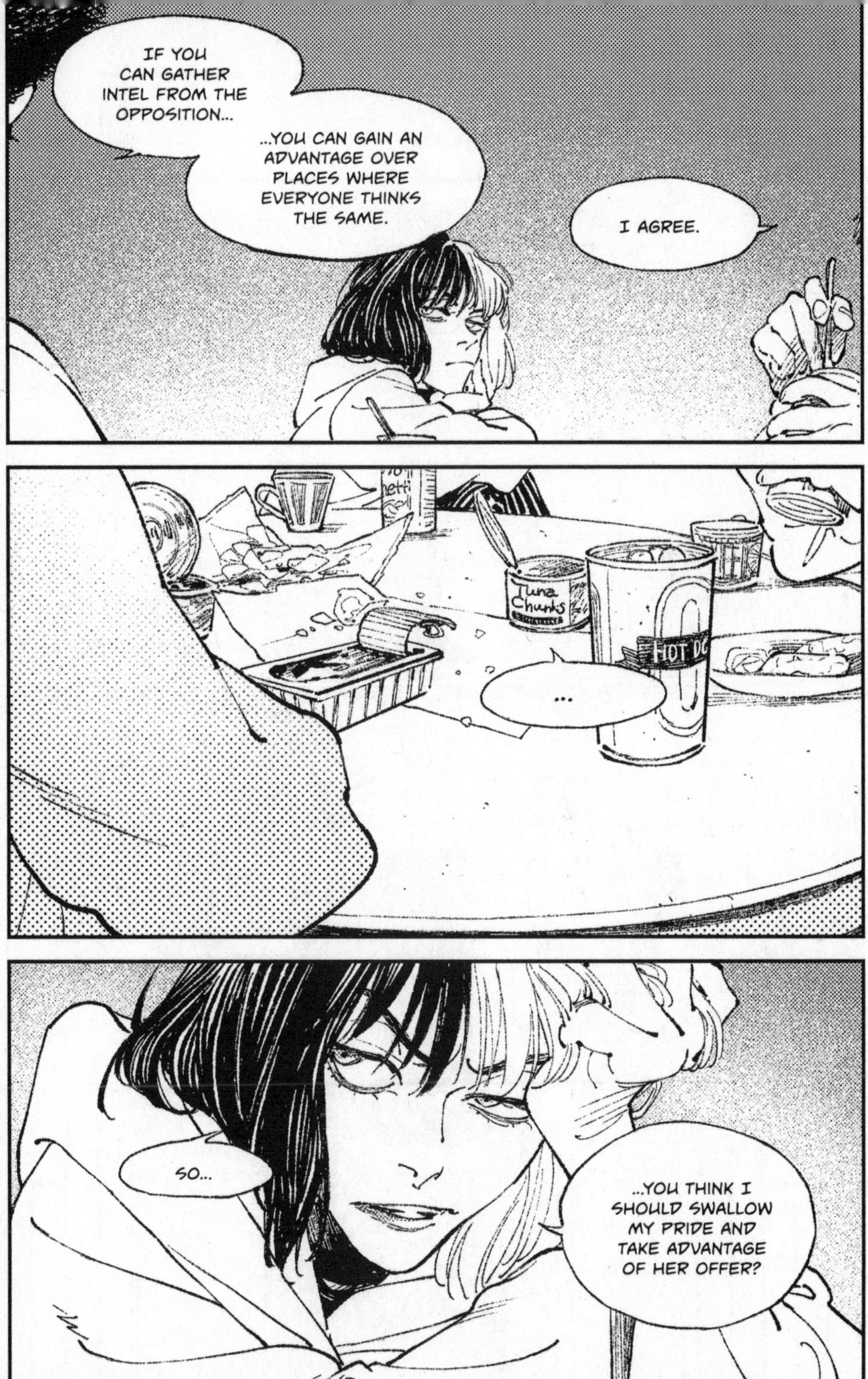
IF YOU CAN GATHER INTEL FROM THE OPPOSITION...
...YOU CAN GAIN AN ADVANTAGE OVER PLACES WHERE EVERYONE THINKS THE SAME.
I AGREE.
Tuna Chunks
...
SO...
...YOU THINK I SHOULD SWALLOW MY PRIDE AND TAKE ADVANTAGE OF HER OFFER?

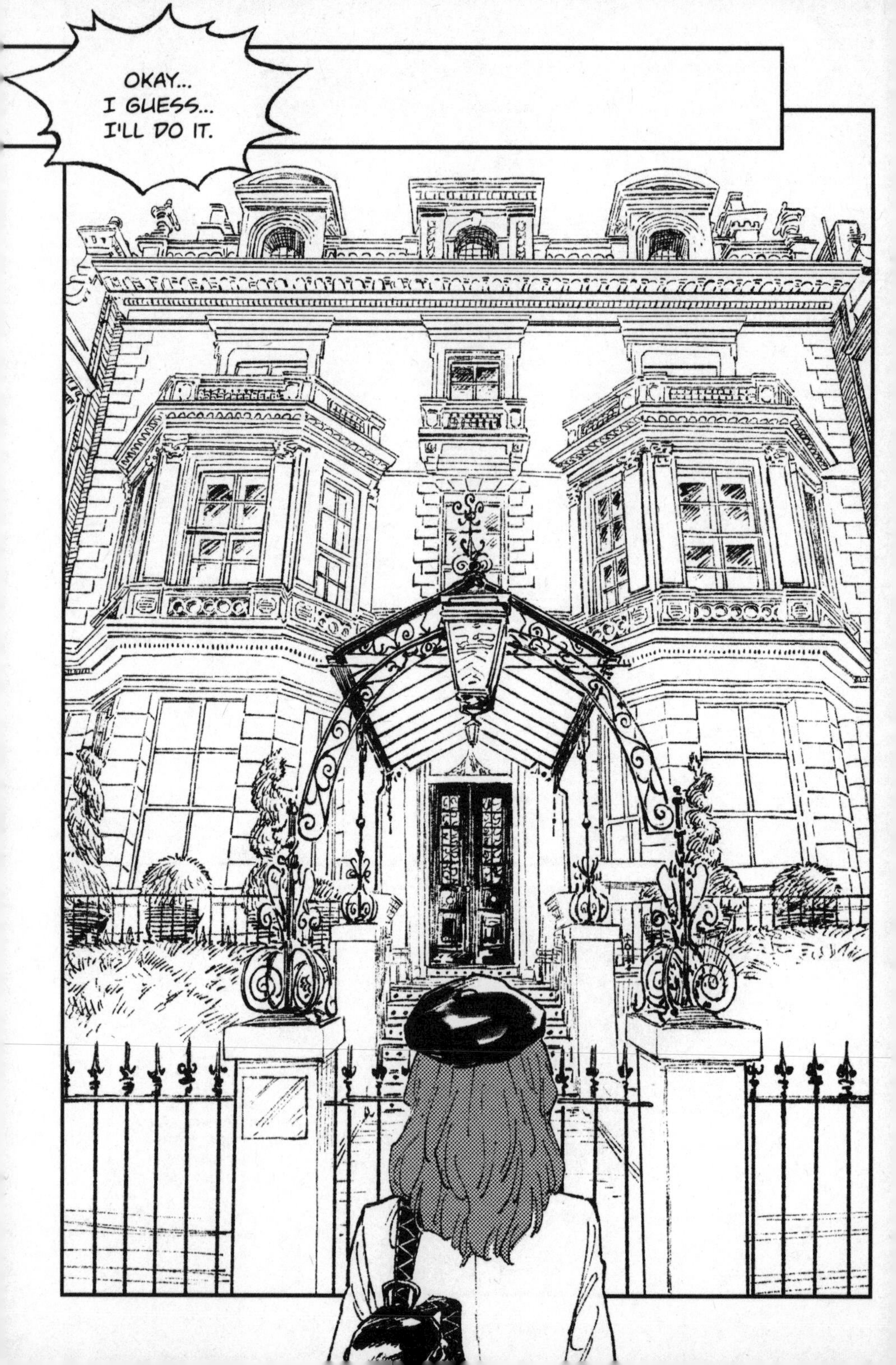
OKAY... I GUESS... I'LL DO IT.

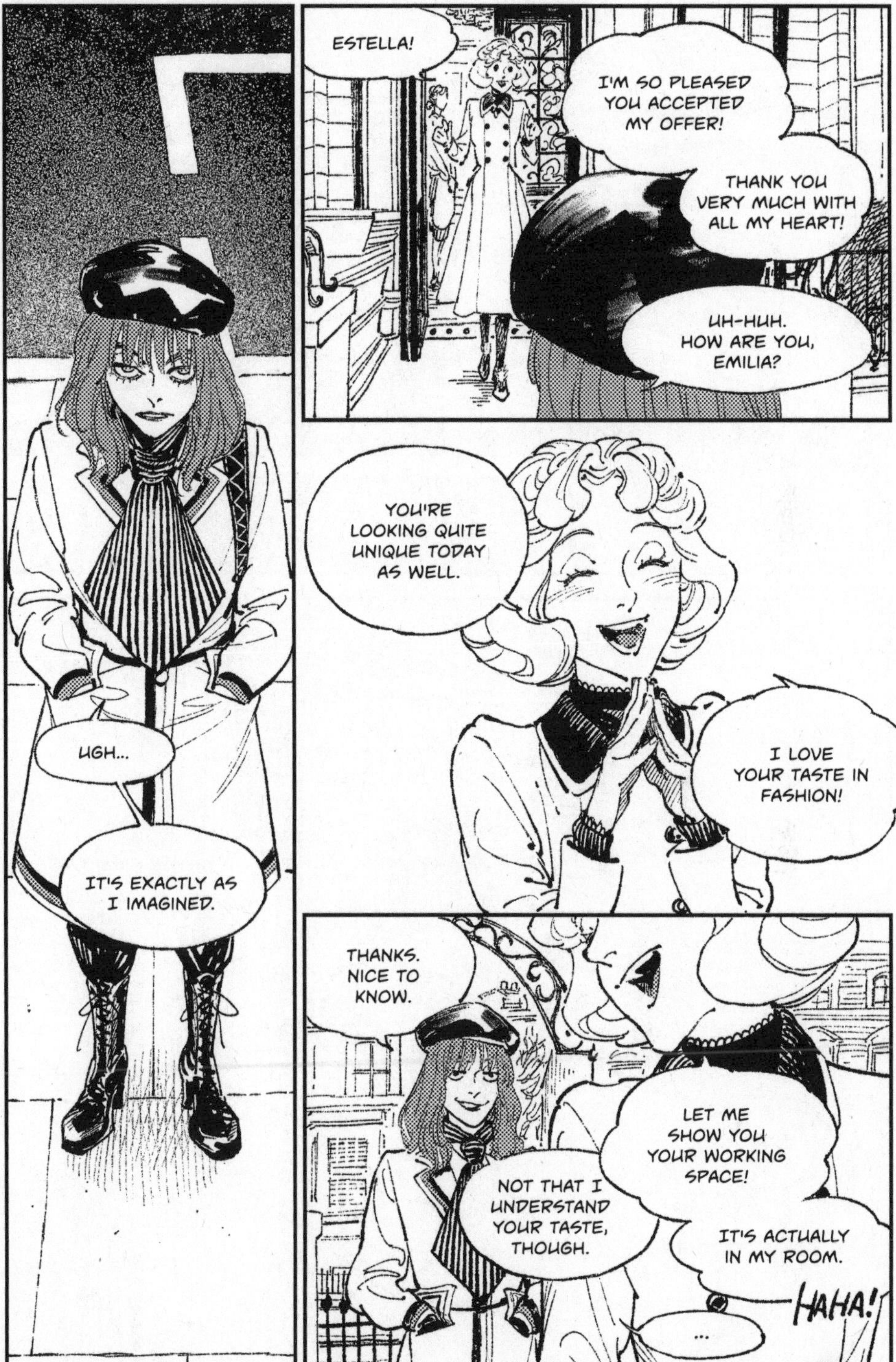
UGH...
IT'S EXACTLY AS I IMAGINED.
ESTELLA!
I'M SO PLEASED YOU ACCEPTED MY OFFER!
THANK YOU VERY MUCH WITH ALL MY HEART!
UH-HUH. HOW ARE YOU, EMILIA?
YOU'RE LOOKING QUITE UNIQUE TODAY AS WELL.
I LOVE YOUR TASTE IN FASHION!
THANKS. NICE TO KNOW.
NOT THAT I UNDERSTAND YOUR TASTE, THOUGH.
LET ME SHOW YOU YOUR WORKING SPACE!
IT'S ACTUALLY IN MY ROOM.
HAHA!
...

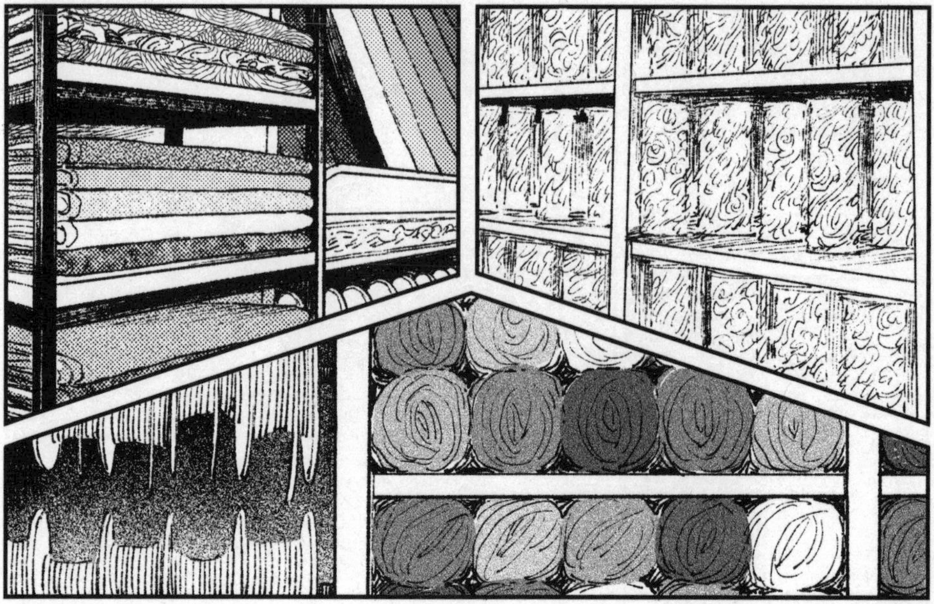

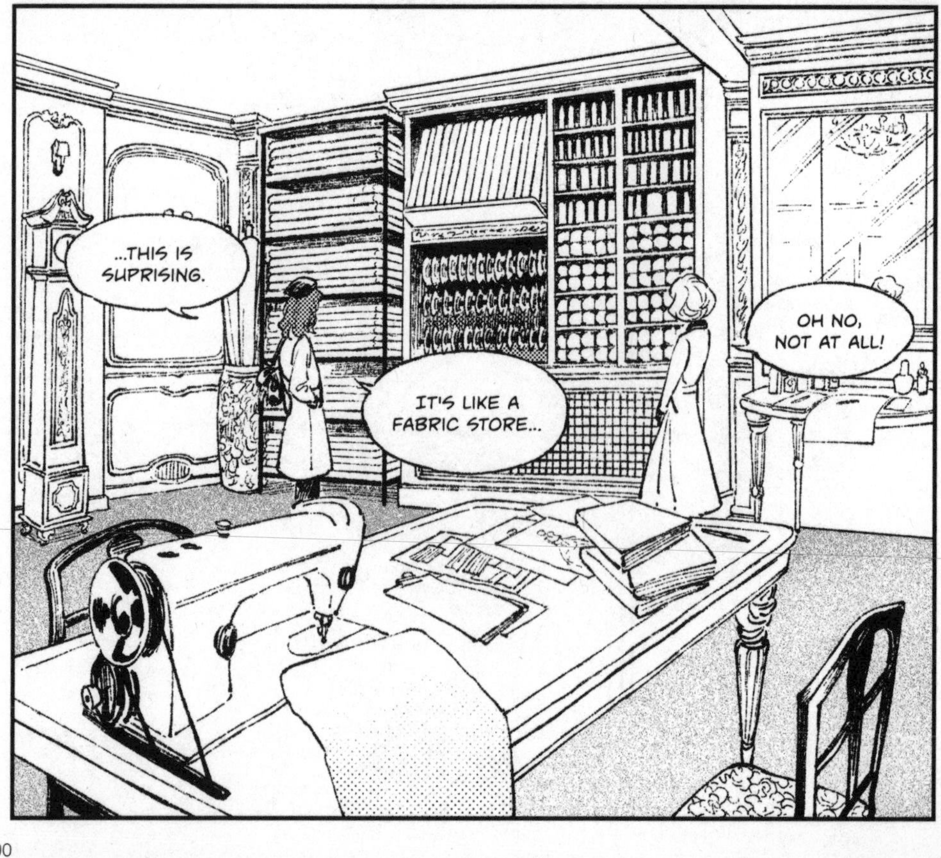
...THIS IS SUPRISING.
IT'S LIKE A FABRIC STORE...
OH NO, NOT AT ALL!

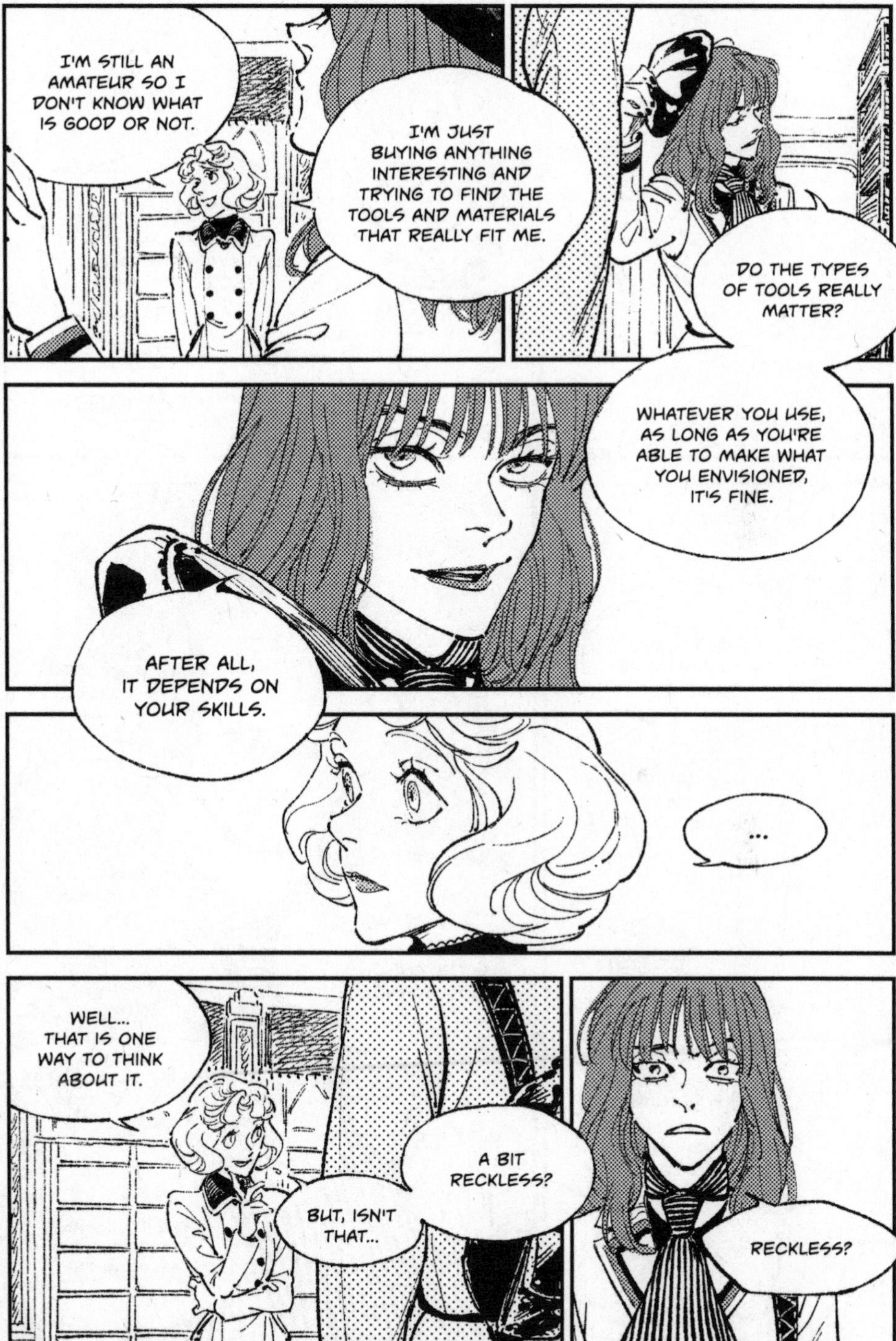
I'M STILL AN AMATEUR SO I DON'T KNOW WHAT IS GOOD OR NOT.
I'M JUST BUYING ANYTHING INTERESTING AND TRYING TO FIND THE TOOLS AND MATERIALS THAT REALLY FIT ME.
DO THE TYPES OF TOOLS REALLY MATTER?
WHATEVER YOU USE, AS LONG AS YOU'RE ABLE TO MAKE WHAT YOU ENVISIONED, IT'S FINE.
AFTER ALL, IT DEPENDS ON YOUR SKILLS.
...
WELL... THAT IS ONE WAY TO THINK ABOUT IT.
BUT, ISN'T THAT...
A BIT RECKLESS?
RECKLESS?

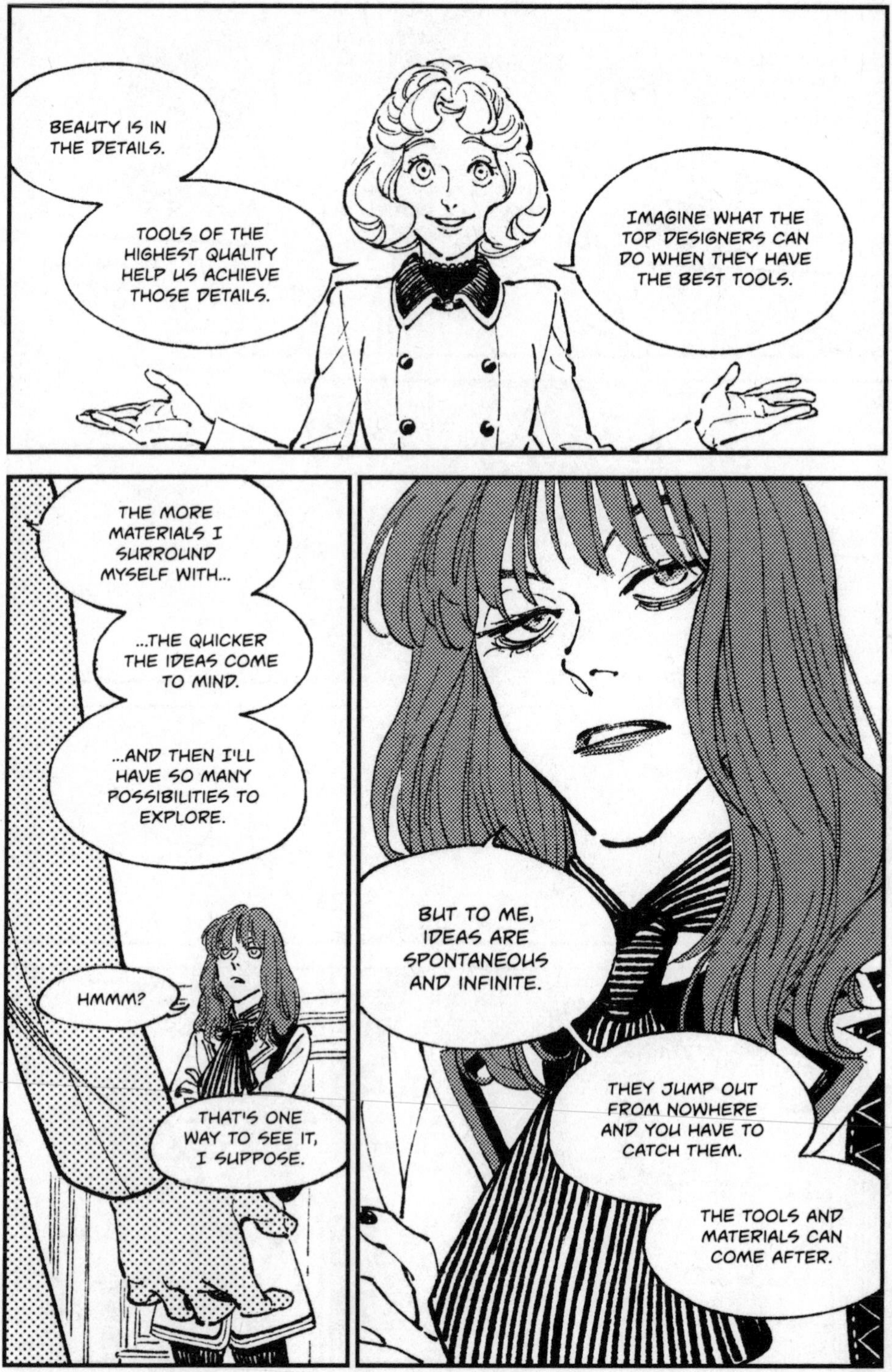
BEAUTY IS IN THE DETAILS.
TOOLS OF THE HIGHEST QUALITY HELP US ACHIEVE THOSE DETAILS.
IMAGINE WHAT THE TOP DESIGNERS CAN DO WHEN THEY HAVE THE BEST TOOLS.
THE MORE MATERIALS I SURROUND MYSELF WITH...
...THE QUICKER THE IDEAS COME TO MIND.
...AND THEN I'LL HAVE SO MANY POSSIBILITIES TO EXPLORE.
HMMM?
THAT'S ONE WAY TO SEE IT, I SUPPOSE.
BUT TO ME, IDEAS ARE SPONTANEOUS AND INFINITE.
THEY JUMP OUT FROM NOWHERE AND YOU HAVE TO CATCH THEM.
THE TOOLS AND MATERIALS CAN COME AFTER.

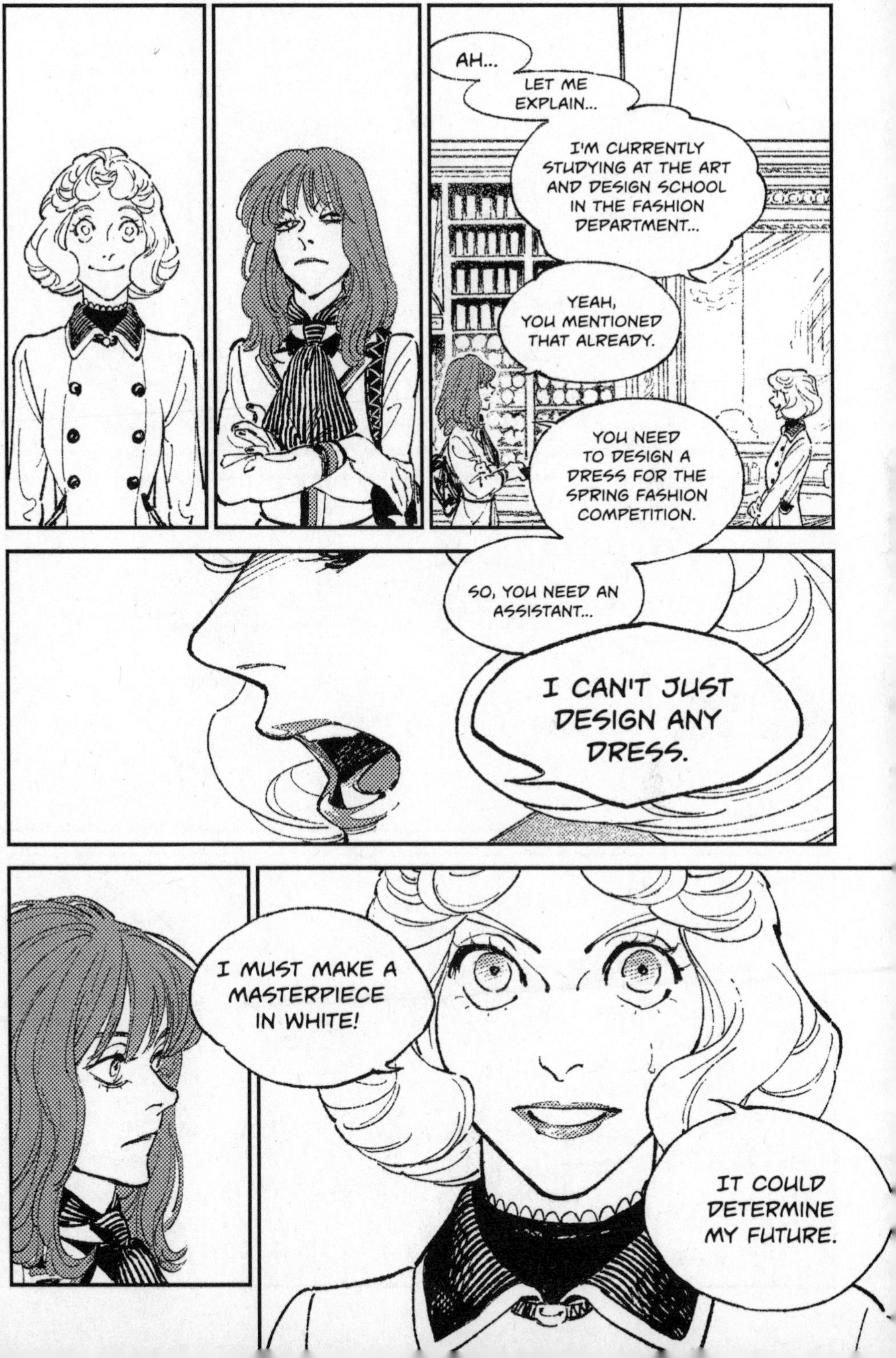
AH...
LET ME EXPLAIN...
I'M CURRENTLY STUDYING AT THE ART AND DESIGN SCHOOL IN THE FASHION DEPARTMENT...
YEAH, YOU MENTIONED THAT ALREADY.
YOU NEED TO DESIGN A DRESS FOR THE SPRING FASHION COMPETITION.
SO, YOU NEED AN ASSISTANT...
I CAN'T JUST DESIGN ANY DRESS.
I MUST MAKE A MASTERPIECE IN WHITE!
IT COULD DETERMINE MY FUTURE.

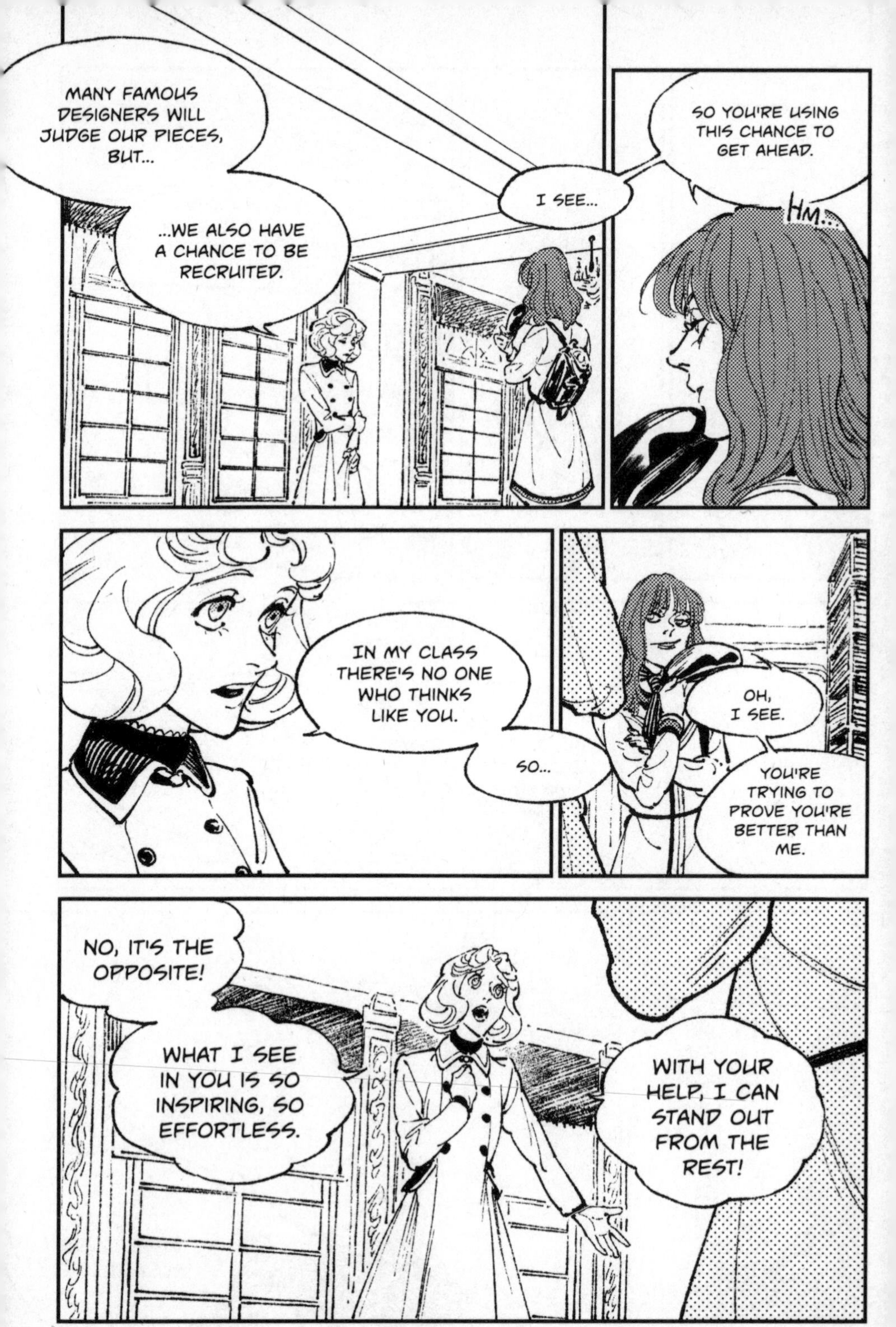
MANY FAMOUS DESIGNERS WILL JUDGE OUR PIECES, BUT...
...WE ALSO HAVE A CHANCE TO BE RECRUITED.
I SEE...
SO YOU'RE USING THIS CHANCE TO GET AHEAD.
HM...
IN MY CLASS THERE'S NO ONE WHO THINKS LIKE YOU.
SO...
OH, I SEE.
YOU'RE TRYING TO PROVE YOU'RE BETTER THAN ME.
NO, IT'S THE OPPOSITE!
WHAT I SEE IN YOU IS SO INSPIRING, SO EFFORTLESS.
WITH YOUR HELP, I CAN STAND OUT FROM THE REST!

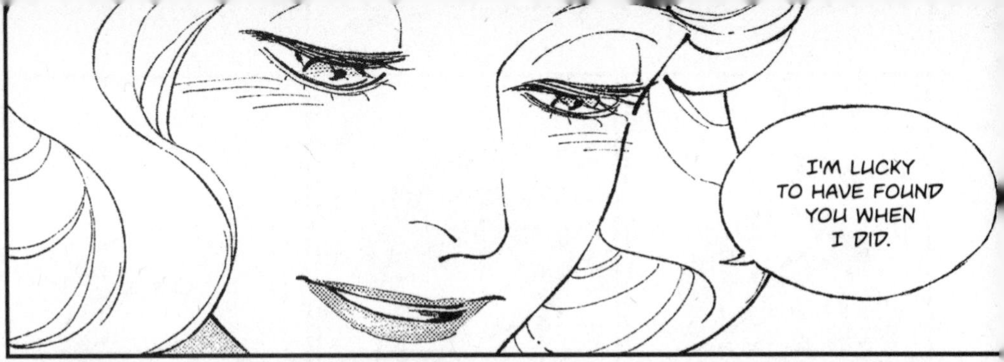
I'M LUCKY TO HAVE FOUND YOU WHEN I DID.

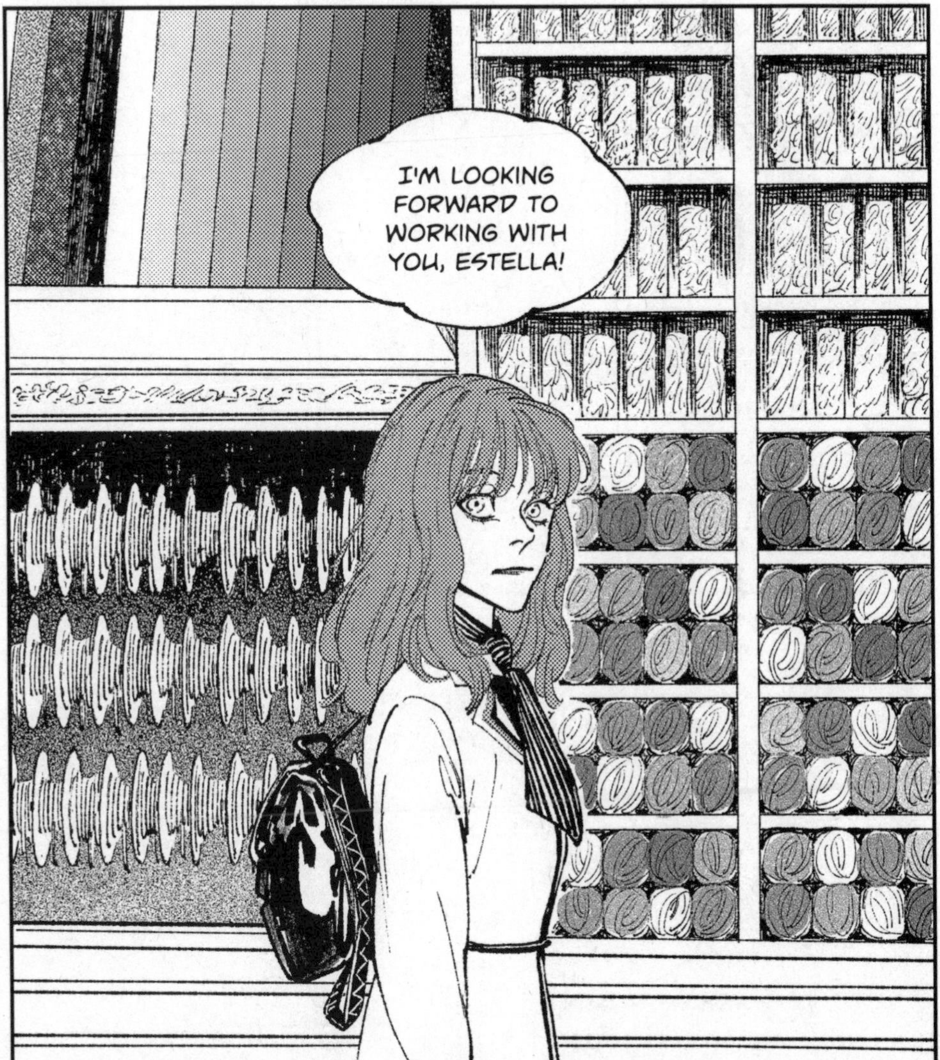
I'M LOOKING FORWARD TO WORKING WITH YOU, ESTELLA!

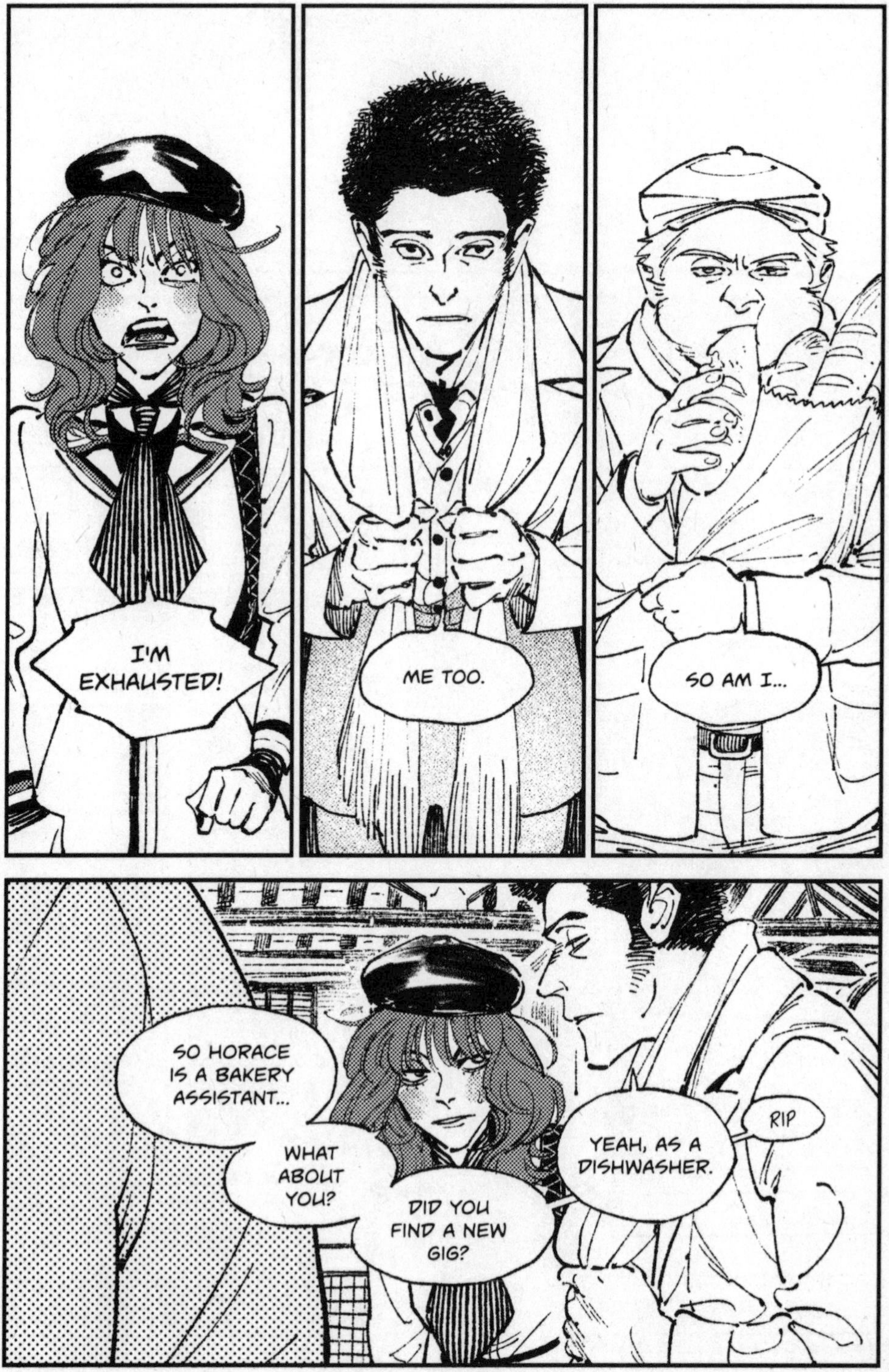
I'M EXHAUSTED!
ME TOO.
SO AM I...
SO HORACE IS A BAKERY ASSISTANT...
WHAT ABOUT YOU?
DID YOU FIND A NEW GIG?
YEAH, AS A DISHWASHER.
RIP

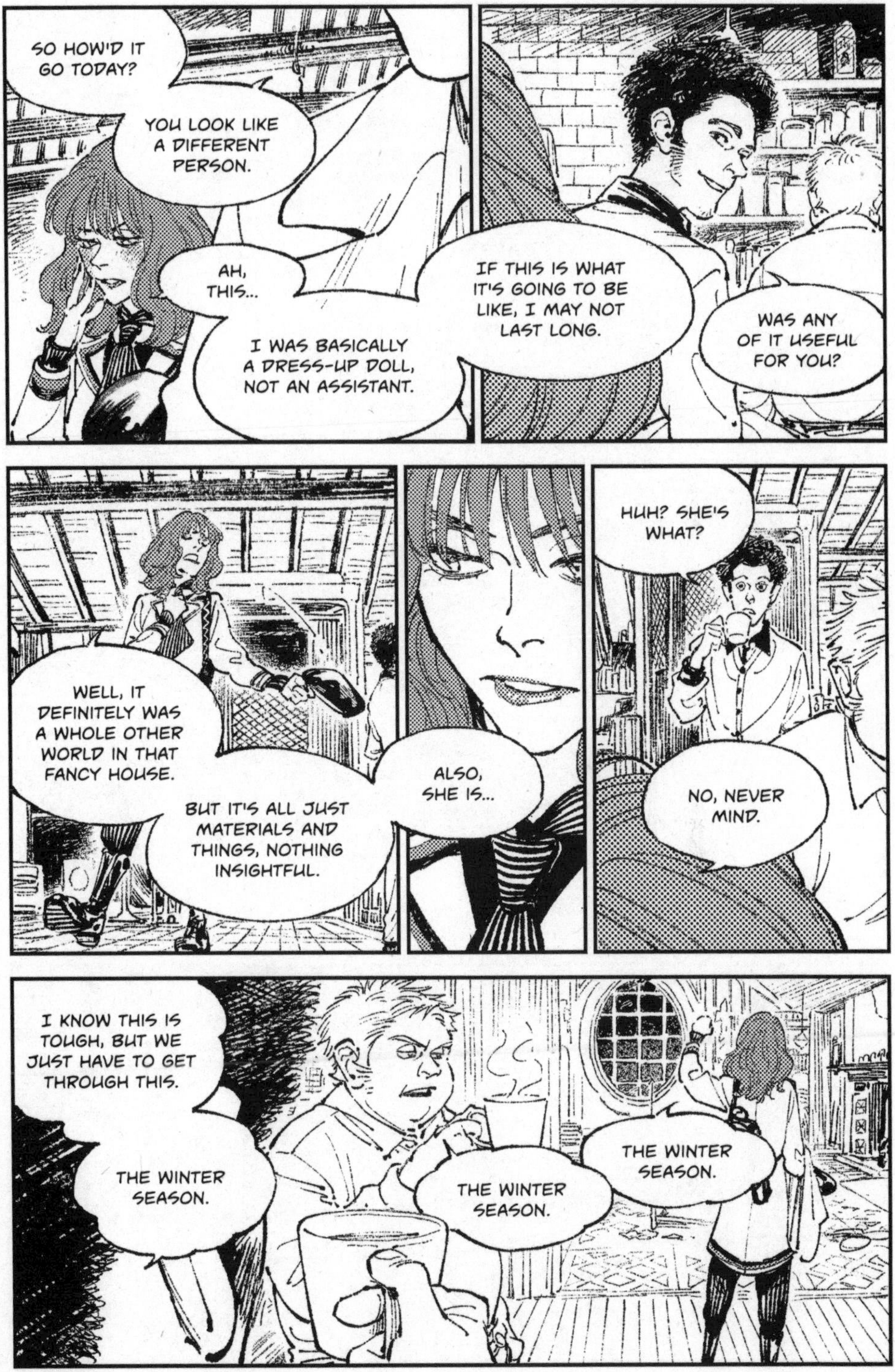
SO HOW'D IT GO TODAY?
YOU LOOK LIKE A DIFFERENT PERSON.
AH, THIS...
I WAS BASICALLY A DRESS-UP DOLL, NOT AN ASSISTANT.
IF THIS IS WHAT IT'S GOING TO BE LIKE, I MAY NOT LAST LONG.
WAS ANY OF IT USEFUL FOR YOU?
WELL, IT DEFINITELY WAS A WHOLE OTHER WORLD IN THAT FANCY HOUSE.
BUT IT'S ALL JUST MATERIALS AND THINGS, NOTHING INSIGHTFUL.
ALSO, SHE IS...
HUH? SHE'S WHAT?
NO, NEVER MIND.
I KNOW THIS IS TOUGH, BUT WE JUST HAVE TO GET THROUGH THIS.
THE WINTER SEASON.
THE WINTER SEASON.
THE WINTER SEASON.

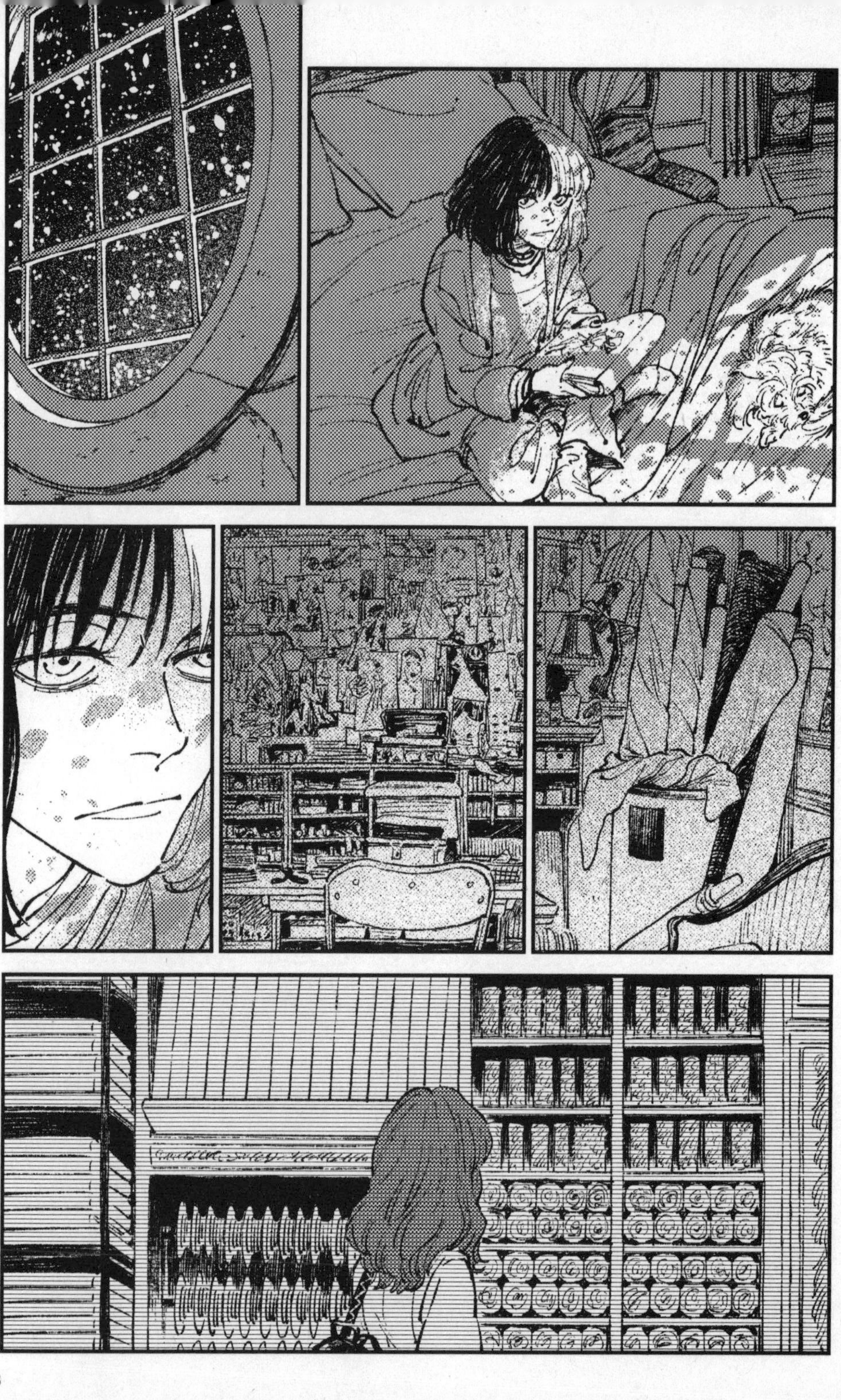

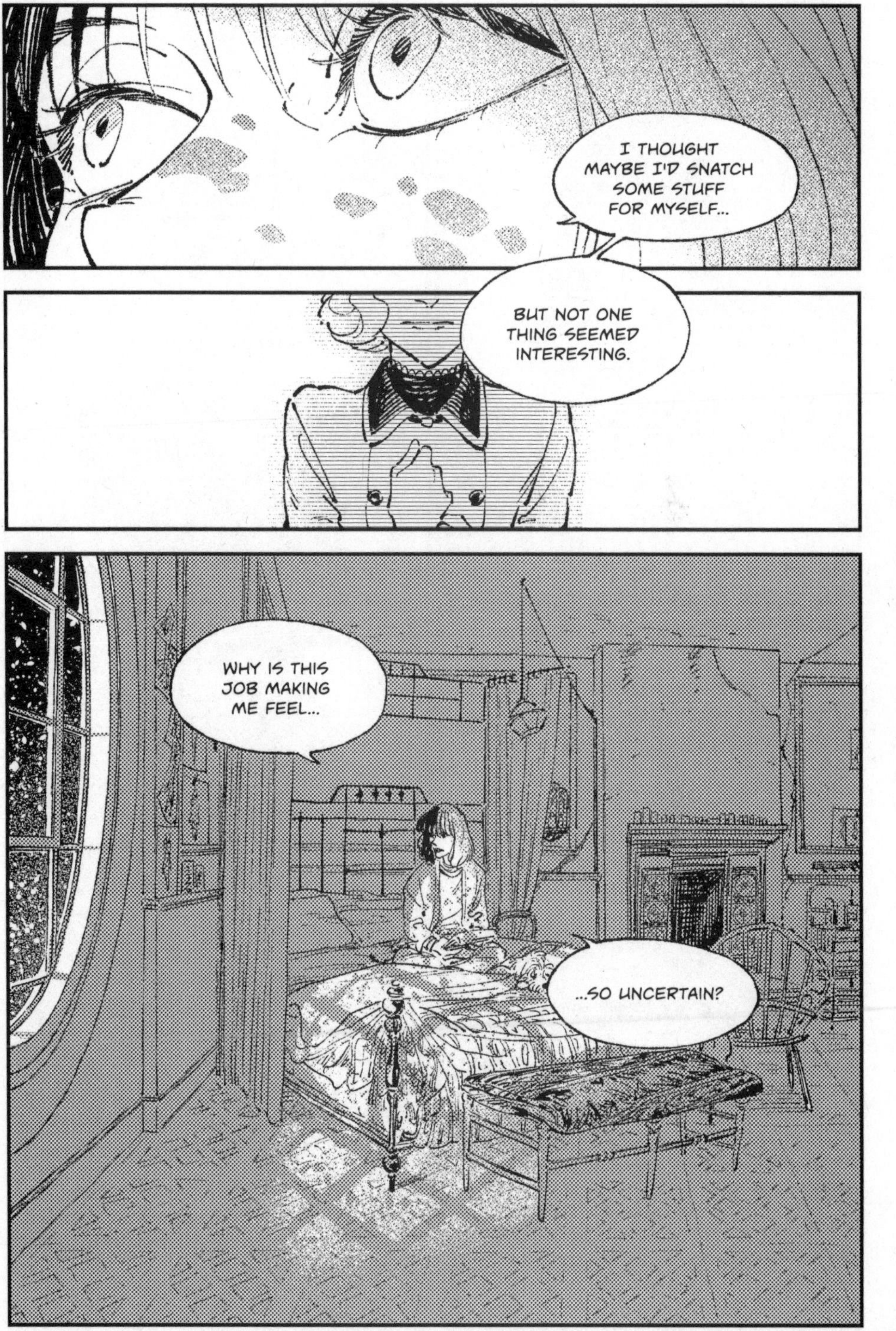
I THOUGHT MAYBE I'D SNATCH SOME STUFF FOR MYSELF...
BUT NOT ONE THING SEEMED INTERESTING.
WHY IS THIS JOB MAKING ME FEEL...
...SO UNCERTAIN?

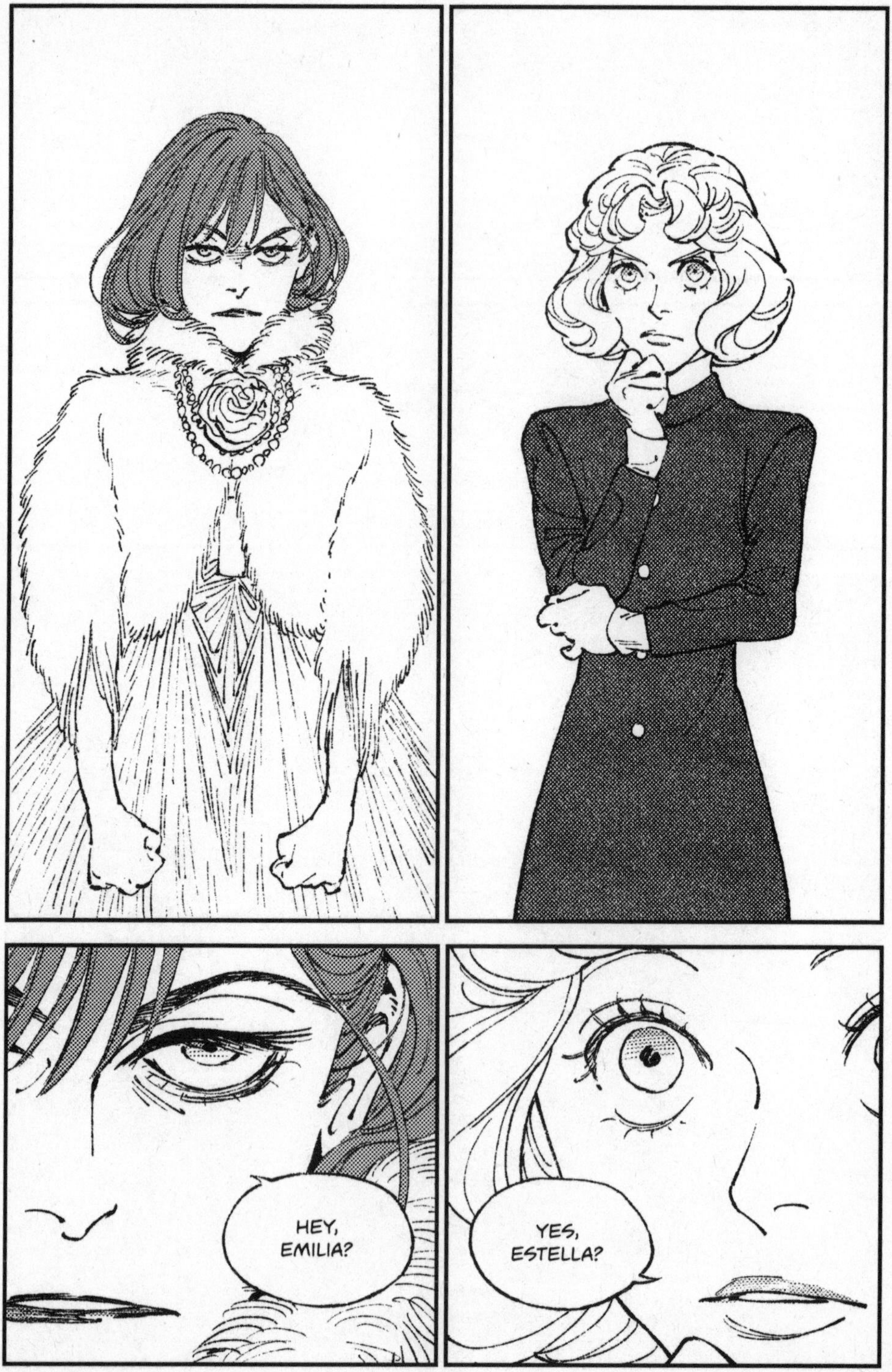
HEY,
EMILIA?
YES,
ESTELLA?

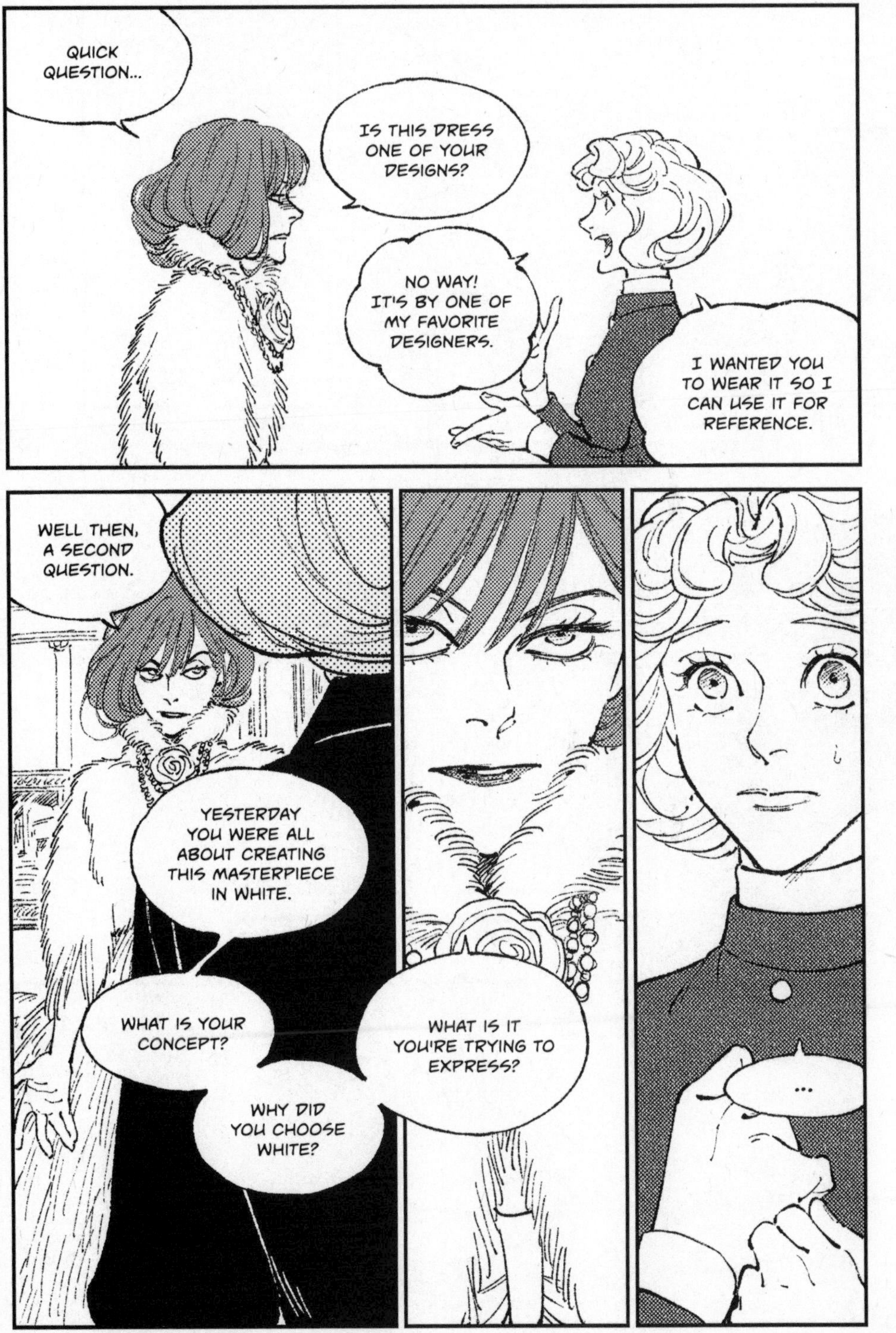
QUICK QUESTION...
IS THIS DRESS ONE OF YOUR DESIGNS?
NO WAY! IT'S BY ONE OF MY FAVORITE DESIGNERS.
I WANTED YOU TO WEAR IT SO I CAN USE IT FOR REFERENCE.
WELL THEN, A SECOND QUESTION.
YESTERDAY YOU WERE ALL ABOUT CREATING THIS MASTERPIECE IN WHITE.
WHAT IS YOUR CONCEPT?
WHY DID YOU CHOOSE WHITE?
WHAT IS IT YOU'RE TRYING TO EXPRESS?
...

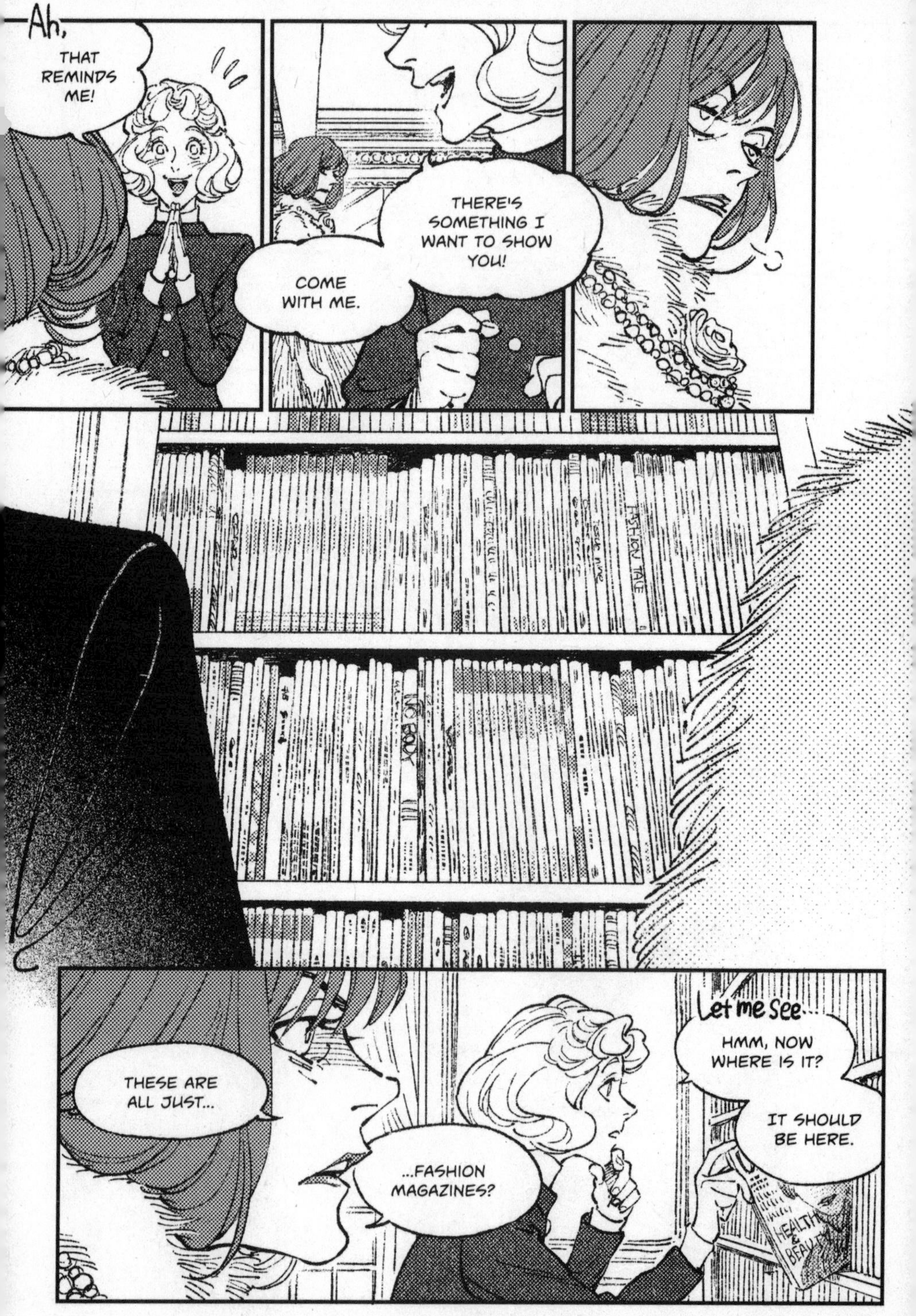
Ah,
THAT REMINDS ME!
THERE'S SOMETHING I WANT TO SHOW YOU!
COME WITH ME.
FASHION TALE
THESE ARE ALL JUST...
...FASHION MAGAZINES?
Let me see...
HMM, NOW WHERE IS IT?
IT SHOULD BE HERE.
HEALTH & BEAUTY

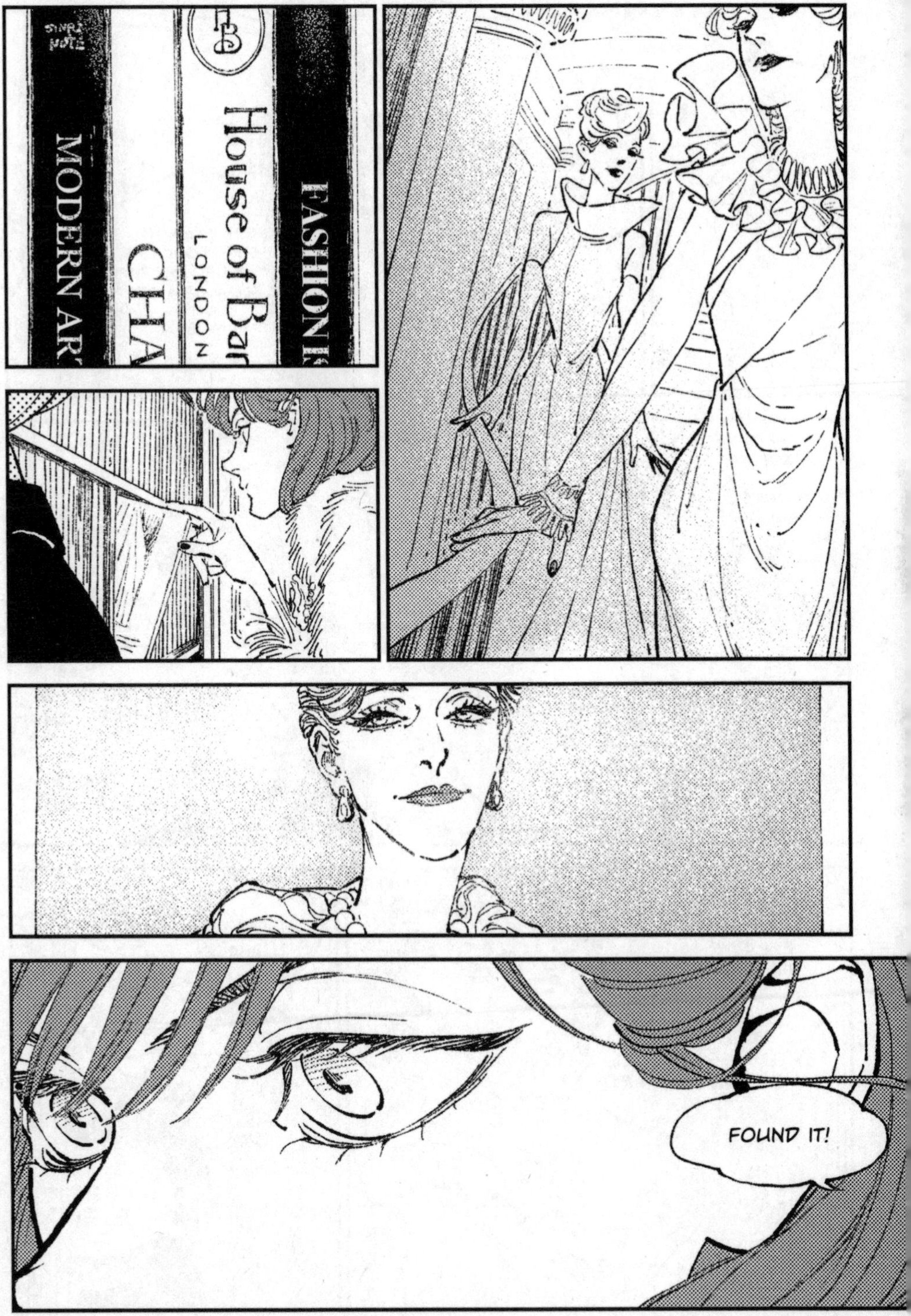
LONDON
FOUND IT!

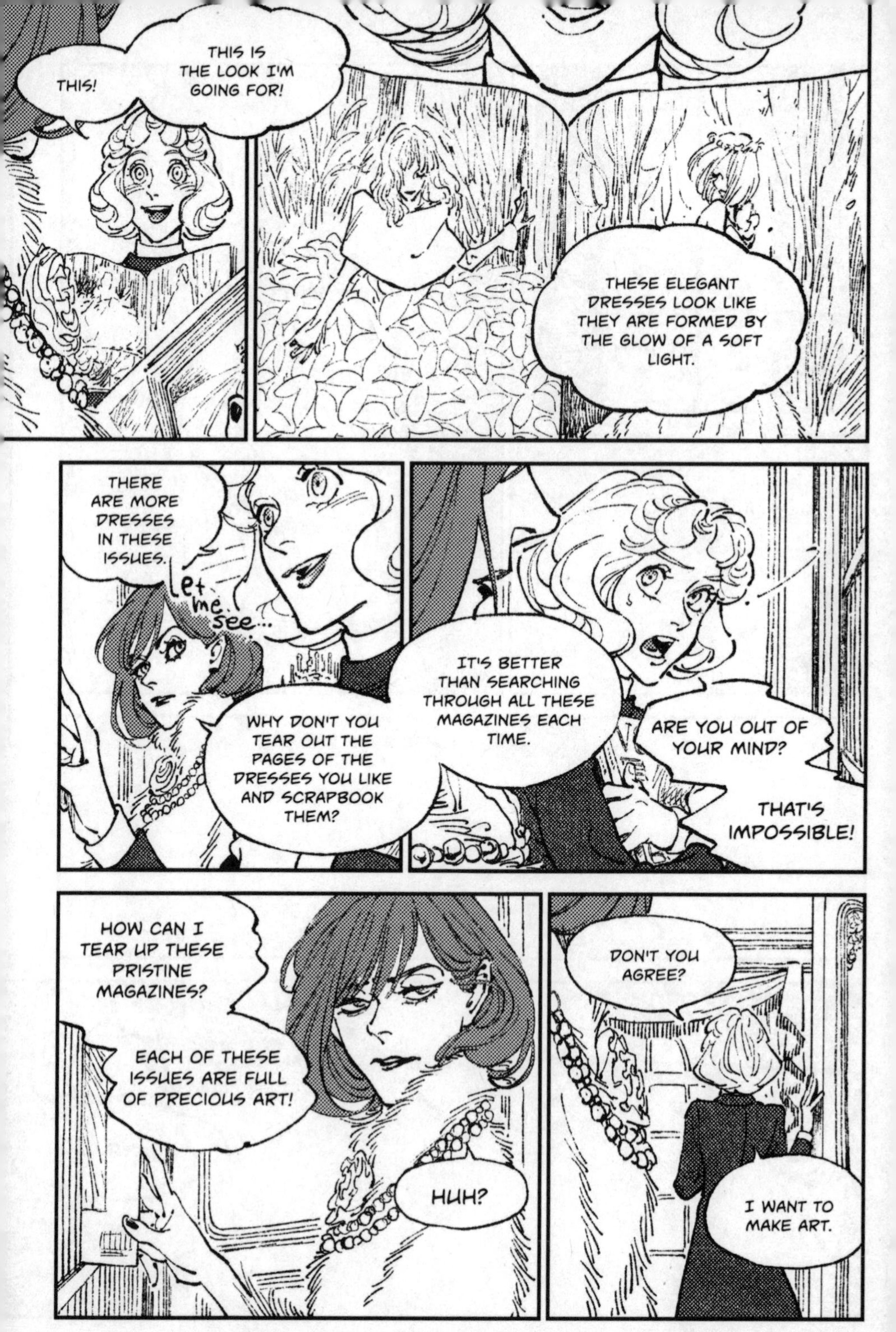
THIS!
THIS IS THE LOOK I'M GOING FOR!
THESE ELEGANT DRESSES LOOK LIKE THEY ARE FORMED BY THE GLOW OF A SOFT LIGHT.
THERE ARE MORE DRESSES IN THESE ISSUES.
Let me see...
WHY DON'T YOU TEAR OUT THE PAGES OF THE DRESSES YOU LIKE AND SCRAPBOOK THEM?
IT'S BETTER THAN SEARCHING THROUGH ALL THESE MAGAZINES EACH TIME.
ARE YOU OUT OF YOUR MIND?
THAT'S IMPOSSIBLE!
HOW CAN I TEAR UP THESE PRISTINE MAGAZINES?
EACH OF THESE ISSUES ARE FULL OF PRECIOUS ART!
HUH?
DON'T YOU AGREE?
I WANT TO MAKE ART.

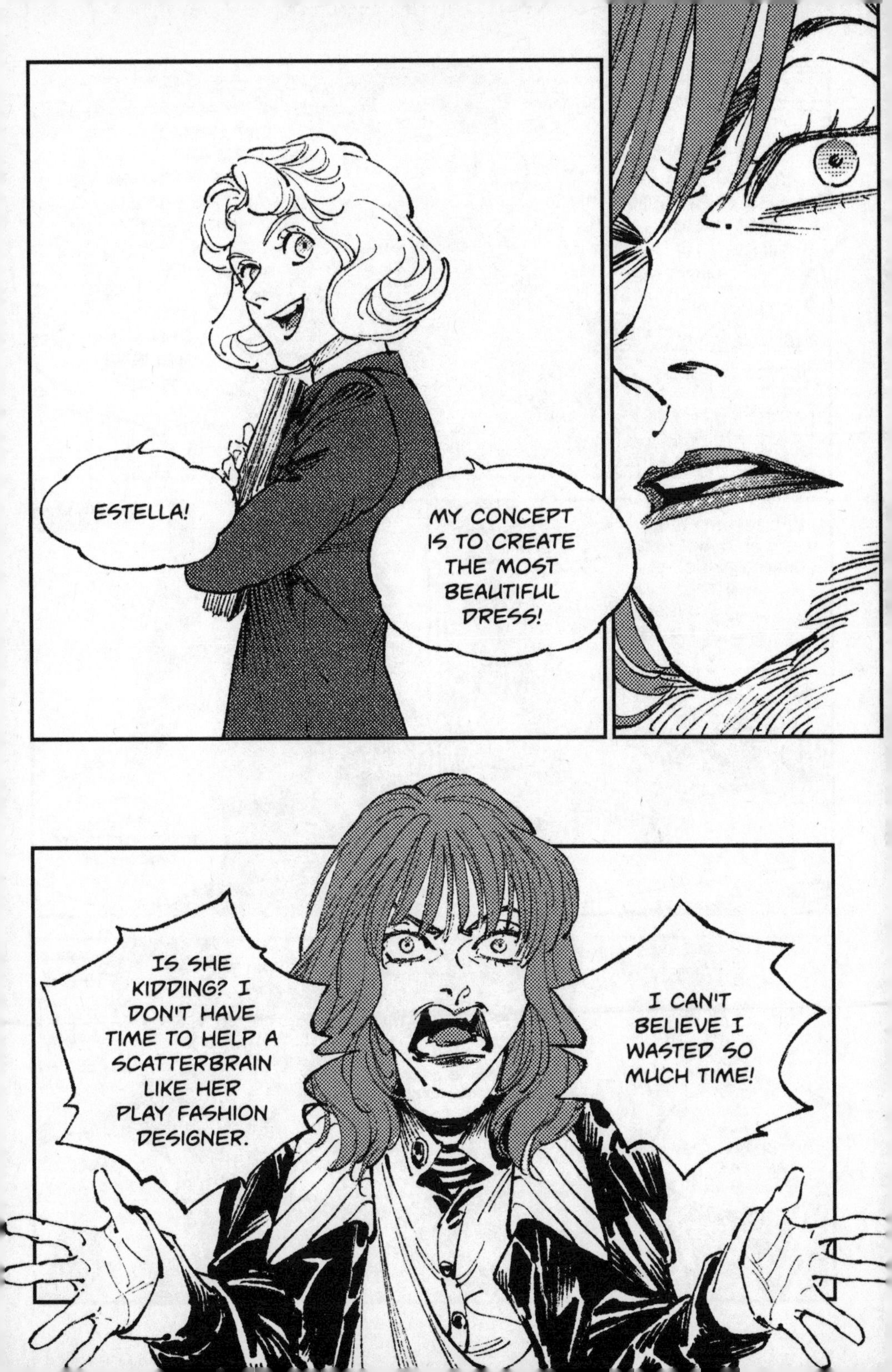
ESTELLA!
MY CONCEPT IS TO CREATE THE MOST BEAUTIFUL DRESS!
IS SHE KIDDING? I DON'T HAVE TIME TO HELP A SCATTERBRAIN LIKE HER PLAY FASHION DESIGNER.
I CAN'T BELIEVE I WASTED SO MUCH TIME!

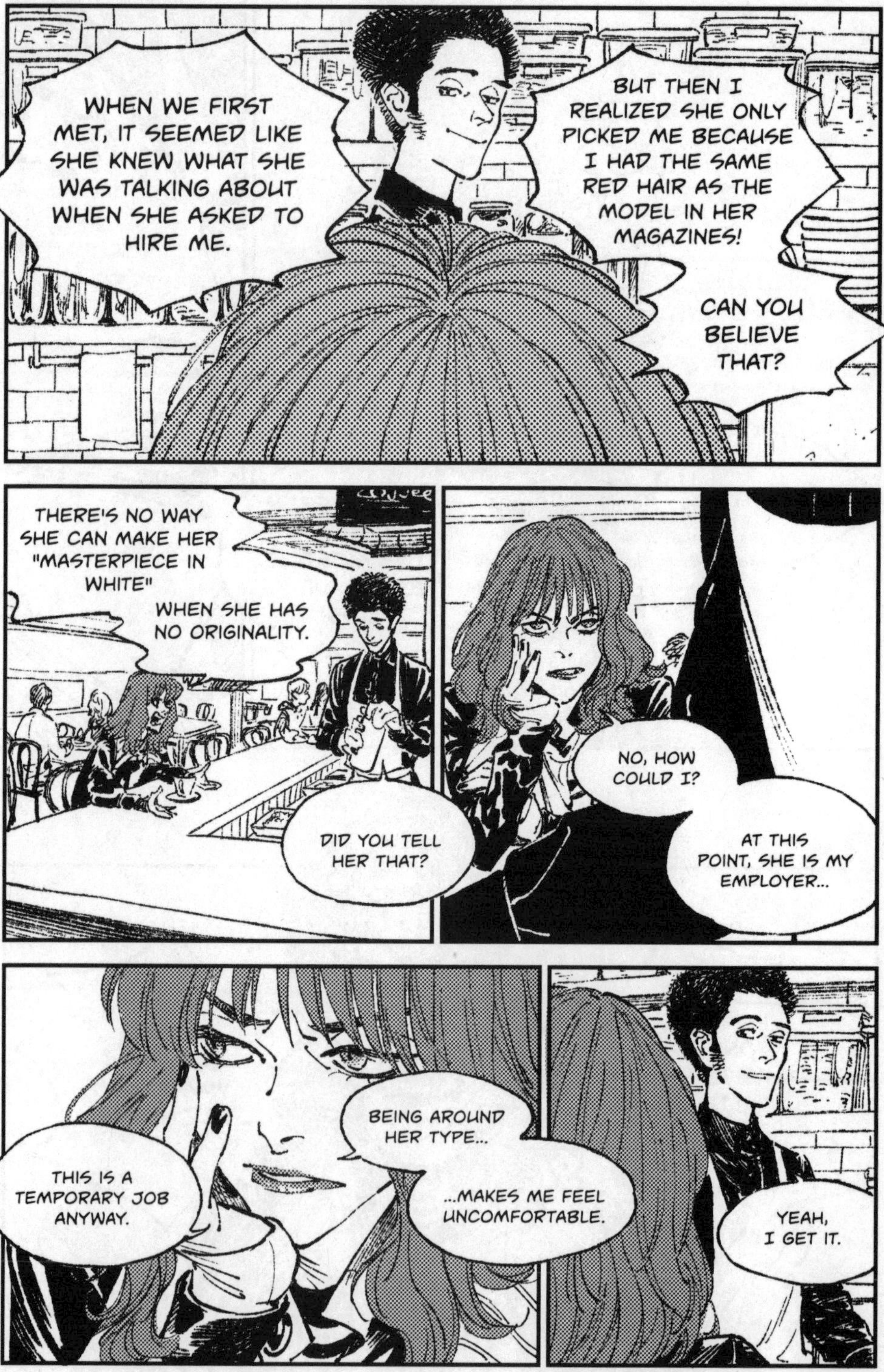
WHEN WE FIRST MET, IT SEEMED LIKE SHE KNEW WHAT SHE WAS TALKING ABOUT WHEN SHE ASKED TO HIRE ME.
BUT THEN I REALIZED SHE ONLY PICKED ME BECAUSE I HAD THE SAME RED HAIR AS THE MODEL IN HER MAGAZINES!
CAN YOU BELIEVE THAT?
THERE'S NO WAY SHE CAN MAKE HER "MASTERPIECE IN WHITE"
WHEN SHE HAS NO ORIGINALITY.
DID YOU TELL HER THAT?
NO, HOW COULD I?
AT THIS POINT, SHE IS MY EMPLOYER...
THIS IS A TEMPORARY JOB ANYWAY.
BEING AROUND HER TYPE...
...MAKES ME FEEL UNCOMFORTABLE.
YEAH, I GET IT.

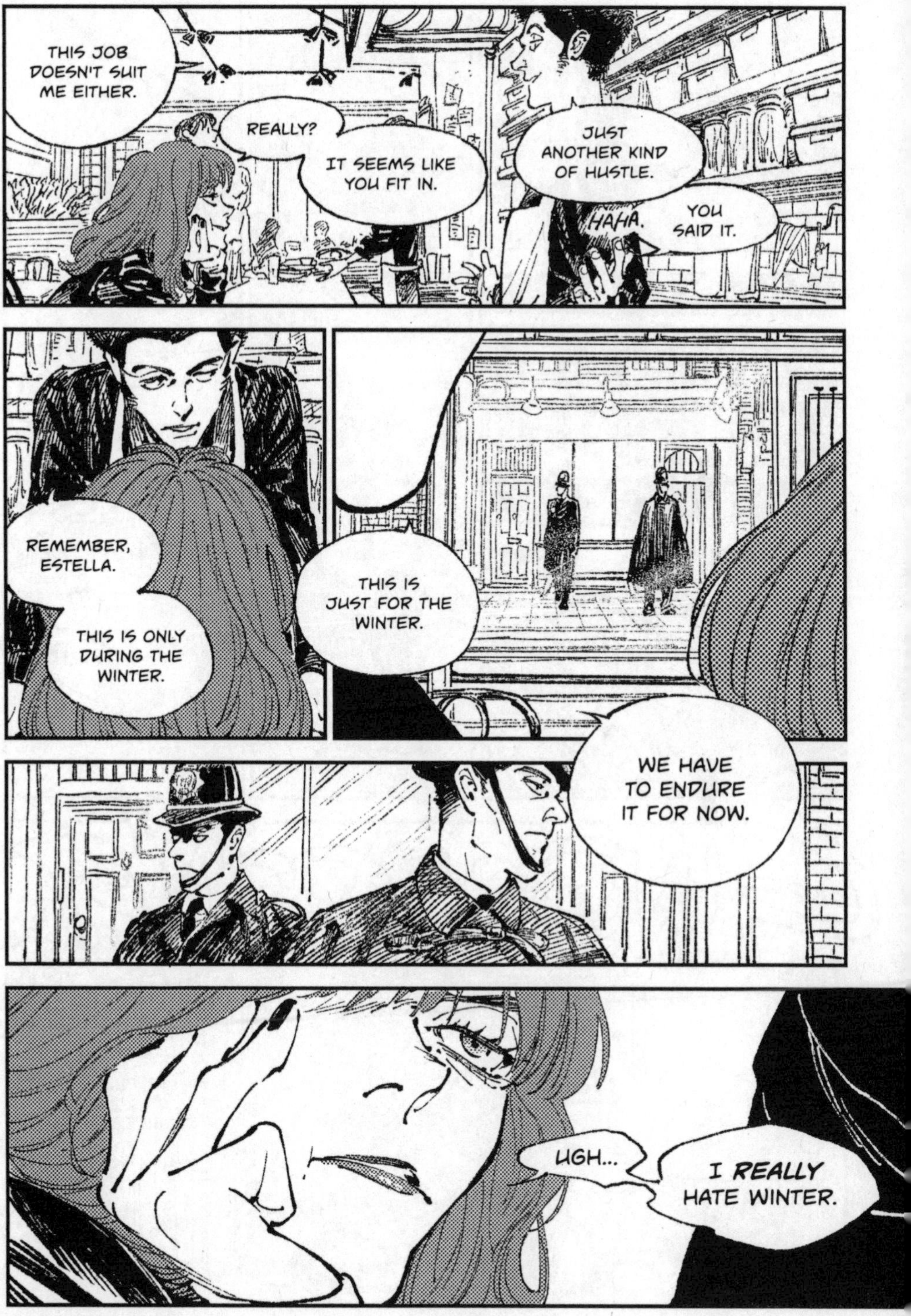
THIS JOB DOESN'T SUIT ME EITHER.
REALLY?
IT SEEMS LIKE YOU FIT IN.
JUST ANOTHER KIND OF HUSTLE.
HAHA.
YOU SAID IT.
REMEMBER, ESTELLA.
THIS IS ONLY DURING THE WINTER.
THIS IS JUST FOR THE WINTER.
WE HAVE TO ENDURE IT FOR NOW.
UGH...
I *REALLY* HATE WINTER.

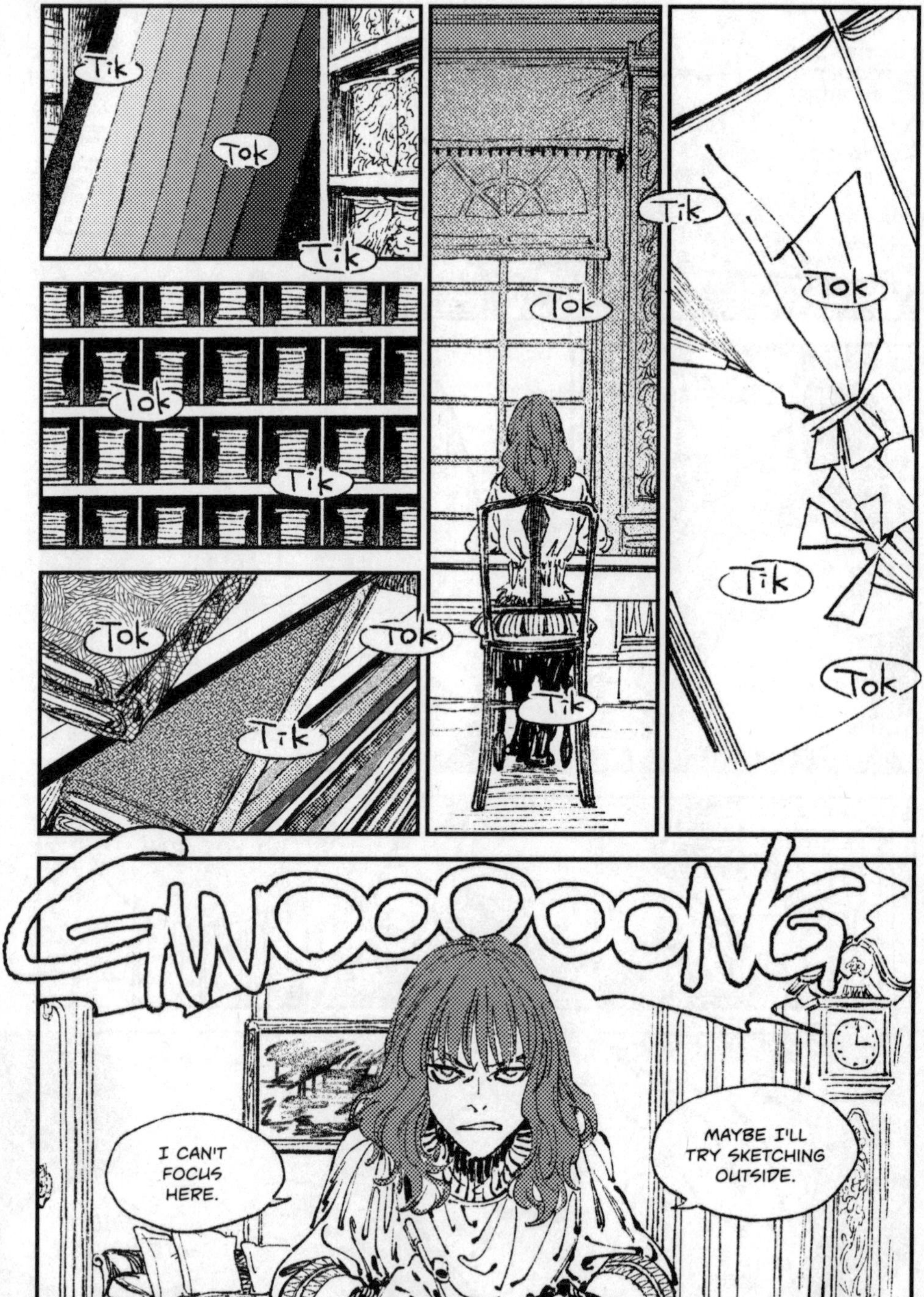
Tik
Tok
Tik
Tok
Tik
Tok
Tok
Tik
Tok
Tik
Tik
Tok
Tik
Tok
GWOOOOONG
I CAN'T FOCUS HERE.
MAYBE I'LL TRY SKETCHING OUTSIDE.

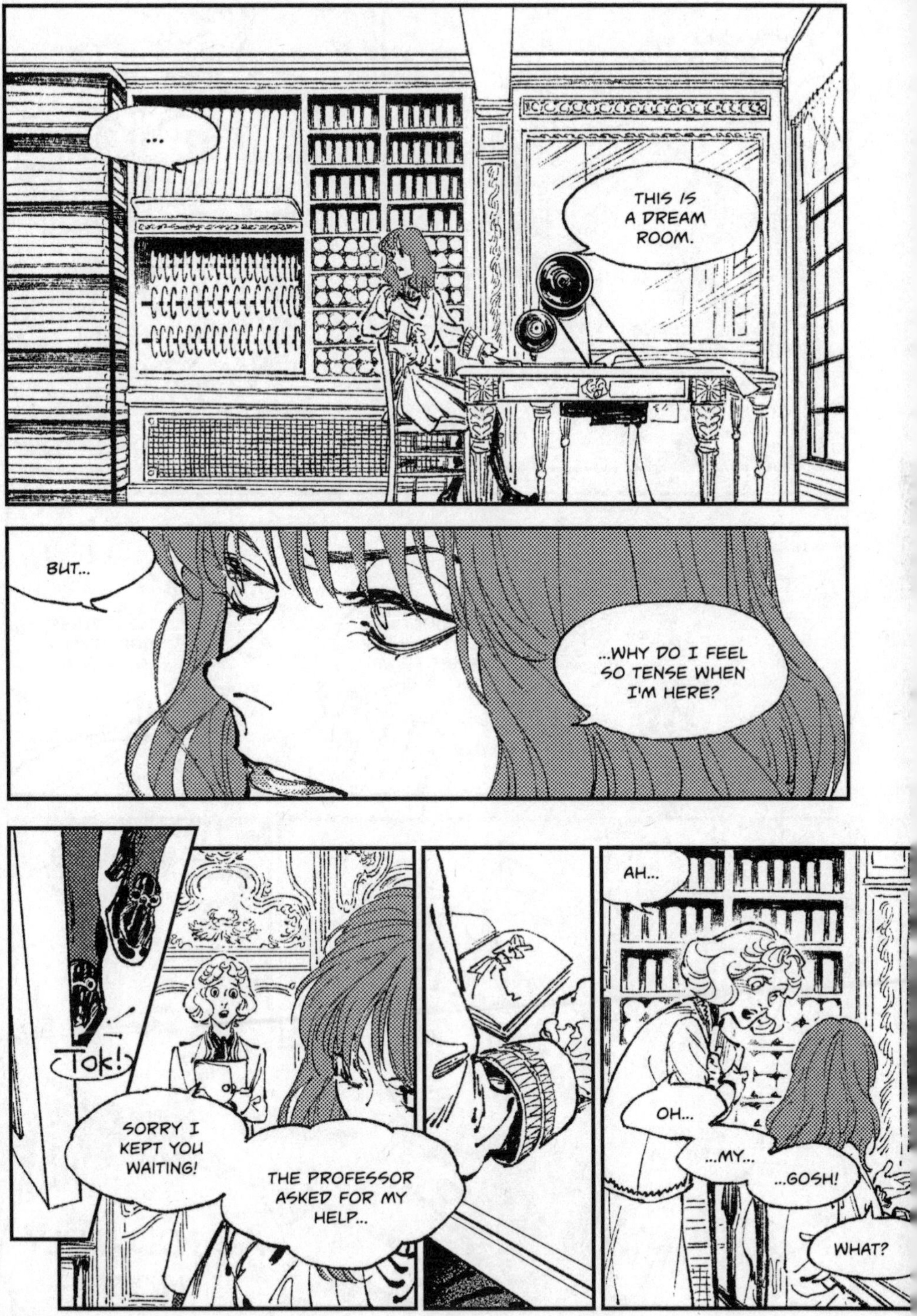
...
THIS IS A DREAM ROOM.
BUT...
...WHY DO I FEEL SO TENSE WHEN I'M HERE?
TOK!
SORRY I KEPT YOU WAITING!
THE PROFESSOR ASKED FOR MY HELP...
AH...
OH...
...MY...
...GOSH!
WHAT?

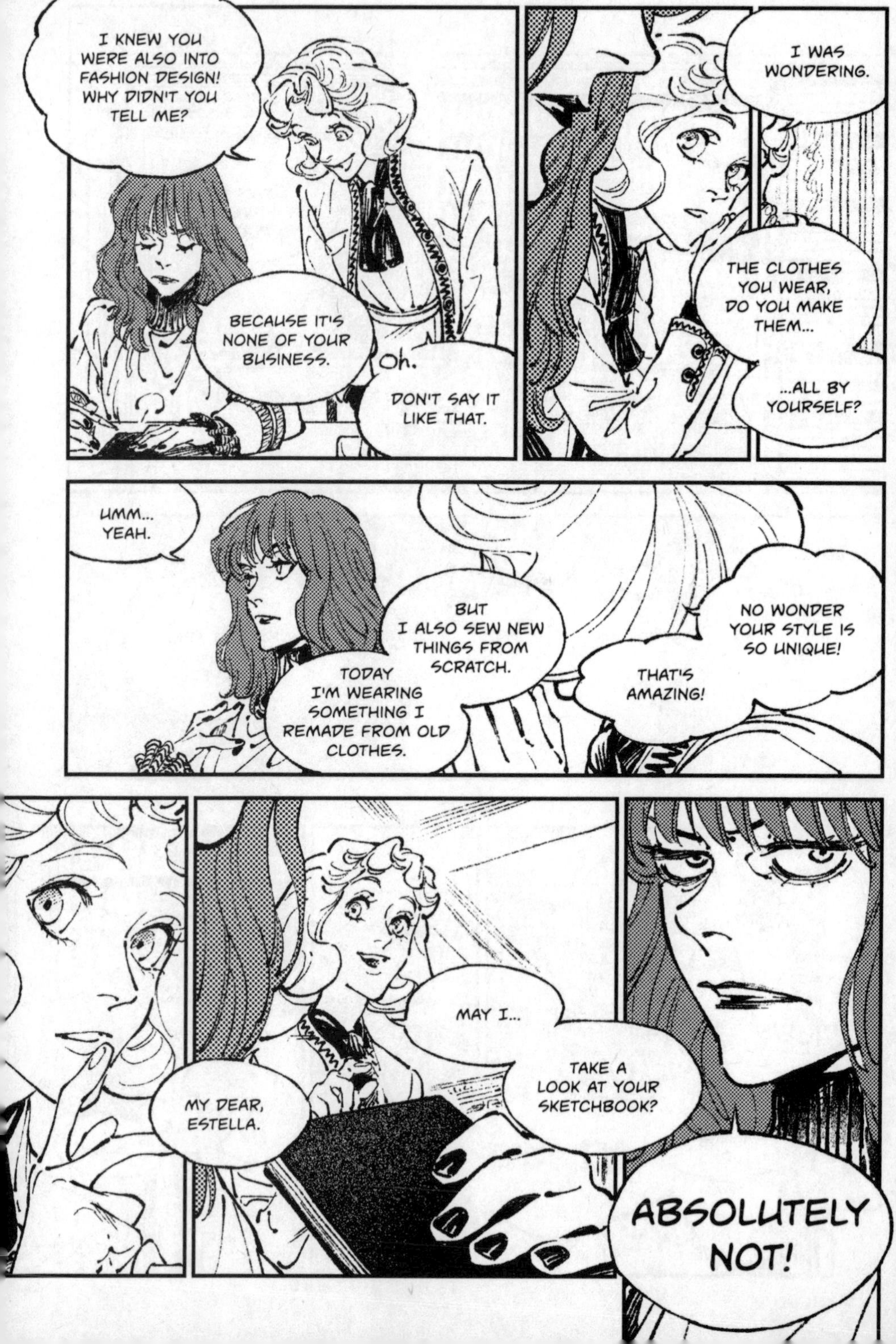
I KNEW YOU WERE ALSO INTO FASHION DESIGN! WHY DIDN'T YOU TELL ME?
BECAUSE IT'S NONE OF YOUR BUSINESS.
Oh.
DON'T SAY IT LIKE THAT.
I WAS WONDERING.
THE CLOTHES YOU WEAR, DO YOU MAKE THEM...
...ALL BY YOURSELF?
UMM... YEAH.
BUT I ALSO SEW NEW THINGS FROM SCRATCH.
TODAY I'M WEARING SOMETHING I REMADE FROM OLD CLOTHES.
NO WONDER YOUR STYLE IS SO UNIQUE!
THAT'S AMAZING!
MY DEAR, ESTELLA.
MAY I...
TAKE A LOOK AT YOUR SKETCHBOOK?
ABSOLUTELY NOT!

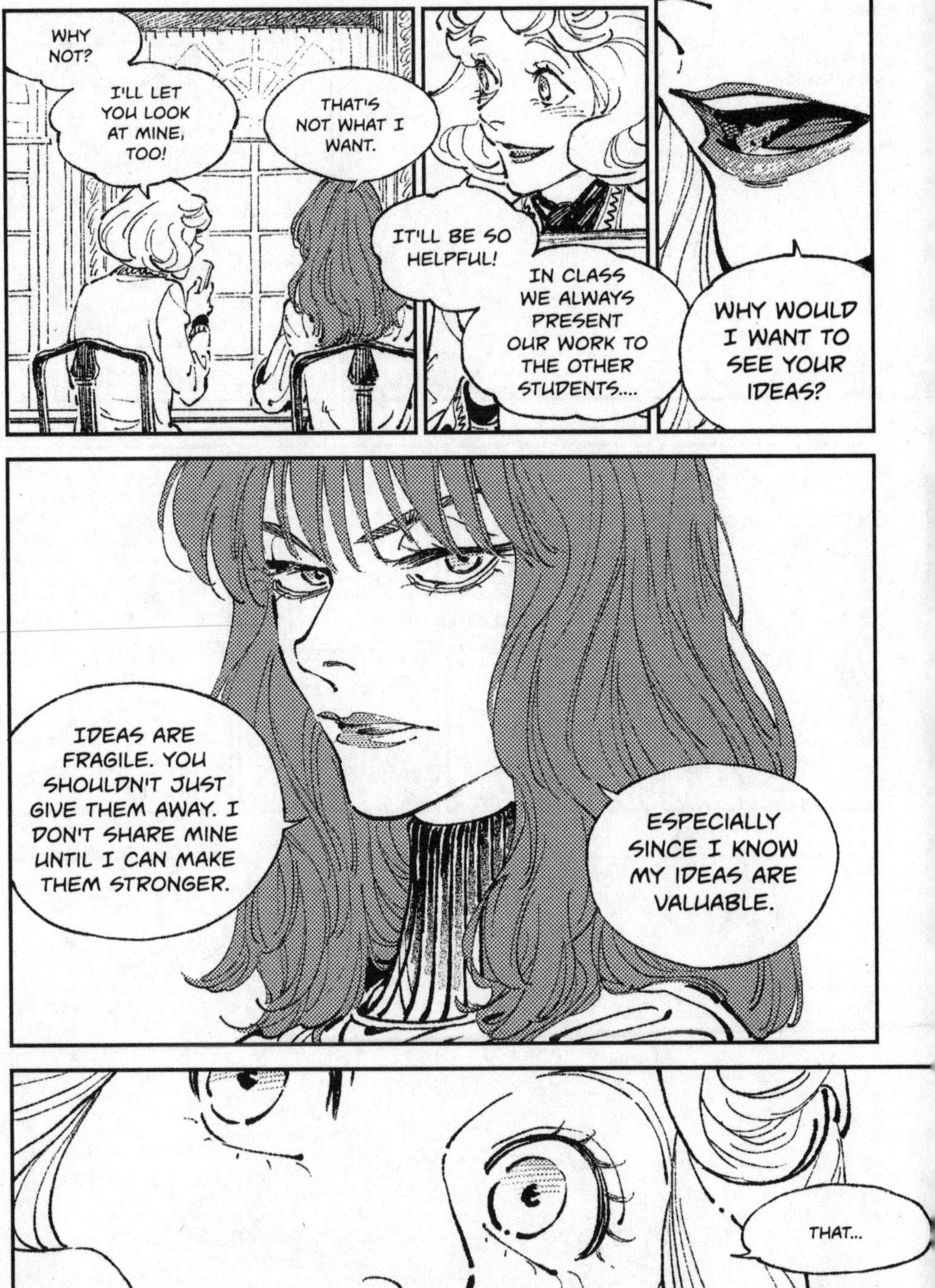
WHY NOT?
I'LL LET YOU LOOK AT MINE, TOO!
THAT'S NOT WHAT I WANT.
IT'LL BE SO HELPFUL!
IN CLASS WE ALWAYS PRESENT OUR WORK TO THE OTHER STUDENTS....
WHY WOULD I WANT TO SEE YOUR IDEAS?
IDEAS ARE FRAGILE. YOU SHOULDN'T JUST GIVE THEM AWAY. I DON'T SHARE MINE UNTIL I CAN MAKE THEM STRONGER.
ESPECIALLY SINCE I KNOW MY IDEAS ARE VALUABLE.
THAT...

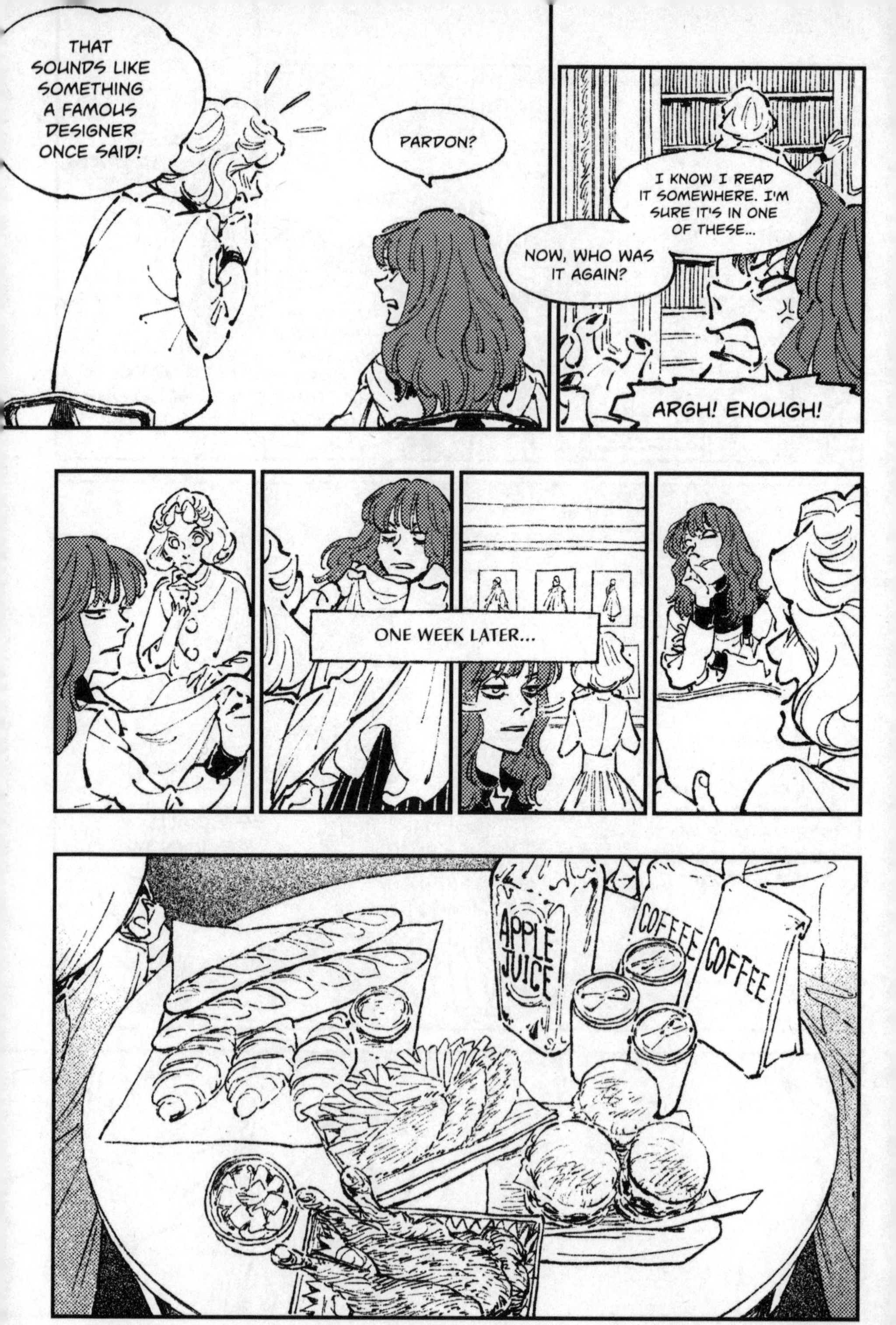
THAT SOUNDS LIKE SOMETHING A FAMOUS DESIGNER ONCE SAID!
PARDON?
I KNOW I READ IT SOMEWHERE. I'M SURE IT'S IN ONE OF THESE...
NOW, WHO WAS IT AGAIN?
ARGH! ENOUGH!
ONE WEEK LATER...
APPLE JUICE
COFFEE
COFFEE

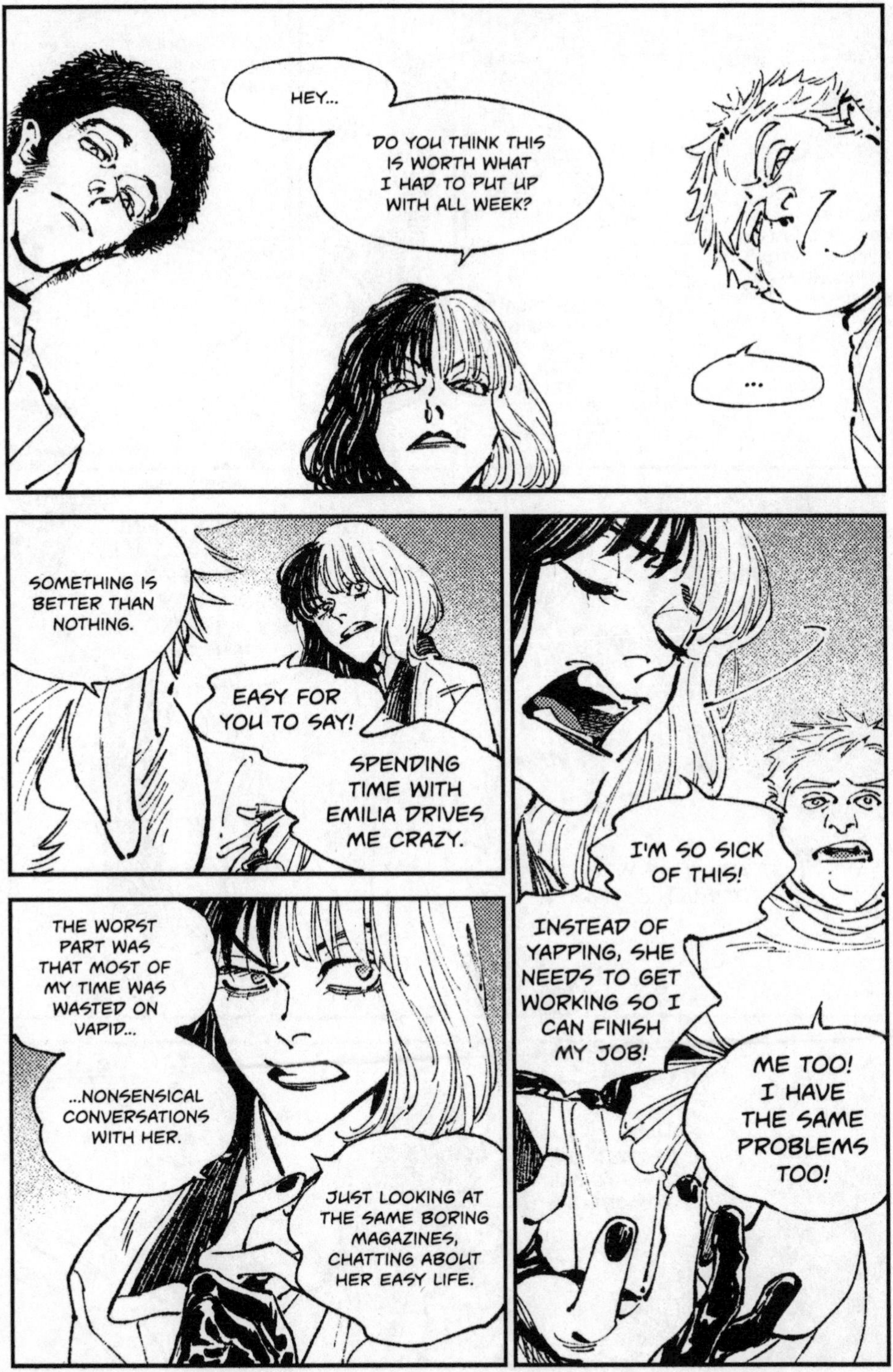
HEY...
DO YOU THINK THIS IS WORTH WHAT I HAD TO PUT UP WITH ALL WEEK?
...
SOMETHING IS BETTER THAN NOTHING.
EASY FOR YOU TO SAY!
SPENDING TIME WITH EMILIA DRIVES ME CRAZY.
THE WORST PART WAS THAT MOST OF MY TIME WAS WASTED ON VAPID...
...NONSENSICAL CONVERSATIONS WITH HER.
JUST LOOKING AT THE SAME BORING MAGAZINES, CHATTING ABOUT HER EASY LIFE.
I'M SO SICK OF THIS!
INSTEAD OF YAPPING, SHE NEEDS TO GET WORKING SO I CAN FINISH MY JOB!
ME TOO! I HAVE THE SAME PROBLEMS TOO!

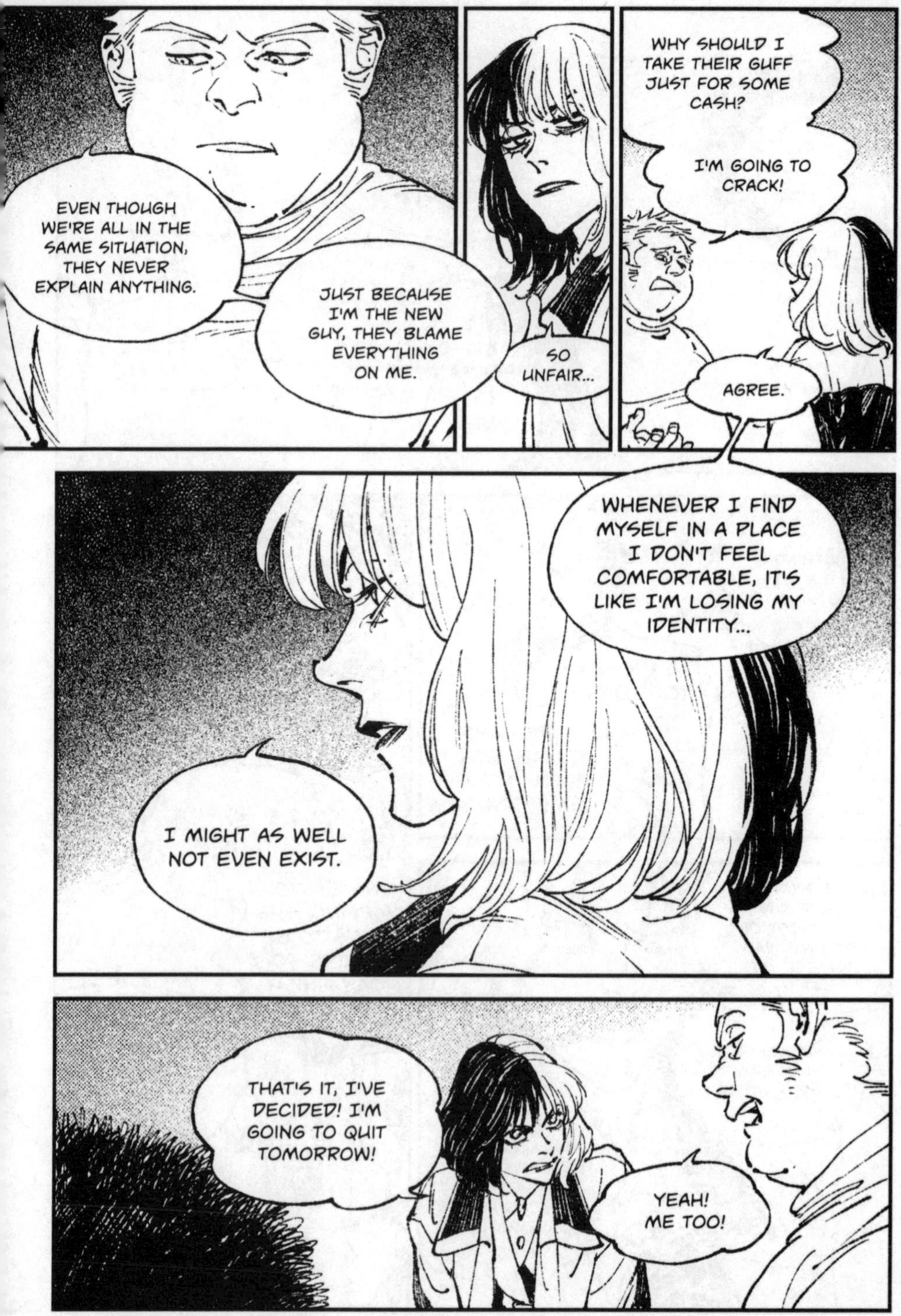
EVEN THOUGH WE'RE ALL IN THE SAME SITUATION, THEY NEVER EXPLAIN ANYTHING.
JUST BECAUSE I'M THE NEW GUY, THEY BLAME EVERYTHING ON ME.
SO UNFAIR...
WHY SHOULD I TAKE THEIR GUFF JUST FOR SOME CASH?
I'M GOING TO CRACK!
AGREE.
WHENEVER I FIND MYSELF IN A PLACE I DON'T FEEL COMFORTABLE, IT'S LIKE I'M LOSING MY IDENTITY...
I MIGHT AS WELL NOT EVEN EXIST.
THAT'S IT, I'VE DECIDED! I'M GOING TO QUIT TOMORROW!
YEAH! ME TOO!

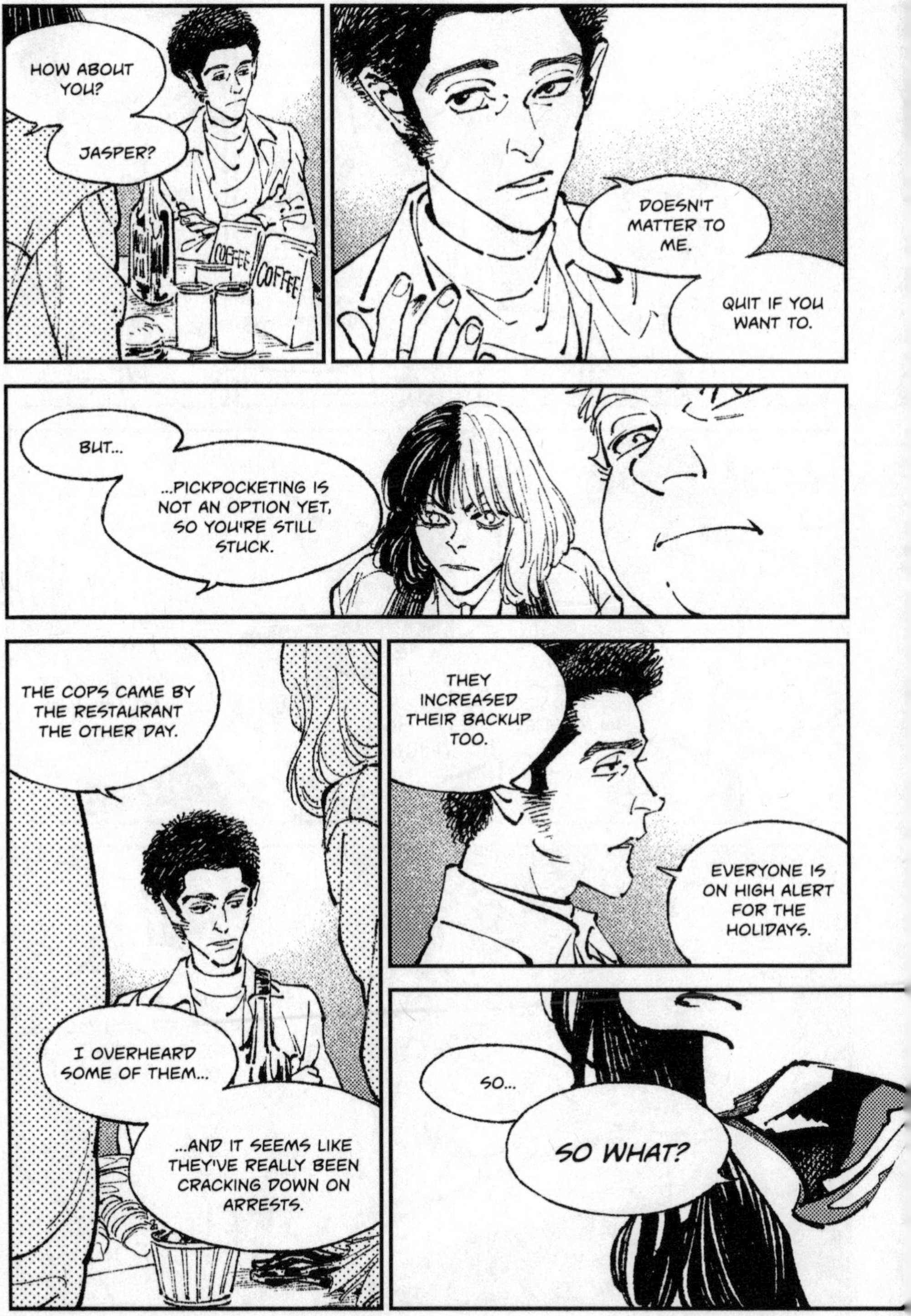
HOW ABOUT YOU?
JASPER?
DOESN'T MATTER TO ME.
QUIT IF YOU WANT TO.
BUT...
...PICKPOCKETING IS NOT AN OPTION YET, SO YOU'RE STILL STUCK.
THE COPS CAME BY THE RESTAURANT THE OTHER DAY.
I OVERHEARD SOME OF THEM...
...AND IT SEEMS LIKE THEY'VE REALLY BEEN CRACKING DOWN ON ARRESTS.
THEY INCREASED THEIR BACKUP TOO.
EVERYONE IS ON HIGH ALERT FOR THE HOLIDAYS.
SO...
SO WHAT?

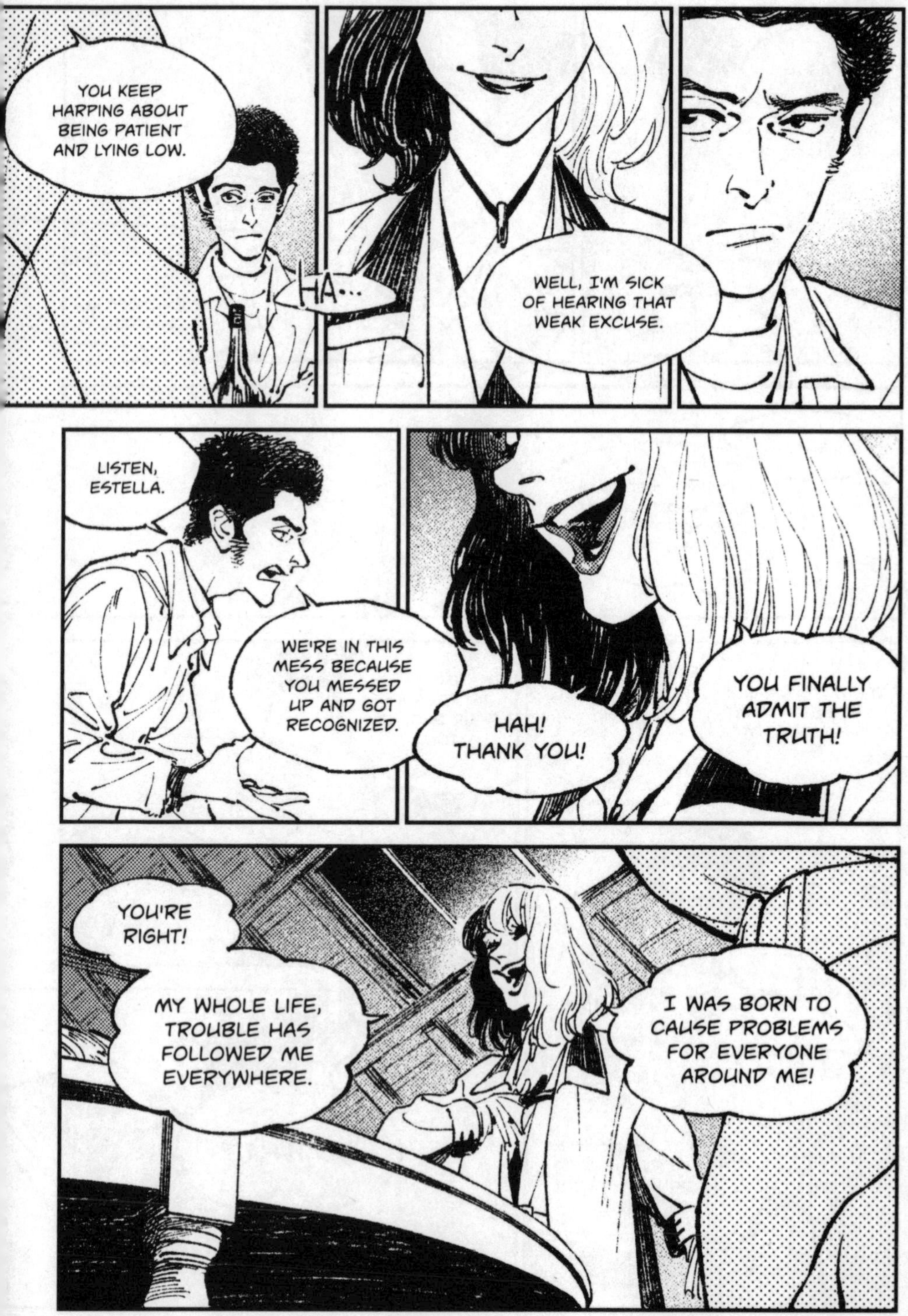
YOU KEEP HARPING ABOUT BEING PATIENT AND LYING LOW.
HA...
WELL, I'M SICK OF HEARING THAT WEAK EXCUSE.
LISTEN, ESTELLA.
WE'RE IN THIS MESS BECAUSE YOU MESSED UP AND GOT RECOGNIZED.
HAH! THANK YOU!
YOU FINALLY ADMIT THE TRUTH!
YOU'RE RIGHT!
MY WHOLE LIFE, TROUBLE HAS FOLLOWED ME EVERYWHERE.
I WAS BORN TO CAUSE PROBLEMS FOR EVERYONE AROUND ME!

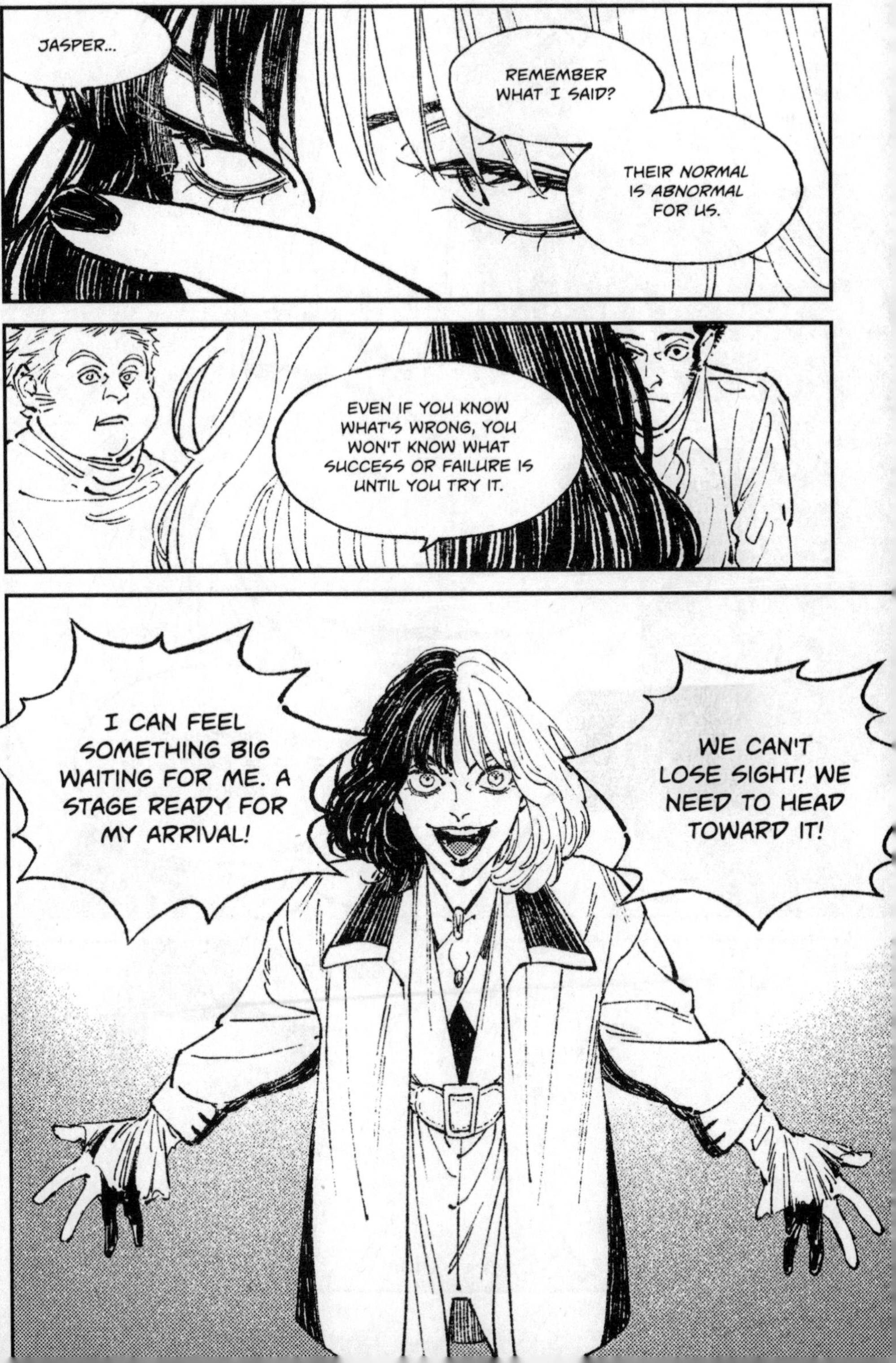
JASPER...
REMEMBER WHAT I SAID?
THEIR *NORMAL* IS *ABNORMAL* FOR US.
EVEN IF YOU KNOW WHAT'S WRONG, YOU WON'T KNOW WHAT SUCCESS OR FAILURE IS UNTIL YOU TRY IT.
I CAN FEEL SOMETHING BIG WAITING FOR ME. A STAGE READY FOR MY ARRIVAL!
WE CAN'T LOSE SIGHT! WE NEED TO HEAD TOWARD IT!

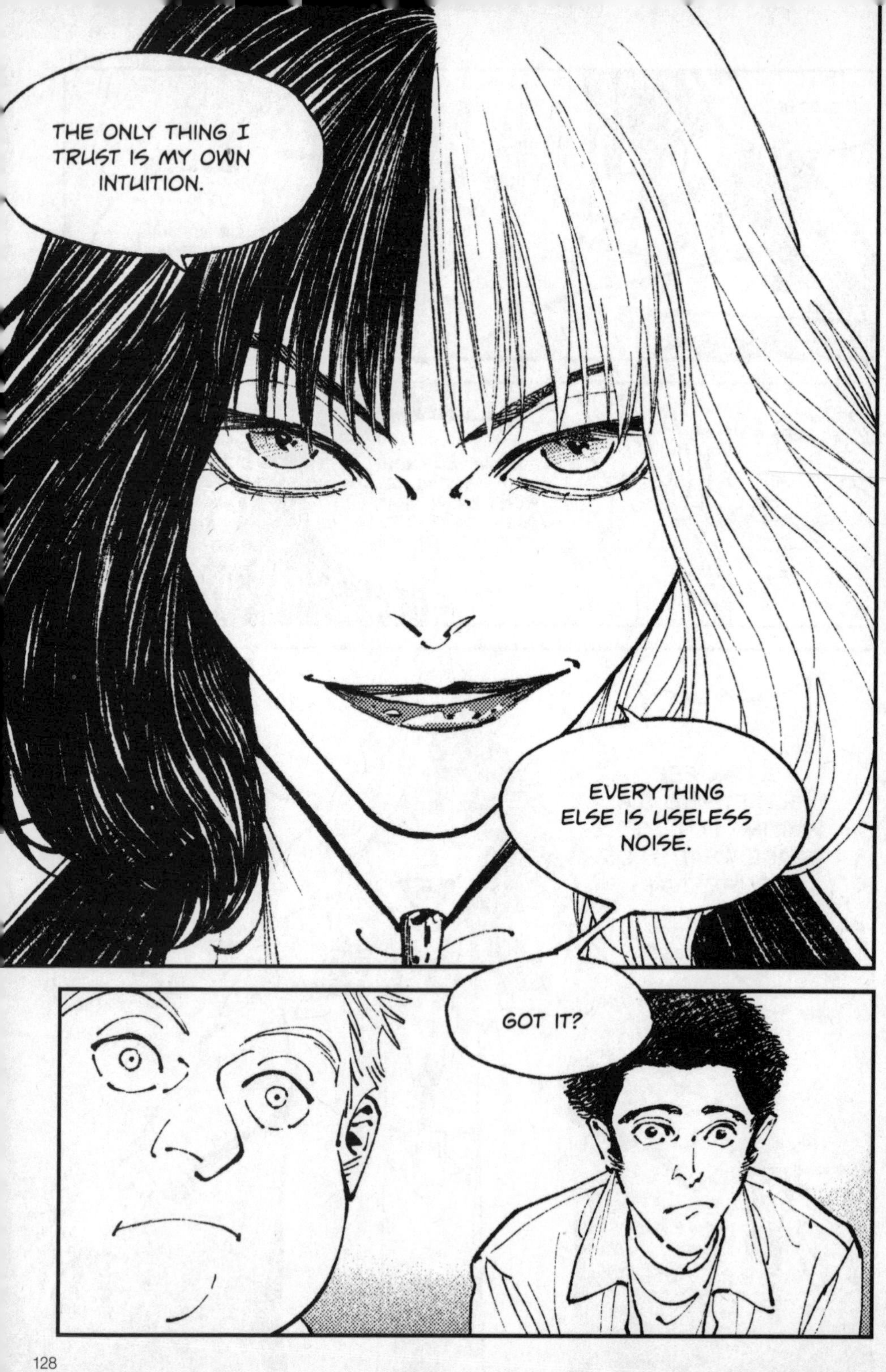
THE ONLY THING I TRUST IS MY OWN INTUITION.
EVERYTHING ELSE IS USELESS NOISE.
GOT IT?

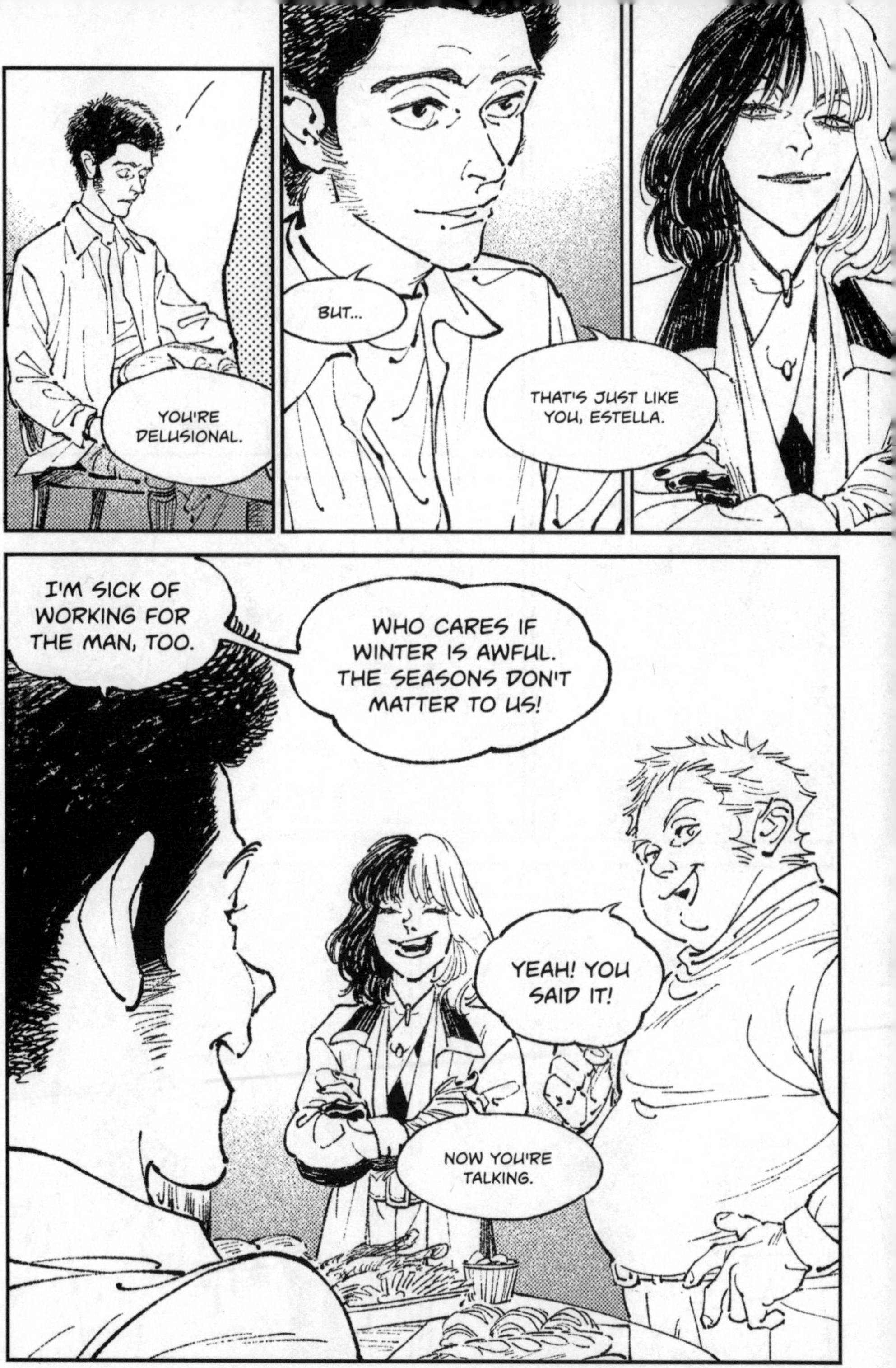
YOU'RE DELUSIONAL.
BUT...
THAT'S JUST LIKE YOU, ESTELLA.
I'M SICK OF WORKING FOR THE MAN, TOO.
WHO CARES IF WINTER IS AWFUL. THE SEASONS DON'T MATTER TO US!
YEAH! YOU SAID IT!
NOW YOU'RE TALKING.

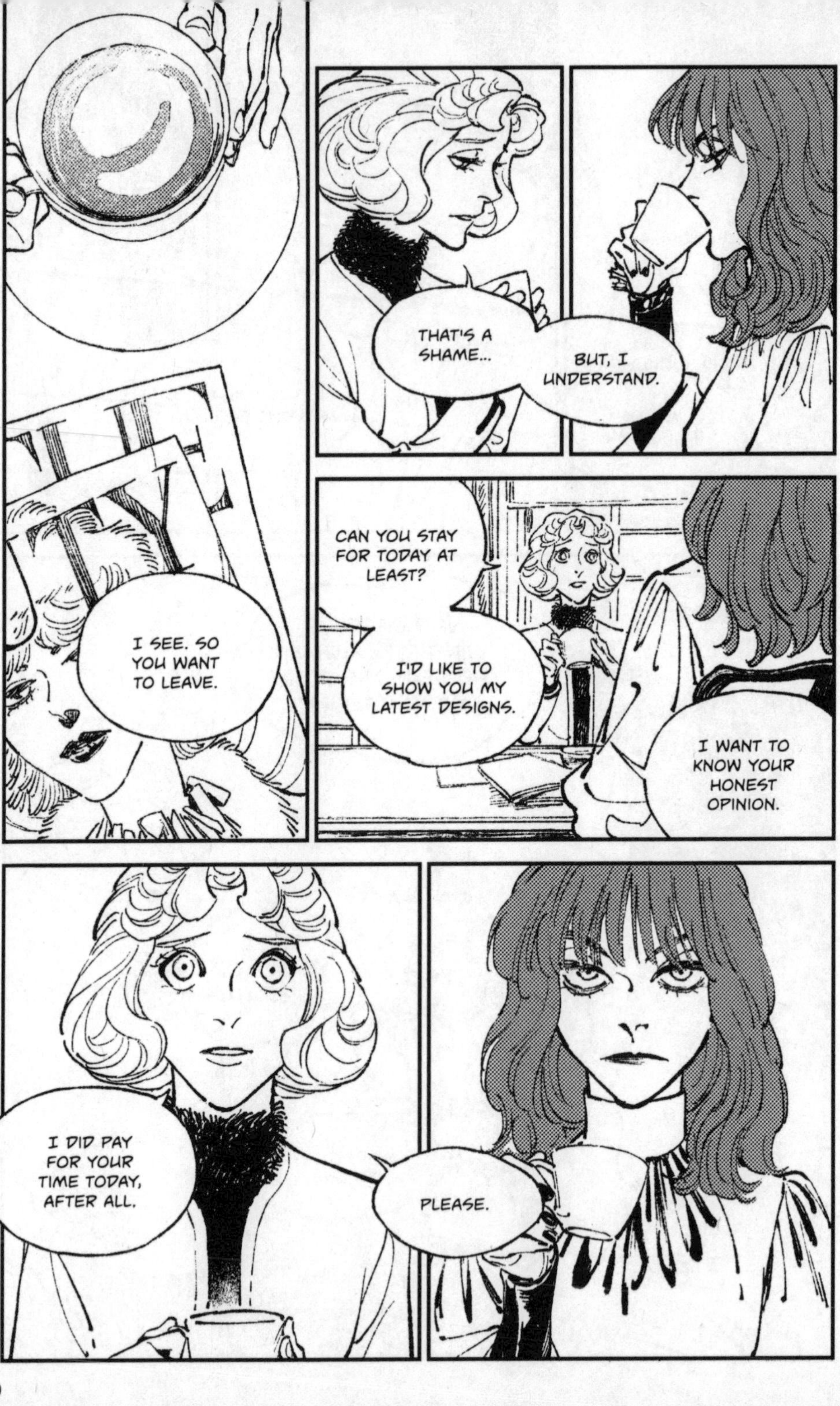
I SEE. SO YOU WANT TO LEAVE.
THAT'S A SHAME...
BUT, I UNDERSTAND.
CAN YOU STAY FOR TODAY AT LEAST?
I'D LIKE TO SHOW YOU MY LATEST DESIGNS.
I WANT TO KNOW YOUR HONEST OPINION.
I DID PAY FOR YOUR TIME TODAY, AFTER ALL.
PLEASE.

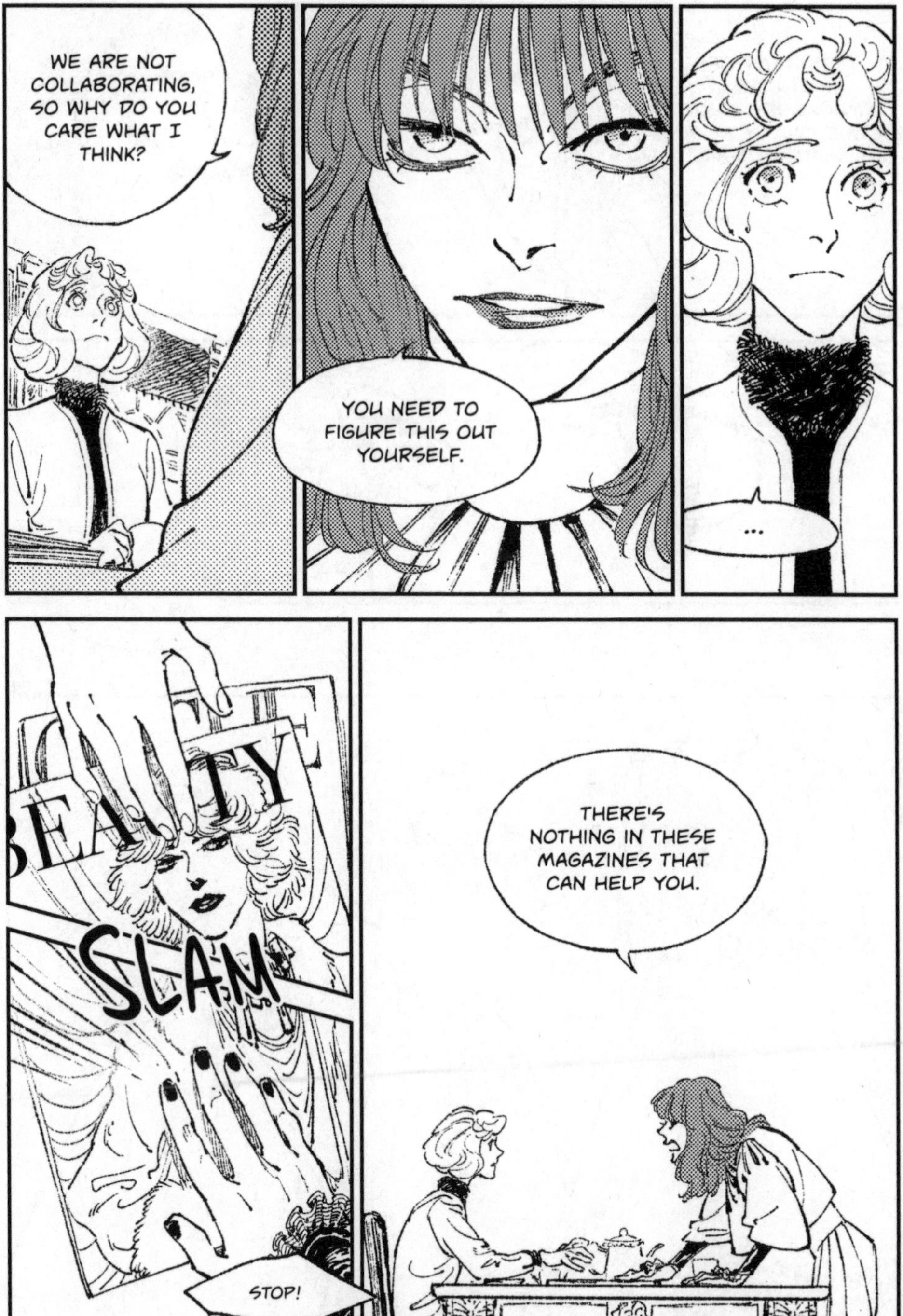
WE ARE NOT COLLABORATING, SO WHY DO YOU CARE WHAT I THINK?
YOU NEED TO FIGURE THIS OUT YOURSELF.
...
SLAM
STOP!
THERE'S NOTHING IN THESE MAGAZINES THAT CAN HELP YOU.

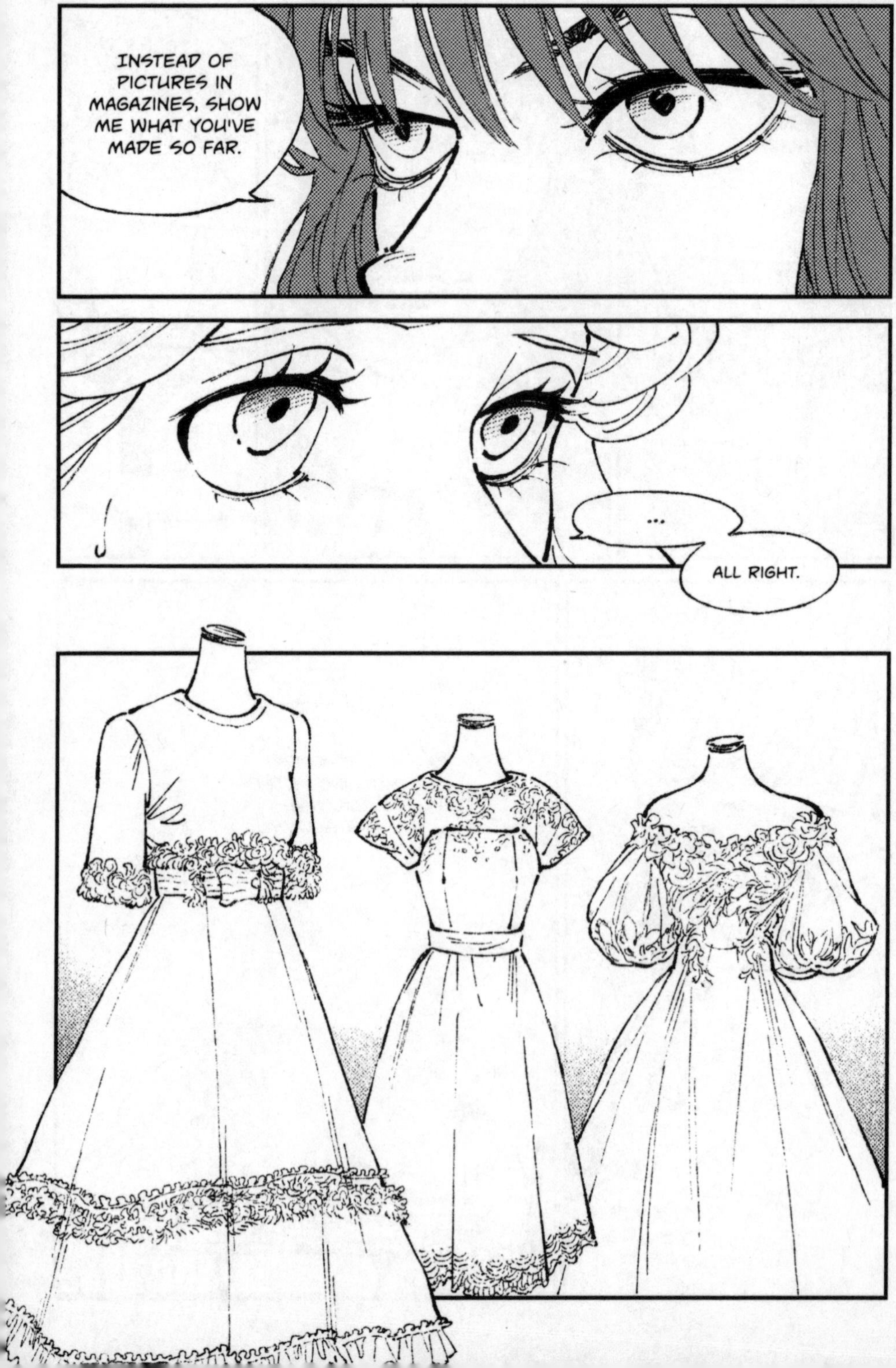
INSTEAD OF PICTURES IN MAGAZINES, SHOW ME WHAT YOU'VE MADE SO FAR.
...
ALL RIGHT.

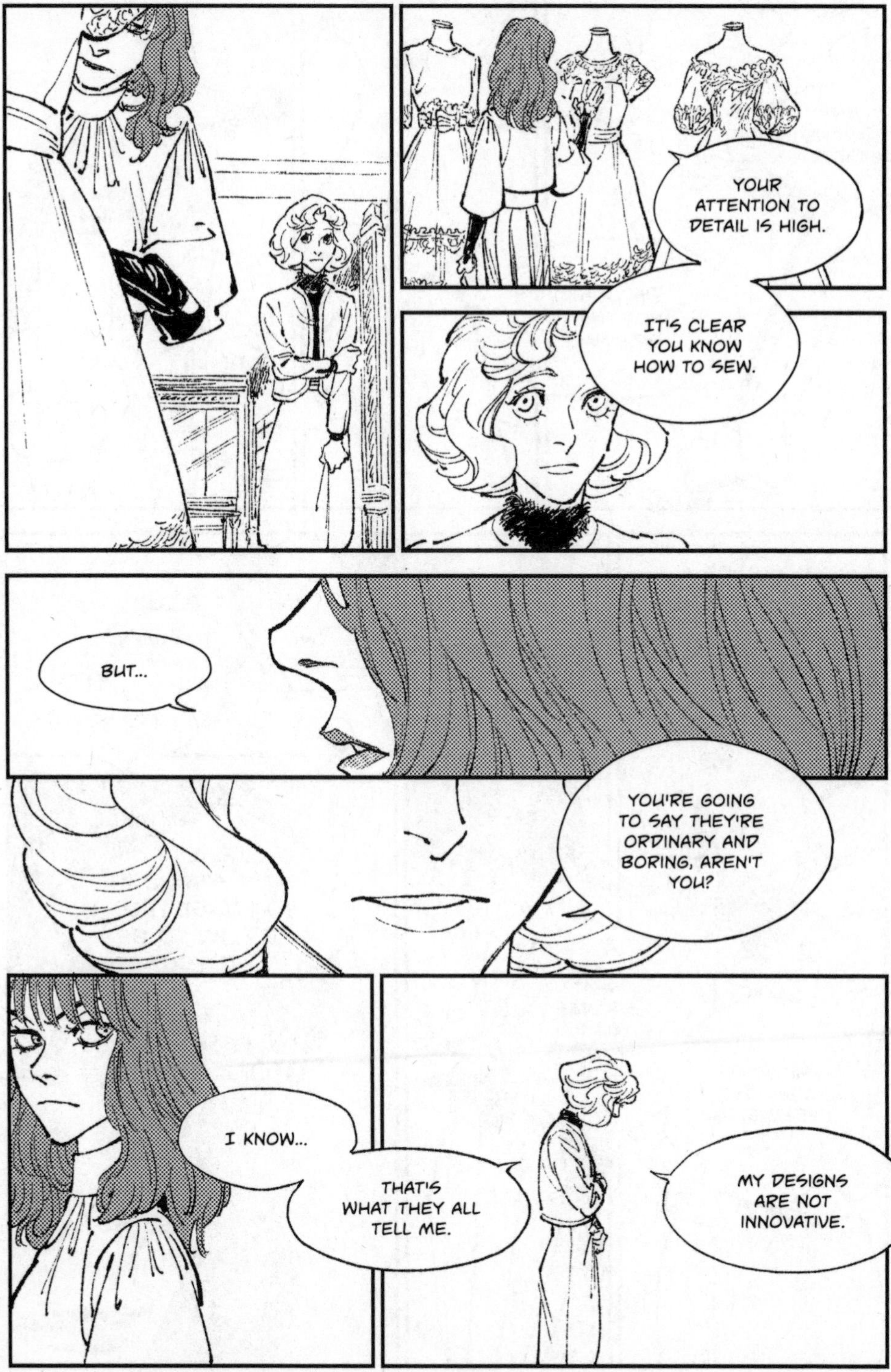
YOUR ATTENTION TO DETAIL IS HIGH.
IT'S CLEAR YOU KNOW HOW TO SEW.
BUT...
YOU'RE GOING TO SAY THEY'RE ORDINARY AND BORING, AREN'T YOU?
I KNOW...
THAT'S WHAT THEY ALL TELL ME.
MY DESIGNS ARE NOT INNOVATIVE.

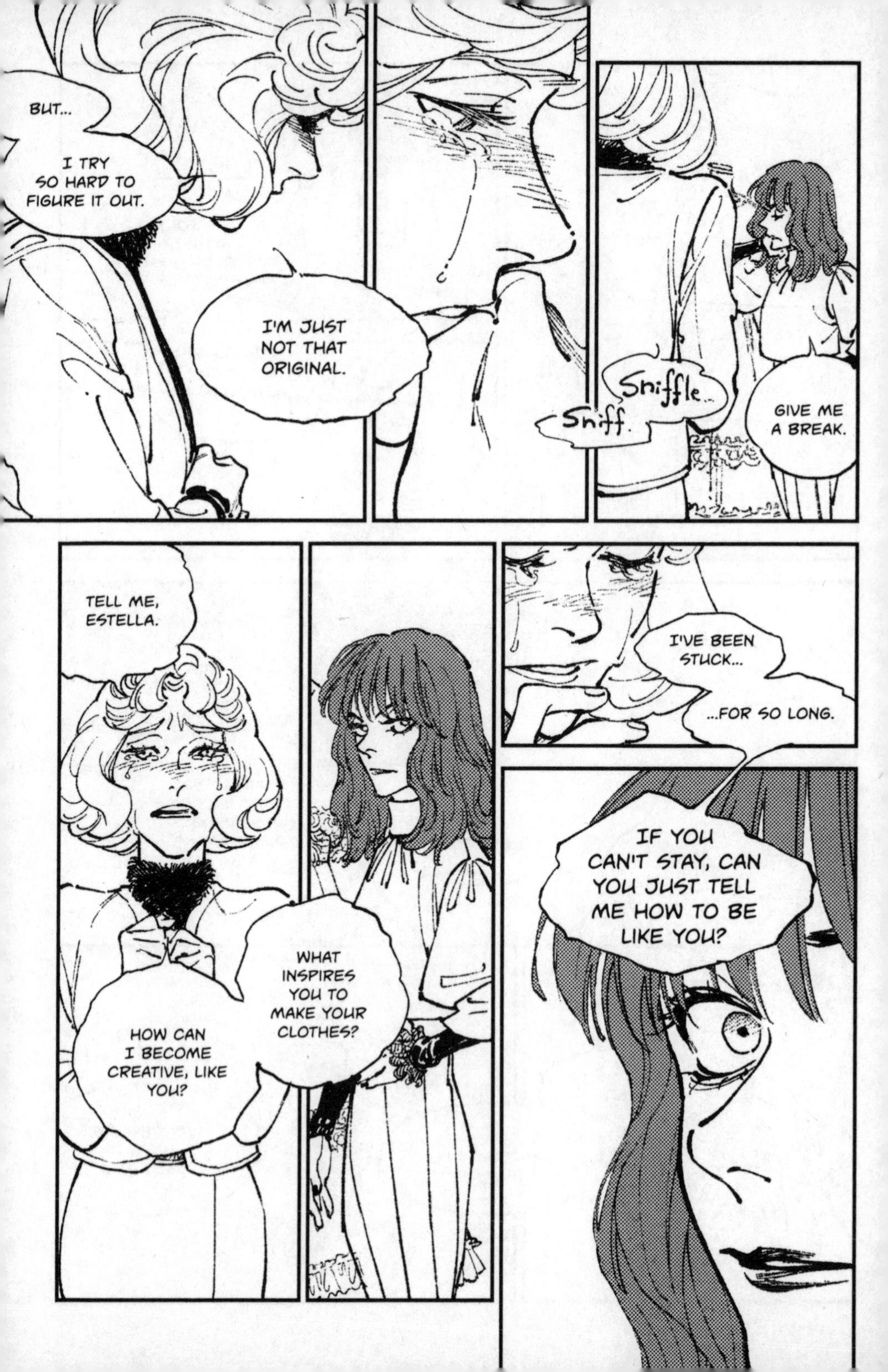
BUT...
I TRY SO HARD TO FIGURE IT OUT.
I'M JUST NOT THAT ORIGINAL.
Sniffle...
Sniff.
GIVE ME A BREAK.
TELL ME, ESTELLA.
HOW CAN I BECOME CREATIVE, LIKE YOU?
WHAT INSPIRES YOU TO MAKE YOUR CLOTHES?
I'VE BEEN STUCK...
...FOR SO LONG.
IF YOU CAN'T STAY, CAN YOU JUST TELL ME HOW TO BE LIKE YOU?

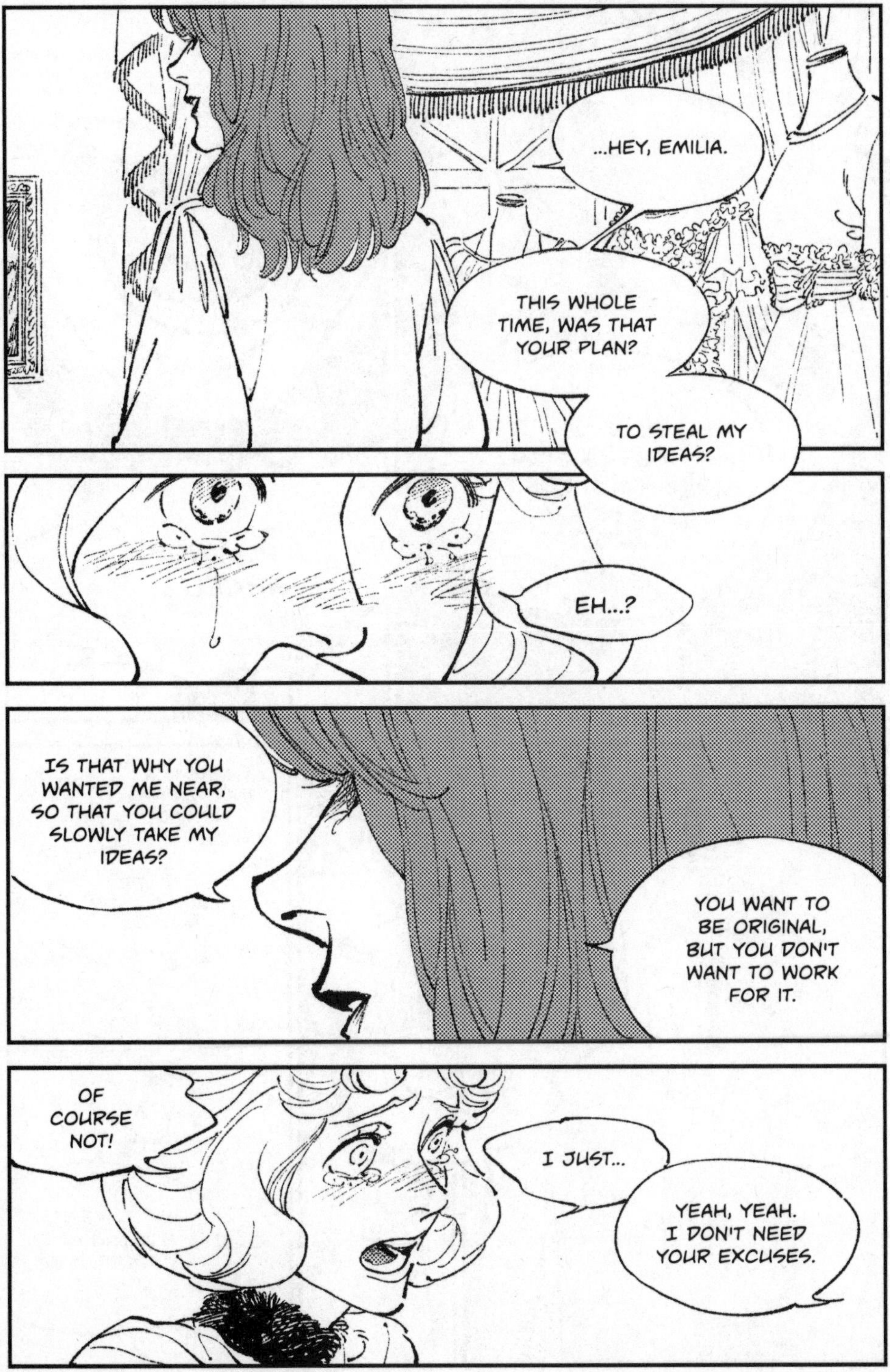
...HEY, EMILIA.
THIS WHOLE TIME, WAS THAT YOUR PLAN?
TO STEAL MY IDEAS?
EH...?
IS THAT WHY YOU WANTED ME NEAR, SO THAT YOU COULD SLOWLY TAKE MY IDEAS?
YOU WANT TO BE ORIGINAL, BUT YOU DON'T WANT TO WORK FOR IT.
OF COURSE NOT!
I JUST...
YEAH, YEAH. I DON'T NEED YOUR EXCUSES.

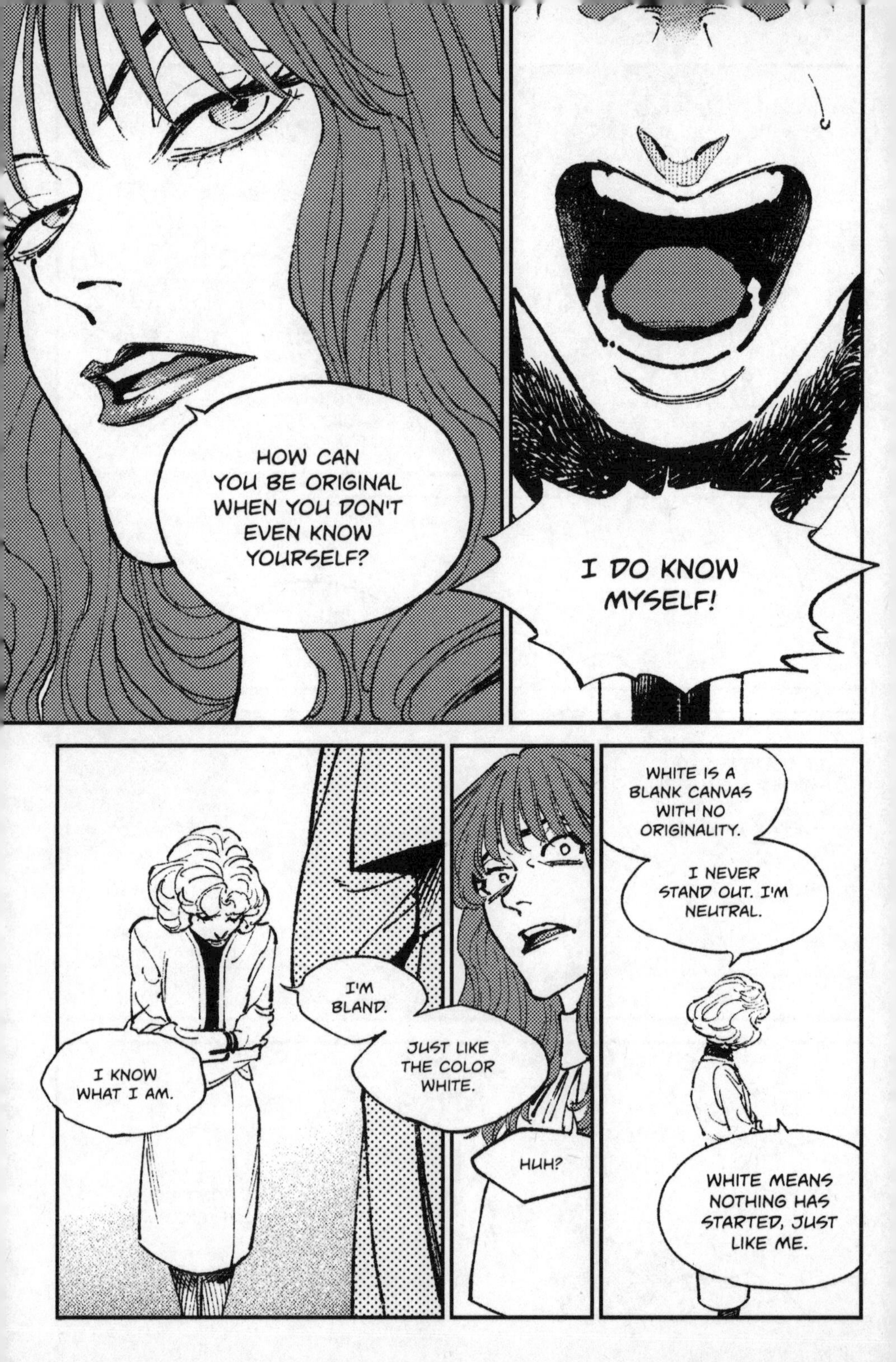
HOW CAN YOU BE ORIGINAL WHEN YOU DON'T EVEN KNOW YOURSELF?
I DO KNOW MYSELF!
I KNOW WHAT I AM.
I'M BLAND.
JUST LIKE THE COLOR WHITE.
HUH?
WHITE IS A BLANK CANVAS WITH NO ORIGINALITY.
I NEVER STAND OUT. I'M NEUTRAL.
WHITE MEANS NOTHING HAS STARTED, JUST LIKE ME.

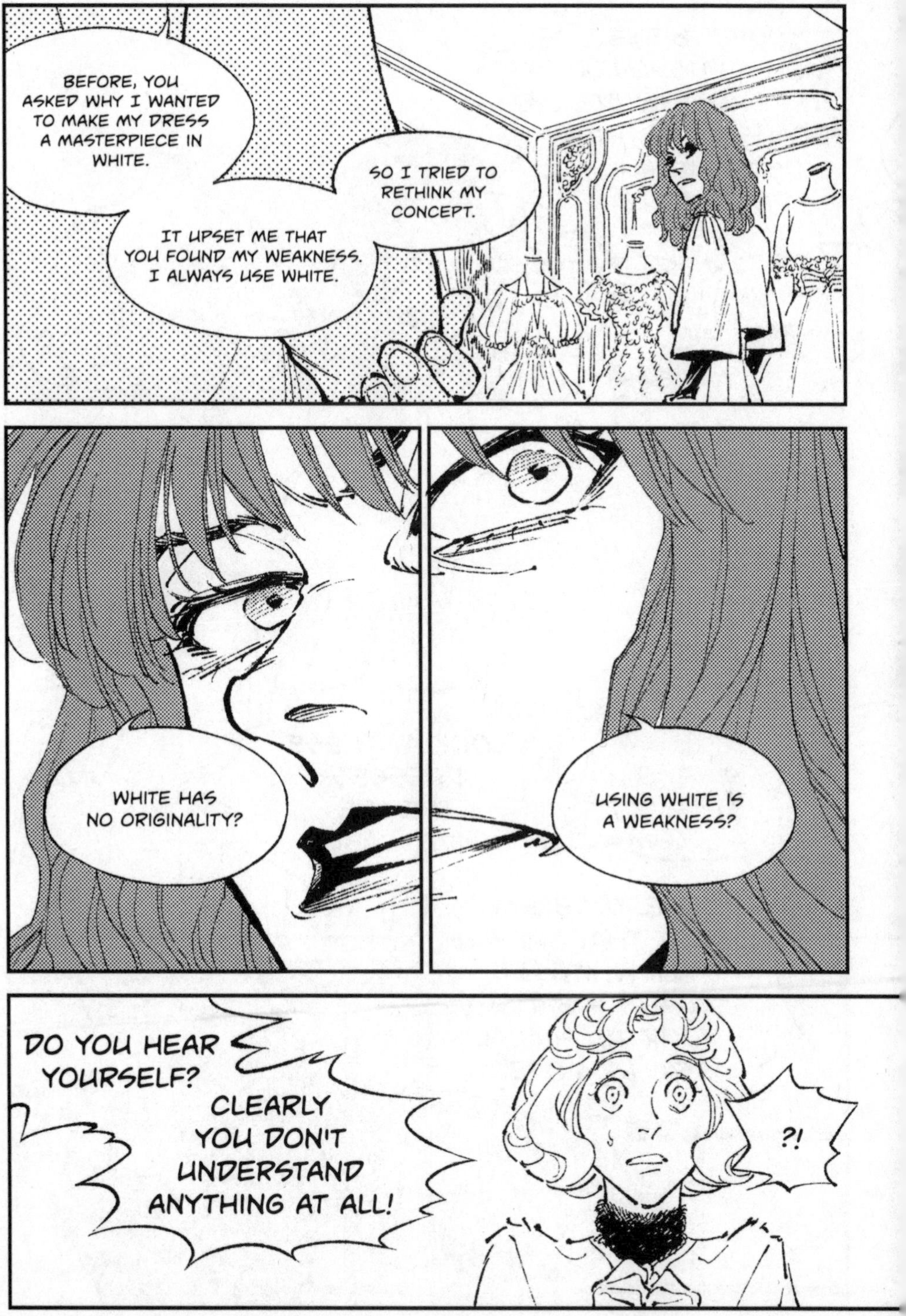
BEFORE, YOU ASKED WHY I WANTED TO MAKE MY DRESS A MASTERPIECE IN WHITE.
IT UPSET ME THAT YOU FOUND MY WEAKNESS. I ALWAYS USE WHITE.
SO I TRIED TO RETHINK MY CONCEPT.
WHITE HAS NO ORIGINALITY?
USING WHITE IS A WEAKNESS?
DO YOU HEAR YOURSELF?
CLEARLY YOU DON'T UNDERSTAND ANYTHING AT ALL!
?!

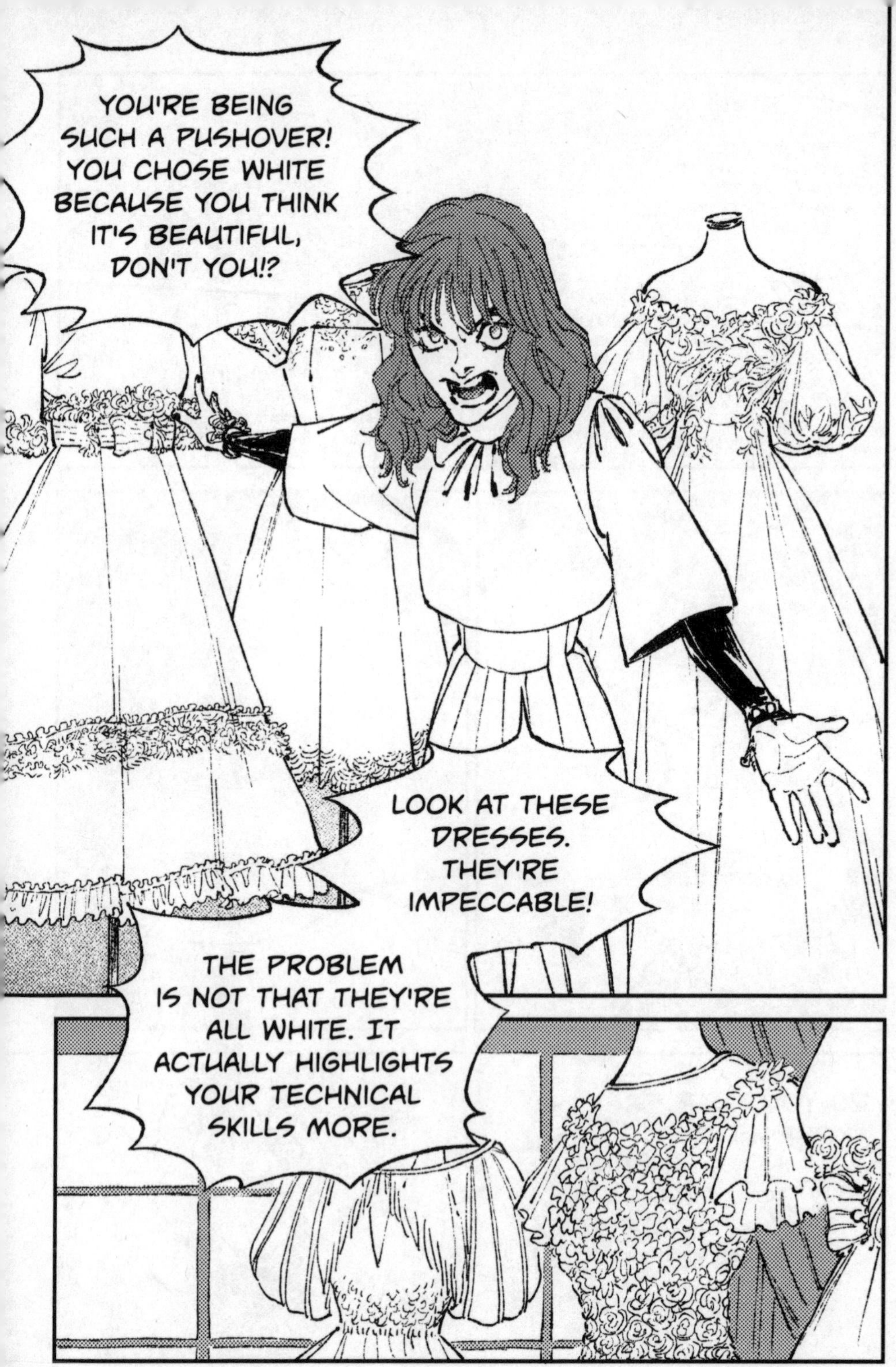
YOU'RE BEING SUCH A PUSHOVER! YOU CHOSE WHITE BECAUSE YOU THINK IT'S BEAUTIFUL, DON'T YOU!?
LOOK AT THESE DRESSES. THEY'RE IMPECCABLE!
THE PROBLEM IS NOT THAT THEY'RE ALL WHITE. IT ACTUALLY HIGHLIGHTS YOUR TECHNICAL SKILLS MORE.

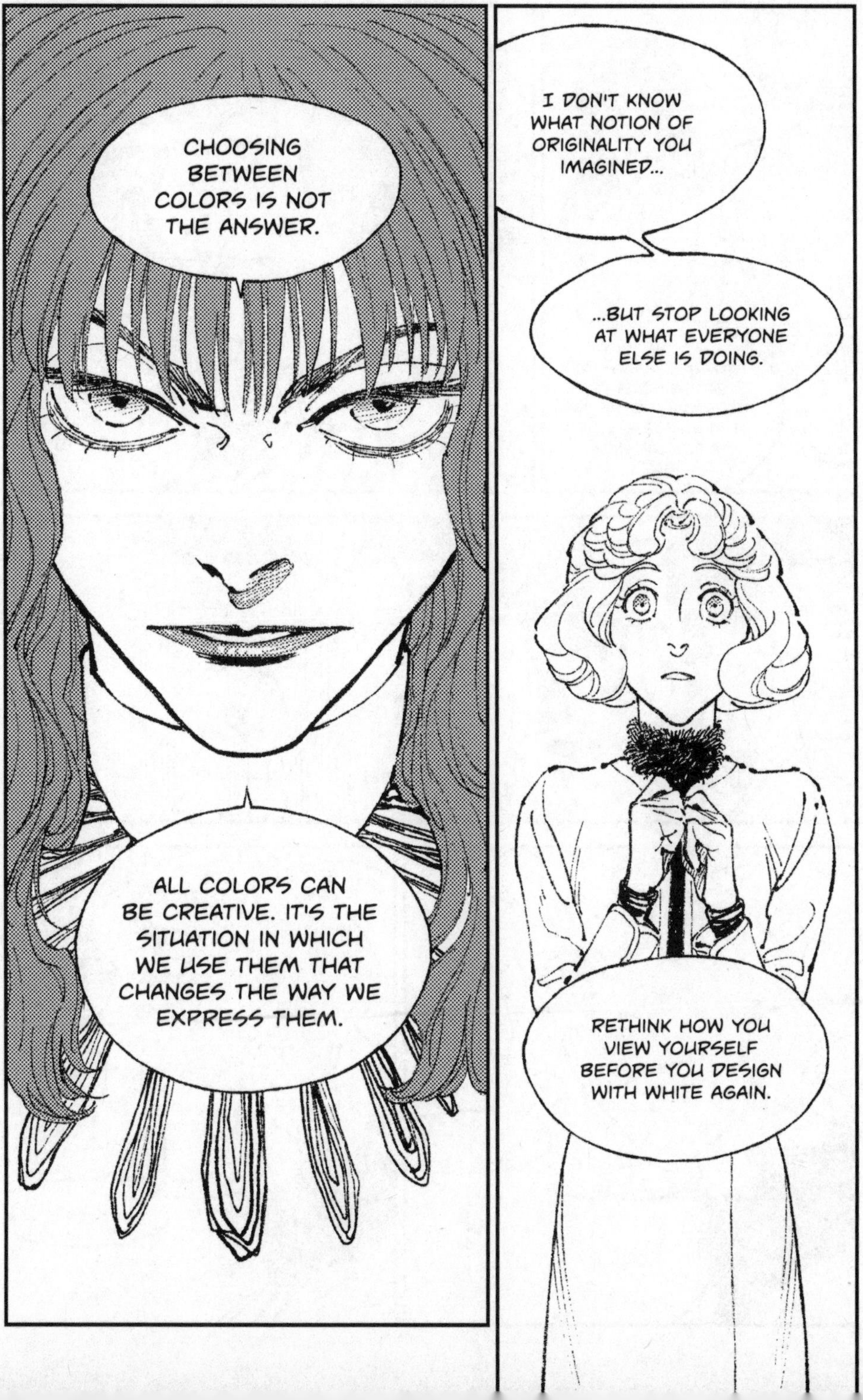
CHOOSING BETWEEN COLORS IS NOT THE ANSWER.
ALL COLORS CAN BE CREATIVE. IT'S THE SITUATION IN WHICH WE USE THEM THAT CHANGES THE WAY WE EXPRESS THEM.
I DON'T KNOW WHAT NOTION OF ORIGINALITY YOU IMAGINED...
...BUT STOP LOOKING AT WHAT EVERYONE ELSE IS DOING.
RETHINK HOW YOU VIEW YOURSELF BEFORE YOU DESIGN WITH WHITE AGAIN.

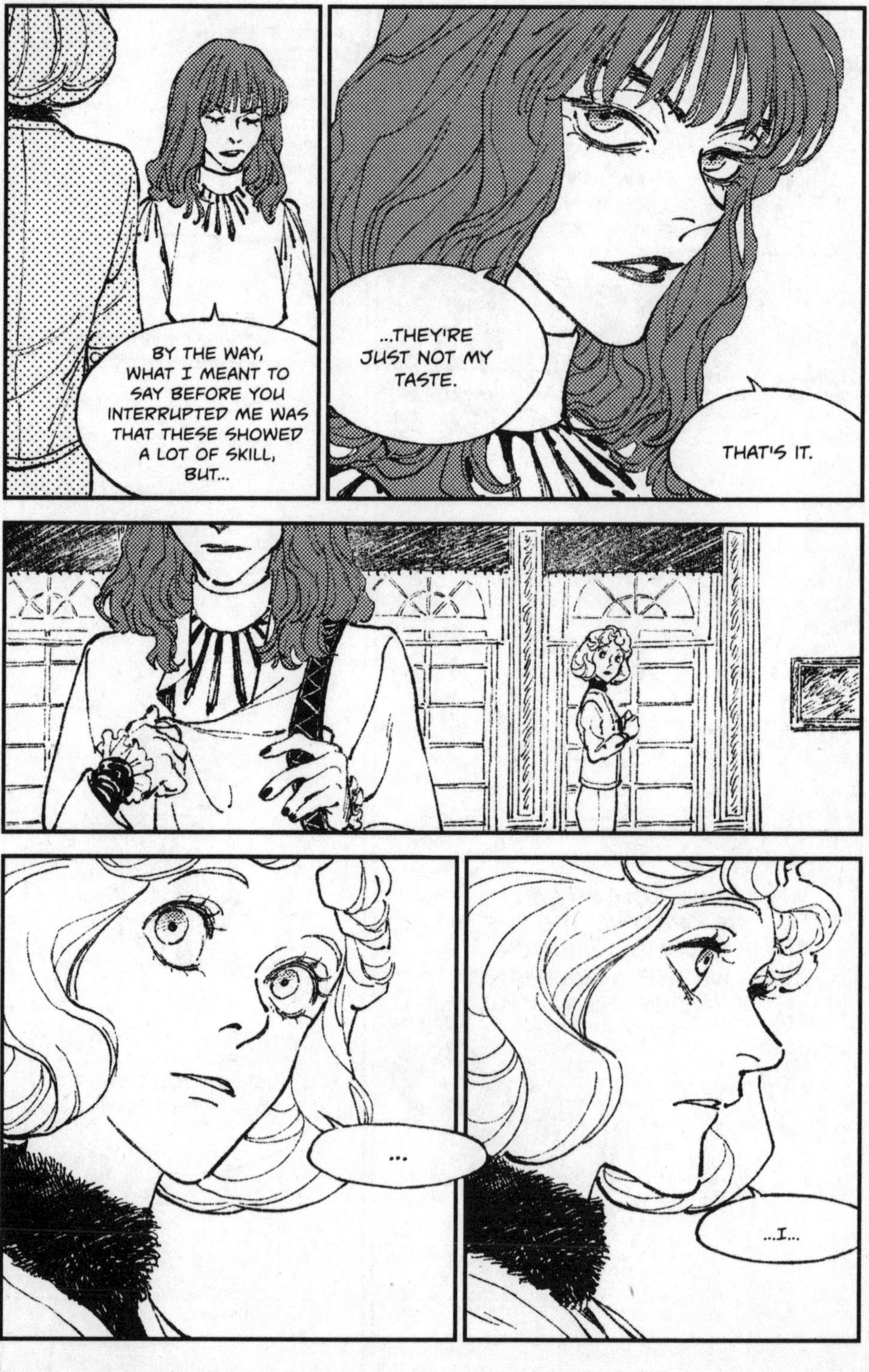
BY THE WAY, WHAT I MEANT TO SAY BEFORE YOU INTERRUPTED ME WAS THAT THESE SHOWED A LOT OF SKILL, BUT...
...THEY'RE JUST NOT MY TASTE.
THAT'S IT.
...
...I...

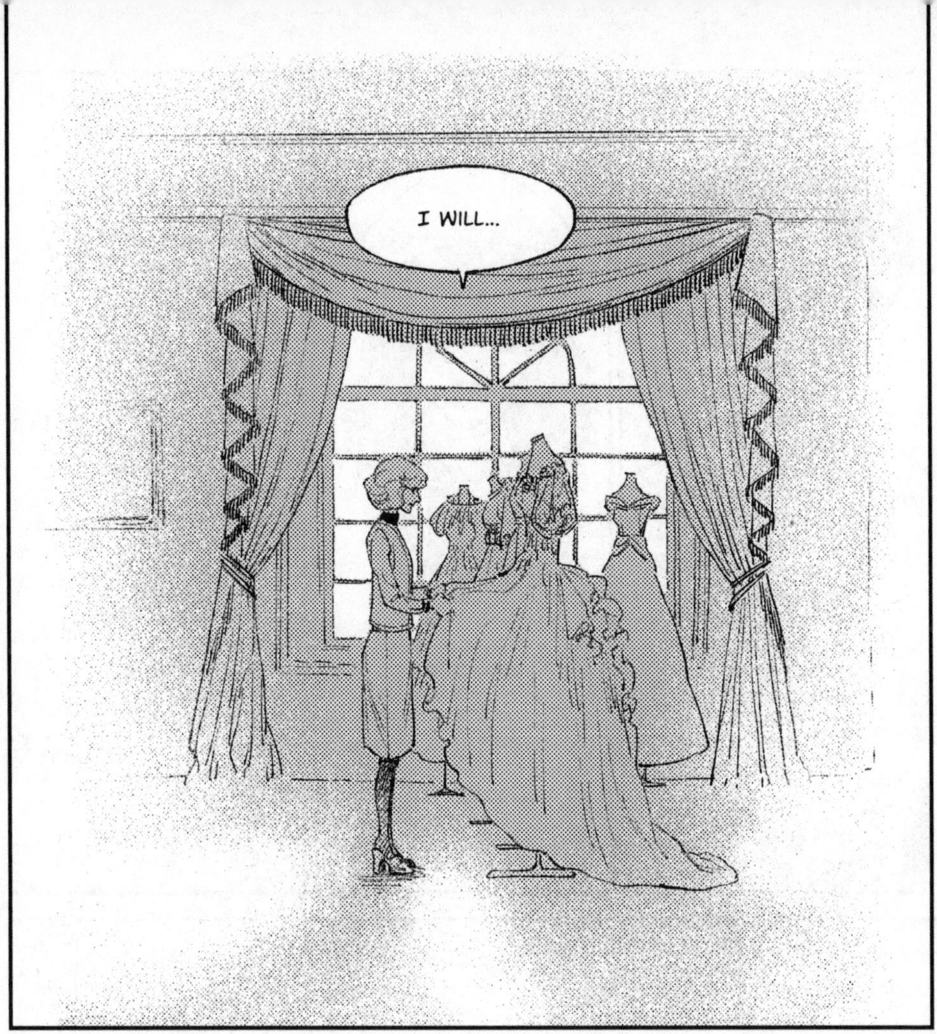
I WILL...
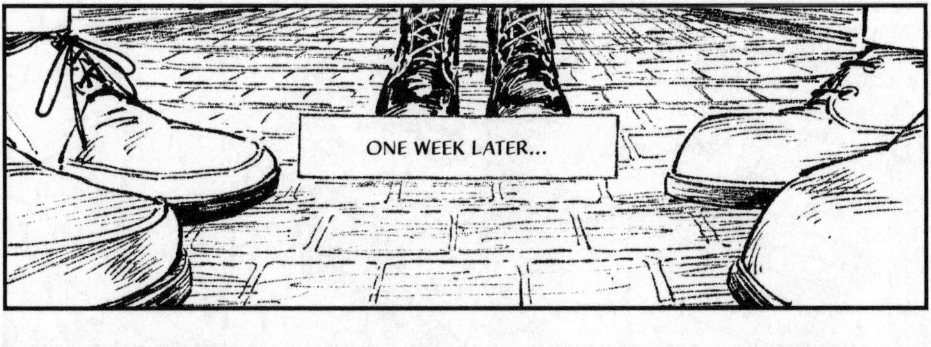
ONE WEEK LATER...

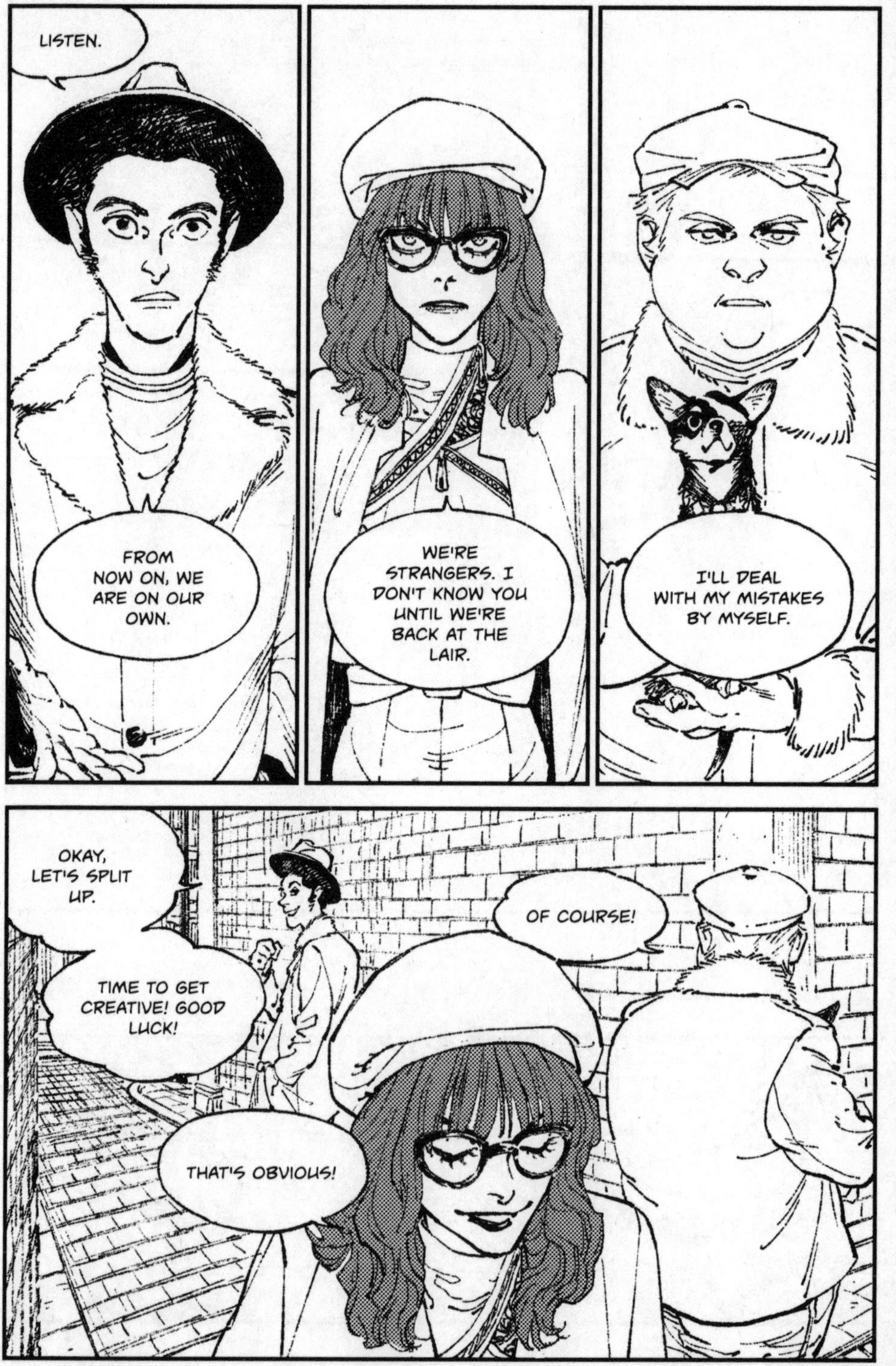
LISTEN.
FROM NOW ON, WE ARE ON OUR OWN.
WE'RE STRANGERS. I DON'T KNOW YOU UNTIL WE'RE BACK AT THE LAIR.
I'LL DEAL WITH MY MISTAKES BY MYSELF.
OKAY, LET'S SPLIT UP.
TIME TO GET CREATIVE! GOOD LUCK!
OF COURSE!
THAT'S OBVIOUS!

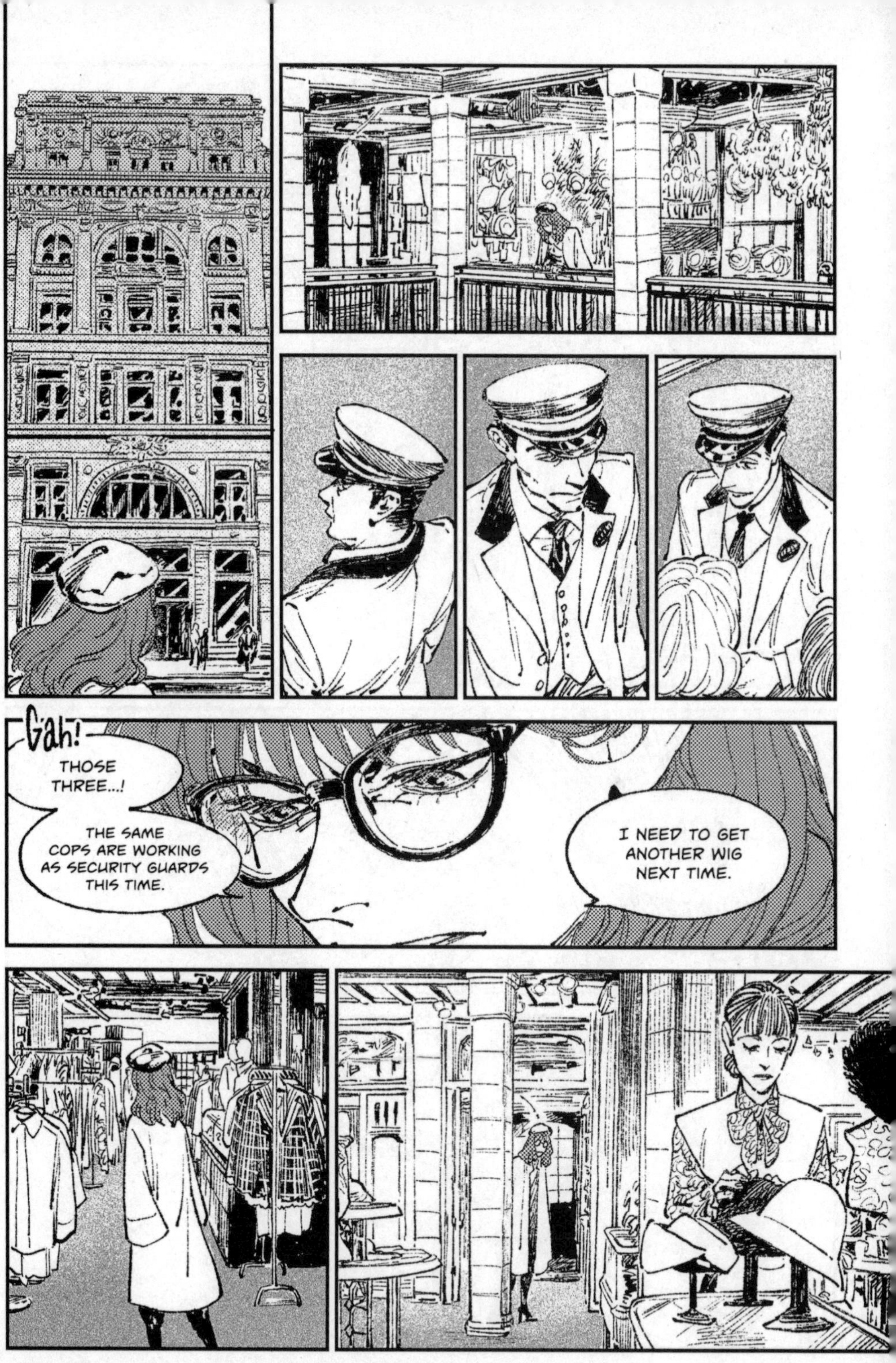
Gah!
THOSE THREE...!
THE SAME COPS ARE WORKING AS SECURITY GUARDS THIS TIME.
I NEED TO GET ANOTHER WIG NEXT TIME.

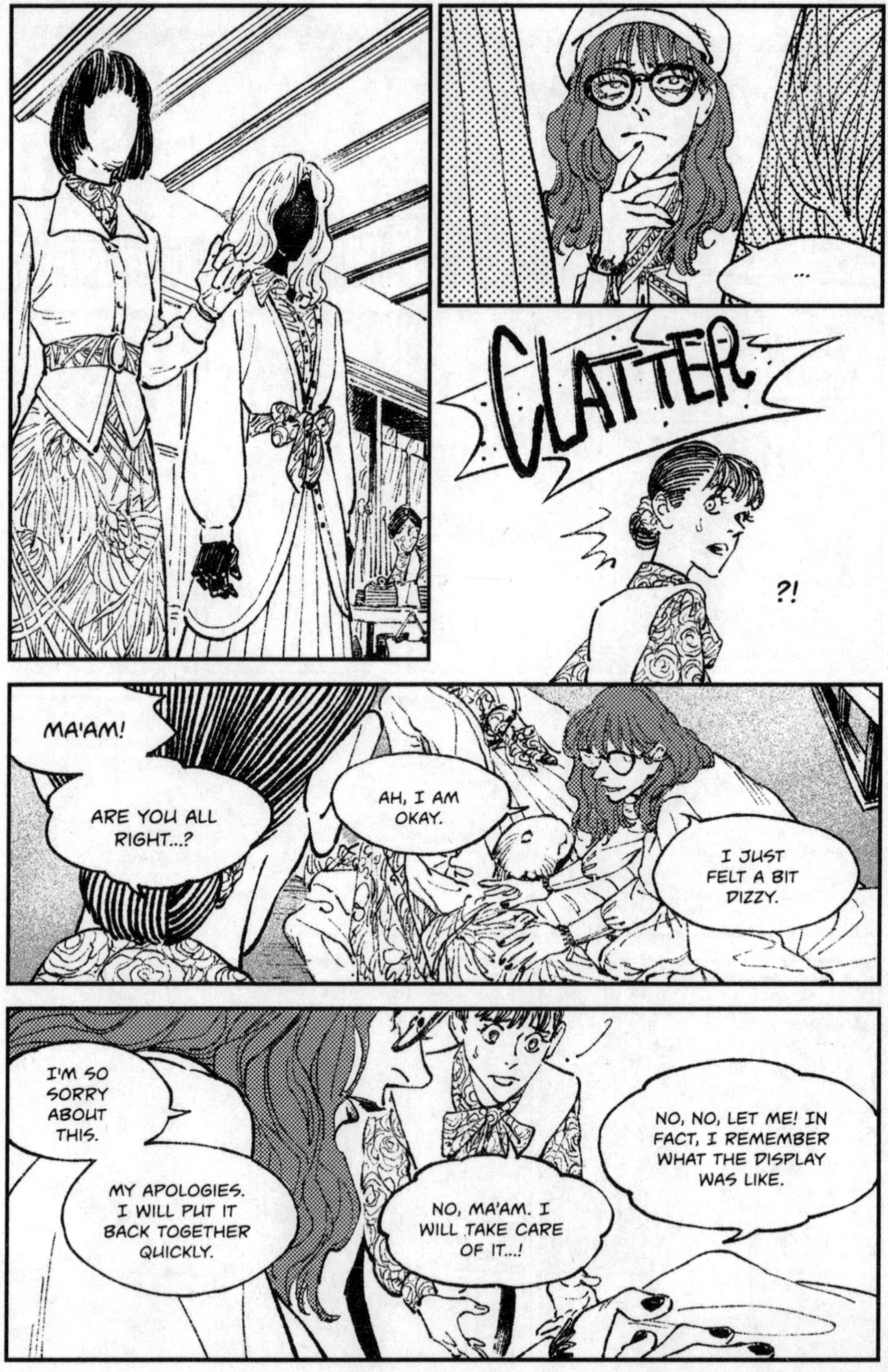
...
CLATTER
?!
MA'AM!
ARE YOU ALL RIGHT...?
AH, I AM OKAY.
I JUST FELT A BIT DIZZY.
I'M SO SORRY ABOUT THIS.
MY APOLOGIES. I WILL PUT IT BACK TOGETHER QUICKLY.
NO, MA'AM. I WILL TAKE CARE OF IT...!
NO, NO, LET ME! IN FACT, I REMEMBER WHAT THE DISPLAY WAS LIKE.

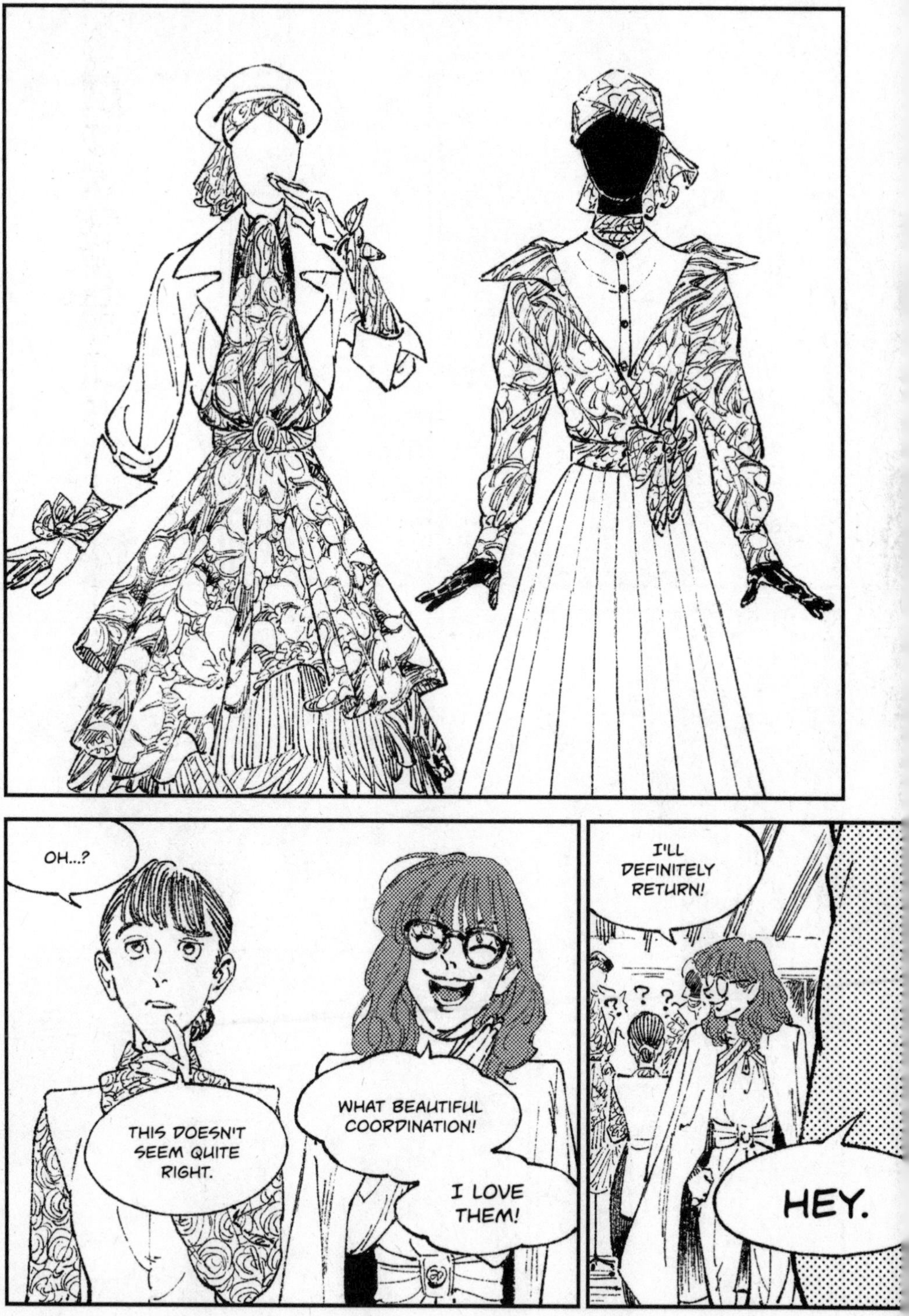
OH...?
THIS DOESN'T SEEM QUITE RIGHT.
WHAT BEAUTIFUL COORDINATION!
I LOVE THEM!
I'LL DEFINITELY RETURN!
? ?
HEY.

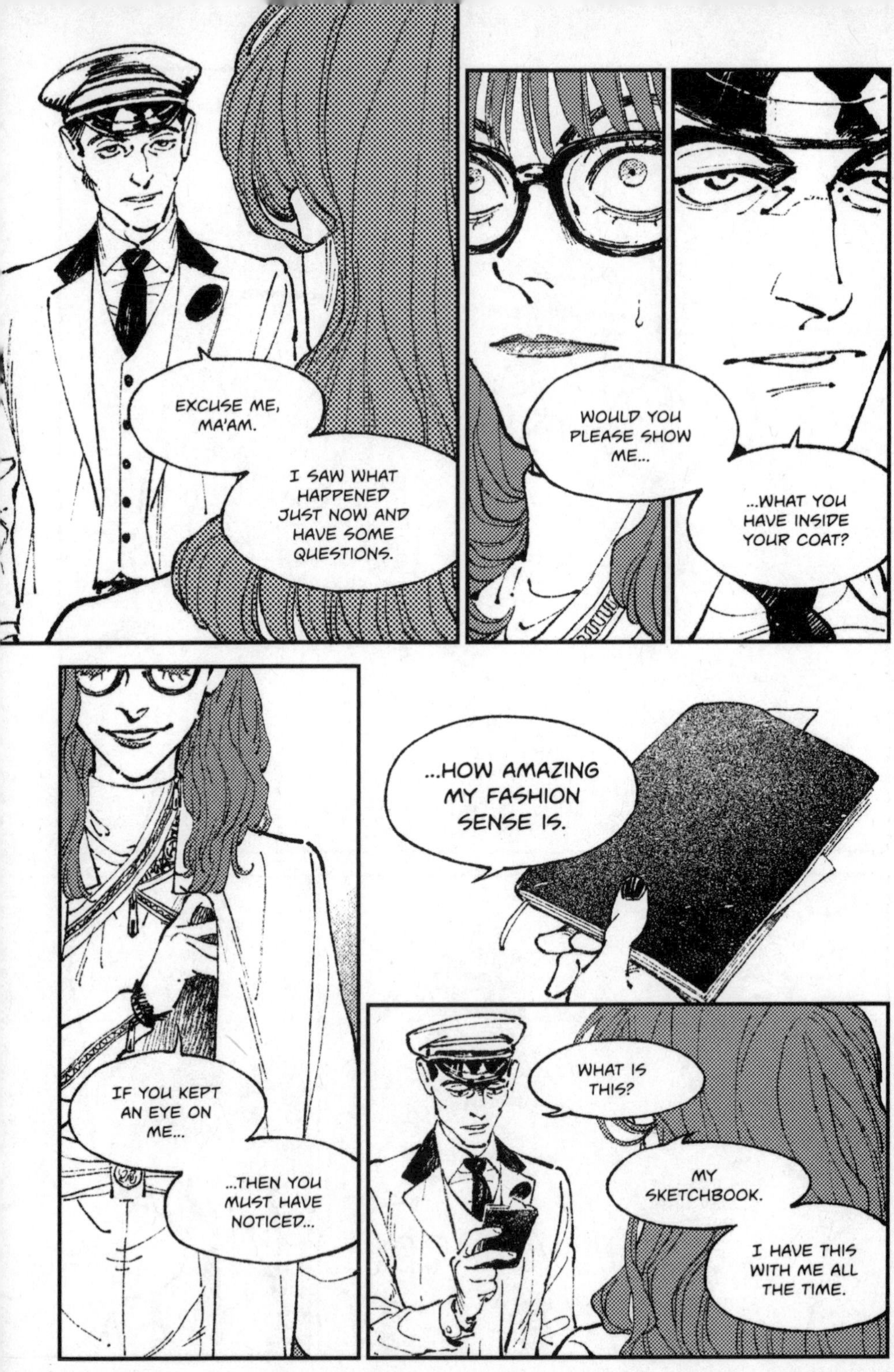
EXCUSE ME, MA'AM.
I SAW WHAT HAPPENED JUST NOW AND HAVE SOME QUESTIONS.
WOULD YOU PLEASE SHOW ME...
...WHAT YOU HAVE INSIDE YOUR COAT?
IF YOU KEPT AN EYE ON ME...
...THEN YOU MUST HAVE NOTICED...
...HOW AMAZING MY FASHION SENSE IS.
WHAT IS THIS?
MY SKETCHBOOK.
I HAVE THIS WITH ME ALL THE TIME.

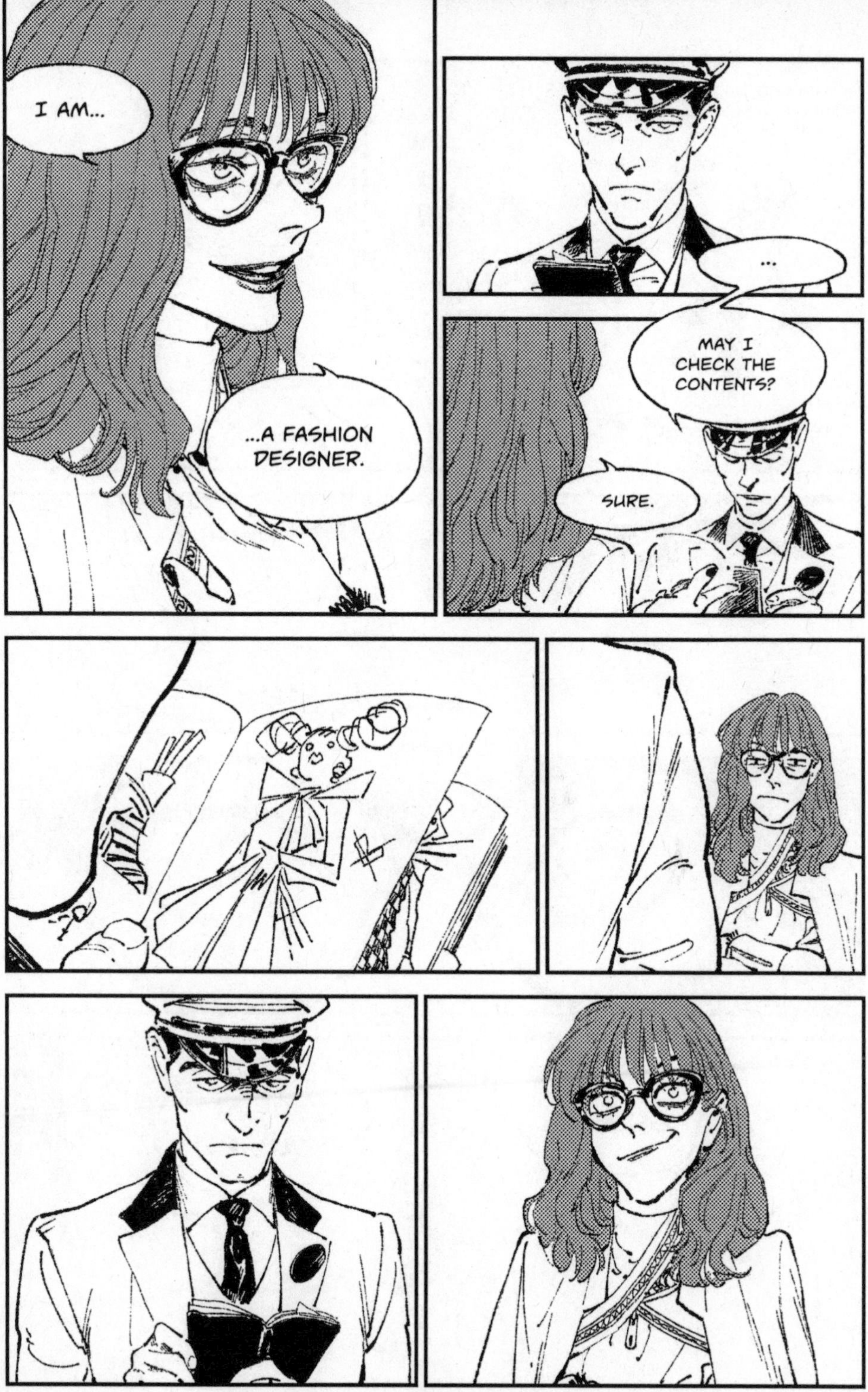
I AM...
...A FASHION DESIGNER.
...
MAY I CHECK THE CONTENTS?
SURE.

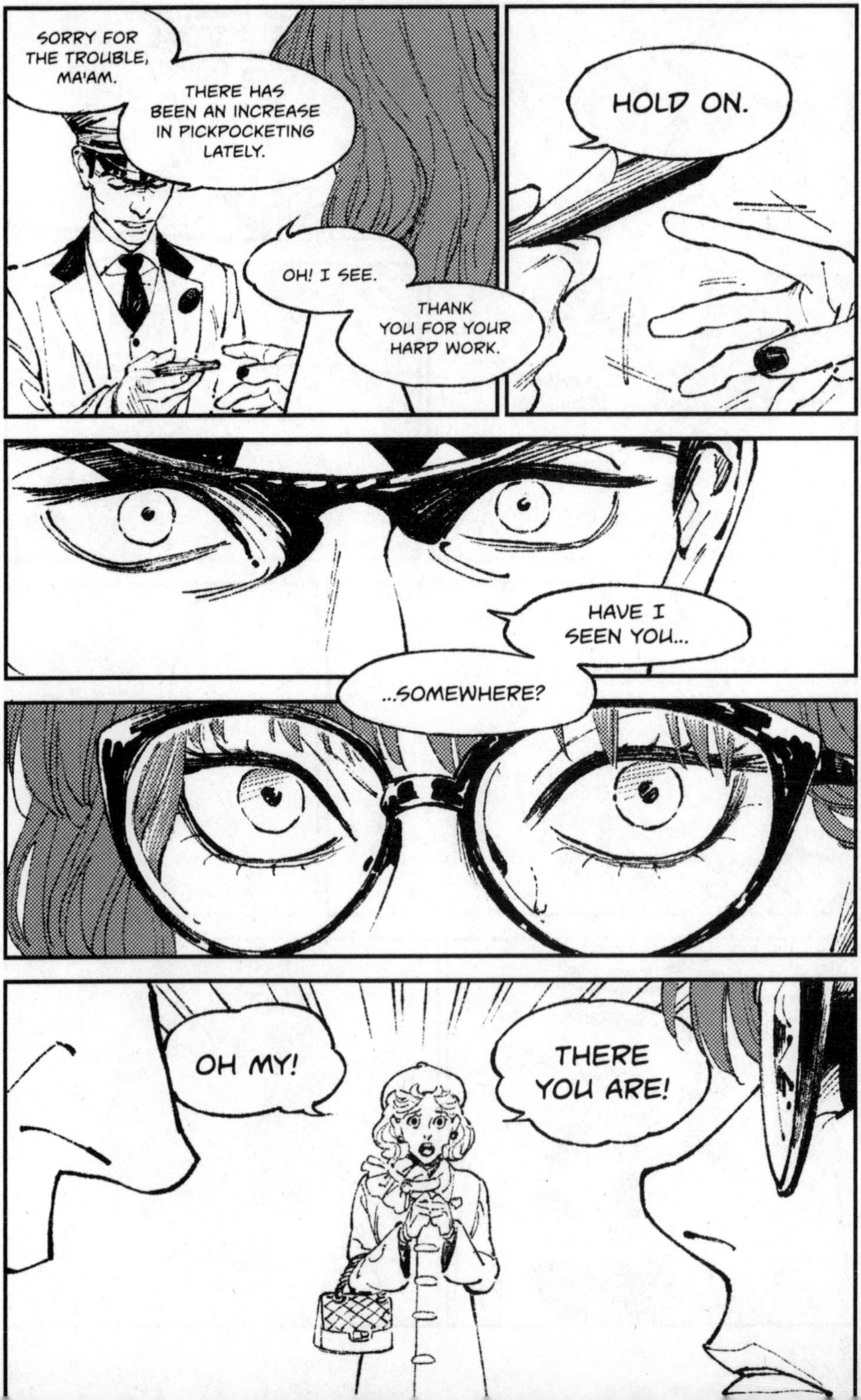
SORRY FOR THE TROUBLE, MA'AM.
THERE HAS BEEN AN INCREASE IN PICKPOCKETING LATELY.
OH! I SEE.
THANK YOU FOR YOUR HARD WORK.
HOLD ON.
HAVE I SEEN YOU...
...SOMEWHERE?
OH MY!
THERE YOU ARE!

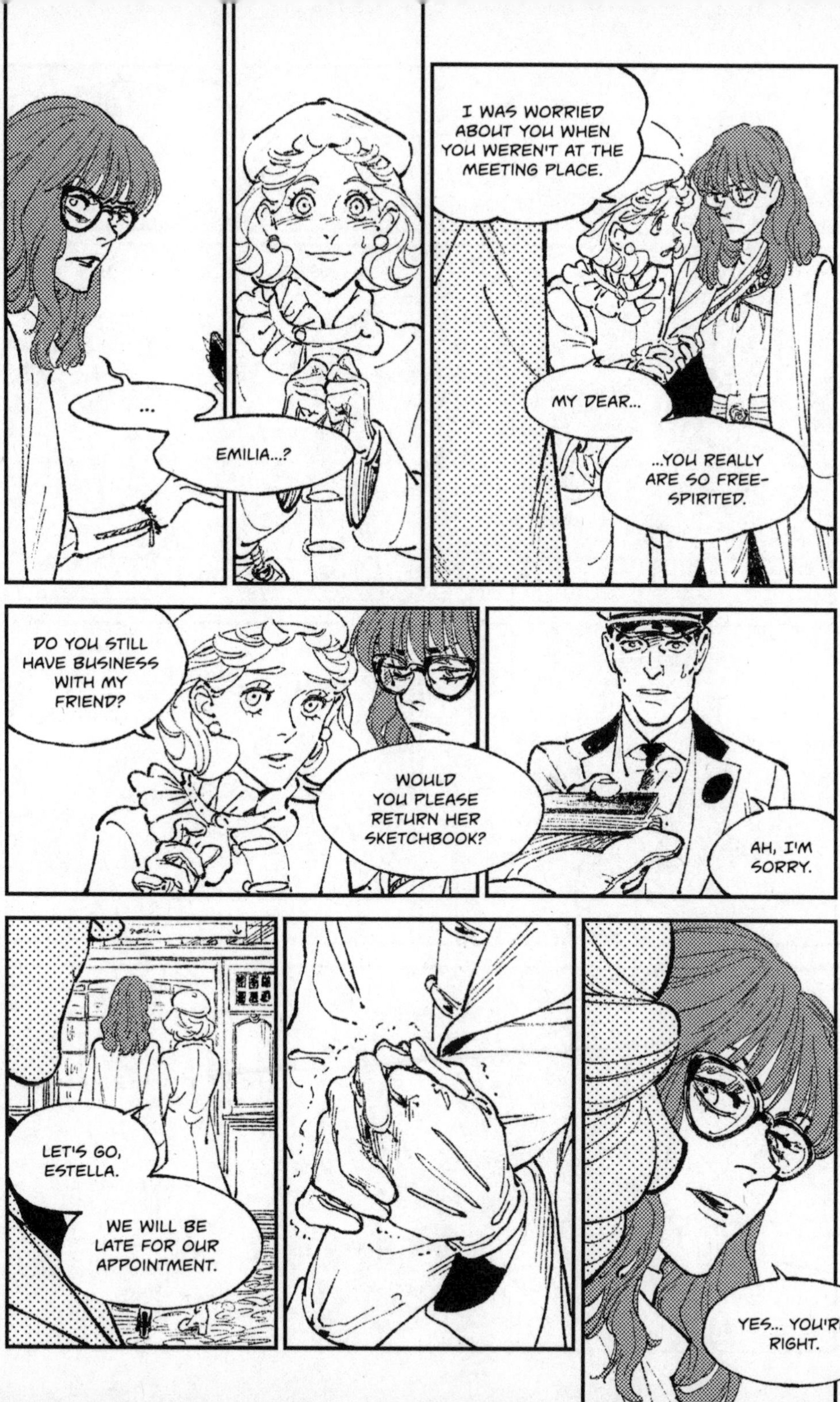
...
EMILIA...?
I WAS WORRIED ABOUT YOU WHEN YOU WEREN'T AT THE MEETING PLACE.
MY DEAR...
...YOU REALLY ARE SO FREE-SPIRITED.
DO YOU STILL HAVE BUSINESS WITH MY FRIEND?
WOULD YOU PLEASE RETURN HER SKETCHBOOK?
AH, I'M SORRY.
LET'S GO, ESTELLA.
WE WILL BE LATE FOR OUR APPOINTMENT.
YES... YOU'RE RIGHT.

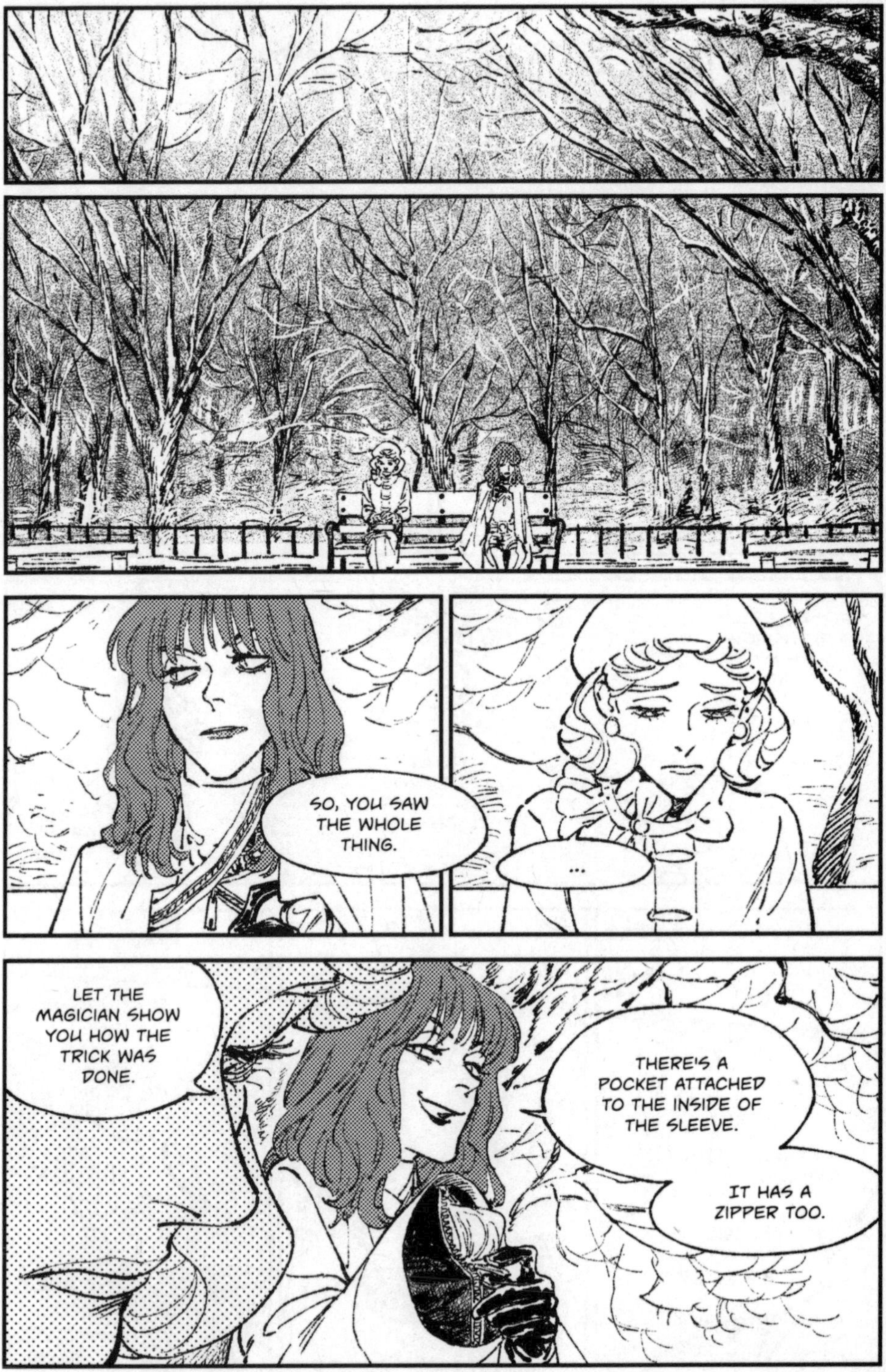
SO, YOU SAW THE WHOLE THING.
...
LET THE MAGICIAN SHOW YOU HOW THE TRICK WAS DONE.
THERE'S A POCKET ATTACHED TO THE INSIDE OF THE SLEEVE.
IT HAS A ZIPPER TOO.

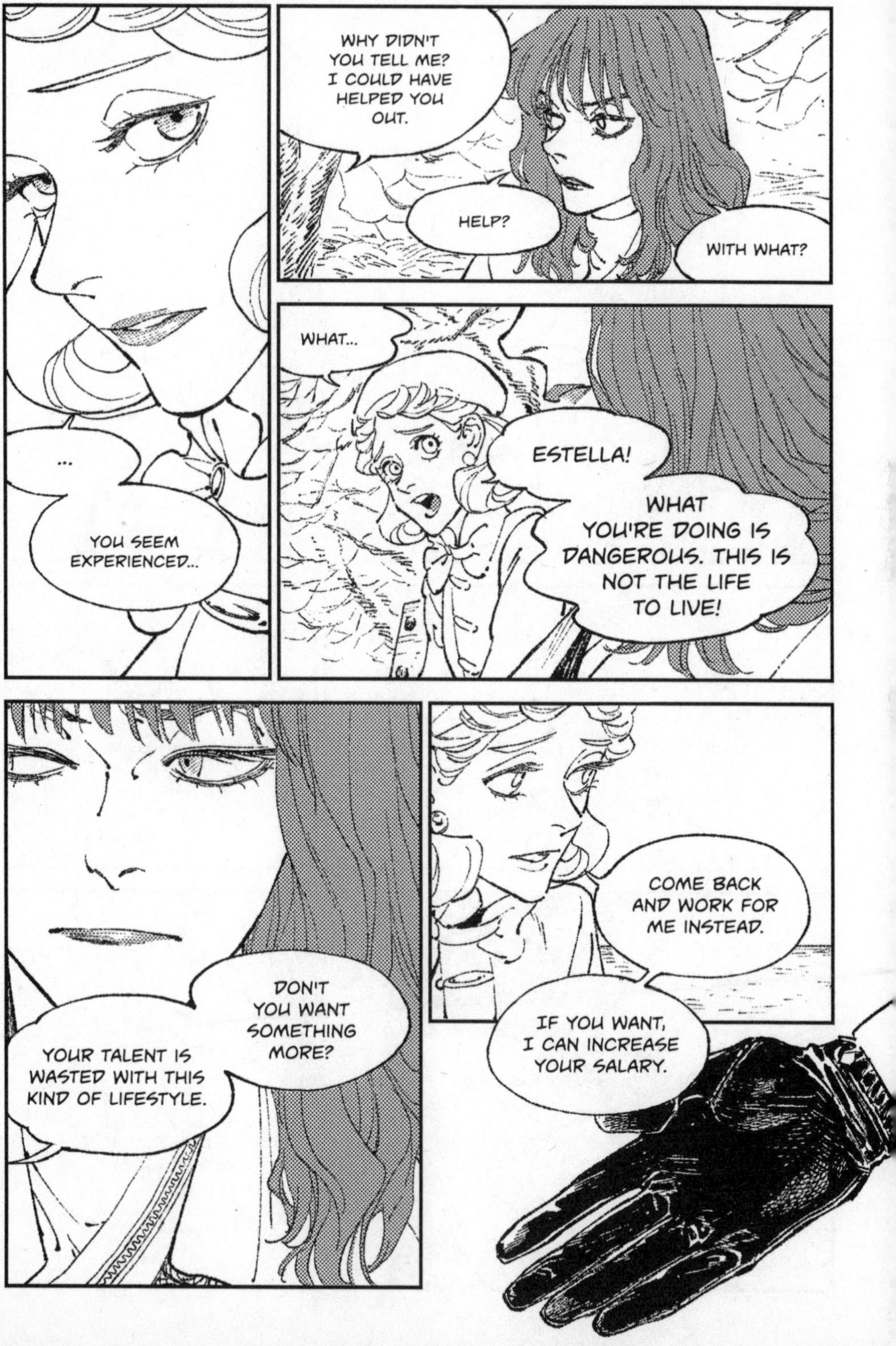
WHY DIDN'T YOU TELL ME? I COULD HAVE HELPED YOU OUT.
HELP?
WITH WHAT?
...
YOU SEEM EXPERIENCED...
WHAT...
ESTELLA!
WHAT YOU'RE DOING IS DANGEROUS. THIS IS NOT THE LIFE TO LIVE!
YOUR TALENT IS WASTED WITH THIS KIND OF LIFESTYLE.
DON'T YOU WANT SOMETHING MORE?
COME BACK AND WORK FOR ME INSTEAD.
IF YOU WANT, I CAN INCREASE YOUR SALARY.

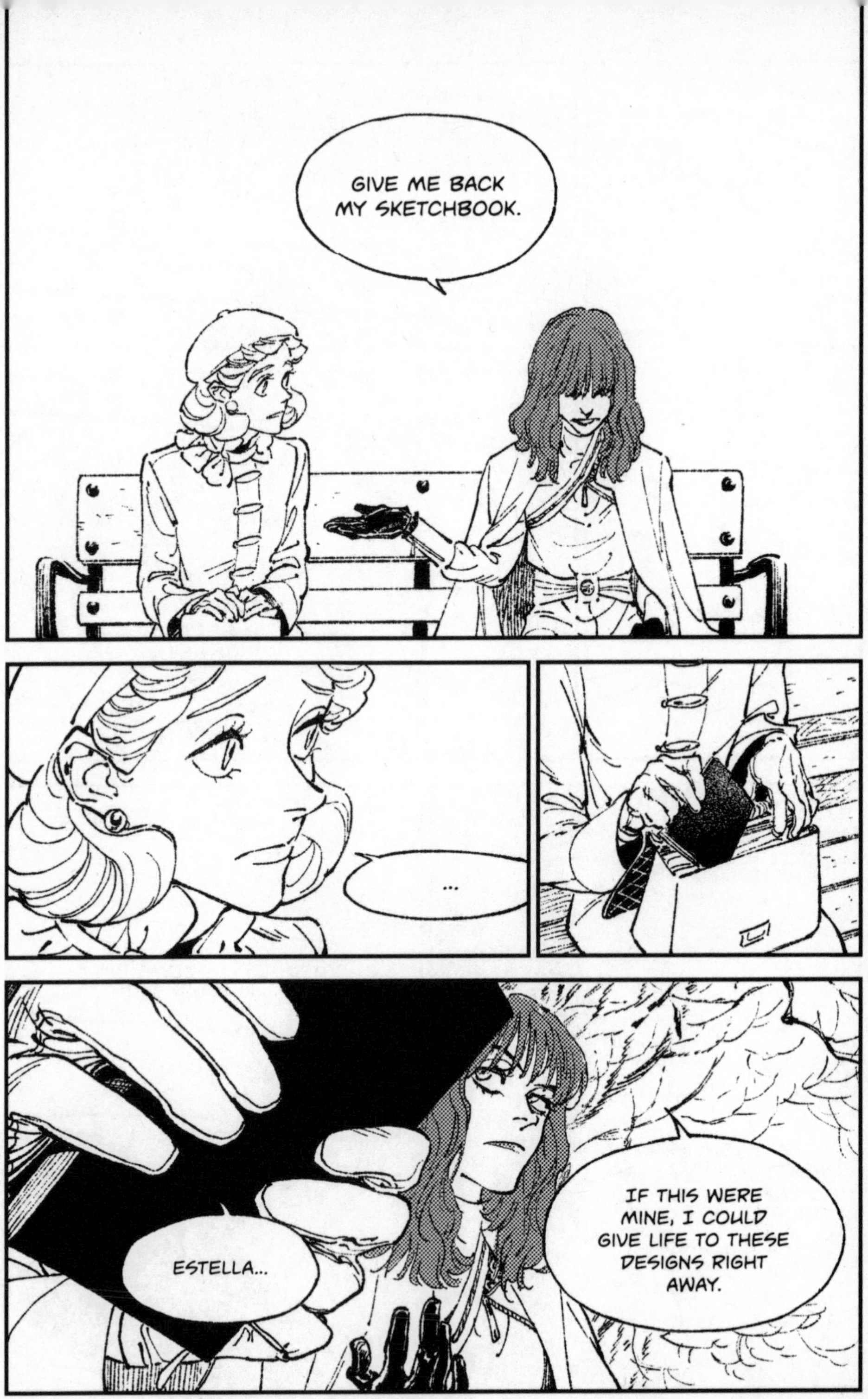
GIVE ME BACK MY SKETCHBOOK.
...
IF THIS WERE MINE, I COULD GIVE LIFE TO THESE DESIGNS RIGHT AWAY.
ESTELLA...

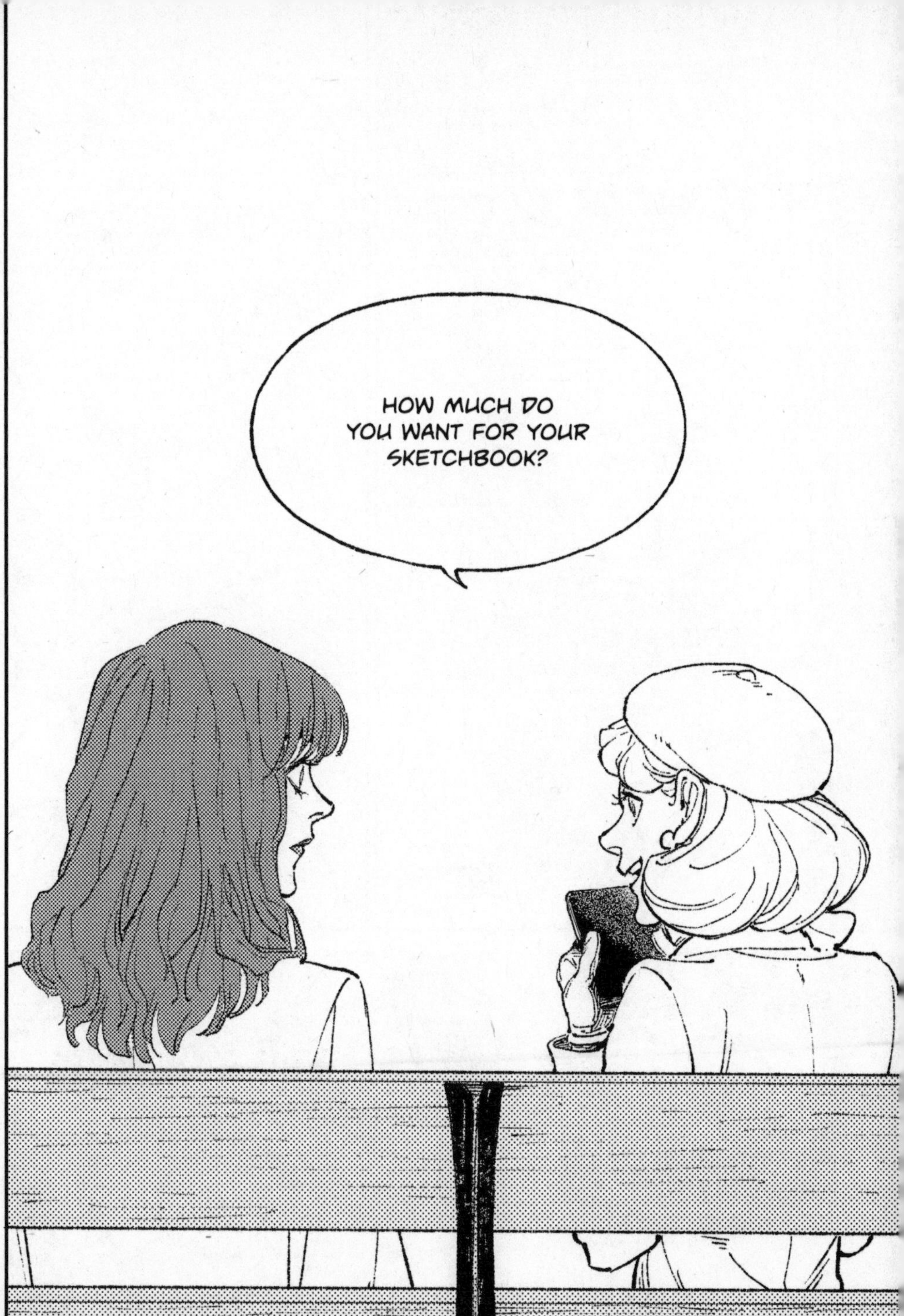
HOW MUCH DO YOU WANT FOR YOUR SKETCHBOOK?

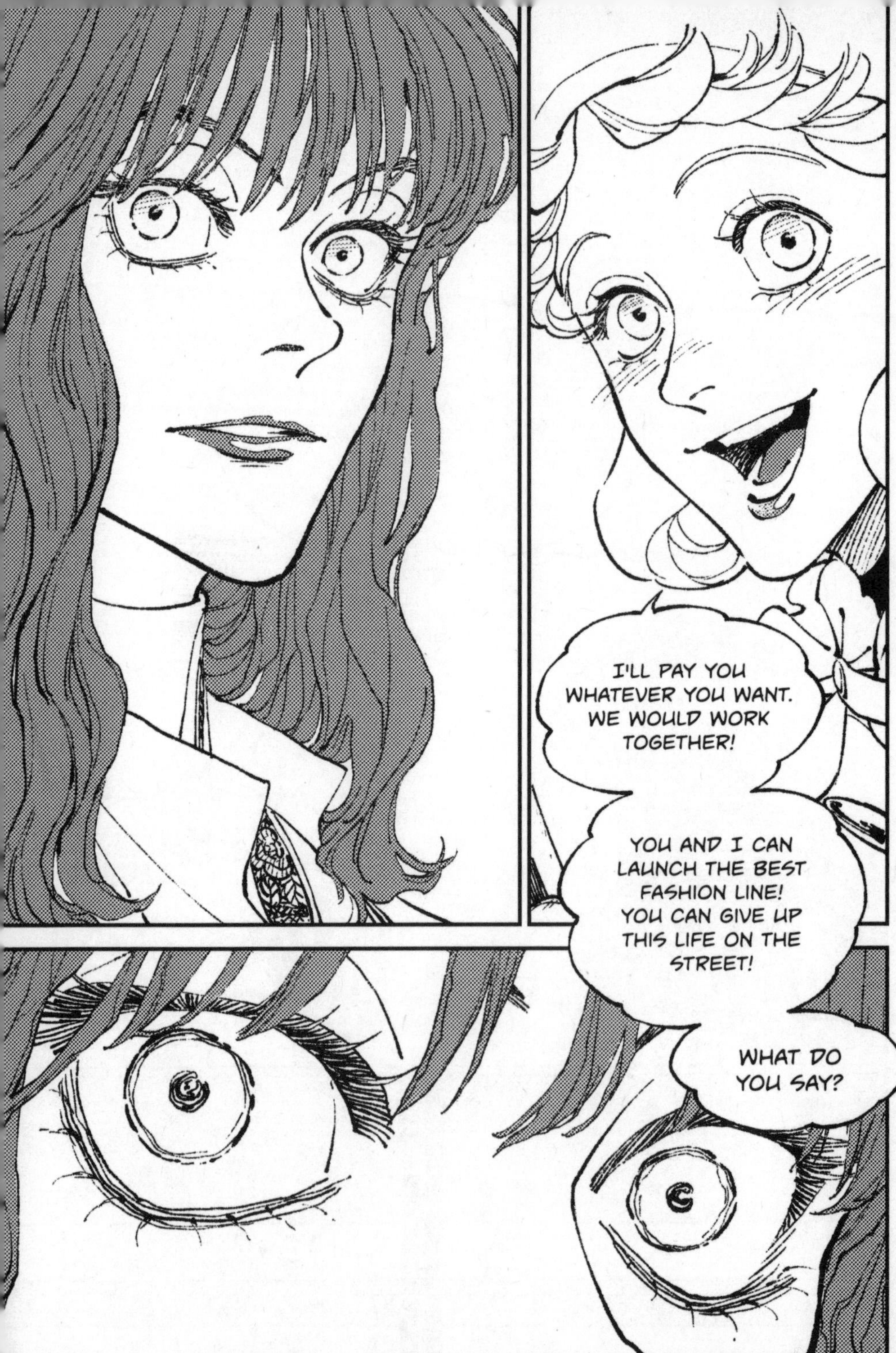
I'LL PAY YOU WHATEVER YOU WANT. WE WOULD WORK TOGETHER!
YOU AND I CAN LAUNCH THE BEST FASHION LINE! YOU CAN GIVE UP THIS LIFE ON THE STREET!
WHAT DO YOU SAY?

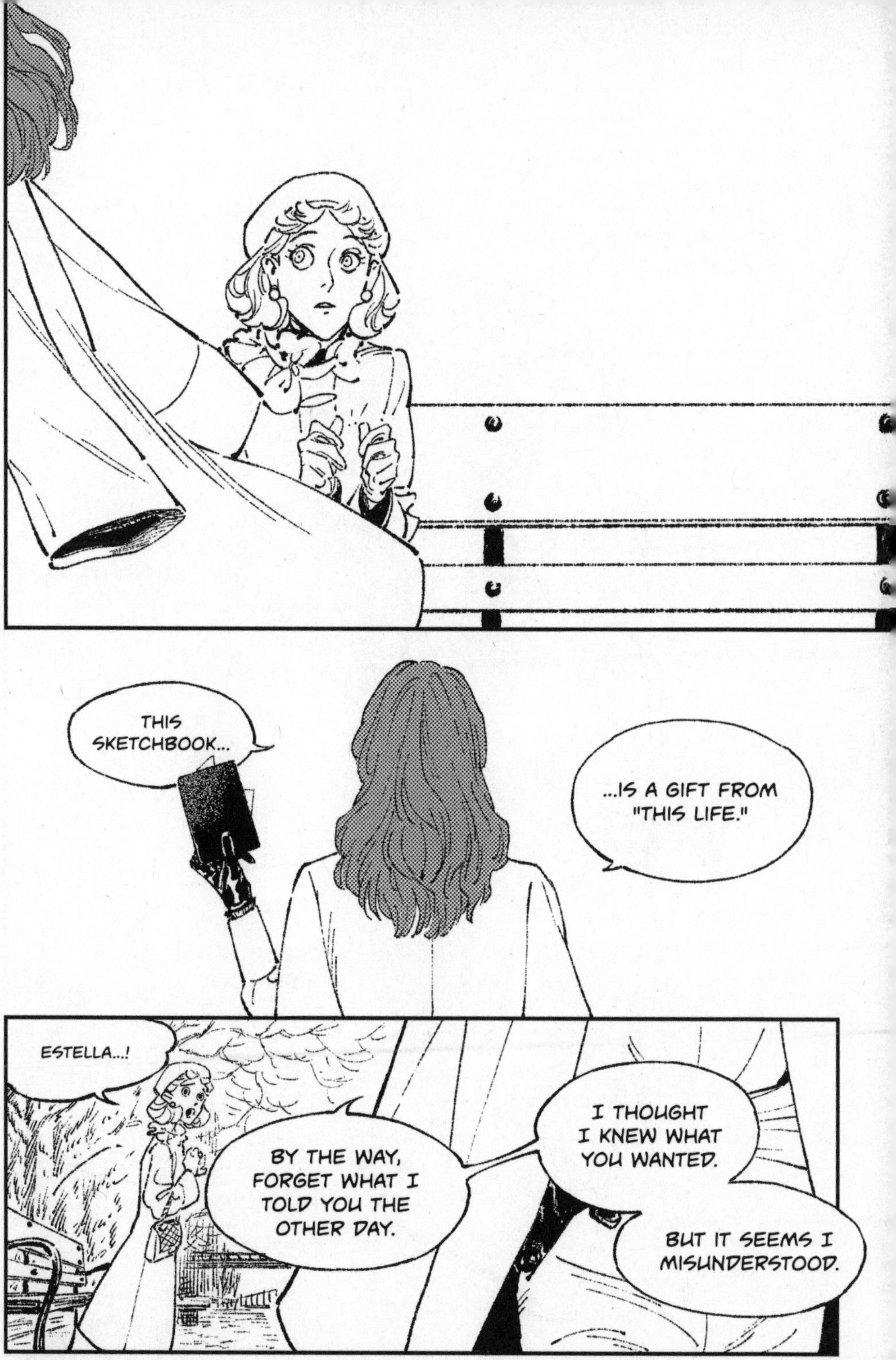
THIS SKETCHBOOK...
...IS A GIFT FROM "THIS LIFE."
ESTELLA...!
BY THE WAY, FORGET WHAT I TOLD YOU THE OTHER DAY.
I THOUGHT I KNEW WHAT YOU WANTED.
BUT IT SEEMS I MISUNDERSTOOD.

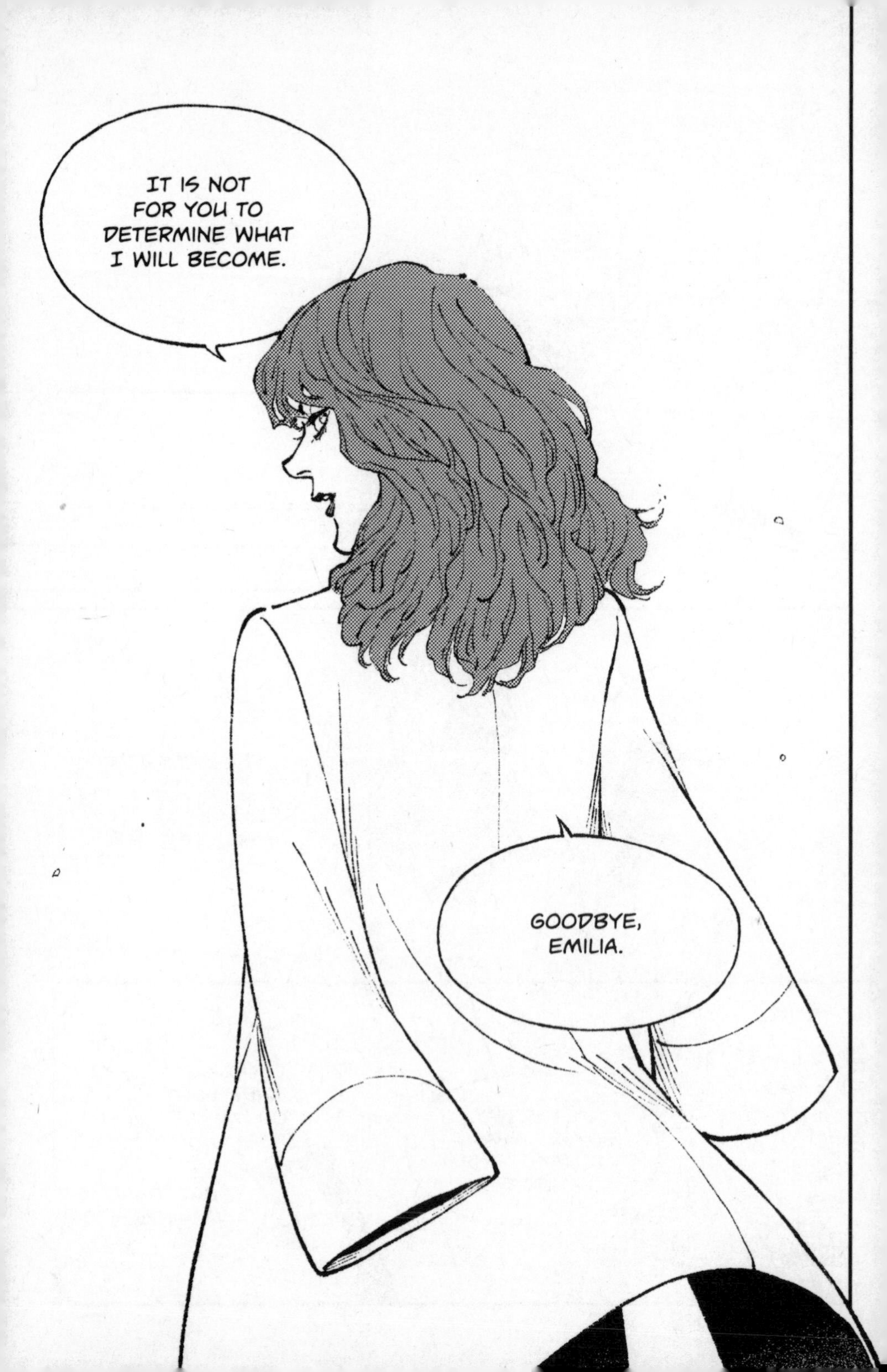
IT IS NOT FOR YOU TO DETERMINE WHAT I WILL BECOME.
GOODBYE, EMILIA.

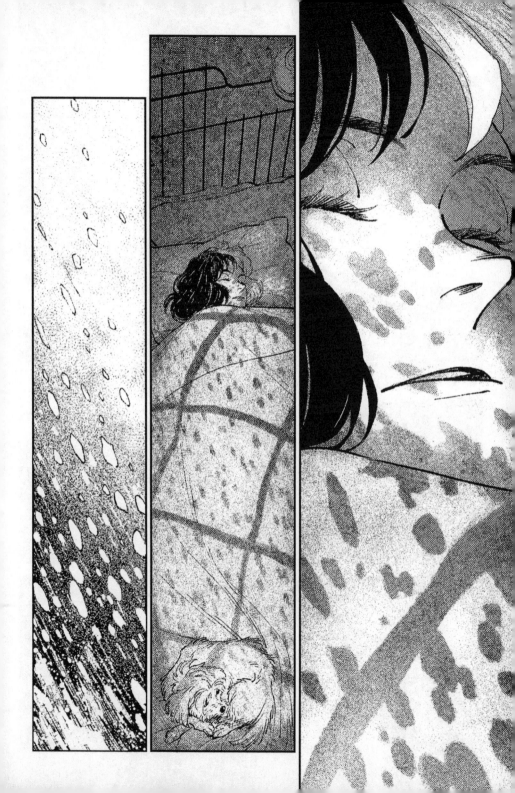

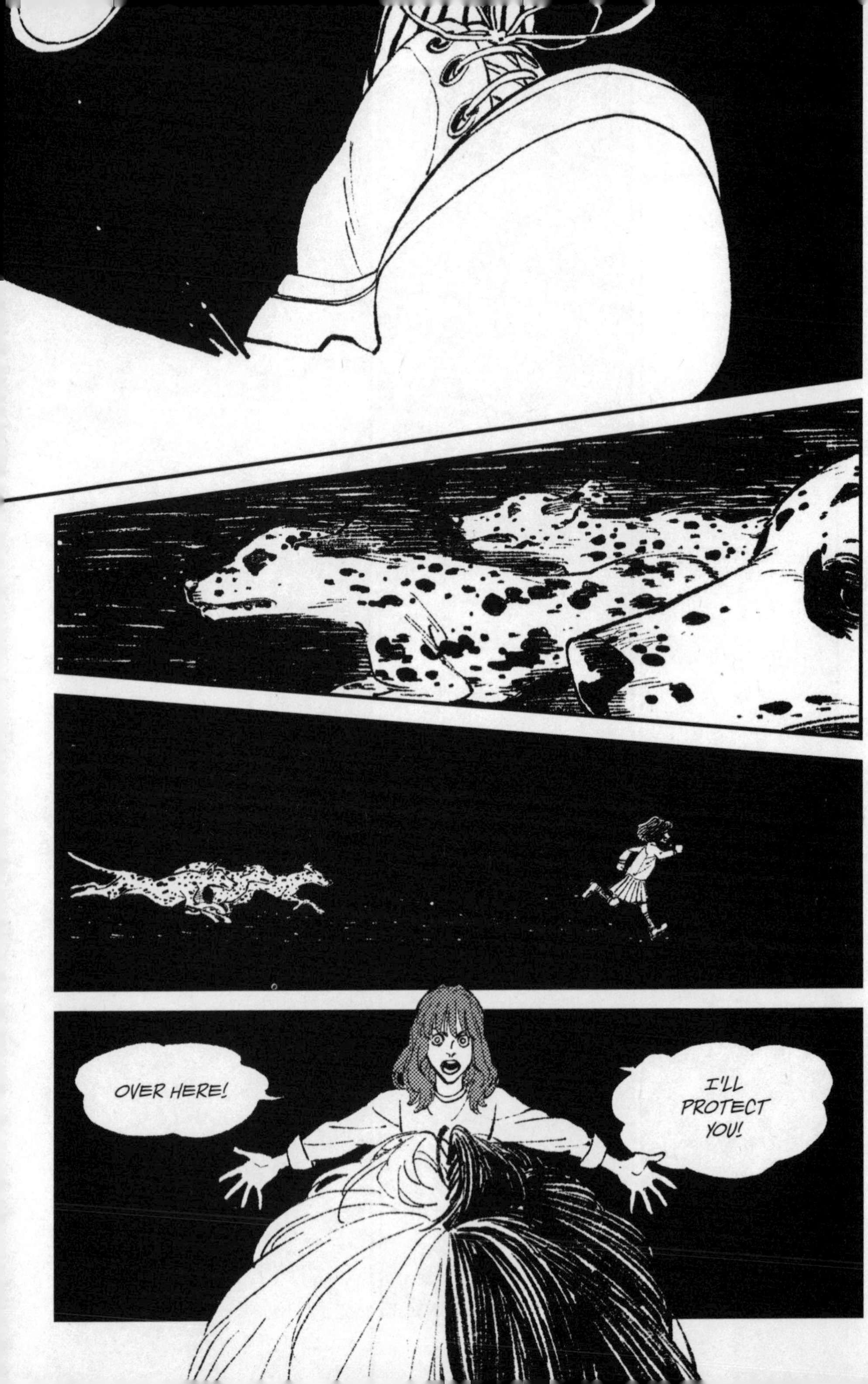
OVER HERE!
I'LL PROTECT YOU!

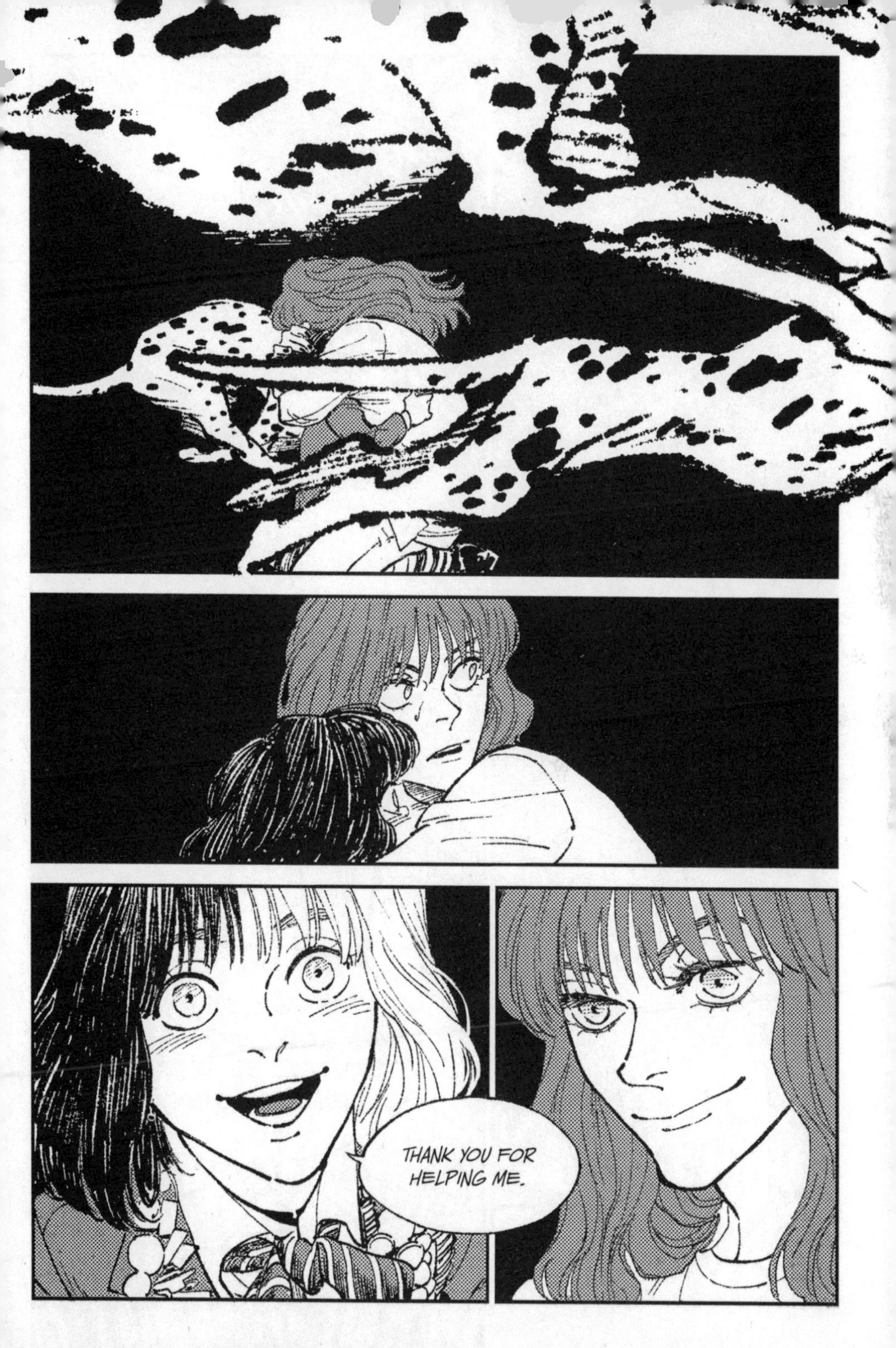
THANK YOU FOR HELPING ME.

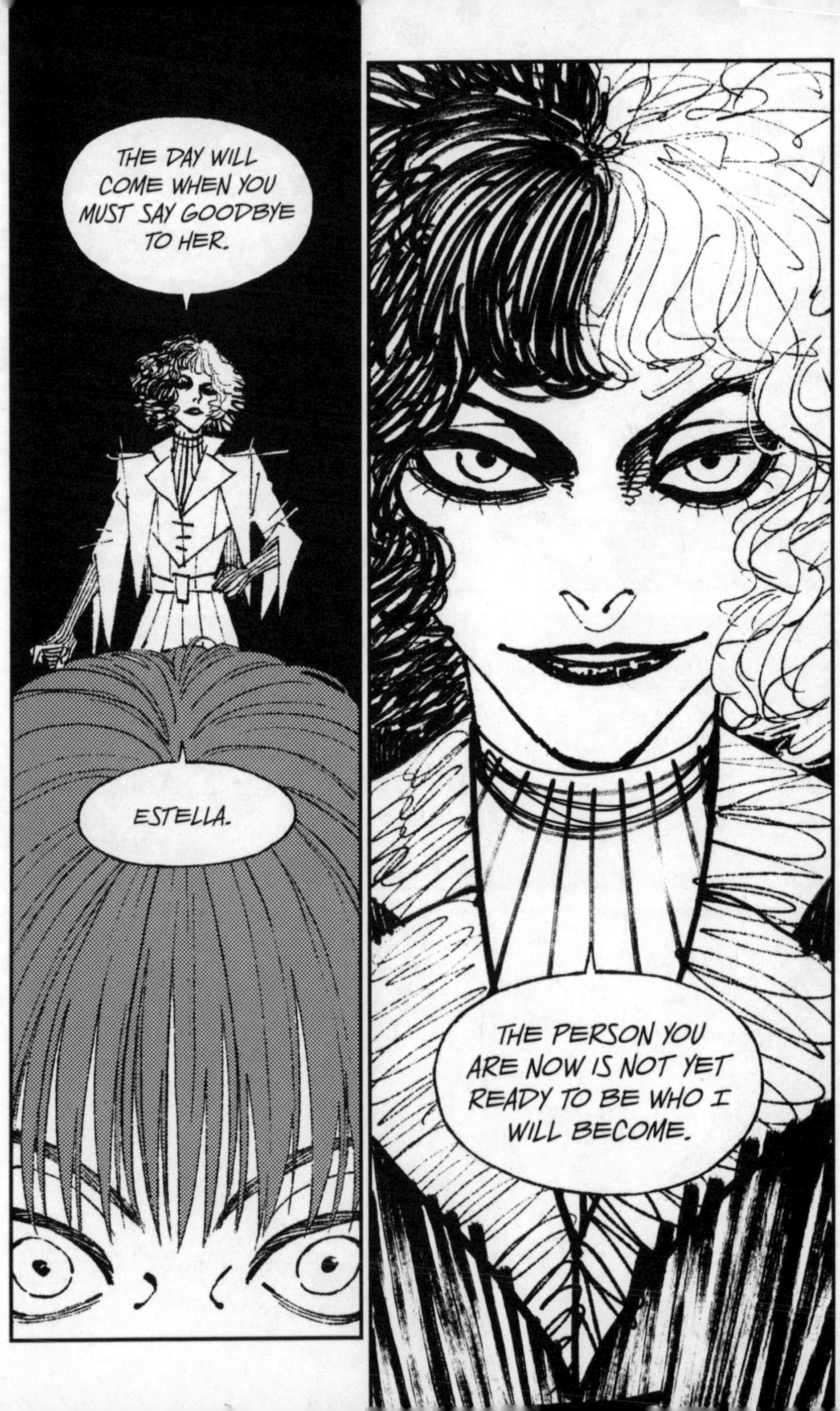
THE DAY WILL COME WHEN YOU MUST SAY GOODBYE TO HER.
ESTELLA.
THE PERSON YOU ARE NOW IS NOT YET READY TO BE WHO I WILL BECOME.

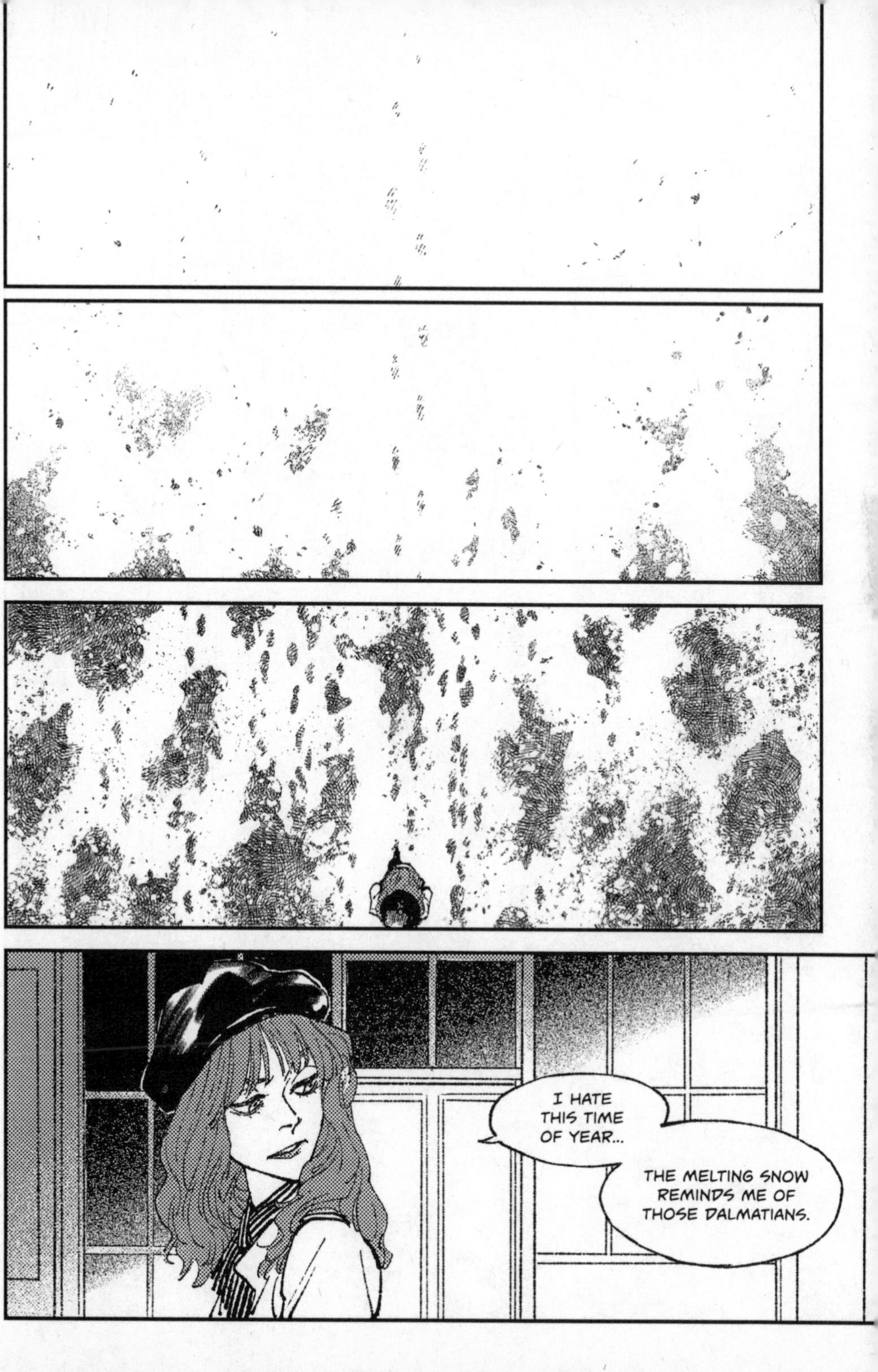
I HATE THIS TIME OF YEAR...
THE MELTING SNOW REMINDS ME OF THOSE DALMATIANS.

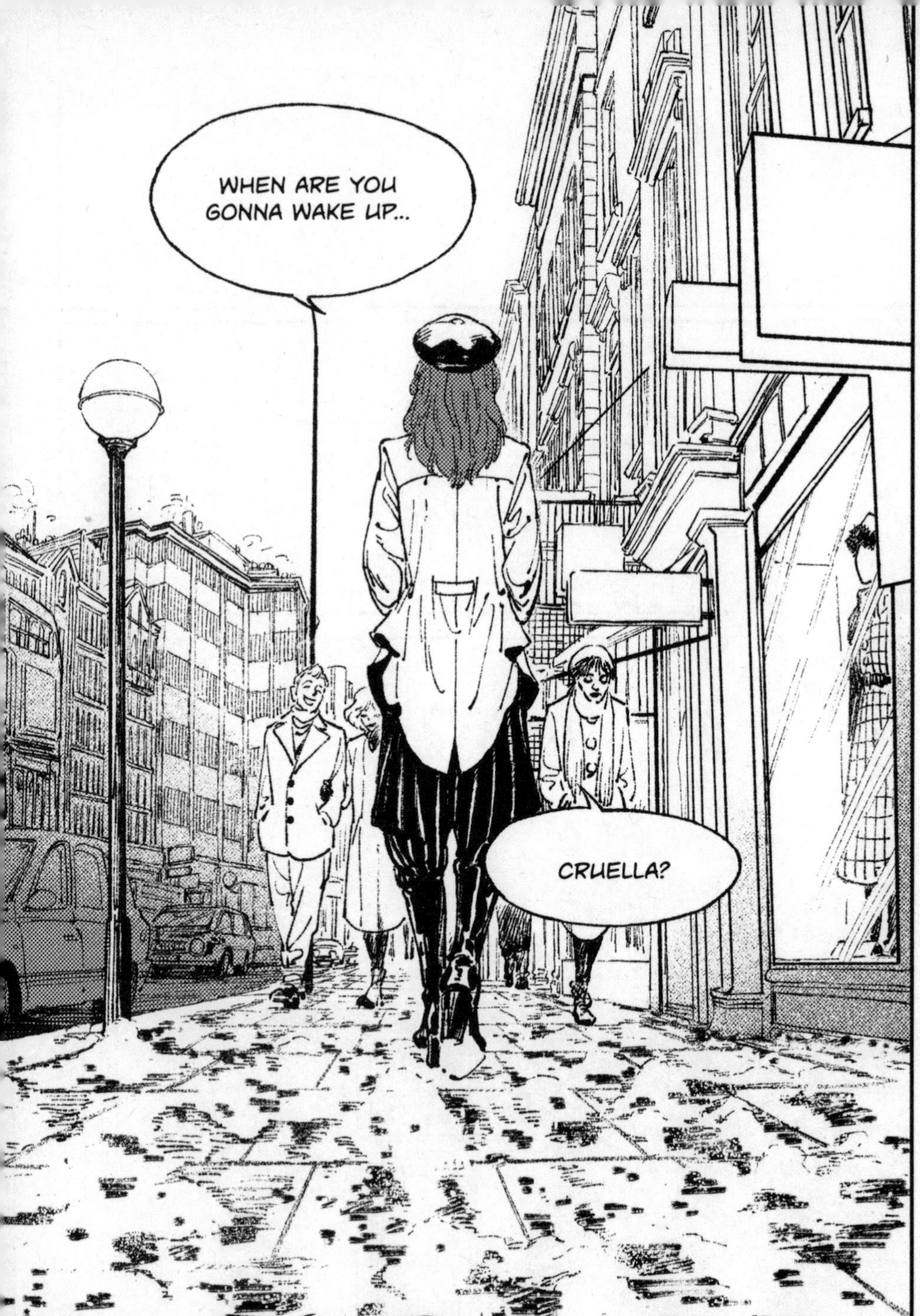
WHEN ARE YOU GONNA WAKE UP...
CRUELLA?

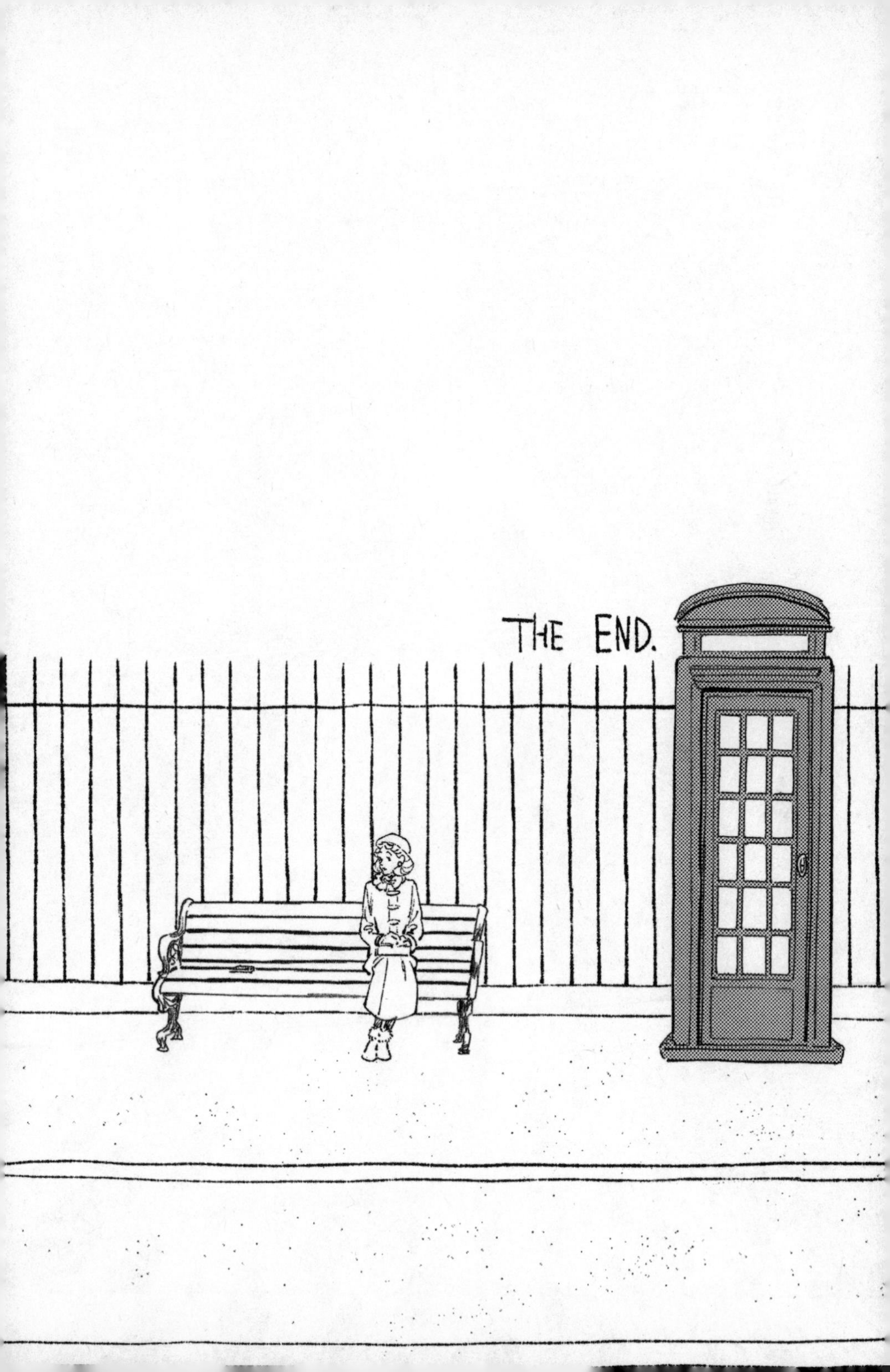
THE END.

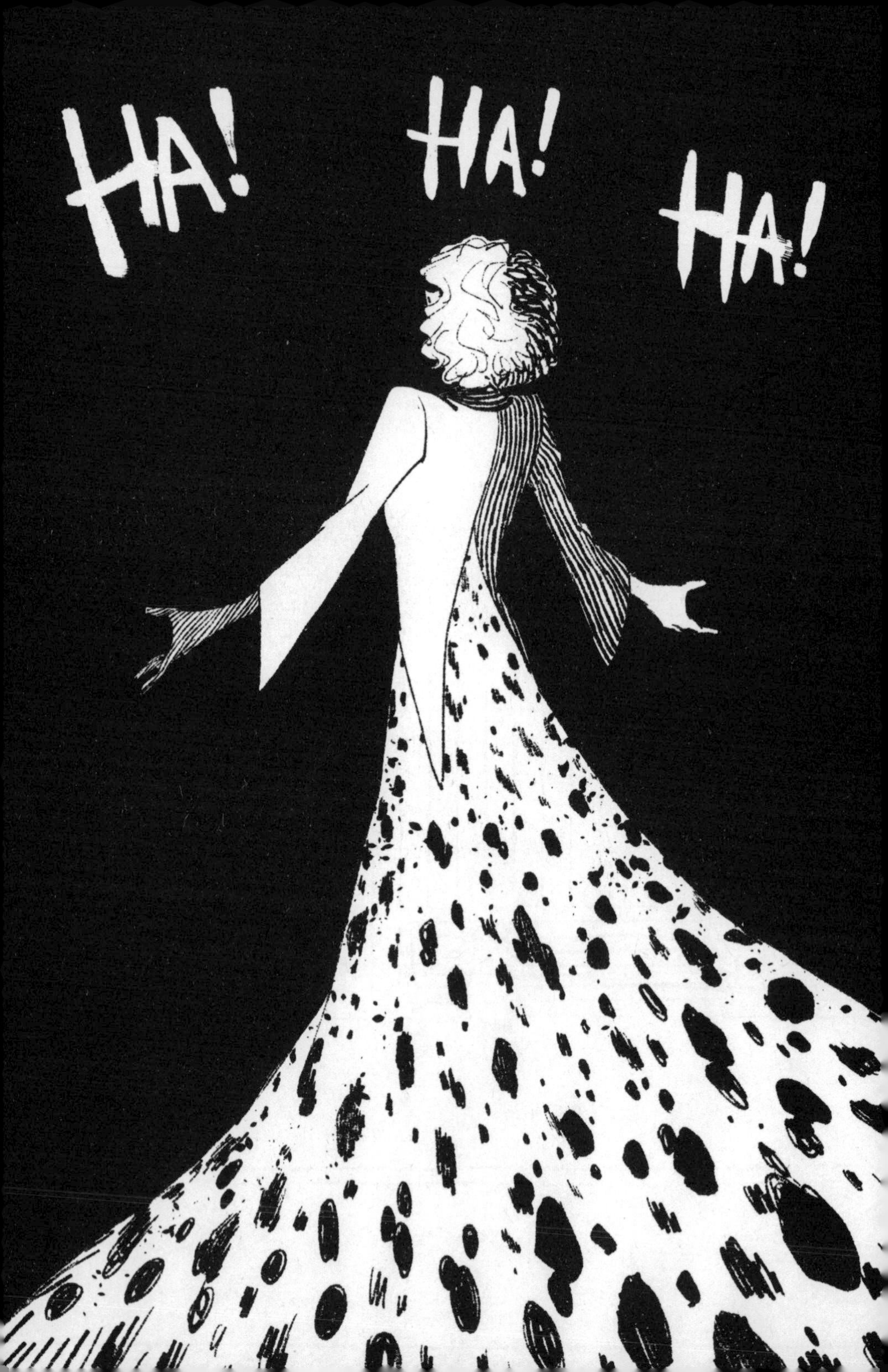
HA!
HA!
HA!

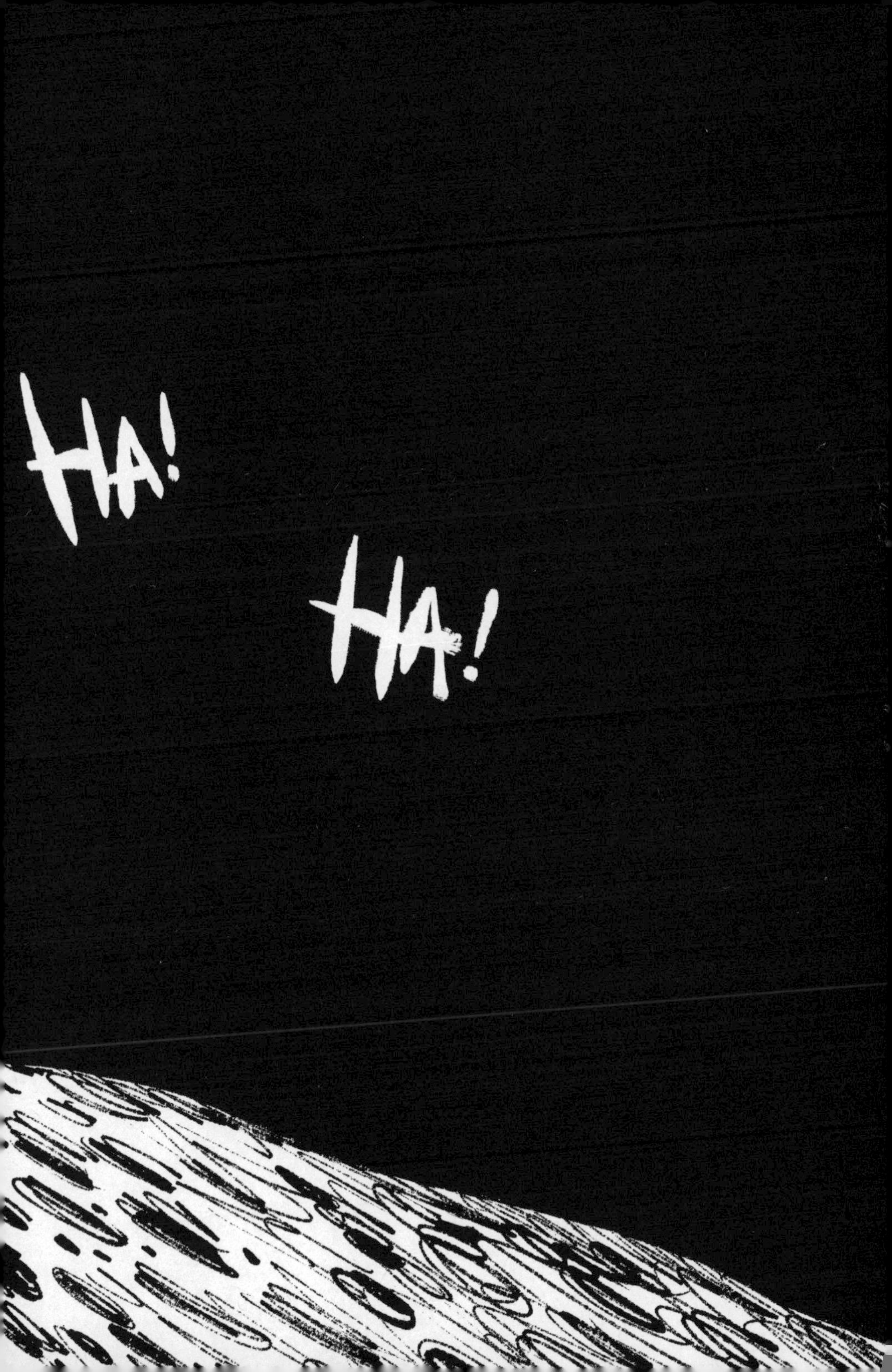
HA!
HA!

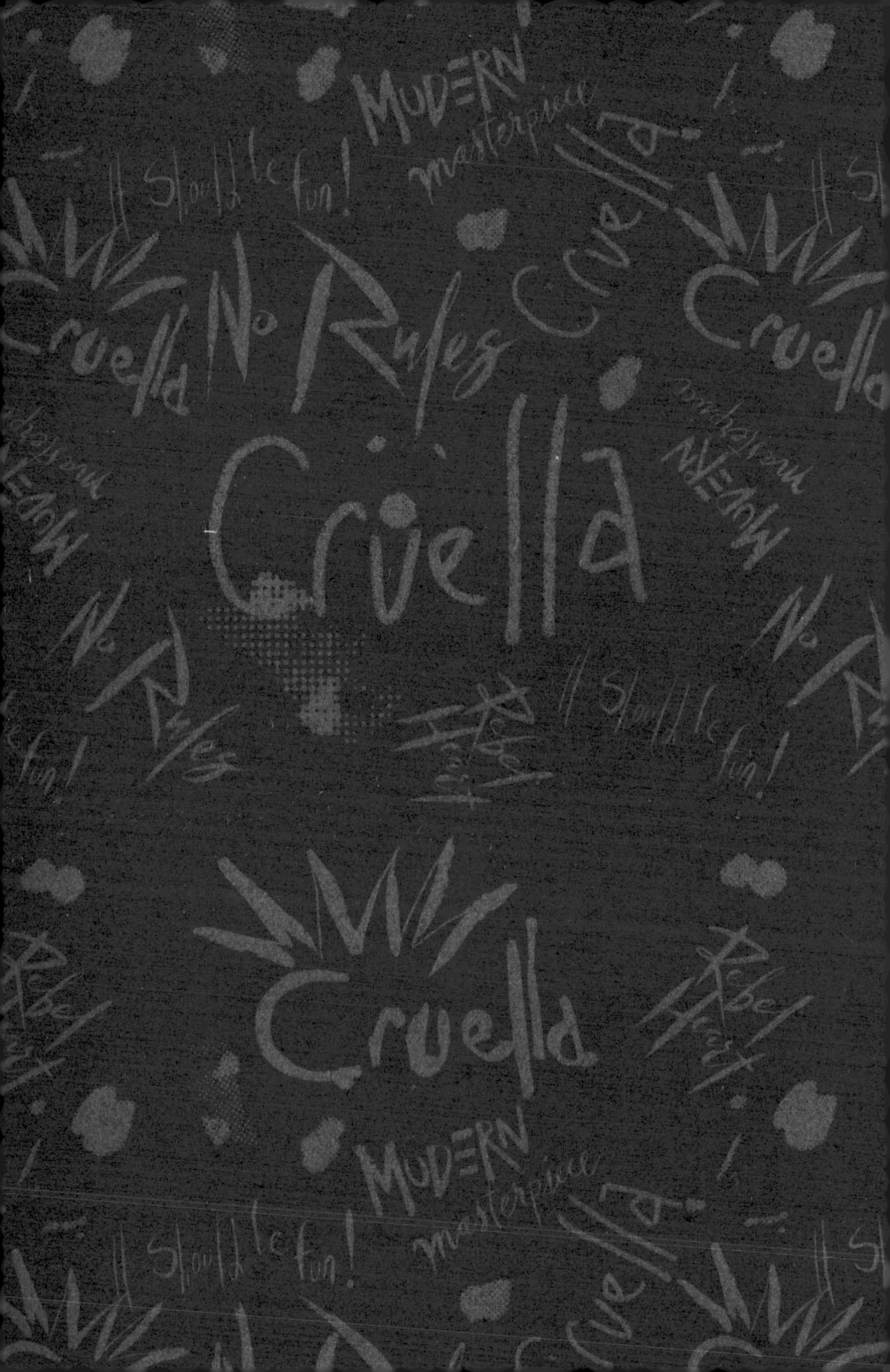
Cruella
No Rules
It should be fun!
Modern masterpiece
Rebel Heart

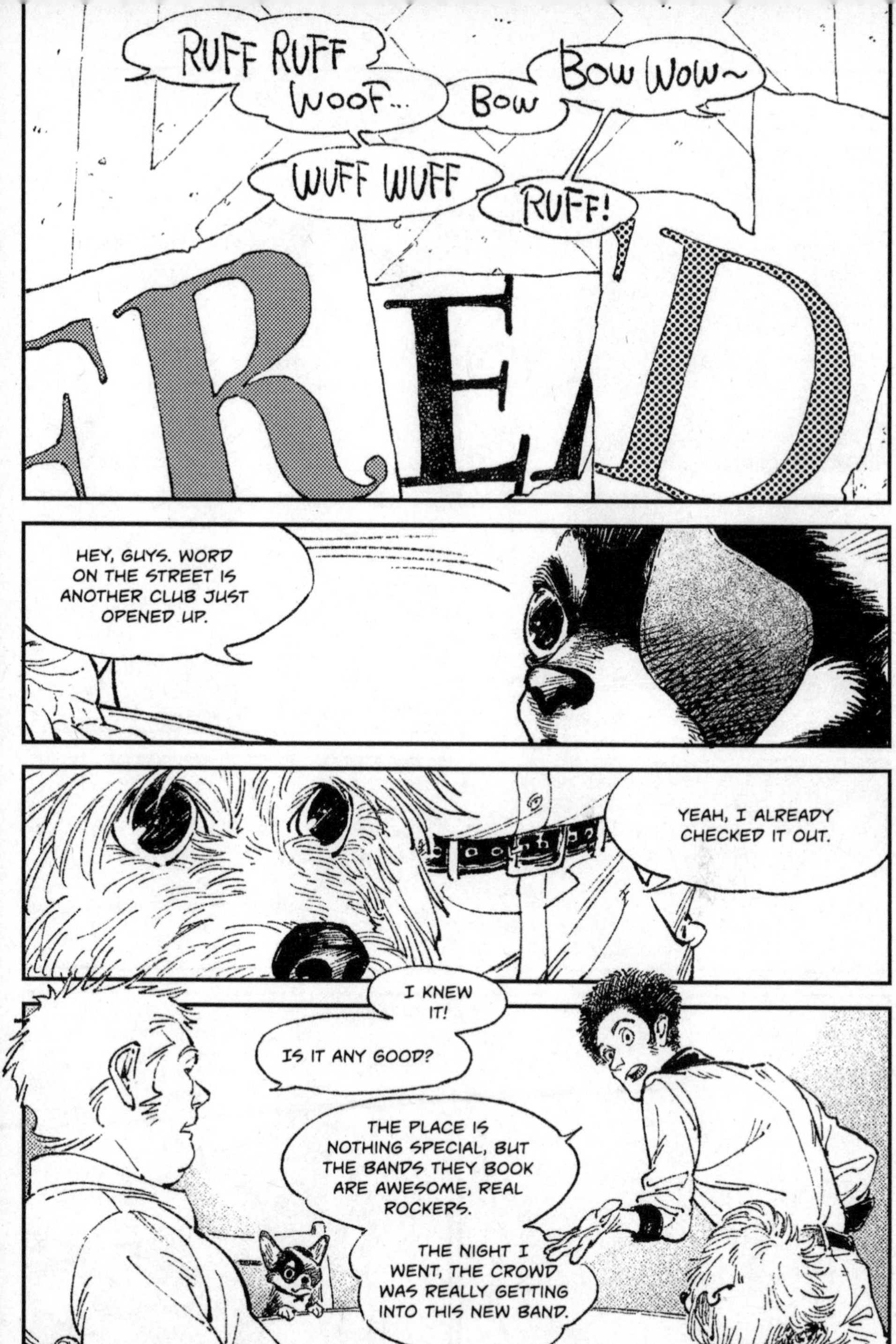
RUFF RUFF WOOF...
BOW
BOW WOW~
WUFF WUFF
RUFF!
RED
HEY, GUYS. WORD ON THE STREET IS ANOTHER CLUB JUST OPENED UP.
YEAH, I ALREADY CHECKED IT OUT.
I KNEW IT!
IS IT ANY GOOD?
THE PLACE IS NOTHING SPECIAL, BUT THE BANDS THEY BOOK ARE AWESOME, REAL ROCKERS.
THE NIGHT I WENT, THE CROWD WAS REALLY GETTING INTO THIS NEW BAND.

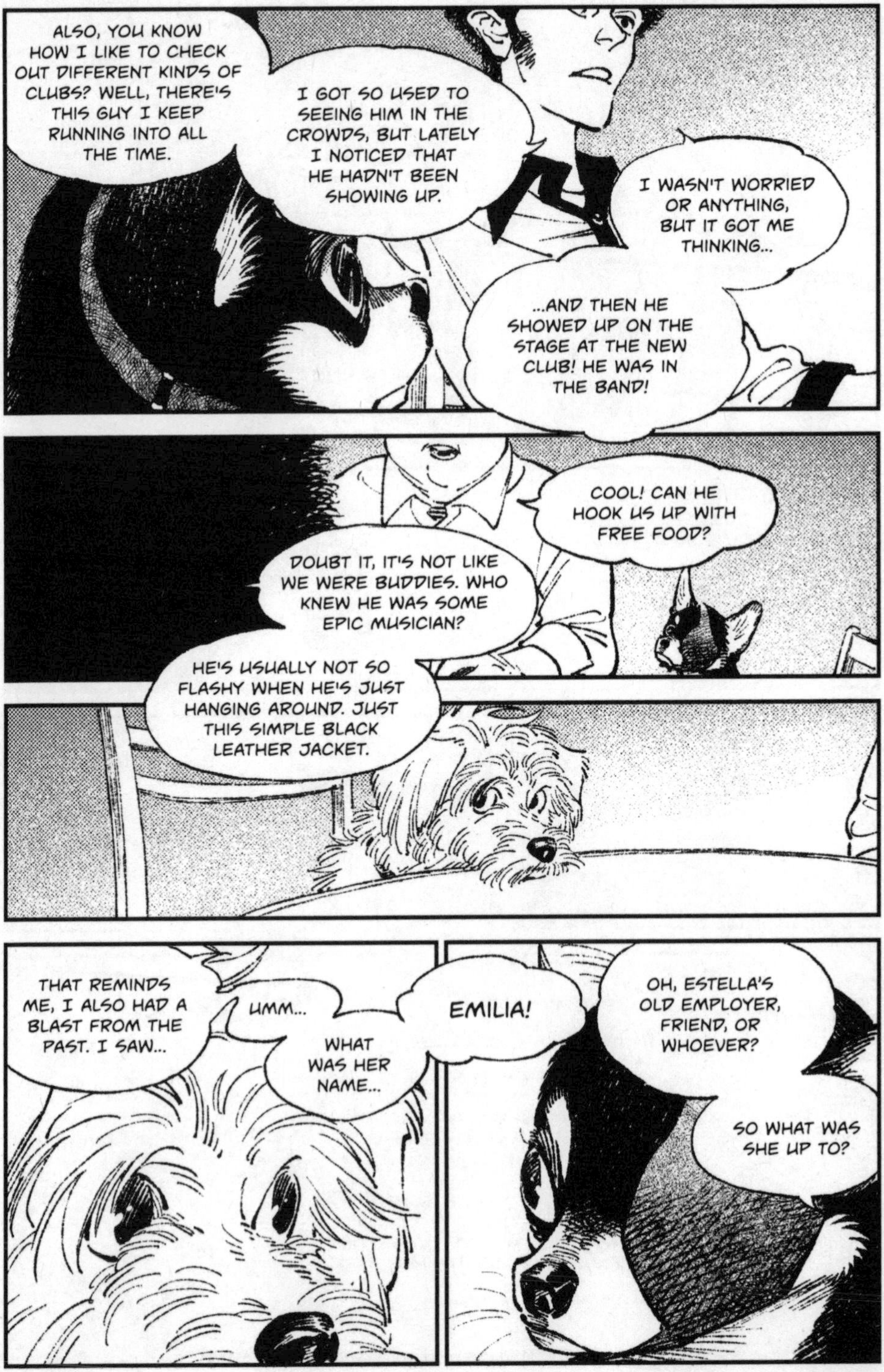
ALSO, YOU KNOW HOW I LIKE TO CHECK OUT DIFFERENT KINDS OF CLUBS? WELL, THERE'S THIS GUY I KEEP RUNNING INTO ALL THE TIME.
I GOT SO USED TO SEEING HIM IN THE CROWDS, BUT LATELY I NOTICED THAT HE HADN'T BEEN SHOWING UP.
I WASN'T WORRIED OR ANYTHING, BUT IT GOT ME THINKING...
...AND THEN HE SHOWED UP ON THE STAGE AT THE NEW CLUB! HE WAS IN THE BAND!
COOL! CAN HE HOOK US UP WITH FREE FOOD?
DOUBT IT, IT'S NOT LIKE WE WERE BUDDIES. WHO KNEW HE WAS SOME EPIC MUSICIAN?
HE'S USUALLY NOT SO FLASHY WHEN HE'S JUST HANGING AROUND. JUST THIS SIMPLE BLACK LEATHER JACKET.
THAT REMINDS ME, I ALSO HAD A BLAST FROM THE PAST. I SAW...
UMM...
WHAT WAS HER NAME...
EMILIA!
OH, ESTELLA'S OLD EMPLOYER, FRIEND, OR WHOEVER?
SO WHAT WAS SHE UP TO?

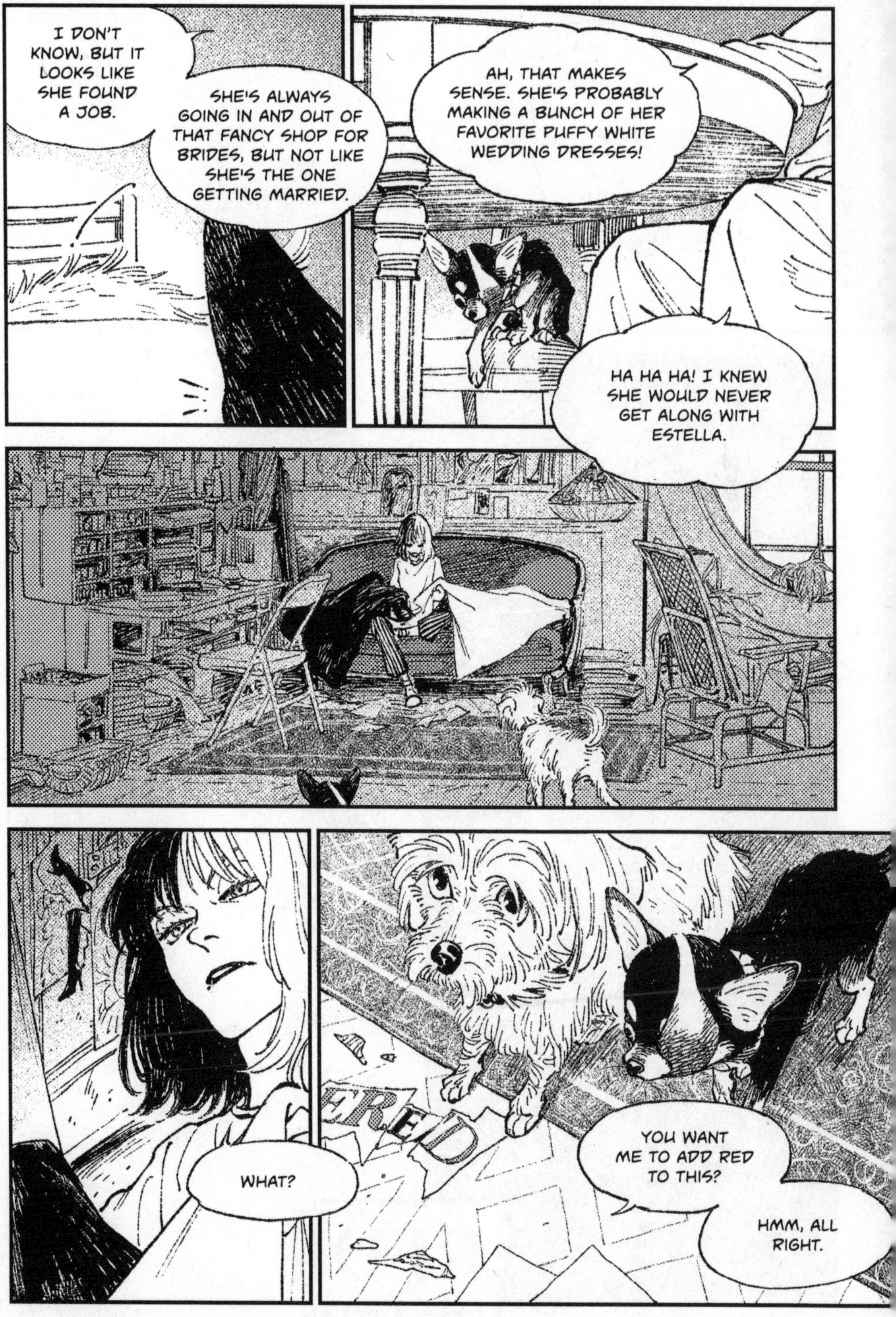

I DON'T KNOW, BUT IT LOOKS LIKE SHE FOUND A JOB.
SHE'S ALWAYS GOING IN AND OUT OF THAT FANCY SHOP FOR BRIDES, BUT NOT LIKE SHE'S THE ONE GETTING MARRIED.
AH, THAT MAKES SENSE. SHE'S PROBABLY MAKING A BUNCH OF HER FAVORITE PUFFY WHITE WEDDING DRESSES!
HA HA HA! I KNEW SHE WOULD NEVER GET ALONG WITH ESTELLA.
WHAT?
YOU WANT ME TO ADD RED TO THIS?
HMM, ALL RIGHT.

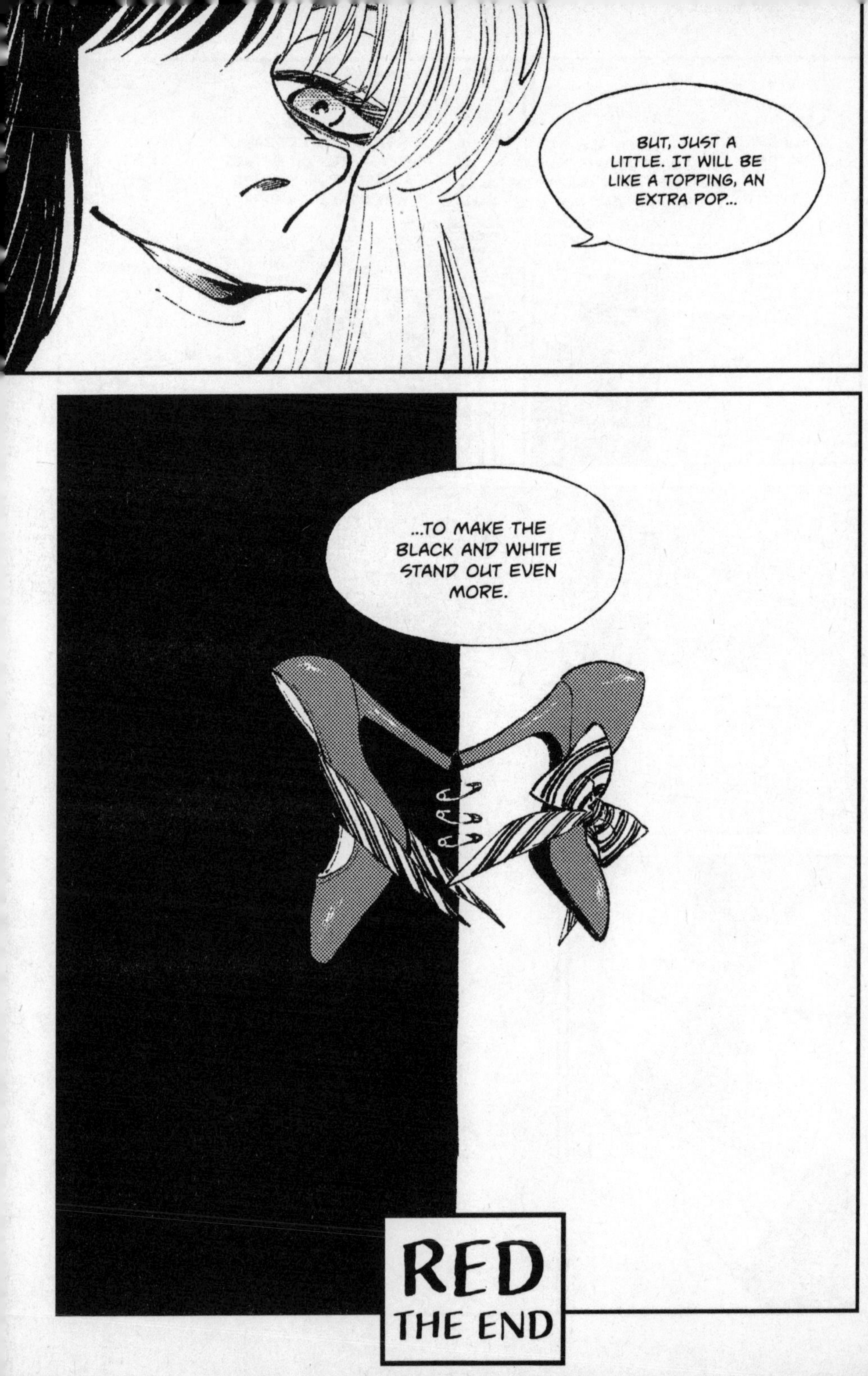
BUT, JUST A LITTLE. IT WILL BE LIKE A TOPPING, AN EXTRA POP...
...TO MAKE THE BLACK AND WHITE STAND OUT EVEN MORE.
RED THE END

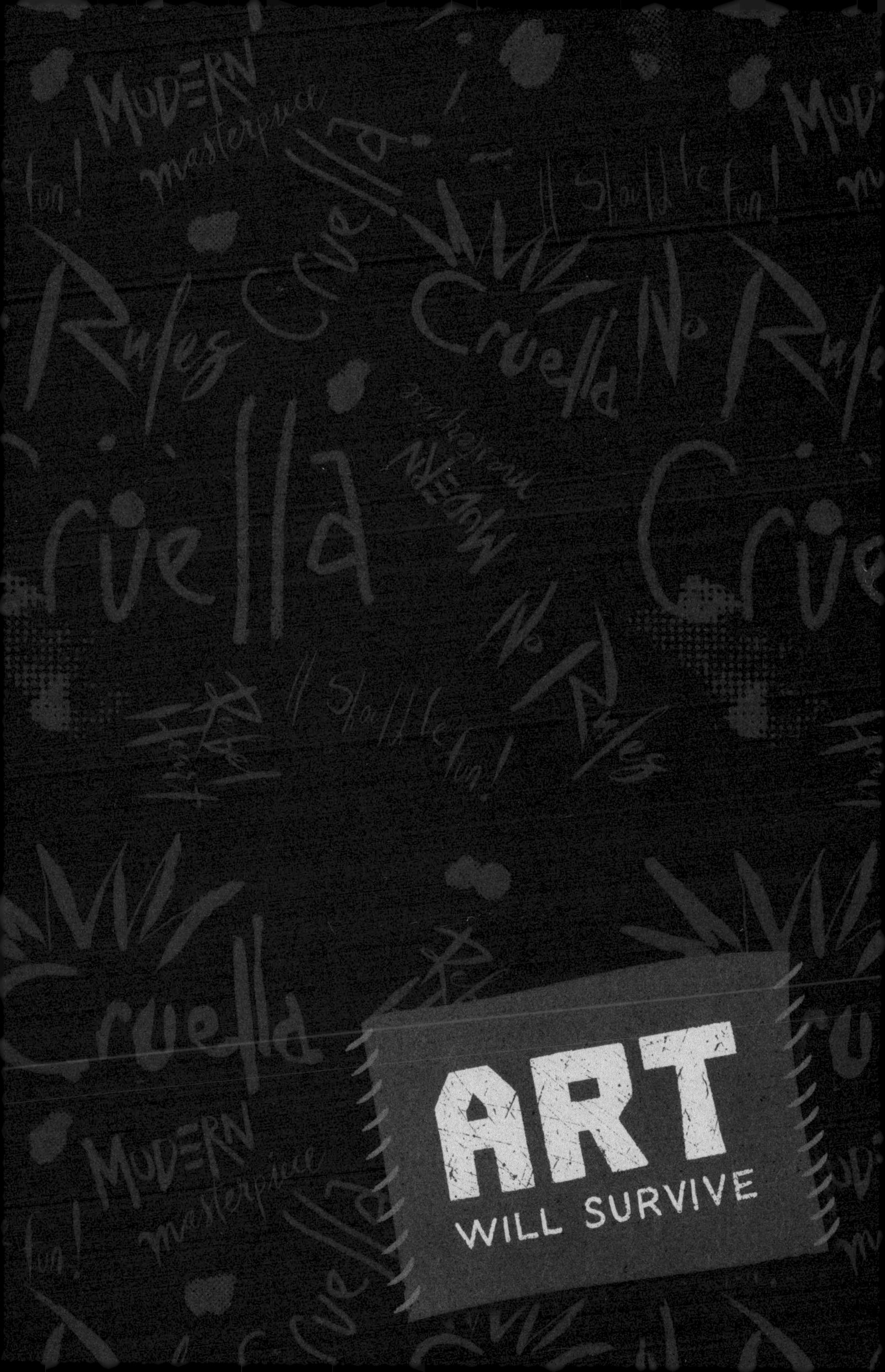
ART
WILL SURVIVE

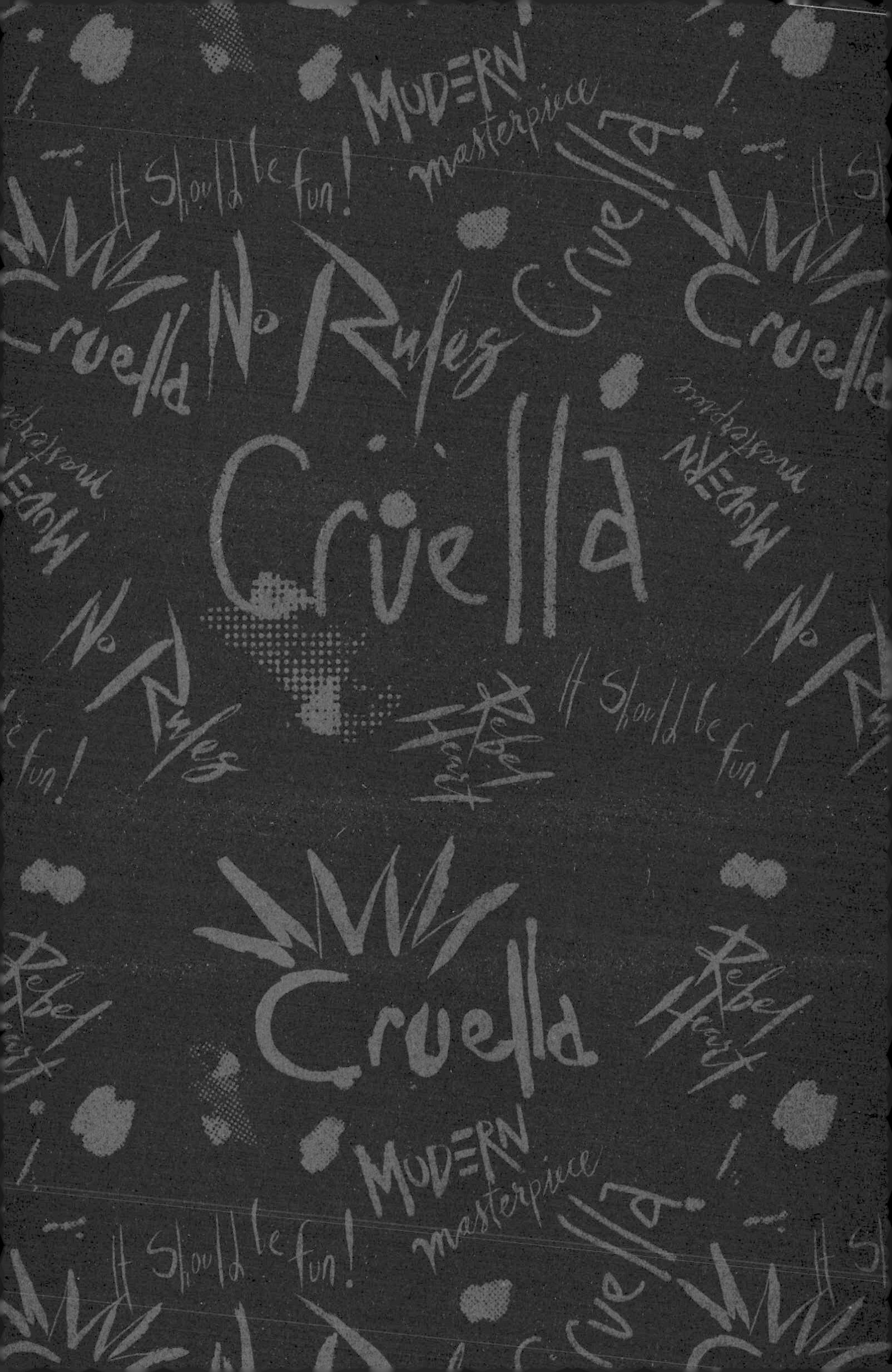
MODERN masterpiece
It should be fun!
No Rules
Cruella
Rebel Heart

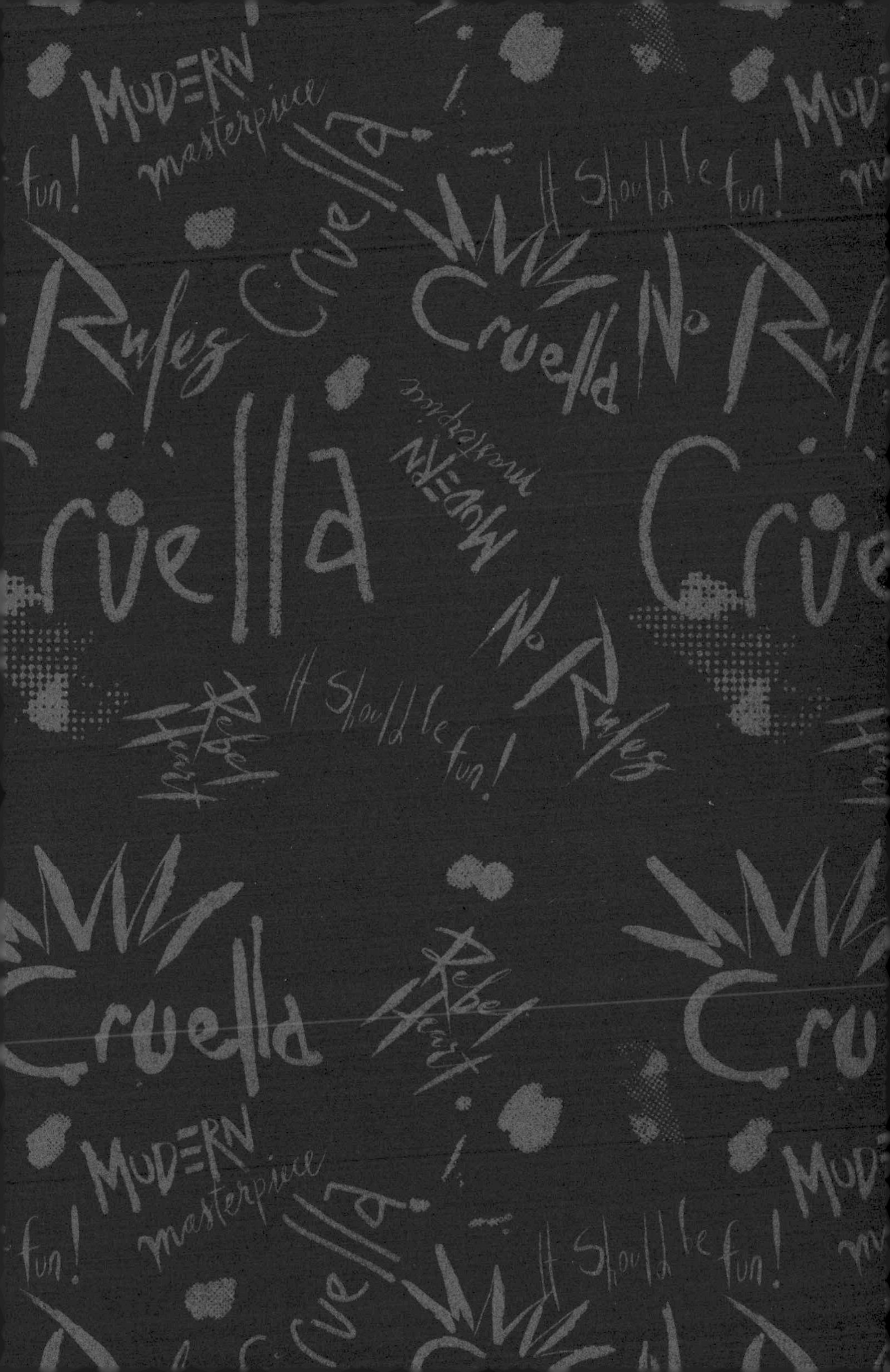
Cruella
No Rules
Modern masterpiece
It should be fun!
Rebel Heart

HACHI ISHIE

Hachi Ishie is a manga artist from Japan who recently published her original series *Rojiura Brothers*. *Disney Cruella: Black, White, and Red* is her first publication for the U.S.

Disney Cruella THE MANGA

BLACK, WHITE, AND RED

VIZ MEDIA EDITION

BY HACHI ISHIE

Special thanks to Christopher Troise, Eugene Paraszczuk,
Behnoosh Khalili, Dale Kennedy, Sarah Huck, Emily Shartle

ADDITIONAL TRANSLATION / Satsuki Yamashita
LETTERING / Erika Terriquez
COVER & INTERIOR DESIGN / Alice Lewis
COPY EDITOR / Justin Hoeger
EDITORS / Mayuko Hirao, Fawn Lau

PRINTED IN THE U.S.A.

PUBLISHED BY VIZ MEDIA, LLC
P.O. BOX 77010
SAN FRANCISCO, CA 94107

10 9 8 7 6 5 4 3 2
FIRST PRINTING, AUGUST 2021
SECOND PRINTING, AUGUST 2021

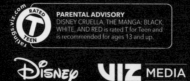

Disney   VIZ MEDIA

viz.com

THE MANGA TIE-IN TO DISNEY'S ANIMATED HIT, *FROZEN 2!*

DISNEY
FROZEN II
⇤ THE MANGA ⇥

Adapted by
ARINA TANEMURA